The Wine Roads of France

The Wine Roads
of
FRANCE

MARC AND KIM MILLON

Photographs by Kim Millon

Grafton Books

A Division of HarperCollins*Publishers*

To Guy

GraftonBooks
A Division of HarperCollins*Publishers*
77–85 Fulham Palace Road
Hammersmith, London W6 8JB

First published 1989 by the Thorsons Publishing Group Limited
This edition published by GraftonBooks 1991

British Library Cataloguing in Publication Data

Millon, Marc
 The wine roads of France: the complete companion guide. –
 New ed.
 1. France. Wine-growing regions – Visitors' guides
 I. Title   II. Millon, Kim
 914.404838

ISBN 0-246-13749-5

Printed in Great Britain by
Butler & Tanner Ltd, Frome, Somerset

CONTENTS

INTRODUCTION

*T*here is something magical about the wine regions of France. Every year, in areas throughout the country as beautiful as they are varied, a minor miracle occurs as the juice from mere grapes is transformed into something quite wonderful: wine. First the Greeks, then the Romans, established the principal vineyards of France, many of which have been continuously cultivated to this day. The results of their efforts have been valued for millennia as one of the great products of human civilization.

Wine may be simply the fermented juice of the grape, yet what variety exists within that basic equation! France, the greatest wine-producing nation in the world, offers a range as full, as varied, and as subtle as the many dabs of paint on an Impressionist palette: ranging in colour, from apple green to deep gold; from cherry red to near black; from the merest blush of pink to something altogether darker and fuller, yet still not quite red; and in taste from lemon sharp to unctuously honeyed; from the flavour of fresh-squeezed grapes to something so complex in bouquet and texture that it defies definition and leaves us gasping in wonder.

Pale, dry white wines; magical sparklers with tiny bubbles which seem to rise for ever and ever; glorious sweet wines with a rare haunting aroma that comes from 'rotten' grapes; forceful orange-tinged rosés; wines left to bake in the hot Midi sun before being macerated with pungent herbs; sweet, robust *apéritif* wines whose fermentation has been muted with the addition of grape brandy; youthful fruity *primeurs* meant to be joyously imbibed within days or weeks of the harvest; and deeper, classic *vins de garde*, wines for laying down 10, 15, 20 years or more: these and many others are the wines of France.

Right *The Dordogne near Bergerac.*

Left *The wine roads of France.*

As varied as the wines are the wine regions themselves. From the tortuously steep, sun-scorched vineyards of Banyuls on the Spanish border, to the manicured, green and golden slopes of Alsace, near Germany; from sea-fresh Muscadet to the alpine vineyards of Arbois; from the grand châteaux of Bordeaux to the multi-owned patchwork that is Burgundy; from rugged Gascony, where the thin local wines are distilled into fiery Armagnac, to the Renaissance landscape of the Loire; from quiet, introverted Champagne to boisterous outdoor Provence, where people live, eat, work, and play *en plein air*: that vines — free-standing or trained on wires; short, close-planted, or high and wide; ancient, gnarled, and as thick as a man's thigh, or young, spindly, wispy — grow in all these places may seem to be the only factor that unites them.

But there is one more undeniable aspect: where the vine grows, life is good and the wine regions of France — yes, all of them — share an essential outlook that is above all warm and welcoming, where the simple art of living well is unsurpassed.

The Wine Roads of France

Les Routes du Vin

*T*he wine roads of France lead directly to and through these wonderful regions. Many are actually sign-posted, and take you on small tracks or little country lanes direct to *chez viticulteur*. Some may make only a pleasant hour or two's detour from a journey, others can be the journey itself, a route to be followed intimately for days or even weeks.

A wine circuit placard in the Mâconnais.

All along the many thousands of kilometres of wine roads there are literally hundreds of wine producers who will be encountered. Many are individual small or large *propriétaires-récoltants* — that is, grape growers who make and bottle wines from their own harvest, *propre récolte*, and who sell these wines themselves. A *propriétaire-récoltant* may scratch a living from just a few hectares of vines (a hectare is the metric equivalent of about 2½ acres), making only enough wine for family consumption plus a small additional surplus to sell to passers-by; or he may be the owner of a famous château known throughout the world whose wine is in such demand that it is virtually earmarked for customers even before each year's grapes are picked.

Such wines, made and bottled by the producer himself, are designated estate-bottled, domaine-bottled or château-bottled. Additionally, almost half of all French wine is commercialized through merchants or *négociants* who may purchase and elevate wines to maturity, then bottle and market them under their own label: the wine tourist and traveller should by no means overlook this important and abundant source of both fine and everyday wines. In Burgundy, Alsace, Champagne, and elsewhere, such *négociants* are often the famous names that are best known abroad, who produce well-respected wines that are the standard-bearers of each region; as such, they often have the best organized facilities for visiting and tasting.

In other cases, growers may band together to form a collective *cave coopérative* that invests in modern wine-making machinery for an entire commune or village. While such 'wine factories', on the face of it, may hardly seem picturesque they are an equally essential part of the wine industry in France, often the centre of the local economy and village life. As such, visits to *caves coopératives*, with their red and white concrete fermentation vats, their lengths of plastic hose, and their vats where wine is pumped into jerrycans or *cubitainers* irreverently from a nozzle, are an equally exciting part of the French wine scene. The wines, in most cases, are well-made and often surprisingly high quality.

Propriétaires-récoltants, négociants, négociants-éleveurs, caves coopératives: all can be visited, cellars and vineyards toured, and wines tasted and purchased. We include the addresses and visiting details for over 350 of them, chosen for their excellence (wines that we know and have enjoyed, or which are consistent medal winners at the great wine fairs in Paris, Mâcon, Bordeaux, and elsewhere); for their facilities or willingness to welcome interested wine tourists (many fine and famous wine producers are notable absentees, simply because they don't have the time, inclination, or presumably the need to receive visitors); and/or for their proximity to the sign-posted wine roads or suggested routes. We have had considerable assistance in this selection from the many professional wine bodies in each of the regions.

However, this collection of wine producers, we stress, makes no claim to being exhaustive, exclusive, or comprehensive: there are many other wine producers who will be encountered and visited. We are thus certain that intrepid wine travellers will soon begin gathering their own personal list of favourites — in effect, writing their own 'Wine Roads of France'.

The cellars of Pierre Riffault, a small propriétaire-récoltant *in Sancerre.*

While larger firms may welcome visitors primarily as a public relations exercise — especially the great Champagne and Cognac houses, as well as some famous Bordeaux châteaux and Burgundian *négociants-éleveurs* — smaller growers, those who produce simple wines as well as grand, may undoubtedly open their premises to the public for the not insignificant direct sales that result. Certainly the French themselves have always enjoyed going direct to the source to purchase their wines and, indeed, the British have been returning home with French wine — a few bottles or a couple of hogsheads — since at least the time when much of France itself came under the rule of the English sovereign.

Make no mistake, wine travellers and visitors should never feel arm-twisted into making unwanted purchases, but they ought none the less to be sensitive to the situation. The wine grower who gives up his Saturday morning to show you around his cellars and who offers his wines for tasting, deserves more than a mere smile and a handshake: if you like the wines you will probably want to purchase a couple of bottles or a carton of six to take back home; but if you don't, or if you cannot carry the wine back with you then an offer to pay for the wines that you tasted will go a long way to maintaining the *entente cordiale*. While we are certain that considerable savings can be made by purchasing wine direct, do always check the prices being charged to ascertain whether or not they really are cheaper than at home.

We have visited, spoken over the telephone, or corresponded with every wine producer in this book; they themselves have supplied the visiting information which forms its core and they have indicated that they are all willing to receive visitors at the hours or on the conditions indicated. The larger firms may have permanent guides on hand in summer months for visits without appointment. In other cases, it is simply a question of turning up and knocking on the door. Where indicated, a telephone call may be necessary because otherwise there may be no one there to receive visitors.

A telephone call might also be the only way to actually find some of the more remote properties. Certainly, many are actually located directly on the wine roads and we have tried to give detailed directions where possible. However, do bear in mind that many wine growers' properties, houses or estates are in the country, or in tiny communes or hamlets, not in the larger towns which are given as their postal addresses (the prefixed number is the French postal code), thus adding an adventure element to finding some of them. We hope that this will not prove too frustrating; indeed we feel that 'hunting out' wine producers on or off the wine roads is part of the enjoyment of exploring the wine regions of France. It will be essential to use the recommended Michelin maps for detailed navigation.

We have indicated those wine growers or establishments where English is spoken: however, that does not mean that someone is on hand at all times (it may be only a single member of the staff, or even a son or daughter who has learned English at school). We have invariably found that a little French goes a very long way and if you make the effort you will obviously have a lot more fun.

Tasting Wine

*W*hen wine professionals and buyers visit France to taste wines, they may have hundreds or thousands of pounds, dollars, or gulden riding on their fleeting sensory judgements. In some cases they may be judging wines not only on how they taste now but on how they will develop over the course of the next decade or more. But most of us who visit the wine regions to taste wine direct at the source do so for the sheer enjoyment of it, and for the future enjoyment that a bottle or bottles purchased will bring, whether at a roadside picnic or back at home. Tasting wine for us, therefore, need not be a particularly scientific exercise: it is primarily simply about considering whether or not this wine or that gives us pleasure. We perceive that pleasure through our senses: sight, that is the colour, clarity, and general appearance; smell, the primary fruit aromas and developing bouquet; taste, the flavours and impressions on the palate; even touch, that is the feel and length of the wine in the mouth. Tasting wine may be simply a case of saying 'yes, I like that one'; 'no, don't think much of that'. Or it can be altogether more considered, a question of why you like a wine, how does it compare with similar examples or different vintages, or what specific viticultural or oenological factors have contributed to its character?

Certainly, those who taste large numbers of wines regularly must spit in order to maintain clear heads, not to mention driving licences. Tyros to this active and challenging sport may find that it is not quite as easy as it looks and may well soil shirts, shoes, wives, or four-year-olds while learning. But rest assured, few wine growers will be offended if you spit on their cellar floor. If you are tasting wine in their kitchen or sitting room, that may be another matter!

Drinking and Driving

Jus de Raisin and *Pétillant de Raisin*

*I*n France the laws against drinking and driving are as severe as they are in the United Kingdom. But drivers or non-drinkers need not feel totally left out. In many wine regions, non-alcoholic drinks are made from the grape and can be tasted and purchased. They can be excellent. In Monbazillac, for example, *jus de raisin* is made from the same noble grape varieties (Sémillon, Sauvignon, and Muscadelle) as that great *vin liquoreux*: deep gold in colour, rich in natural sugars, and with fine honeyed and floral flavours, this non-alcoholic grape juice is as delicious in its own way as the wine itself. In the Gaillac region, the wine producers make *pétillant de raisin*, another grape juice which gains its natural sparkle through fermentation in the bottle, resulting in a lively mousse and only a tiny amount of alcohol; usually about 1 per cent but guaranteed not more than 3 per cent. Very clean, drier than other grape juices, this is another excellent drink which drivers and non-drinkers alike can happily tipple till the cows come home. Other such grape juices are made throughout the wine regions of France. Ask for them and try them.

Restaurants

Wine Producers' (and our own) Recommendations

*B*ased on the not unreasonable assumption that the wine producers themselves are the best ones to advise on where to eat and drink in their own locality, we asked every one that we met, spoke to, or corresponded with to recommend their favourite local restaurants, and most of them were more than happy to oblige. These recommended restaurants, together with those which we have known and enjoyed ourselves over the course of some years' annual travel to France, form the core of the Restaurant section. They range from the very simplest family-run establishments where *vignerons* in orange or blue overalls are not out of place at midday, to the very grandest — and most expensive — temples of gastronomy in France. We have since visited,

The Gazinni family, who run a simple but welcoming ferme-auberge *in Monbazillac.*

or corresponded directly with, all of the restaurants included to ensure that our practical information is as up-to-date and correct as possible at the time of going to press. However, closing days do change from time to time so a telephone call in advance is always advisable before making a long detour or journey.

Since prices fluctuate (always in one direction — up) we have followed a simple rating based on the price of a full three or four course meal at the time of going to press: under 75F, **Very Inexpensive;** 75–150F, **Inexpensive;** 150–250F, **Moderate;** 250–400F, **Expensive;** over 400F, **Very Expensive.**

Enjoyment

Ripe Gamay grapes in Beaujolais.

*T*he wine regions of France will always be special to us. When we were young newlyweds, we came to Alsace on our honeymoon. It was only a brief interlude, a stop for a few days en route from Venice back to Britain by train, but how wonderful it was! It was early autumn and we stayed in a little hotel in the heart of the Bas-Rhin. The speckled Riesling grapes, the Gewürztraminer, Pinots, and others were not yet ripe, but there was a sense of anticipation in the wine villages like Andlau, Dambach-la-Ville and Riquewihr, a feeling of waiting and preparation. I can well remember our very first sip of Gewürztraminer (it was in the Restaurant Arnold, a superb, half-timbered old inn run by the Arnold family, themselves wine growers at Itterswiller): we were astounded, for the 'Gewürz' was a revelation, a wonder that such an enormous floral bouquet and mouth-filling, pungent flavour, combined with a clean, bone-dry finish, could come from the juice of grapes alone. Gewürztraminer may well be considered an 'obvious' wine by connoisseurs, but that discovery, in our youthful exuberance many years ago, was incredibly exciting: the slender, green-stemmed goblet, beaded with cold and shimmering brightly, seemed to promise all that lay before us, waiting to be discovered as if for the very first time!

Those who have not yet discovered the charms of the wine regions of France have a very special, exciting treat awaiting them. Others who return to the wine regions year after year may find that their pleasures and charms, like good wine, only improve with age.

Topsham, Devon, England

HM Customs and Excise

For those purchasing wine to be brought into the UK for their own personal use, the following guidance may be of use.

Wine (like all articles acquired abroad) is currently liable on importation into the UK to both duty and VAT at the appropriate rates. The allowances relating to alcoholic drinks purchased duty-paid in France (or other Member States) are currently as follows for adults:

Goods obtained duty- and tax-paid in the EC
1½ litres of alcoholic drinks over 22 per cent vol. (38.8° proof)
or
3 litres of alcoholic drinks not over 22 per cent vol. *or* fortified *or* sparkling wine
plus
5 litres of still table wine.

Furthermore, if no spirits or fortified or sparkling wines are imported, then those allowances can be used to increase the table wine allowance. This means, in effect, that if table wines are purchased duty- and tax-paid in France, a traveller may then import for his own use, without incurring extra charges, 8 litres or about 10½ 75 cl bottles or 11½ 70 cl bottles.

If over these allowances, then it is necessary to report to the Red Channel. Excise charges for wines purchased duty- and tax-paid in France are currently payable at the following rates per litre, plus 15 per cent VAT on the value of the wine:

Still table wine	£1.10
Fortified wine	£1.90
Sparkling wine	£1.82

The Completion of the Single Market: After 1 January, 1993
After the completion of the Single Market (to come into effect 1 January, 1993), the situation for the private individual purchasing wine in a Member State should become much more favourable. HM Customs and Excise advise (in a working paper):

> After the completion of the Single Market, private individuals will expect and should be able to purchase, in person and for their personal use, excise goods in another Member State that have borne the duty of that Member State. Provided that these purchases were obtained only on a duty-paid basis and were genuinely for private purposes and not for subsequent resale, there would be no further liability to excise duty in the Member State of consumption. In order to provide a sensible and

practical borderline to distinguish between private and commercial quantities, thresholds may have to be established for the quantities of excisable goods allowed to travellers without payment of duty in the country of destination/consumption.

While at the time of writing such threshold limits have not yet been established, we understand this to mean, in principle, that private individuals will be able to purchase wine in sensible quantities for importation and private consumption in Britain with no further liability to excise duties. Indeed, it is envisaged that no physical frontiers (and no Green or Red Channels) will exist between Member States after the completion of the Single Market.

UK Customs and Excise procedures nonetheless remain complex. If in doubt, write or telephone your local office for further advice.

French *Appellations:*
Classifications of Quality

It is well known that given half a chance the French will classify anything, from artichokes to chickens to cheese. As far as wine goes, their system of *appellation d'origine contrôlée* (AOC) is probably the most complex, detailed and effective of any in the world. The reasoning is that geographical location, or *terroir* (an all-embracing term which encompasses soil and microclimate) is the keynote to quality and individual character. Thus, the system of AOC attempts to pinpoint the origin of a wine, either broadly by region (Bourgogne or Bordeaux), or more specifically by commune or village (Vosne-Romanée or Pauillac) or even, in exceptional cases, by individual parcel or vineyard (La Romanée-Conti, Château-Grillet). The accepted implication is that the more precise the *appellation* the greater the wine, for only the best wines are able to make individual statements unique to their *terroir.*

The system of *appellation d'origine contrôlée* not only defines wines by their exact geographical locations, it also lays down certain rigid strictures, including permitted grape varieties, as well as rules relating to methods of cultivation, production and amounts of yield per hectare. The latter is certainly an important quality factor, for if the harvest is not limited then the resulting overproduction will dilute character and quality, leading to bland, indifferent wines. The system of *appellation contrôlée*, furthermore, protects by law quality wine producers from having their rightful and hard-earned *appellations* stolen: it is clearly illegal for wine producers from the Midi to call their wines Bordeaux or Burgundy.

Vin Delimité de Qualité Supérieure (VDQS) is a slightly lesser category, rated just below *appellation d'origine contrôlée* status, but none the less it should be read as a guarantee of quality for the consumer. As with AOC wines, VDQS must come from carefully defined regions, and adhere to strictures regarding grape varieties cultivated, methods of production, yield, and minimum alcohol levels.

Vin de Pays is the final recognized classification of French wine, a grade higher than simple '*vin de table*' but less complex than the exclusive wines which have earned AOC and VDQS status. None the less, the same principles apply: the wine must come from a specific named area and from specified grape varieties. It must be produced in limited quantities and it must have a minimum alcoholic content.

Telephone Numbers

Since going to press, all French telephone numbers have been modified to include the area code, shown in brackets as the first two digits. Therefore, it is now only necessary, when dialling either between *départements* or within the same *département*, to dial the full eight-digit figure.

Key to Maps

☐ Wine Properties to visit. (Note that this location is based on the postal village in the address and that many properties are located in the surrounding countryside or hamlets. Enquire at local information offices, or telephone for detailed directions.)

🍽 Restaurants.

M Museums and Wine Museums.

⌂ Maisons du Vin (professional organizations which serve to promote the interests of that area's wine growers; they can often provide much useful information, or assist with appointments and visits if necessary).

ALSACE

Introduction

Right *A characteristic Alsatian house.*

*A*lsace is the prettiest wine region in France. Here, in the far north-eastern corner of the country, the lower slopes of the Vosges mountains, as well as much of the valley floor and the broad, flatter plains extending to the Rhine, are covered with vines. As far as the eye can see, and with scarcely a break along the entire 125-km (75-mile) long sign-posted *Route du Vin d'Alsace* a striated sea of green connects wine village with wine village, from Marlenheim near Strasbourg, through Colmar, the 'wine capital' of the region, way down to Thann, nearly on the border with the ancient Franche-Comté.

The villages, with their scores of medieval half-timbered houses, sandstone town halls and churches, window-boxes filled with delicate trailing geraniums, stone fountains, towers topped with stork-nests and tall pointed steeples which peek over the hills from one to another, are absolutely charming. In every village along the *Route* there are scores of small individual wine growers, urging you to stop and taste wines made from their own harvest — *propre récolte* — in cellars or at tables set up in shaded wine gardens. Larger *négociants* — grower-shippers who are well known worldwide — offer both visits to cellars, as well as tall, green-stemmed goblets of wine to thirsty tourists and wine lovers alike. Even the *caves coopératives* here are exceptionally welcoming: many have pleasant tasting salons with red-checked tablecloths where you can sit all day if you like, working your way through a delightful but manageable range of Alsatian wines. Some even have adjoining restaurants and *winstubs* where you can sample the regional specialities accompanied by their wines.

For, as befits a great wine region, Alsace today is also one of the country's top gastronomic areas. Not only are there countless such good, informal *winstubs* and restaurants offering the hearty Alsatian basics — *choucroute, baekhoffa, tarte à l'oignon*, and much else — in addition, there is an ever-growing number of fine and elegant starred establishments which blend

Left *Riquewihr.*

elements of *nouvelle* with traditional cuisine to result in a style unique to the region.

Today Alsace is quiet, beautiful and at peace. Yet it is impossible to forget, while here, how much the region suffered in the not so distant past. Military cemeteries in Ammerschwihr, Bergheim, and elsewhere call to mind the men of Alsace, *morts pour la France*. Towns such as Mittelwihr and Bennwihr were virtually razed to the ground during the fierce fighting for the Colmar Pocket in 1944. Tiny Riquewihr, which miraculously escaped significant damage, lost no fewer than 50 local men in the last war and 60 in 1914–18. In the last century alone Alsace was snatched by Germany in 1871 after the Franco–Prussian War; repossessed by the French after World War I; annexed by the Nazis and submitted to four years of brutal Germanization; and finally returned to France after Hitler's defeat.

The region today is undoubtedly and vociferously French (the 'Marseillaise', after all, was composed by a young French army officer, Rouget de Lisle, while stationed at Strasbourg in 1792 and was originally called *Chant de l'Armée du Rhin*). Yet in spite of its tragic past, one does not sense any smouldering feelings of bitterness and resentment. There is, after all, an essential natural affinity between the peoples of the Rhineland. The villages of Baden-Württemberg across the river are almost mirror images reflected in the Rhine; the local languages from each area are not dissimilar Germanic dialects. And for the wine growers at least such attitudes would be self-defeating: signs offering *Weinproben* are as common — and as lucrative — as those which try to lure passing trade with their proclamations of *dégustation*.

Orientation

Strasbourg, the capital of Alsace, is located about 450 km (280 miles) from Paris. Colmar, the 'capital' of the wine region, is a further 60 km (38 miles) south of Strasbourg. By car from Paris, take the A4 *autoroute* to Metz, then the A32/34 to Strasbourg. Comfortable driving time is about 6 hours, though the vineyards of Champagne could be toured *en route*. Alternatively, take the N4 all the way to Strasbourg via Nancy, or at Nancy, the N59 to Séléstat.

There are several TEE trains each day between Paris and Strasbourg: journey time is under 3 hours. There are good local connections between Strasbourg and Colmar, with stops at Séléstat.

International and domestic flights land at Strasbourg Entzheim airport, conveniently located near the start of the *Route du Vin*.

While most visitors will wish to spend at least some time in Strasbourg, wine-travellers will be most comfortable in Colmar, or else in any number of small wine villages along the *Route du Vin*. Others may choose to relax in the forests and mountains of the Vosges.

Michelin Map 87

To us, Alsace may seem on the far eastern fringe of France, but in reality the Rhineland is an historic and strategic *carrefour*, a crossroads at the very heart of Europe (a fact recognized by the siting of the EEC's European Parliament in Strasbourg). For northern Europeans (from Germany, the Netherlands, and Scandinavia) it remains a natural corridor to the south. Yet surprisingly few English-speaking visitors come to Alsace; to many this alone may be reason enough to spend time here, but there are more and better reasons as well.

Alsatian Wine and the Wars

During the wars over the last century, Alsace suffered profoundly. Not only were the villages and vineyards destroyed by fierce fighting, a further blow to the wine growers was that the subsequent changes of nationality led to the loss of traditional markets and changes in emphases and priorities of wine making. After the Franco–Prussian War in 1871, when the region was annexed to Germany, the growers were forced to grub up their traditional noble grape varieties and replace them with lesser, high-yielding vines that were able to produce strong and plentiful but bland wines to satisfy the near-legendary thirst of the conquerors. So complete was this transformation of the vineyard that in 1918 when the region became part of France once more, nearly the entire Alsace vineyard was planted with lesser grape varieties, primarily Chasselas and Sylvaner.

'When we were annexed to Germany, we lost our identity', says Jean Hugel, of Hugel et Fils, one of the region's foremost grower-shippers, whose family has been making wine in Riquewihr since 1639. 'Each time we changed nationality, we lost our customers. The Germans have different drinking habits to us.'

This situation was not rectified until after the devastation of World War II. At that time, the Alsatian growers took the courageous decision to replant the ruined vineyards primarily with the traditional noble *cépages*. Now more than 70 per cent of the vineyard is planted with Riesling, Tokay d'Alsace (Pinot Gris), Gewürztraminer, Muscat, Pinot Blanc, and Sylvaner. These varietals produce classic French dry white wines which are meant to be consumed with meals (unlike semi-sweet and sweet German wines, which are best enjoyed on their own).

Today the wine growers and grower-shippers of Alsace are reaping the benefits of that courageous decision and of what must seem to them a near-lifetime of stability and peace.

The Wines of Alsace

Alsace or
Vin d'Alsace AOC

*T*his is the basic *appellation* for the quality wines of the region. Most wines which are entitled to this *appellation* are also sold under the name

of the grape variety from which they are produced (see below). With the exceptions of the small amounts of red and rosé wine produced from the Pinot Noir, the Alsace vineyard is noted for its strong, dry white wines which embody the distinctive fruity and aromatic characteristics of each of the individual grape varieties from which they are made. The minimum alcoholic content of 10° is often exceeded. The words *Vins Fins*, *Vins Nobles* or *Alsace Grand Vin* may indicate wines with a slightly higher alcoholic content than this minimum.

The wines of Alsace gained official *appellation d'origine* status only in 1962. They must be bottled in the region in the distinctive, elegant green-glass Alsatian *flûte*.

Permitted Grape Varieties

The following grape varieties can all be mentioned on the label. The first four produce the most distinctive and best wines of Alsace.

Muscat   Muscat is probably the least well known of the Alsace noble grape varieties for it only makes up a very small proportion of the plantation; in recent years even this small amount has been decreasing. Though elsewhere this delicious grape is associated with very sweet dessert wines (Muscat de Beaumes-de-Venise, Muscat de Rivesaltes, for example), the Muscat in Alsace creates an opulently scented, exquisite wine with an enormous and expansive bouquet, yet which is fermented out completely, to result in a bone-dry, highly aromatic wine. Muscat d'Alsace is a relative rarity which should be sought; it is best drunk as an *apéritif*. The little village of Voegtlinshoffen, near Colmar, is considered foremost for the Muscat.

Gewürztraminer   Gewürztraminer produces the most easily recognizable and initially most appealing of Alsace wines. The flowery, spicy, sometimes peppery, aroma of the grape can be light and attractive in some wines, or considerably heavier, even overpowering in others. '*Gewürz*' means spice, and indeed this wine shares that certain pithy, rich, almost oriental opulence of Alsace wines at their best. Though the Gewürztraminer produces primarily dry wines, in exceptional years excellent *vendange tardive* are also made. Gewürztraminer is planted widely throughout the Alsace vineyard but yields its finest, most elegant examples from the heart of the vineyard some 15 km to the north and south of Colmar.

Riesling   Riesling is universally acknowledged as the *cépage* capable of producing the very finest wines in Alsace, characterized foremost by a certain class and elegance which comes from a combination of the attractive and distinctive ripe scent of the Riesling, a great depth of flavour, and an underlying backbone of firm acidity and alcohol. As elsewhere in the world, this capricious late-ripening variety is difficult to cultivate and only reaches great heights on the finest and best-exposed slopes and in the best years only. *Grands Crus* Rieslings as well as selected *cuvée* Rieslings from individual houses from the best years thus represent the pinnacle of the Alsace vineyard. Great Rieslings can be laid down like red wines to improve and develop for 7–10 years or more. As in Germany, Riesling has the further ability to benefit from *pourriture noble*, and thus exceptional late-harvest wines are produced when conditions allow. Rieslings from Ribeauvillé, Riquewihr, Hunawihr, Kaysersberg, and Andlau are all highly prized.

Tokay d'Alsace or **Pinot Gris**   Tokay is the traditional Alsatian name for the grape known elsewhere as Pinot Gris. However, due to possible confusion with the great Hungarian dessert wine of Tokaj (to which it bears no similarity whatsoever) the wine growers have been compelled gradually to replace this traditional name with the less evocative Pinot Gris on the label. The Tokay–Pinot Gris (as some producers now indicate) is capable of producing immense wine, the most full-bodied of all Alsace wines, and an able partner to the robust and hearty foods of the region: deep yellow in colour, relatively low in acid, with a warm, spicy bouquet and exceptionally rich flavour. The best examples can be aged for considerable periods. In exceptional years, fine late-harvest wines are also produced.

Pinot Blanc   Pinot Blanc, known also as Klevner, is a long-standing, classic *cépage* of the Alsace vineyard, though in the past it was generally deemed capable of producing only minor everyday wines. In recent years, it has been planted extensively thoughout the region. Pinot Blanc produces clean, dry wine that may lack the obvious varietal characteristics, and especially the elegance and finesse, of wines from the above noble varieties but which none the less has considerable distinction in its own right. Full-bodied and well-flavoured, Pinot Blanc d'Alsace is an able partner to food. It is still relatively inexpensive.

ALSACE

Sylvaner   Long considered the everyday workhorse of the Alsace vineyard, the Sylvaner grape is a large-cropper which produces quantities of straightforward white wines particularly favoured by the Alsatians themselves. Sylvaner is often available by the *pichet* in *winstubs*, a straightforward, uncomplicated accompaniment to *choucroute, tarte à l'oignon* and other such dishes. However, in certain areas, especially around Mittelbergheim on the *lieu-dit* known as Zotzenberg, it is capable of producing wines of considerable finesse and depth.

Pinot Noir   The classic grape of Burgundy is planted in small quantities in Alsace, which is, apart from Champagne, the northernmost vineyard in France. The wines which result, therefore, are on the whole extremely light, more often rosé than red. However, in exceptional years red wines with considerable depth of colour and flavour can be produced, though usually only in small quantities, aged in wood, and hoarded by the wine growers for their own enjoyment. Lighter Pinot Noirs can be pleasant picnic wines, drunk slightly chilled. Pinot Noir from Ottrott, a small village in the hills above Obernai, is considered among the best.

Lesser Grape Varieties   Chasselas, known also as Gutadel, was in former times, especially under the Germans, planted extensively throughout the region: pockets remain and the grapes are generally used to make blended wines sold by the *pichet*. Chasselas gradually is being replaced, primarily with Pinot Blanc. Other lesser grape varieties include Knipperlé and Auxerrois.

Vin d'Alsace
Edelzwicker AOC

Edelzwicker is a wine made from a blend of the so-called noble grape varieties. In practice, however, this usually means a high proportion of Sylvaner, perhaps some Pinot Blanc, and Chasselas. At its best, it is a refreshing jug wine to be drunk on the spot.

Alsace Grand Cru
AOC

This superior *appellation* came into being officially only in 1975 and can be applied to wines produced from Riesling, Muscat, Tokay, or Gewürztraminer from certain delimited areas only. The harvest must not exceed 70 hectolitres/hectare though in practice the growers making the finest wines restrict this yield considerably further. The wines must also have a higher minimum alcohol content. Such *Grands Crus* from certain vineyards and slopes known as *lieux-dits* have the right to use these approved names on the bottle. A list of 25 *lieux-dits* was agreed in 1983 and a further 22 were added in 1986. These two lists are shown below, given in order following the *Route du Vin d'Alsace* from north to south.

Grands Crus established in 1983

Lieu-dit	*Commune or Communes*
Altenberg de Bergbieten	Bergbieten
Kirchberg de Barr	Barr

Wiebelsberg	Andlau
Kastelberg	Andlau
Moenchberg	Andlau and Eichhoffen
Gloeckelberg	Rodern and St-Hippolyte
Kanzlerberg	Bergheim
Altenberg de Bergheim	Bergheim
Geisberg	Ribeauvillé
Kirchberg de Ribeauvillé	Ribeauvillé
Rosacker	Hunawihr
Sonnenglanz	Beblenheim
Schlossberg	Kaysersberg and Kientzheim
Sommerberg	Niedermorschwihr and Katzenthal
Brand	Turckheim
Hengst	Wintzenheim
Eichberg	Eguisheim
Hatschbourg	Hattsatt and Voegtlinshoffen
Goldert	Gueberschwihr
Spiegel	Bergholtz and Guebwiller
Kessler	Guebwiller
Saering	Guebwiller
Kitterlé	Guebwiller
Ollwiller	Wuenheim
Rangen	Thann and Vieux-Thann

Grands Crus established in 1986

Lieu-dit	*Commune or Communes*
Steinklotz	Marlenheim
Engelberg	Dahlenheim
Altenberg de Wolxheim	Wolxheim
Zotzenberg	Mittelbergheim
Muenchberg	Nothalten
Winzenberg	Blienschwiller
Frankstein	Dambach-la-Ville
Praelatenberg	Orschwiller
Osterberg	Ribeauvillé
Froehn	Zellenberg
Schoenenbourg	Riquewihr
Sporen	Riquewihr
Mandelberg	Mittelwihr
Markrain	Bennwihr
Mambourg	Sigolsheim
Wineck-Schlossberg	Katzenthal
Steingrubler	Wettolsheim
Pfersigberg	Eguisheim

ALSACE

Steinert
Vorbourg
Zinnkoepflé
Pfingstberg

Pfaffenheim
Rouffach-Westhalten
Westhalten-Soultzmatt
Orschwihr

Crémant d'Alsace AOC

*A*lsace sparkling wine produced by the *méthode champenoise*. Many of the larger houses produce such wines which are invariably clean and well made, if not over distinguished.

Cuvée Réserve; Cuvée Tradition; Réserve Personelle, etc.

*U*ntil the addition of the *Grand Cru appellation*, wine producers had no means of denoting wines of superior quality. Even this system is not wholly satisfactory, since it applies to wines from particular *lieux-dits*. Therefore, an individual hierarchy of quality has developed whereby growers and *négociants* market both their 'straight' varietals, e.g. Riesling d'Alsace, Gewürztraminer d'Alsace, etc., as well as selected superior *cuvées* which bear individual *marques* or names, such as *cuvée tradition, cuvée réserve, réserve personelle, Cuvée des Comtes d'Eguisheim*, and others. Such wines have undergone a more rigorous selection and are almost always worth paying more for.

Vendange tardive

*T*he term *vendange tardive* literally means 'late harvest' and signifies that grapes have been left on the vines considerably longer than normal with a corresponding increase in ripeness, sugar, and potential alcohol. Alsace *vendange tardive* wines generally retain greater or lesser amounts of residual sugar, depending on how fully they are fermented out, though on the whole they are quite high in alcohol, often over 14°. This balance between residual sugar and alcohol is crucial; but when it is just right, such wines are rare nectars indeed.

Sélection des grains nobles

*W*hile *vendange tardive* wines are Alsatian equivalents of German *Spätlese* and *Auslese*, the *selection des grains nobles* are even higher up the quality scale, like *Beerenauslese* and *Trockenbeerenauslese* wines produced only in very few exceptional years and only after the vineyard has been harvested in several successive tries. Each time only those bunches, or individual grapes, which are extremely overripe and have been affected by *pourriture noble* are collected. The wines made from such unpromising-looking shrivelled grapes are intensely concentrated, great dessert wines, both extremely rare and hugely expensive.

Les Eaux-de-Vie d'Alsace

Eaux-de-Vie d'Alsace

*I*n addition to wine, Alsace is the centre for the production of fine *eaux-de-vie*, distilled mainly from the abundant fruit which grows in this fertile region: *poire william* (William pear), *quetsch* (blue plums), *mirabelle* (yellow plums), *framboise* (raspberries), *fraise* or *fraise de bois* (strawberries or wild strawberries), *houx* (holly), *coing* (quince), and much else. They are expensive, since to make the real article requires huge amounts of fruit, but they are true essences, embodying the very intensity and aroma of the fruits from which they are made.

Marc d'Alsace
Gewürztraminer AOC

A s in all wine regions, *marc* is produced by the distillation of the residue left after pressing the grapes. *Marc d'Alsace Gewürztraminer* is entitled to its own *appellation* for this distinctive grape results in a particularly pungent and aromatic fire-water.

Les Vins Sigillés

Each year the Confrérie St-Etienne, the pre-eminent wine organization in Alsace, organizes a large tasting in its headquarters in the Château of Kientzheim. The aim is to discover those wines which represent the highest quality and which demonstrate the most typical characteristics of each of the various grape varieties and styles. The best wines are awarded the *sigillé* and are entitled to a numbered seal of quality which is usually attached above the bottle's label.

These wines are subsequently registered with the Confrérie and the representative bottles are stored in its *oenothèque*. Consumers who have any doubts or queries about the quality of such wines may contact the Confrérie direct. The *sigillé* of the Confrérie Saint-Etienne is thus a highly valued seal of quality and a further guarantee for the consumer.

There is a wine museum in the Château that is open to the public.

Ⓜ Musée du Vignoble et du Vin d'Alsace
Château de la Confrérie St-Etienne
68240 Kientzheim
tel: (89) 78 21 36
Open 15 June–31 October daily 10–12h; 14–18h.

The Wine Road of Alsace

Route du Vin d'Alsace

In Brief The *Route du Vin d'Alsace* is about 125 km (75 miles) long, running along the eastern flank of the lower Vosges from Marlenheim to Thann in the *départements* of Bas-Rhin and Haut-Rhin. The *Route* is well sign-posted throughout. There are literally hundreds of tasting opportunities along the

ALSACE

way. If time is limited, the prettiest part of the wine road, and the area which generally produces the best wines, is to be found in the Haut-Rhin, from Ribeauvillé to Guebwiller, south of Colmar. In the Bas-Rhin, there are pretty wine villages and fine wines to be found particularly between Barr and Dambach-la-Ville. While Strasbourg has no shortage of hotels of all categories, we suggest that Colmar, long considered capital of the wine trade, makes a more suitable and enjoyable base. Alternatively, there are scores of charming hotels located right along the *Route du Vin d'Alsace*. Some of these are listed in the Restaurant section.

Any tour of Alsace will probably begin in Strasbourg, capital of the region, headquarters of the Council of Europe and home of the EEC Parliament. Strasbourg today may be a modern and important industrial and cultural centre, but the essential character of prosperous and wealthy medieval *bourg* remains. The magnificent spiny sandstone Gothic cathedral dominates an old quarter that is particularly charming, with its dark, stone-paved streets lined with former merchants' houses. Bourgeois tastes, then as now, are amply catered for, with shops selling *foie gras*, wine, the range of pork *charcuterie* for which the city is famous, and much else. The Maison Kammerzell in the place de la Cathédrale is one of the finest Renaissance houses, dating from 1467. Today it is a *winstub-restaurant* where you can enjoy typical dishes in a unique atmosphere. The nearby Petite France quarter was once an area of artisans and tanners; today these restored houses and workshops overhang a system of quiet canals: come here to sip goblets of wine at terraces overlooking the water. Or else, order a cool *demi* of beer (the best in France is brewed in Alsace) and just watch the world go by.

The *Route du Vin d'Alsace* begins at Marlenheim, just 20 km (13 miles) from Strasbourg (leave on the N4 in the direction of Paris). At Marlenheim we gain an immediate first glimpse of the splendour of the Alsace vineyard: the well-exposed flank known as Steinklotz which dominates the town has recently been awarded *Grand Cru* status. Marlenheim offers a sign-posted footpath through its vineyards.

From Marlenheim, the wine road meanders through little wine towns such as Wangen, Westhoffen, Traenheim, Bergbieten, and Dangolsheim, but this upper stretch of the *Route* cannot sustain the concentrated riches of the vine which are offered further south: fine wines *are* produced here but vineyards compete with other agricultural crops — wheat, hops, and sunflowers.

Molsheim and Obernai are the first two large wine towns in the upper section of the *Route*. Molsheim is an ancient university town set amongst orchards as well as fields of vines; it is also a convenient starting place for excursions into the Vosges mountains. In Obernai, fine old buildings such as the fifteenth-century Corn Market and the Town Hall Assembly Chamber are noteworthy but the most dominant feature is the enormous Kronenbourg brewery on the town's outskirts. Stop in Obernai to purchase the essentials of a classic Alsatian picnic before continuing into the heart of the vineyards.

Right *Alsace*.

Ottrott, Heiligenstein, Barr, Mittelbergheim, Andlau and Dambach-la-Ville all produce fine wines. The geology in this particular niche of the vineyard is so complex that in each commune certain grapes thrive better than others. Ottrott is known foremost for its Pinot Noir wines, the unusual *rouge d'Ottrott*, said to be the best 'red' wine in Alsace. Barr is reputed above all for its fine Gewürztraminers. The Sylvaner, usually deemed capable of producing sound if rather unexciting wine, yields richer examples with considerable finesse from the Zotzenberg *Grand Cru* of Mittelbergheim. Andlau boasts no fewer than three *Grand Crus*, all planted with Riesling: yet Kastelberg, Wiebelsberg, and Moenchberg, each produce wines of strikingly individual character from this great grape, the results of their totally unique soil compositions and exposure. The Frankstein of Dambach-la-Ville is another particularly fine *lieu-dit*: for those wishing to explore it at closer range, there is a sign-posted footpath which leads from the market square through the vineyards.

St-Hippolyte is a picturesque medieval town nestling below the commanding Haut-Koenigsbourg. Drive up to this somewhat overzealously restored castle for a superb view over the vineyards to the flatter plains of the Rhine. If it is not too hazy, the slopes of the *Schwarzwald* (Black Forest) are visible in the east.

While excellent individual wines, such as the above, come from the Bas-Rhin, it is generally agreed that the Haut-Rhin is the finer stretch

Haut-Koenigsbourg.

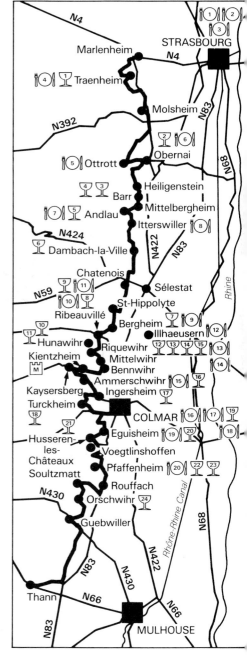

of the wine road. Here the mountains are slightly higher, the microclimates more sheltered and favourable than in the Bas-Rhin where vast quantities of basic Alsace varietals are produced from the flatter plains. A principal town in this lower stretch, and an excellent touring centre, is Ribeauvillé. The three castles of Ribeaupierre which rise behind the town are an important landmark of the Alsatian countryside. Ribeauvillé hosts a lively wine festival on the last Saturday and Sunday of July, while the *Fête des Ménétriers* is held at the beginning of September. Pipers weave their way through the stone-paved streets and the town's fountain overflows with free wine. Ribeauvillé has three

Riquewihr.

Grands Crus: Kirchberg, Geisberg, and Osterberg, while the prestigious Clos du Zahnacker (the exclusive domaine of the town *cave coopérative*) though not classified as such, is an exceptional *lieu-dit* planted with a mixture of Riesling, Gewürztraminer, and Tokay. The grapes are all harvested together to result in a non-varietal wine that combines the characteristics of each.

Riquewihr is one of the finest and most perfectly preserved villages along the *Route*. Miraculously, in spite of the almost total destruction of neighbouring villages, Riquewihr escaped unscathed from the fierce fighting which took place here towards the end of the last war. This ancient walled town, with its numerous medieval and Renaissance half-timbered houses and stone-paved streets, is surrounded by some of the finest vineyards of the region, especially Sporen and Schoenenbourg. Riquewihr is the home of individual growers as well as of some of the region's best-known *propriétaires-négociants* — grower-shippers — including Jean Hugel et Fils, Dopff au Moulin, Dopff et Irion, and Preiss-Zimmer. The town's ramparts are still almost wholly intact: located in one section is the so-called Robber's Tower, complete with an authentic torture chamber.

After Riquewihr come the small towns of Mittelwihr and Bennwihr. Both suffered extensive damage in the war, particularly the latter which was almost completely razed to the ground. Yet today, except for its strikingly hideous modern church, Bennwihr has been rebuilt in a traditional style which hardly looks out of place.

Kientzheim and Kaysersberg both lie in a deep valley which pierces into the broad flank of the Vosges: here they profit from some extremely well-exposed south-facing slopes such as the Schlossberg, noted above all for its Riesling. Kientzheim is the headquarters of the Confrérie St-Etienne, the most important wine fraternity in the region. In its headquarters in the château there is a wine museum. Kaysersberg, further up the valley, is a popular and lively town, and the birthplace of the Nobel Prize winner Dr Albert Schweitzer.

Ammerschwihr was also extensively damaged in the last war and today presents a somewhat grim and sad face, under the shadow of its famous Kaefferkopf. A once lovely Renaissance façade is all that remains from the former *Hôtel de Ville*; there are a few stout round towers and some fine old houses, but almost everything else here was destroyed and subsequently rebuilt. Ammerschwihr is the home of one of the region's greatest restaurants, Aux Armes de France.

The largest town along the wine road, Colmar has long been considered the capital of the wine trade. Here, as much as anywhere else, the fusion of French and Germanic tradition, architecture, and culture is evident; explore the moody medieval quarter, with its leaning, painted, and intricately carved houses and shops, and the area known as 'Petite Venise', where a little canal threads its way through shaded streets. Visitors should not miss the Unterlinden Museum with its Isenheim altar, a true masterpiece.

The wine road continues south from Colmar, often branching off from the too-busy N83 to loop through more pretty and welcoming wine villages. Make a detour (on D10 from Turckheim) to Munster, where you can buy the famous cheese direct from the farms which make it. From here you can continue further into the mountains to explore beautiful walking country and the lakes which are such popular resorts for the French: Lac de Gérardmer, Lac de Longemer, and the smaller Lac Blanc.

Further south, Eguisheim and Husseren-les-Châteaux are both highly regarded wine villages, the latter perches below the ruins of three castles. Voegtlinshoffen is particularly noted for its fine Muscat wines. Pfaffenheim has a fine *cave coopérative* offering *Grands Crus* such as Goldert and Steinert. Soultzmatt boasts the highest vineyard in Alsace, the *Grand Cru* Zinnkoepflé, while Guebwiller leads to the beautiful Florival, valley of flowers. Thann is the final village on the wine road, and boasts a ruined castle, Gothic church, an old tower locally famous for its colony of nesting storks, and rich, spicy wines.

Alsatian wine garden.

Dégustation: Stop to Taste; Stop to Buy

All along the *Route du Vin* there are scores of wine producers to visit, both individual growers who make and market their own wines (*propriétaires-viticulteurs*), and grower-merchants (*propriétaires-négociants*) who both own their own vineyards and purchase additional grapes from other growers. About one-third of the region's production comes from *caves coopératives*. Alsace wines have long been considered one of the bargain quality wines of France but this does not mean that they are ever really cheap: quality never is. While the 'straight' Alsace varietals remain relatively inexpensive, they may not necessarily represent the best buys. Special *cuvée* wines (*cuvée tradition, réserve, etc.*) are usually only a few francs extra per bottle, and the extra selection which goes into them is almost always worth paying for.

ALSACE

Appointments are not generally necessary for those who simply want to taste and possibly purchase, though for more in-depth visits, a telephone call is always advisable. The list below follows the *Route du Vin* from north to south.

1 Cave Vinicole de Traenheim
RN422
67310 Traenheim
tel: (88) 50 67 27
Hours: Mon–Fri 8–12h; 14–18h.
This *cave coopérative* near the start of the wine road produces a full range of Alsace wines including the *Grands Crus* Altenberg de Bergbieten and Altenberg de Wolxheim.
English spoken.

2 Jean-Paul Seilly & Fils
8, rue du Gal Gouraud
67210 Obernai
tel: (88) 95 55 80
Hours: by appointment.
Full range of Alsace wines, and also the village speciality known as *vin du pistolet d'Obernai*, produced from a blend of noble grapes. M. Seilly is a member of the *Confrérie de la Veritable Tarte Flambée* — this unique speciality, cooked in a wood-fired oven, can be sampled on certain days in the adjacent *Caveau du Vigneron Restaurant*.
Charge for *dégustation*.
English spoken.

3 Domaine Klipfel
6, ave de la Gare
67140 Barr
tel: (88) 08 94 85
Hours: Daily 10–12h; 14–18h. Telephone call preferred.
Charge for *dégustation*.
This grower-merchant produces a full range of Alsace wines, including the *Grand Cru* Kirchberg as well as occasional *sélection de grains nobles*. Tasting and meals in the *caves* can be arranged for groups.
English spoken.

4 Alsace Willm, SA
32, rue du Docteur-Sultzer
67140 Barr
tel: (88) 08 19 11
Hours: Mon–Fri 8–12h; 14–17h.
Charge for *dégustation*.

Large and well-known producer of the full range of Alsace wines and the *Grand Cru* Kirchberg.
English spoken.

André and Rémy Gresser
2, rue de l'École
67140 Andlau
tel: (88) 08 95 88
Hours: Daily 10–19h.
Rémy Gresser is an enthusiast, committed wine maker, and champion of the *Grands Crus* of Alsace. Learn about the effects of soil and microclimate here, for all three of Andlau's Riesling *Grands Crus* are produced: Wiebelsberg, Kastelberg and Moenchberg.
English spoken.

Willy Gisselbrecht & Fils
route du Vin
67650 Dambach-la-Ville
tel: (88) 92 41 02
Hours: Mon–Fri 8–12h; 14–17h.
The commune of Dambach-la-Ville has the largest area under vines in the region. Willy Gisselbrecht is a grower-merchant who makes wines from both his own harvest — *propre récolte* — as well as from grapes purchased from others in this area. Full range of Alsace wines, including Crémant d'Alsace and *vendange tardive*.

Gustave Lorentz SA
35, Grande Rue
68750 Bergheim
tel: (89) 73 63 08
Hours: Mon–Fri 8–12h; 14–18h. Sat 8–12h.
Appointment necessary only for groups larger than six. The pretty fortified village of Bergheim hosts a Gewürztraminer festival each August. Gustave Lorentz's wine from that distinctive grape, especially the *Grand Cru* Altenberg de Bergheim, is highly regarded, as is the full range of wines. The Lorentz family have been in Bergheim since the fourteenth century.
English spoken.

Cave Coopérative de Ribeauvillé
2, route de Colmar
68150 Ribeauvillé
tel: (89) 73 61 80
Hours: Daily 9–12h; 14–17h.
Full range of Alsace wines, including Crémant d'Alsace, can be tasted in a pleasant salon of this large *cave coopérative*. Sole proprietor of the Clos du Zahnacker. The *cave coopérative* is also the proprietor of a nearby *winstub-restaurant*, Auberge 'Au Zahnacker'.
English spoken.

ALSACE

Grands Vins d'Alsace Louis Sipp
5, Grande Rue
68150 Ribeauvillé
tel: (89) 73 60 00
Hours: March–October by appointment.
Full range of Alsace wines and *eaux-de-vie* from this well-respected *viticulteur-négociant*. *Grands Crus* Kirchberg and Osterberg.
English spoken.

David Ermel & Fils
30, route de Ribeauvillé
68150 Hunawihr
tel: (89) 73 61 71
Hours: Daily 8–18h.
This small family *propriétaire-viticulteur* produces the full gamut of Alsace wines, including Crémant d'Alsace as well as Marc de Gewürztraminer and *eau-de-vie de quetsch*. Parking near the stork refuge.
English spoken.

Cave Vinicole de Hunawihr
48, route de Ribeauvillé
68150 Hunawihr
tel: (89) 73 61 67
Hours: Mon–Fri 8–12h; 14–18h. Appointment preferable.
Full range of Alsace wines, including the *Grand Cru* Rosacker and *vendange tardive*.
English spoken.

The premises of Hugel & Fils, established in Riquewihr since 1639.

Hugel & Fils SA
68340 Riquewihr
tel: (89) 47 92 15
Hours: Mon–Thur 8–12h; 13h30–17h30. Fri 8–12h.
Appointment essential to visit the cellars. Retail shop open during above hours.
One of the most famous grower-merchants, established in Riquewihr since 1639. In addition to the always sound 'straight' Hugel range of varietals, there are also finer selected wines which have undergone more vigorous selection: *cuvée tradition* and *réserve personnelle*, the latter designation applying to superb wines

produced only in exceptional years. In those years when conditions are favourable, Hugel produces some of the region's finest late-harvest wines: *vendange tardive* and *sélection de grains nobles*. So rare are the latter, produced from individually selected over-ripe grapes, that since 1865 there have been only 10 vintages.
English spoken.

13

Dopff Au Moulin
2, rue J.-Preiss
68340 Riquewihr
tel: (89) 47 92 23
Hours: Daily 8–12h; 14–18h.
One of the larger Alsace grower-shippers, established in Riquewihr in 1574, Dopff Au Moulin have helped to promote the region's image at home and abroad. A full range of Alsace wines is produced, including straight varietals as well as wines from the firm's own vineyards and *Grands Crus* such as Schoenenbourg, Sporen, and Brand de Turckheim. Dopff Au Moulin were the pioneers of sparkling Alsace wines and visitors see the *cave* where still wines undergo secondary fermentation in the bottle by the *méthode champenoise*. Late-harvest wines and *eaux-de-vie* are also produced. Dopff is the proprietor of the restaurant 'Au Moulin' in the centre of this delightful village.
Charge for visit and *dégustation*.
English spoken.

14

Dopff & Irion
Château de Riquewihr
68340 Riquewihr
tel: (89) 47 92 51
Hours: Daily Easter to October 9–19h.
Another large grower-merchant producing well-known and well-liked wines both from its own domaines (Riesling Les Murailles, Gewürztraminer Les Sorcières, Pinot Gris Les Maquisards, and Muscat Amandiers) and from grapes purchased from neighbouring growers.
Charge for visit and *dégustation*.
English spoken.

15

SARL Jean Preiss-Zimmer
42, rue du Général de Gaulle
68340 Riquewihr
tel: (89) 47 92 58
Hours: Daily 8–11h30; 13h30–17h.
This long-standing family firm produces a full range of Alsace wines. Proprietor of Winstub 'Au Tire-Bouchon'.
Charge for *dégustation*.
English spoken.

ALSACE

16 Les Caves J. B. Adam
5, rue de l'Aigle
68770 Ammerschwihr
tel: (89) 78 23 21
Hours: Mon–Sat 8–12h; 14–18h.
The town of Ammerschwihr, severely damaged in the war, sits below its famous *lieu-dit*, the well-exposed slope known as the Kaefferkopf. J. B. Adam is a family firm of *propriétaires-négociants* which has been making wine for 14 generations. They produce the full Alsace range, including, of course, the Kaefferkopf.
English spoken.

17 Cave Coopérative d'Ingersheim
1, rue Georges Clemenceau
68000 Ingersheim
tel: (89) 27 05 96
Hours: Mon–Thur 8–12h; 13h30–17h. Fri 8–12h; 13h30–16h.
From April to September weekend visits including *dégustation* arranged by appointment.
Full range of Alsace wines and Crémant d'Alsace.
Charge for *dégustation*.
English spoken.

18 Charles Schleret
1–3 route d'Ingersheim
68230 Turckheim
tel: (89) 27 06 09
Hours: Daily except Sun afternoon from 8–12h; 13h30–19h.
Appointment preferred.
Full range of Alsace wines.

19 Domaine Viticole de la Ville de Colmar
2, rue du Stauffen
68000 Colmar
tel: (89) 79 11 87
Hours: Mon–Fri 8–12h; 14–18h. Weekends by appointment.
The Domaine Viticole de la Ville de Colmar was created out of the crisis which the wine growers found themselves in after the Franco–Prussian War ended in 1870. The vineyards had been destroyed by war; the Germans did not want to promote Alsace wines at the expense of their own from the Mosel and Rhine; and these factors coincided with the outbreak of phylloxera (see p.267). The vineyards were thus falling into ruin and it was for this reason that the Domaine Viticole, known formerly as the Institut Oberlin after its founder, Philippe Christian Oberlin, came into being. Its primary objectives were to re-introduce the noble *cépages* and to fight against the maladies of the vineyard. Today these roles have been taken over by the professional bodies of Alsace

but the Domaine's 14 hectares are still exploited for the production and sale of fine wines.

20 Maison Léon Beyer
2, rue de la 1ère Armée
68420 Eguisheim
tel: (89) 41 41 05
Hours: Mon–Fri 8–12h; 14–17h.
Appointment essential.
One of the oldest and most respected houses in Alsace, the Maison Léon Beyer is a *propriétaire-négociant* with considerable vineyard holdings, especially around this lovely and popular town. A full range of wines is produced, with the finest sold under the prestige labels *Cuvée des Comtes d'Eguisheim* and *Cuvée d'Ecaillers*. There is a tasting *caveau* open to all in July and August. English spoken.

21 Kuentz-Bas SA
14, route du Vin
68420 Husseren-les-Châteaux
tel: (89) 49 30 24
Hours: Mon–Fri 9–12h; 13–18h. Sat 9–12h.
Visits by appointment only.
Situated high above the Alsatian plain, along the *Route des Cinq Châteaux* which dominate above, Husseren is a particularly pretty village which gives splendid views over the Alsace vineyard. Kuentz-Bas is another large and well-respected *maison* producing the full Alsace range. Tasting *caveau* open May–September.
English spoken.

22 Cave Vinicole de Pfaffenheim
Pfaffenheim
68250 Rouffach
tel: (89) 49 61 08
Hours: Mon–Sat 8–12h; 14–19h. Sun 10–12h; 14–19h.
This serious and well-respected *cave coopérative* produces a fine range of Alsace wines, including the *Grands Crus* Steinert and Goldbert. Many wines have been awarded medals as well as the *sigillés* from the Confrérie St-Etienne.

23 François Runner
1, rue de la Liberté
Pfaffenheim
68250 Rouffach
tel: (89) 49 62 89
Hours: Daily except Sun.
Typical family *propriétaire-viticulteur* producing the full Alsace range. Charge for wine consumed on the premises.
English spoken.

ALSACE

Vignobles P. Reinhart
7, rue du Printemps
68500 Orschwihr
tel: (89) 76 95 12
Hours: Mon–Sat 9–12h; 14–20h.
Small family exploitation with full Alsace range made exclusively from own harvest — *propre récolte*.
A little English spoken.

Distillerie Artisanale

A. Legoll
route de Villé
67730 Chatenois
tel: (88) 85 66 90
Hours: Visits by appointment.
The art of traditional Alsatian distillation can be seen and sampled at this fine family business. *Eaux-de-vie de cerise, quetsch, framboise, poire william, marc de Gewürztraminer* have all won many awards.

The *Grands Crus* of Alsace

Although official recognition of superior individual vineyards and slopes has only been given with the granting of the *Grand Cru appellation* in 1975 and the subsequent classification of individual sites in 1983 and 1986, to the growers whose families have tended vines here for centuries and generations, there has never been any doubt that certain *lieux-dits* were indeed exceptional.

The Kastelberg vineyard in Andlau was documented as long ago as 1064, the Moenchberg as early as 1214, the Altenberg of Bergheim in 1394, the Kaefferkopf in 1328, and so on, these few examples thus proving that, as in other wine regions of France, individual *terroirs* have long been valued. It was only after World War II that the producers began to market their wines varietally, that is by the names of the single grape variety only.

While the simplicity of Alsace varietal wines has long been appreciated and admired (especially in contrast to the tortured complexities of, say, Burgundy), the development of the *Grands Crus* is most welcome, for this now adds a further tier of enjoyment to drinking Alsace wine. Any wine bearing the *Grand Cru appellation* is produced from grapes grown on exceptional and recognized sites, to more stringent and exacting requirements. When well made and in favourable years, such a wine will carry its own individual signature: the flavour and character of its unique *terroir*.

Wine Festivals

Last Sunday in March	Presentation of new wines	Eguisheim
Early May	Wine Festival	Molsheim
End of May	Wine Festival	Guebwiller
2nd Sunday in June	Kugelhopf Festival	Ribeauvillé
Mid July	Wine Festival	Barr
1st Saturday in July	Open *Caves*	Dambach-la-Ville
Sunday after 14 July	Fête des Guinguettes d'Europe	Husseren-les-Châteaux
Before last weekend in July	Wine Festival	Ribeauvillé
Before last weekend in July	Riesling Festival	Riquewihr
End of July	Wine Festival	Wettolsheim
Last weekend in July	Wine Festival	Mittelbergheim
1st weekend in August	Wine Festival	Turckheim
1st Sunday in August	Fête des Amandiers	Mittelwihr
Weekend of 15 August	'Mini' Wine Fair	Obernai
1st fortnight in August	Wine Festival	Dambach-la-Ville
Last Sunday in August	Vintage Festival	Eguisheim
1st Sunday in September	Fête des Ménétriers	Ribeauvillé
Beginning of September	Fête du Riesling	Wolxheim
During the vintage (1–15 October)	Fête des Vendanges	Barr Hunawihr Itterswiller Katzenthal Niedermorschwihr Obernai Rosheim Marlenheim
2nd weekend in October	Wine Festival	Molsheim
3rd Sunday in October	Fête des Vendanges	Marlenheim Obernai

A L S A C E

37

Regional Gastronomy

The cuisine of Alsace, like its wines, developed out of the historic turbulence which has shaped the region itself. Influences from Germany as well as from France are readily apparent, yet foremost Alsace presents a cuisine which is all its own.

For example, that favourite but often pedestrian German staple *sauerkraut* here translates into *choucroute garnie* and becomes a veritable feast: lightly pickled cabbage simmered slowly in Riesling and garnished with as many as nine different types of meat, sausages, and other *charcuterie*. *Baekhoffa* is another typical hearty Alsatian one-pot meal, an earthenware dish packed solid with an assortment of beef, pork, lamb, and mutton, all generously soused in wine, and layered together with potatoes, vegetables, and herbs. In the past this used to be carried to the town baker's oven, hence the name, but today, cooked for hours, if not overnight, in homes and restaurants, it is still a substantial and mouth-watering feast not to be missed.

Neither of these typical Alsatian foods would appear out of place on tables across the Rhine. Yet alongside them appear foods such as that greatest French delicacy *foie gras*, the fattened liver of goose or duck, as well as other archetypal Gallic stand-bys such as *escargots* — snails from the vineyard cooked with garlic butter and chopped parsley. Another favourite is *coq au Riesling*, a fine variation of the French chicken-in-wine favourite, here flamed first in brandy, then simmered in a delicate sauce of Riesling d'Alsace and cream. Freshwater fish stews (*matelotes*) are similarly prepared: combinations of pike, tench, river eel, and trout cooked in wine then finished lightly with cream.

The pork butchers of Alsace demonstrate the skills of both their German counterparts by creating an enormous range of *wurst*-like sausages, including *saucisse de Strasbourg* (lightly smoked, pork and beef), *cervelas* (fine pork sausage studded with pistachios or hazelnuts), sausages flavoured with caraway seeds, versions of *bratwurst*, *knackwurst*, and liver sausages; French skills are apparent in the range of *pâtés*, *terrines*, *fromage de tête*, *boudins*, and, especially, *tourtes* — meat-filled pies which make such excellent picnic fare.

Another typical dish which should not be missed is the *tarte flambée*, also known as *le flammekueche*. Of all the Alsatian specialities, this is one of the simplest and most delicious: a round or rectangle of bread dough, covered with *fromage blanc* and cream, sprinkled with *lardons* and cooked onions, seasoned with salt, pepper, and oil, then cooked over the flames of a wood-fired oven. This basic recipe varies between each village and household. There is even a society to safeguard its authenticity: *La Confrérie de la Véritable Tarte Flambée d'Alsace*. There are a number of restaurants and *winstubs* which authentically prepare the *tarte flambée* but only on certain days of the week.

The *tarte flambée* is an example of a simple country dish which once formed part of the weekly diet for the farmers and hill folk of the region and which is now embraced with gusto no longer just by the locals but by city dwellers and tourists. Game from the forests of the Vosges has always been

Le Menu.

an important mainstay in the local diet, too, and restaurants reflect this fondness by offering, in season, wild boar, venison, partridge, and hare, cooked in *civets*, rich stews flavoured with wild mushrooms and thickened with blood, or served *à l'alsacienne*, on a bed of *choucroute*.

The Alsatians are masters of pastry skills and their range of both savoury and sweet tarts is almost unrivalled. *Tarte à l'oignon* is sublimely simple, sweet, and delicious. And the whole catalogue of fruit-filled tarts in a *pâtisserie* window is one of the prettiest sights in France: tarts made with yellow plums, blueberries, bilberries, cherries, raspberries, and much else. Alongside these are the famous *kugelhopfs*, yeast cakes baked in their distinctive fluted moulds, the classic Alsatian breakfast.

Kugelhopf, a classic Alsatian yeast cake.

The basics of the Alsatian kitchen are handled well throughout the region, in simple restaurants and *winstubs*: indeed, if you stick to the regional foods, it is difficult to go wrong. Additionally, Alsace has become a highly regarded gastronomic mecca, and there are numerous fine and elegant restaurants serving *nouvelle*-inspired foods alongside traditional. The region, too, with its grassy meadows full of wildflowers, its lakes and woods and quiet roads through the vineyards, is picnic country *par excellence*.

Restaurants (Map p.27)

Maison Kammerzell
16, place de la Cathédrale
67000 Strasbourg
tel: (88) 32 42 14
Open daily.
In the shadow of the Gothic cathedral, this splendid Alsatian dwelling built in 1427 is a classified historic monument. The ground floor is decorated with murals painted by the artist Leon Schnug, which lend a particular atmosphere to this typical *winstub* where local specialities are served, including *choucroute*, *foie gras* and *escargots maison*. The upper floors serve a mixture of *nouvelle cuisine* and traditional, with imaginative dishes such as *saumon marine au citron vert sur lit de choucroute*.
Moderate

Maison des Tanneurs
42, rue Bain-aux-Plantes
67000 Strasbourg
tel: (88) 32 79 70

A L S A C E

Closed Sun and Mon; 22 December–23 January; 27 June–7 July.
A centuries-old craftsman's workshop, now a fine restaurant directly on the Ill, serving all regional specialities and Alsace wines.
Moderate

3

Restaurant 'Zum Strissel'
5, place de la Grande Boucherie
67000 Strasbourg
tel: (88) 32 14 73
Closed Sun and Mon.
Typical *winstub* near the Cathedral serving regional specialities and *grillades* together with a good selection of Alsace wines *en pichet*.
Inexpensive

Le Pique-Nique

Tarte à l'oignon Alsatian onion tart. Purchase small individual tarts or slices to eat hot or cold.

Tourte alsacienne Pork, wine, and herb pie.

Foie gras The best place to eat this delicacy is in a good restaurant where the fresh, fattened livers of goose or duck (raised in the region again after a period of relative local scarcity) will be *mi-cuit* — only delicately cooked and still slightly pink in the middle. Good *charcuteries* will sell that particular Alsatian speciality *pâté de foie gras en croute*, a fine mixture of goose liver and pork baked in a *brioche* pastry. Many shops offer tins or ceramic terrines of *foie gras*, as well. Though never as fine as when freshly prepared, this is the most convenient picnic fare. Remember: *bloc* means whole pieces of goose liver; *mousse* is a puréed mixture which, though less expensive, is considerably less fine.

Jambon de montagne Air-dried mountain ham, usually smoked.

Pretzels Large, bready pretzels, salted or sweet.

Kugelhopf The classic yeast-raised *brioche* of Alsace, delicious for breakfast with a tot of *eau-de-vie d'Alsace*.

Munster The great cheese of Alsace and as fitting an accompaniment to a picnic as to the end of a great meal. This round, flat rind-washed cheese is made in the Vosges slopes around the town of the same name as well as in its surrounds. Mild when young, it gains an intense and rich aroma and strong flavour with age. In the region, it is often eaten sprinkled with caraway seeds.

4

Restaurant Loejelgücker
17, rue Principale
67310 Traenheim
tel: (88) 50 38 19
Closed Tue; month of February.
Near the start of the *Route du Vin* serving typical dishes such as *sandre au Riesling*, *foie gras maison*, *escargots*. Recommended by the Cave Coopérative de Traenheim.
Inexpensive to Moderate

5

Beau Site
place de l'Église
67350 Ottrott
tel: (88) 95 80 61
Restaurant closed Sun evening.
This geranium-bedecked hotel-restaurant serves traditional and typical cooking, accompanied by *rouge d'Ottrott*, the red wine for which the village is famous.
Moderate

6

Caveau du Vigneron
18, rue du Gal Gouraud
67210 Obernai
tel: (88) 95 53 10
Open daily.
Wine grower J. Seilly's rustic *caveau* serves own wines, simple typical foods, and specialities such as the *tarte flambée* (only on Fri, Sat and Sun night).
Inexpensive

7

Le Relais de la Poste
Winstub-Restaurant
1, rue des Forgerons
67140 Andlau
tel: (88) 08 95 91
Closed Mon; Tue midday.
A welcoming *relais* along the *Route du Vin* whose enthusiastic owner-chef maintains the essential casual and good-humoured atmosphere of the authentic *winstub*. Specialities include *baekhoffa* and *foie gras maison*. Recommended by Rémy Gresser.
Moderate

8

Hôtel–Restaurant Arnold
98, route du Vin
67140 Itterswiller
tel: (88) 85 50 58
Restaurant closed Sun evening; Mon.
In the heart of the vineyards, at the foot of the Vosges mountains, this hotel–

restaurant is an old favourite. Restaurant serves all the Alsatian specialities, but the *baekhoffa* (only on Thur and Sat), is worth making a detour for. Riesling and Sylvaner wines are home-produced from vineyards in front of the hotel. Recommended by Willy Gisselbrecht.
Moderate

9 Wistub du Sommelier
51, Grande Rue
68750 Bergheim
tel: (89) 73 69 99
Closed Sun.
M. Jean-Marie Stoeckel was the '*Meilleur Sommelier de France*' in 1972 so it is not surprising that this typical *winstub* has a fine choice of Alsace wines, including many served by the glass. Good regional menu. Recommended by Gustave Lorentz.
Inexpensive to Moderate

10 Auberge 'Au Zahnacker'
8, rue du Gal de Gaulle
68150 Ribeauvillé
tel: (89) 73 60 77
Open daily from 1 June to 31 October.
This restaurant is owned by the *Cave Coopérative de Ribeauvillé* which is located just across the road. Simple *winstub* on one side, restaurant on the other, there is also a pleasant outdoor terrace where meals or wines of the *coop* are served in fine weather.
Inexpensive to Moderate

11 Les Vosges
2, Grande Rue
68150 Ribeauvillé
tel: (89) 73 61 39
Closed Mon; January–February.
Chef Joseph Matter prepares classic elegant cuisine with an Alsatian accent: *matelote de sandre et sole, pièce de boeuf au Pinot Noir*. Recommended by Trimbach, Louis Sipp.
Moderate to Expensive

12 Winstub–Restaurant 'Au Tire-Bouchon'
rue du Gal de Gaulle
68340 Riquewihr
tel: (89) 47 91 61
Open daily in season. Closed Tue midday; Wed November–May.
Small, unpretentious typical *winstub* serving Alsatian dishes like *quennelles de foie* (liver dumplings) and *tourte vigneronne* together with wines exclusively from the proprietor, Preiss-Zimmer.
Inexpensive

13 Le Sarment d'Or
4, rue du Cerf
68340 Riquewihr
tel: (89) 47 92 85
Closed Mon.
In the heart of old Riquewihr, a very pleasant old *logis* serving *matelote de poissons 'Sarment d'Or', foie gras à la gelée au Tokay, feuilleté d'escargots.*
Moderate

14 Auberge de l'Ill
rue de Collonges
68150 Illhaeusern
tel: (89) 71 83 23
Closed Mon eve; Tue; February; first week in July.
Situated on the banks of the Ill, surrounded by lovely flowered gardens, this is one of the very finest and loveliest restaurants in France, specializing in a unique and elegant blend of Alsatian classic and *nouvelle cuisine*: *brioche de foie gras, mousseline de grenouilles, noisettes de chevreuil.*
Very Expensive

15 Hôtel–Restaurant Aux Armes de France
1, Grande Rue
68770 Ammerschwihr
tel: (89) 47 10 12
Closed Wed; Thur midday.
Famous Alsatian temple of gastronomy in a famous Alsace wine town: specialities include *foie gras d'oie 'Aux Armes de France', filet de sole aux nouilles, la canette de Barbarie au miel et aux épices, la pièce de boeuf au Pinot Noir.*
Expensive

16 Restaurant Au Fer Rouge
52, Grande Rue
68000 Colmar
tel: (89) 41 37 24
Closed Sun eve; Mon.
Nouvelle cuisine in the old part of Colmar; wide range of Alsace and other French wines. Recommended by Jean Hugel.
Moderate to Expensive

17 La Maison des Têtes
19, rue des Têtes
68000 Colmar
tel: (89) 24 43 43
Closed Sun eve; Mon.
A landmark in old Colmar, the panelled dining room in this fine Renaissance

ALSACE

house is separated into little private alcoves. The full range of Alsatian specialities and wines.

Moderate

18 Restaurant au Trois Poissons
15, quai de la Poissonnerie
68000 Colmar
tel: (89) 41 25 21
Closed Wed.
Fish restaurant in the Petite Venise part of town specializing in *matelote, friture,* and *bouillabaisse.*

Inexpensive to Moderate

19 Caveau d'Eguisheim
3, place du Château-St-Léon
68420 Eguisheim
tel: (89) 41 08 89
Closed Wed eve and Thur.
This typical Alsatian house, built in 1603 opposite the château where Pope Leo IX was born, serves Alsatian specialities, cuisine based on the daily market produce, and game in season. Wines mainly from this fine commune. Recommended by Maison Léon Beyer.

Moderate to Expensive

20 Relais 'Au Petit Pfaffenheim'
1, rue de la Chapelle
68250 Pfaffenheim
tel: (89) 49 62 06
Closed Mon eve; Tue.
Specialities include *foie gras* and *truite au bleu aux girolles en papillote.* Recommended by François Runner.

Moderate

Winstub.

Winstubs

The *winstubs* or *wistubs* of Alsace are unique (both spellings are used). Foremost, they originated as places where friends could gather to meet and talk. Talking, as we all know, dries the throat, so a glass of wine — or two, or three — was taken to relieve any discomfort. Surely, though, no one wants to drink without a bite to eat . . . Thus, the wines of Alsace, served *en pichet* were accompanied by the simple plates of the region: a slice of *tarte à l'oìgnon*, some herrings marinated in cream, a few piping hot liver dumplings, some *charcuterie*, or slabs of Munster cheese. *Winstubs* first appeared in Strasbourg in the old quarter around the cathedral and they were very popular with students. Today they are found in half-timbered houses in almost every village along the *Route du Vin d'Alsace*. Though many are open at midday, *winstubs* are at their best and liveliest in the evenings.

Additional Information

Et pour en savoir plus . . .

Comité Interprofessionnel des Vins d'Alsace
8, place de Lattre-de-Tassigny
68000 Colmar
tel: (89) 41 06 21

Office de Tourisme
10, place Gutenberg
67000 Strasbourg
tel: (88) 32 57 07

Office de Tourisme
4, rue Unterlinden
68000 Colmar
tel: (89) 41 02 29

ALSACE

BORDEAUX

Introduction

Couvent des Cordeliers, St-Emilion.

*B*ordeaux is the greatest vineyard in the world. All across the vast Gironde *département* (the largest in France) there are over 100,000 hectares of vines planted. Each autumn it takes a veritable army of over a third of a million *vendangeurs* to bring in the sun-ripened grapes: *paniers* and plastic tubs overflowing with small tough-skinned Cabernet Sauvignon; purple Merlot; pungent Sauvignon; shrivelled, rotten Sémillon; fragrant Muscadelle; and others. These grapes, when pressed and vinified, yield on average a phenomenal 500 million bottles of wine each year: red, white, golden, and pink; famous château-bottled wines which are as fine and as expensive as any on earth; and great rivers of everyday wines which are drunk without fuss and pretension. These facts, combined with the region's proximity to the fine sandy beaches of the Atlantic and its access to the hinterland of Périgord and the Gers, makes it understandably one of the most popular in France for wine travellers and tourists.

The Gironde estuary, formed by the convergence of two great rivers, the Dordogne and Garonne, shapes the region: a pointed crest of land rearing out into the Bay of Biscay, its soil scoured into gravel, pebbles, sand, and other alluvial deposits left here over past millennia. The tall majestic pine forests behind the Atlantic seaboard shelter the vineyards from harsh winds, while the rivers provide the necessary and optimum growing conditions and microclimates. 'The vine likes to see the water', they say in Bordeaux, and indeed vineyards are rarely out of sight of its many rivers: planted on the gentle hills on either side of the Gironde, as well as along both banks of the Dordogne and Garonne and on the lands in between — literally *entre deux mers*. Smaller tributaries play their role, too: the tiny Cirons, for example, contributes just that special autumnal combination of early morning mist and warm afternoon sun which causes the formation of *pourriture noble* and thus

Right *Bordeaux.*

46

The Hundred Years' War

The Hundred Years' War lasted from 1337 until 1453 and during that long period intense fighting took place intermittently over much of south-western and western France. At the root of the war was the marriage of Henry II to Eleanor of Aquitaine; this gave the English a substantial stronghold on French soil which was to last some 300 years. The English monarchs, moreover, refused to pay homage to the Kings of France by recognizing their feudal suzerainty over the fief of Aquitaine.

The fighting began in 1337 when the French King Philip IV seized the English-held duchy of Guyenne, part of Aquitaine. Edward III of England, together with his son the Black Prince, then scored a series of initial notable victories. However, by 1375 Edward had lost all of his French possessions except Calais, Bordeaux, Bayonne, and Brest.

Over the next decades, there was much further entrenched fighting. Henry V's victory at Agincourt in 1415 finally brought the French throne into English hands, though this triumph was short-lived; after the death of that grandiose and ambitious monarch, Jeanne d'Arc, the Maid of Orléans, rallied the French who gradually reclaimed their territory.

The Bordeaux region remained one of the last English strongholds: a final and decisive battle took place at Castillon, east of St-Emilion, on 17 July 1453. The French, with superior artillery, severely routed the enemy. When Bordeaux itself finally capitulated a further 3 months later, this marked not only the end of English rule in Aquitaine but also the waning of the Middle Ages.

---

contributes to the creation of the great sweet wines of Sauternes.

The Dordogne and the Garonne themselves are great wine rivers too, not just here in Bordeaux, but further inland as well. From Bergerac, the wines of the rich Périgord hinterland used to travel down-river in barrels by barge to Libourne. Inky black wine from Cahors came down the winding Lot river to where it joined the Garonne, and from there travelled, alongside barrels of pungent Armagnac, further down-river to Bordeaux itself. The *quais* of this great capital of the grape have thus been awash with wine for centuries. Some of the most celebrated merchants and shippers of Bordeaux still maintain their headquarters along the Quai des Chartrons.

The vineyards of the Médoc to the north of Bordeaux are virtually a national asset, and wine travellers who traverse the D2 wine road through Margaux, St-Julien, Pauillac, and St-Estèphe, do so almost in awe and homage, for indeed the profusion of famous and elegant châteaux is overwhelming. Other vineyard areas are less imposing, the properties and the wines themselves more accessible. St-Emilion is one of the great little wine towns of France: the '1000 châteaux' which claim to surround the medieval town include not only famous and prestigious *Grands Crus* but many modest and smaller properties as well. The great châteaux of Sauternes retain a certain remote country feel about them. And lesser wine regions, if somewhat overshadowed by the greater and more famous ones, are none the less fruitful grounds for the intrepid wine traveller. There are certainly no shortages of opportunities in Bordeaux for visiting and tasting wines at both *grands* and *petits* châteaux alike.

The British have always had a particular and special relation with the region. For when young Henry Plantagenet (later to become King Henry II of England) married Eleanor of Aquitaine, the region became an English possession. And so it stayed, for some three centuries, during which time the Englishman and his beloved claret — which is simply red Bordeaux wine — became inseparable. Even after English rule in Aquitaine came to an end in 1453, the wine trade continued to prosper. Today, holidaymakers from Britain as well as from throughout France, Europe, and further afield, come to this south-western corner of the country not only just to drink wine, but to hide behind the tall pine forests and sand dunes of the Landes; to explore an ancient and historic land; and to enjoy a regional kitchen which, like its wines, combines aristocratic delights such as oysters, *foie gras*, and lamprey with more accessible everyday pleasures.

Orientation

The most direct route for Paris–Bordeaux is on the A10 *autoroute* which leads there all the way, via Orléans, Tours, Poitiers, and Saintes. The distance is about 580 km (360 miles) and can be covered comfortably in around 6–8 hours. Wine travellers may wish to break the journey either in the vineyards of Touraine or else in Cognac. One option, rather than proceeding directly to the city of Bordeaux, is to cross the Gironde at Royan or Blaye to reach the Médoc direct. The Trans-Gironde company operates both these ferry routes, though it is essential to check the times (tel: (56) 52 63 76).

By train, there is an express service from Paris which completes the journey to Bordeaux in under 4 hours. Bordeaux is on the main Paris–Madrid line so there are frequent trains as well as connections with international services. Bordeaux has its own international airport: Bordeaux Mérignac.

Michelin Maps 71, 75

The Wines of Bordeaux

General *appellations*

*Bordeaux AOC;
Bordeaux Supérieur
AOC*

*B*ordeaux is known above all for its famous and prestigious 'classed growths' but vast amounts of good, straightforward red and white wines are produced under the basic *appellation d'origine contrôlée*. Bordeaux AOC and the slightly higher in alcohol Bordeaux Supérieur AOC are produced throughout the delimited Bordeaux region, and are subjected to rigorous quality control regarding permitted grape varieties, methods of cultivation, maximum yield, and minimum alcohol content. The main permitted grape varieties for red wines are Cabernet Sauvignon, Cabernet Franc, Merlot, and Malbec; white wines are produced primarily from Sémillon, Sauvignon, and Muscadelle. For the visitor to the region in search of good everyday wines, there are literally thousands of producers, ranging from small individual *propriétaires-récoltants* to large *coopératives* who produce such wines alongside the famous flag-bearers of the region: these lesser wines are still remarkably good value.

Bordeaux Clairet AOC

Not to be confused with claret, but rather a recognized *appellation* for a robust and rather fuller rosé wine.

Bordeaux Rosé AOC

Rosé wine made from the classic red grape varieties of Bordeaux: primarily Cabernet Sauvignon, Cabernet Franc, and Merlot. The *Supérieur* designation means slightly higher alcohol content. Not widely encountered outside the Bordeaux region but worth drinking on the spot.

The Médoc and Graves

Médoc AOC:
Haut-Médoc AOC

The Médoc and Haut-Médoc *appellations* apply to red wines from vineyards extending over the triangular peninsula which stretches north-west from Bordeaux to form a point where the Gironde meets the Atlantic. They are noted above all for a rather deep, tough character that combines with subtle and delicate flavours; the greatest have the ability to improve and develop nuances over very long periods of time. The finest wines, bearing the *appellations* of individual communes, lie in the southern half closest to

Bordeaux, and this area is known as the Haut-Médoc. Wines bearing the Haut-Médoc *appellation* on its own are generally considered superior to those bearing the Médoc AOC, the former noted for their deeper colour and greater concentration and intensity of flavours. The dividing line between the two occurs around St-Seurin-de-Cadourne, just north of St-Estèphe.

Small amounts of white wine are produced in the Médoc, but even distinguished wines such as Château Margaux's Pavillon Blanc are only entitled to the basic *appellation* Bordeaux AOC.

Old bottles in the private cellars of Château Margaux.

Margaux AOC	*T*he first great commune of the Haut-Médoc, including Margaux itself, Cantenac, Labarde, Arsac, and Soussins. Margaux wines, often made with a higher proportion of Merlot in addition to Cabernet Sauvignon and Cabernet Franc, are considered by many to be the most feminine and elegant wines of the Médoc. Château Margaux, one of only five *Premiers Grands Crus Classés* wines is the great flag-bearer of the commune.
Moulis AOC or Moulis-en-Médoc AOC	*T*his communal *appellation* applies to vineyards north of Margaux and south of Listrac.
Listrac AOC	*A*nother less well-known communal *appellation* for vineyards east of Margaux.
St-Julien AOC	*D*istinguished wine from the communes of St-Julien, Beychevelle, Cussac, and St-Laurent, located in the mid-Médoc. The wines are considered among the best balanced of all clarets, combining the elegance of Margaux with the forceful body of Pauillac.
Pauillac AOC	*T*he classic wine of the Médoc: deep in colour, with an intense bouquet reminiscent of cedar and blackcurrants, and complex long-lasting flavours. Pauillac wines are generally rich in tannin; this gives them a rather hard and initially unforthcoming character, but a great ability to develop and improve with age. Pauillac has three of the five superlative *Premiers Grands Crus Classés*: Château Latour, Château Lafite-Rothschild, and Château Mouton-Rothschild.
St-Estèphe AOC	*T*he last great wine commune of the Haut-Médoc produces big, meaty wines which may lack the finesse of Margaux and St-Julien, but more than make up for it in body and solidity. These at times hard and austere wines often need considerable age to bring out their best.
Graves AOC	*A* prestigious and vast vineyard, producing both distinguished red clarets and vigorous, forceful dry white wines, the best dry white wines, in fact, in the whole Bordeaux vineyard. The region extends virtually from the outskirts of Bordeaux itself to south of Langon and encloses the sweet wine enclaves of Barsac and Sauternes. Château Haut-Brion has long been considered the greatest wine of Graves, and an equal to the finest from the Médoc, a fact recognized in 1855 when it was granted *Premier Grand Cru Classé* status. Apart from this paragon, the remaining finest wines of Graves — both red and white — were classified in 1953, and this was revised again in 1959 and 1985. The principal and best wine communes of Graves are Pessac, Talence, Villenave d'Ornon, Léognan, Martillac, and Cadaujac. They are allowed to append their name to the Graves *appellation* as in Graves de Pessac AOC. Other Graves communes further south of Bordeaux are a great source of less complicated but fine everyday reds and whites.

BORDEAUX

Sauternes, Barsac and Other *Vins Liquoreux*

Sauternes AOC

*T*he great *vin liquoreux* vineyards of Sauternes and Barsac extend over five communes: Sauternes, Barsac, Preignac, Bommes, and Fargues. The wines produced in the best years are luscious, extremely sweet, and among the finest dessert wines in the world. The grapes used are Sémillon, Sauvignon, and Muscadelle; in the best years these are affected by *pourriture noble* or noble rot, concentrating natural grape sugars and flavours yet reducing yield to miniscule levels. The grapes must be harvested in successive passes through the vineyard, only collecting those which are ripe and super-ripe. The wines retain a high level of residual sugar, but this is balanced both by acidity and a relatively high alcohol content (minimum 12.5°, though often much higher). The wines of Sauternes and Barsac were classified in 1855.

Barsac AOC

*B*arsac is the only other wine commune in this exceptional enclave entitled to its separate *appellation*. There are a number of prestigious classified châteaux which produce great and complex *vins liquoreux*; on the whole, the wines of Barsac have a character which is considered somewhat less opulent and luscious than Sauternes.

Cérons AOC

*T*he *appellation* for neighbouring vineyards north of Barsac which produce similar but much lighter and less distinguished *vins liquoreux*.

The Classification of 1855

The first great classification of Bordeaux wines took place in 1855, ordered by Napoleon III to be in place in time for the great world fair, the *Exposition Universelle de Paris*. This daunting task was achieved by ranking the wines of the Médoc (and one from Graves) and the wines of Sauternes in a classification based on the price that they had historically fetched: the reasoning then was based on the simple precept that the best wines were those that could command the highest prices.

In the case of the Médoc, five superlative tiers of *Grands Crus* were established. Four châteaux were considered in a class of their own, *Premiers Grands Crus Classés*: Margaux, Lafite, Latour, and Haut-Brion. In 1973, a generally recognized omission from this élite list was rectified with the elevation of Mouton-Rothschild. A further 58 châteaux were classified in 1855 as *Deuxièmes*, *Troisièmes*, *Quatrièmes* and *Cinquièmes Crus*: all of them very good, and even great, wines which have come to be known as the prestigious *Crus Classés, Grand Cru Classés* or classed growths. Even today, wines are still referred to based on their position on this list: a fourth growth, or a second growth, for example.

The wines of Sauternes were classified at the same time, and 11 were considered superior or *Premiers Crus* (first growths). One wine alone topped even this exceptional category, Château d'Yquem, which was classified on its own as *Grand Premier Cru*. A further 13 wines were ranked *Deuxièmes Crus* or second growths.

Arguments, certainly, rage today over the continuing value of the 1855 classification: some wines are universally regarded as superior to their placing on that list, while others, say many, no longer deserve their position. There is little doubt that experts today, given the chance would each have their own personal alterations — elevations and demotions — to make: yet surely what is most remarkable is that this great classification still remains, on the whole, an accurate and important benchmark.

Cru Bourgeois

The *Cru Bourgeois*, or bourgeois growths, are wines which were considered below *Grand Cru* status in 1855 but which none the less are recognized for their excellence. The classification of such wines was originally carried out in the early part of this century, though the list was considerably revised in 1966 and 1978. There are three tiers, which have correspondingly more stringent requirements relating to the quality of the wine, château-bottling, maturation and other factors: *Cru Exceptionnel* (the highest such accolade), *Cru Grand Bourgeois*, and *Cru Bourgeois*.

Cadillac AOC

*V*ineyards surrounding the town of Cadillac, on the opposite bank of the Garonne from Cérons, are entitled to their own *appellation*: the wines produced from Sémillon, Sauvignon, and Muscadelle grapes are similar to their great counterparts across the river, though considerably lighter.

Loupiac AOC

*M*inor sweet white wines produced from vineyards just south of Cadillac.

Pourriture Noble

Pourriture noble, or noble rot, occurs in certain conditions only — often during spells of autumn morning mist followed by afternoon sunshine and heat — which encourage a fungus, *Botrytis cinerea*, to attack the grape. *Botrytis* pierces the skin and extracts the water content, causing the grape to shrivel and turn brown and wizened. A bunch of grapes so affected is not a pretty sight, and indeed it must have been a brave or a blind man who first attempted to make wine from them. Yet through this process of 'rotting nobly' the natural grape sugars and flavours are concentrated, the glycerin content is increased, and rare and excitingly intense flavours, smells, and texture are imparted.

BORDEAUX

Ste-Croix-du-Mont AOC

*M*inor sweet wines from vineyards around this particularly lovely hill town south of Loupiac. These wines — Ste-Croix-du-Mont, Loupiac, Cérons, and Cadillac — are only 'lesser' in comparison with the great and concentrated wines produced in the nearby Sauternes vineyards. Well-made examples from good vintages are certainly capable of considerable distinction, and have the ability to age for many years. If they are, on the whole, lighter than Sauternes or Barsac, this means that they can be enjoyed at different times and occasions: as an *apéritif* or even, as the locals do, drunk with food.

St-Emilion, Pomerol and their Satellites

St-Emilion AOC

*G*enerous, full-bodied red wine produced from vineyards on the right bank of the Dordogne, around this famous and picturesque medieval town. A higher proportion of Merlot grapes, in addition to Cabernet Sauvignon and Cabernet Franc is generally used and this results in wines that are fuller and more fleshy, with less high levels of tannin than wines from the Médoc. As such they are usually ready to drink somewhat earlier, for they are rounder and more immediately appealing.

St-Emilion is called 'the land of a 1000 châteaux'; in 1955 its numerous wine-producing estates were classified: 12 are entitled to the illustrious designation *Premiers Grands Crus Classés* (two famous properties top this list and are considered in a class of their own: Château Ausone and Château Cheval Blanc), followed by some 72 *Grands Crus Classés*. Confusingly, there are, furthermore, about 100 or so less distinguished but on the whole fine châteaux entitled to call themselves simply *Grands Crus*.

Montagne-St-Emilion AOC; St-Georges-St-Emilion AOC Lussac-St-Emilion AOC; Parsac-St-Emilion AOC; Puisseguin-St-Emilion AOC

*T*he so-called 'satellites' of St-Emilion are vineyards which extend beyond its delimited boundaries, mainly around these five communes to the north and east. The wines produced are very much in the St-Emilion family style, though they are on the whole lighter and less distinguished. None the less, this compact hinterland is worthy of exploration as there are many fine wines to be found. St-Georges-St-Emilion and Montagne-St-Emilion are generally considered to be the best.

Bordeaux-Côtes de Castillon AOC

*T*he vineyards of the Côtes de Castillon continue on west of St-Emilion and around and beyond the town of Castillon-la-Bataille to the very fringe of where the Bordeaux vineyard meets the vineyard of Bergerac. The red wines produced are similar to St-Emilion in style and are still relatively inexpensive.

Pomerol AOC

*M*ellow, rich red wines of great character, delicacy, and elegance are produced from vineyards lying on a low plateau north-east of Libourne, bordering the St-Emilion vineyard. Like St-Emilion, the wines are produced from a higher proportion of Merlot, which is much softer and faster maturing than Cabernet Sauvignon. The wines which result are among the most delicious and readily appealing of all clarets and they are rightly highly prized throughout the world. Perhaps surprisingly, the great wines of Pomerol have never been classified. Nevertheless, Château Pétrus is the region's greatest flag-bearer, considered on a par with the very greatest *Premiers Crus* of the Médoc; there are, furthermore, at least another 40 wines of comparable *Grand Cru* class.

Lalande de Pomerol AOC

'*S*atellite' Pomerol from vineyards located to the hilly north, produced from a similar blend of grapes and worthy of the family pedigree. In recent years Pomerol has become almost prohibitively expensive; Lalande de Pomerol is a less expensive but sound alternative.

Fronsac AOC and Canon Fronsac AOC

*F*ine solid red wines of the Libournais, less well known — and less expensive — than their aristocratic neighbours of Pomerol and St-Emilion.

Côtes de Francs AOC

*A*ppellation for little-known area at the far end of the St-Emilion vine-yard producing fine under-valued reds primarily from Merlot with some Cabernet.

Other Wines of Bordeaux

Entre-Deux-Mers AOC

*F*resh, inexpensive dry white wines produced in the picturesque, undulating country between the Garonne and Dordogne rivers. The Sauvignon grape predominates in this vast and somewhat wild (compared, for example, with the Médoc) region, and the wines produced are excellent with freshwater fish and especially with oysters from Arcachon.

Graves de Vayres AOC

*N*ot to be confused with Graves AOC from across the river, this *appellation* applies to a small enclave within the Entre-Deux-Mers region on the left bank of the Dordogne producing sound red and dry white wines.

Premières Côtes de Bordeaux AOC

*L*arge narrow band of vineyards parallel with and on the right bank of the Garonne, stretching downstream from Bordeaux as far as St-Macaire. Both quick-maturing fruity red wines as well as some dry white and sweet white wines are produced.

Côtes de Blaye AOC

*V*ineyards situated on the right bank of the Gironde, some 50 km (30 miles) north of Bordeaux, producing excellent everyday dry white wine and some sweet white wine.

Premières Côtes de Blaye AOC

*T*he *appellation* for fruity red and some dry white wines produced from the same area of vineyards as above.

Côtes de Bourg AOC

*G*ood solid reds and whites produced from vineyards north of Bordeaux, in vineyards which are contiguous with those of Cognac.

B O R D E A U X

Ste-Foy-Bordeaux AOC

Nineteen wine communes at the eastern extreme of the Bordeaux vineyard south of Ste-Foy-La-Grande producing both sweet and dry white wines, as well as smaller amounts of fruity reds.

Maisons du Vin

The *Maison du Vin de Bordeaux* is the principal centre for general information and promotion of the region's wines. The smaller *Maisons* promote the wines of their own particular locality. In many cases wines are displayed and can be purchased at fair prices. Some offer *dégustations*, either free of charge or for a small fee. Many of the *Maisons* will arrange appointments and can usually give detailed maps or directions to properties.

Maison du Vin de Bordeaux
1, cours du XXX Juillet
33000 Bordeaux
tel: (56) 52 82 82
Hours: Mon–Fri 8h30–12h30; 13h30–18h30. Sat 9–12h.
Much useful literature, maps and information about all the various Bordeaux wine regions. Wines can sometimes be tasted but not purchased.

Maison du Vin de Margaux
place la Trémoille
33460 Margaux
tel: (56) 88 70 82
Hours: Mon afternoon–Sat 9–12h; 14–18h.
No tasting but display and sale of wines.

Maison du Vin de Pauillac
19, rue du Maréchal Juin
33250 Pauillac
tel: (56) 59 02 92
Hours: Open daily 9h30–12h30; 14–18h30; in season 9–19h.
Display and sale of wines and possibility of tasting.

Maison du Vin de St-Estèphe
place de l'Eglise
St-Estèphe
33250 Pauillac
tel: (56) 59 30 59
Hours: Open daily 10–12h; 14–18h; in season 10–19h.
Display and sale of wines, but no tasting.

Maison du Vin de Graves
rue François Mauriac
33720 Podensac
tel: (56) 27 09 25

Hours: Mon–Fri 8h30–12h30; 13h30–17h30. July and August open daily. Display and sale of wines, tasting only for groups.

Maison du Vin de St-Emilion
place Pierre-Meyrat
33330 St-Emilion
tel: (57) 74 42 42
Hours: Open Mon–Sat 9h30–12h30; 14h30–18h. July–September daily 9h30–12h30; 14h30–19h.
Large selection of wines on display for purchase. Useful maps and literature.

Maison du Vin
Château des Ducs d'Éperon
33410 Cadillac
tel: (56) 27 09 25
Hours: Easter–June Sat and Sun 10–12h; 14h30–18h30. June–September daily.
Tasting, display, and sale of wines of Cadillac, Ste-Croix-du-Mont, Loupiac, Sauternes, and Barsac.

Maison du Sauternes
place de la Mairie
33210 Sauternes
tel: (56) 63 60 37
Not an official *Maison du Vin* but an organization of classed properties where wines can be tasted and purchased.

There are, additionally, small *Maisons du Vin* in Fronsac, Castillon-la-Bataille, Blaye, Lussac, and Montagne.

Wine Festivals

18 January	Fête du St-Vincent	Fairs throughout the Médoc and Graves
May	Wine Festival	Cadillac
End of May	Wine Festival	Montagne-St-Emilion
End of May	Grand Chapitre	Pomerol
June	Wine Festival	St-Selve
July	Wine Festival	Sauveterre-de-Guyenne
July–August	Wine Festival	Castillon-la-Bataille
September	Foire aux Vins de Bordeaux et aux Fromages de France	Langon
End of September	Ban des Vendanges	Villages throughout the Médoc, Graves and St-Emilion

BORDEAUX

The Wine Roads of Bordeaux

Les Routes du Vin de Bordeaux

MÉDOC: *La Route des Châteaux*

In Brief   The *Route des Châteaux* is one of the most famous and well-travelled of all France's wine roads. The round circuit from Bordeaux to St-Yzans-de-Médoc via the D2 wine road, then across to Lesparre and back along the quicker N215 and D1 is about 110 km (70 miles) and can easily be completed in a day, though of course it depends on how many properties are going to be visited and how long one stops for lunch. We suggest visiting no more than two or three properties per day, thus leaving ample time simply for wine châteaux sightseeing. This certainly is the most ostentatious wine road in France, and the profusion of famous and lovely seventeenth- and eighteenth-century châteaux (large country mansions) is really worth seeing.

Many of the famous properties do have facilities for receiving visitors (in summer generally), and there are scores of less well-known wine producers who are quite happy to show wine tourists around in the hope that they will leave with a few bottles or a carton under their arms. However, it has to be said that the Médoc, in our experience, is neither the best organized nor the most welcoming of French wine regions, a pity considering its fame.

Of course, in the greatest properties, treasured wines are scarce and cannot be handed out to all and sundry for tasting; yet considering how much larger the classed growths of the Médoc are compared with their *Grands* and *Premiers Crus* counterparts in the Côte d'Or, the contrast in attitude between the two regions is striking. Perhaps this has something to do with the structure of wine selling in the Médoc as compared with Burgundy: in the Médoc, with its complex and often baffling system of *négociants* and wine merchants who purchase wine *en primeur*, there seems little need here to sell wines direct; in Burgundy, though, even famous growers and *négociants-éleveurs* take time off to welcome visitors for the not inconsiderable direct sales that may result.

Come to the Médoc certainly to pay homage to this famous stretch of vineyards; to enjoy the splendour of its domestic architecture; and to visit wine properties, taste and purchase wines: but do save enough time to explore the other less well-travelled wine roads of Bordeaux as well.

From Bordeaux, find the *Route du Médoc* out of town, then the D2 which leads to the suburb of Blanquefort. Blanquefort is the home of one of the

Médoc.

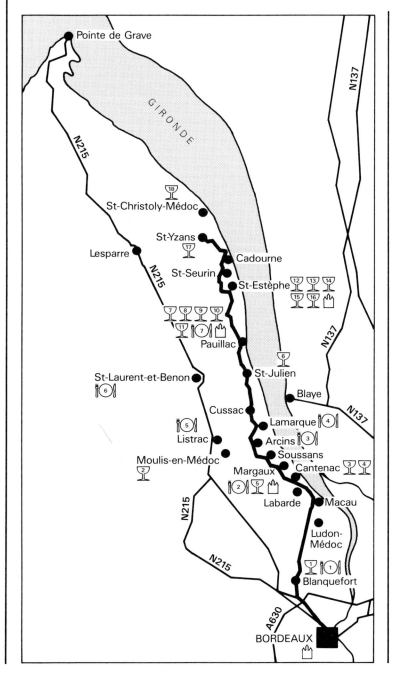

great Bordeaux merchants, Barton & Guestier, whose headquarters are found in the eighteenth-century Château du Déhez. Like other important Bordeaux merchants, Barton & Guestier are *négociants-éleveurs*, which means that the company purchases new young wines which are raised or 'elevated' in their own cellars at Blanquefort and elsewhere, then bottled and sold under their own label. The role which such *négociants-éleveurs* play is an important one in the Bordeaux wine industry, for by working closely with the wine growers a company can develop a range of both everyday and prestigious wines which maintain a consistent house style and quality. For the consumer, therefore, the label of such reliable merchants is a guarantee of quality.

The vineyards of the southern Médoc begin at Blanquefort and continue through the wine communes of Ludon-Médoc and Macau. The wines produced here do not have the right to a communal name but rather bear the area *appellation* Haut-Médoc. None the less, some superlative wines are made at classed properties such as Château La Lagune (third growth) and Château Cantemerle (fifth growth).

Cantenac, however, is the first great wine commune of note, which together with Labarde and Margaux itself, make up the communal vineyard of Margaux, one of the greatest and most famous in the world. Château Prieuré-Lichine at Cantenac (fourth growth) is one of the most welcoming properties in the Médoc. No wine traveller should pass this way without dropping in. Owned by wine writer Alexis Lichine, the Prieuré is open every day of the year and there are bi-lingual hostesses on hand for tours of the first- and second-year wine *chais*. Mr Lichine himself is often 'at home' and happy to meet visitors; there is a shop where the wines can be tasted and purchased together with books and other wine accessories. Other well-known properties here include Château d'Issan (a beautiful moated seventeenth-century property), and Château Palmer, officially only a third growth, but generally acclaimed capable of producing elegant and powerful wines that in the best years can compare to the very greatest.

Château Margaux.

Château Margaux, with its classical Empire façade, really does look like a great château, certainly worthy of its *Premier Grand Cru* status. A visit to Château Margaux impresses upon the visitor the almost unbelievable meticulous care and attention to detail which is necessary to make a great wine. In 1986, for example, the entire Merlot crop was thinned by as much as 50 per cent. Not only did each vine have bunches cut away, leaving only the best formed and exposed, but also even individual leaves were trimmed by hand to maximize exposure to the remaining grapes. Such attention to each vine is obviously a hugely expensive operation. But the intensity and immense concentration of the new wine tasted from the cask demonstrates the benefits: already it is being hailed at Margaux as one of the vintages of the century.

This sort of hand care is essential to making the finest wines, and it is one reason why the greatest deserve to fetch the fantastic prices that they do, year in and year out. In summer months, for example, notice throughout the Médoc, here and in other famous properties in St-Julien and Pauillac, the huge number of manual workers in the vineyards: weeding by hand, pruning and thinning out the vines by hand, spraying by hand. In autumn the grapes are harvested by hand, not by machine. After the harvest, they are further picked over to ensure that only the best-formed bunches and grapes are placed in the vat. Parcels of grapes from different parts of the vineyard are vinified and vatted separately, and the whole only assembled once the lesser wines have been discarded (either to be used as 'second wines' or else declassified further). Clearly, such care and attention can only be carried out by the great wine properties which can afford such luxuries, yet it is these factors, combined with the natural bounty of the Médoc, which makes the best wines so superlative.

The village of Margaux has a *Maison du Vin* where the wines of the commune are on display and available for purchase. Appointments can also be made here to visit properties.

From Margaux, the D2 wine road continues north, though for a time at least there is no particular profusion of great châteaux. Indeed, wine towns such as Arcins, Lamarque, and Cussac may produce good, and even very good, wines, but they themselves are hardly household names. To the west there are two separate wine communes, somewhat further from the Gironde, which are entitled to their own *appellations*: Moulis-en-Médoc and Listrac. Château Chasse-Spleen, a *Cru Exceptionnel* from the former and the two *Crus Bourgeois* Châteaux Fourcas-Hosten and Fourcas-Dupré from the latter are among the better known properties.

At Lamarque there is a convenient ferry across the Gironde to Blaye (another important Bordeaux wine town). The Fort Médoc, located further up the road, is a fascinating seventeenth-century moated ruin; walk out beyond it through the salt pastures of the Médoc to the Gironde itself where the fishing boats with their immense fine nets may be at work. This is a good place for a picnic, to spin out a bottle of wine, or simply to fall asleep for an hour or two.

The vineyards, woods, and villages of the central Médoc give way, suddenly and surprisingly, to another astounding profusion of great wine properties: a giant bottle of wine planted amidst the vines proclaims that we are in St-Julien. In this concentrated and special vineyard, a drive along the D2 is like a drive through the pages of an exclusive club or restaurant wine list. For as the vineyards of St-Julien give way effortlessly into those of Pauillac, the two communes account for no less than 30 — a full half — of all the classed properties of the Médoc.

Some of the finest and best-known châteaux of St-Julien include: Château

Beychevelle itself, a distinguished fourth growth, whose name is supposed to come from the sailor's cry *'baisses les voiles'* — 'lower the sails' in deference to the château's sixteenth-century owner, the Duc d'Eperon, Admiral of France; Château Gloria, only a *Cru Bourgeois* but generally considered of classed growth quality; Château Ducru-Beaucaillou (second growth); Château Talbot (fourth growth named after the region's last British commander, Sir John Talbot, who died unsuccessfully attempting to repel the French at Castillon); Château Langoa-Barton (third growth); and the three Léovilles, all second growths split from one former great estate: Léoville-Barton, Léoville-Las-Cases, and Léoville-Poyferré. The wines of St-Julien are generally considered to combine the manliness and stature of Pauillac with the rounder elegance of Margaux.

Pauillac, though, is undoubtedly the classic claret *par excellence*. It is not mere coincidence that three out of the five outstanding *Premiers Grands Crus Classés* are from this famous wine commune: Château Latour, Château Lafite-Rothschild, and Château Mouton-Rothschild. In addition, Pauillac boasts a further 15 other *Grands Crus Classés*. It comes, therefore, perhaps somewhat as a surprise after the surfeit of elegant and unreal châteaux and considering that some of the wines of Pauillac are among the most expensive and highly regarded in the world, to find that the town of Pauillac itself is rather raw and rough around the edges, a town where workers from the oil refinery and fishermen hang out in waterfront bars. On the outskirts of the village, land is given over to pastures or kitchen gardens, yet on adjoining plots great wines are made. This certainly is one of the enduring mysteries of wine.

The late Baron Philippe de Rothschild was one of the colourful characters and personalities of the wine world, and Château Mouton-Rothschild certainly remains a showpiece of the Médoc. Any wine lover will therefore wish to take the time to write for an appointment to visit here well in advance. The first-year wine *chais* of Mouton is particularly impressive: row after row of light, new Limousin oak *barriques bordelaises* — themselves beautifully crafted, their ends wrapped with chestnut circles, cane whipped around the edges, and the great seal of Mouton embossed on the end panels — extend majestically along the vast, low-lying building. As the wines are topped up, a deep, dark purple stains the bellies of the new wood a striking shade.

One senses throughout the Médoc long-standing links with the past; wine growers here are keenly aware of wine itself as a great civilizing force. Thus, Baron Philippe created the Mouton wine museum to celebrate the cultivation of the vine with a superb and impressive collection of paintings, tapestries, glass, and other wine-associated objects. It is only possible to visit the museum by appointment.

Mouton's great rival, Lafite, is owned by another branch of the Rothschild family, though in truth these days, there is little competition between the five first growth properties whose relations, by all accounts, are based on mutual respect, admiration, and the pleasures of exchanging bottles as well as ideas with one another. Château Lafite-Rothschild is located at the northern end of the Pauillac vineyard, virtually on its boundary with the wine commune

Cellar work at Château Mouton-Rothschild.

of St-Estèphe. The precious 90-hectare vineyard extends around the château itself. The greatest wines of the Médoc have always attracted investors, those who like to collect and hoard wines as much as invest in them. Such a practice may have its opponents and advocates. But consider for a moment the fact that a single bottle of Lafite (albeit a 200-year-old one) recently fetched at auction a record £105,000.

Château Latour stands alone and aloof, far from Mouton and Lafite on the south side of Pauillac virtually in St-Julien. The famous squat tower of the label represents a former watchtower of the sort which lined the Gironde in Plantagenet days and from which lookouts were kept during the Hundred Years' War. The tower that is visible amidst the vines, however, dates from the seventeenth century. Château Latour is a wine which has been famous for its exceptional power and breed literally for centuries.

Like many other great Médoc properties, Latour makes a 'second wine': Les Forts de Latour. The Cabernet Sauvignon (mainly), Cabernet Franc, and Merlot grapes from individual parcels or sections of the vineyard are fermented and all vatted quite separately; then, once the malo-lactic fermentation has been completed, usually around Christmas or after the New Year, a process of rigorous selection and rejection takes place. Such selection is essential not only for the greatest wines, like Latour, but also for many other *Crus Classés* and *Crus Bourgeois* properties, all those who are serious about making the finest wines that their vineyards are capable of. Thus, in this process of selection, only the very finest vats are chosen to become the first, or *grand vin*, those which have the necessary concentration, breed, and characteristics of the estate. Usually such wines come from the oldest vines (a vine can have a productive life span as long as a man's), for they gain increasingly in complexity and character, though at the expense of quantity.

The chosen vats are then assembled and transferred to the new oak barrels where they will age (in the case of Latour) for at least two years before finally being bottled. The remaining, or rejected wine, is consequently assembled, aged, and bottled separately under the 'second label'. It too can be splendid in its own right, in the best properties capable of demonstrating its pedigree, though in a lighter, less concentrated form which necessarily precludes it from greatness. Yet from the consumers' point of view, such 'second wines' can be both considerably less expensive to purchase and also ready to drink far sooner. Today, Latour is owned by a consortium of English and French; unfortunately, the property is not able to offer visits to the general public.

Other well-known classed properties of Pauillac include: Château Pichon-Longueville-Baron and Pichon-Longueville-Lalande (both second growths on the border with St-Julien); Château Duhart-Milon-Rothschild (fourth growth and part of the Lafite empire); and a clutch of fifth growths — Château Batailley, Clerc-Milon, Croizet-Bages, Grand-Puy-Ducasse, Grand-Puy-Lacoste, Haut-Bages-Libéral, Haut-Batailley, Lynch-Bages, Lynch-Moussas, Mouton-Baronne-Philippe, Pédesclaux, and Pontet-Canet. There is a *Maison du Vin* in Pauillac.

The next wine commune along the *Route des Châteaux* is St-Estèphe, the largest of the Médoc *appellations*, with five *Crus Classés* and 40 *Crus Bourgeois* properties and a further 200 growers who are members of the local *cave coopérative*. The wines of St-Estèphe are noted above all for their intense, dark colour and exceptional structure; high in tannin, they can be among the hardest wines of the Médoc which take the longest time to develop. Château Cos d'Estournel is the first great property of the commune, located just past Lafite: you can't miss its outrageous and whimsical French eighteenth-century pagoda. Cos d'Estournel is a second growth. St-Estèphe's other second growth, Montrose, lies further towards the town and closer to the Gironde. Montrose is classic St-Estèphe: a deep, traditional claret which needs considerable ageing. Another well-known St-Estèphe is Château Calon-Ségur. At one time, Calon-Ségur was owned by the Marquis de Ségur, who also owned Lafite and Latour. It was the less famous wine, though, which was the Marquis' favourite, for he reputedly remarked: 'I make wine at Lafite and Latour but my heart lies at Calon'. Thus, the label of Calon-Ségur is enclosed in a heart. Château Cos-Labory and Château Lafon-Rochet, both fourth growths, are the remaining *Crus Classés* of the commune.

St-Estèphe itself is a very pleasant, quiet little town with not all that much to it. The *Maison du Vin* is in the church square and wines can be purchased here.

Beyond St-Estèphe, the transition between the vineyards of the Haut-Médoc and the Médoc is a gradual and not immediately apparent one. The Cabernet vines continue to be trained in favourable sites on elevated ground overlooking the Gironde, and certainly the distinctive pebbly soil around Cadourne, St-Seurin, and even up to St-Yzans appears little different. Yet St-Estèphe is world famous, while these other communes remains virtually unknown. Certainly wines from this extreme end of the Haut-Médoc can be good, and even very good — moreover, because they do not benefit from a well-known *communal appellation* they are often undervalued.

Château Loudenne, washed a glorious shade of pink and with the Union Jack flying proudly, is located at St-Yzans and is one of the most welcoming properties in the Médoc. Any visit to the Médoc should include a stop at this fine property which is a showpiece of Gilbey de Loudenne, a wholly owned subsidiary of International Distillers & Vintners. Visitors are very welcome; given sufficient notice, they may even join staff and employees for lunch.

From St-Yzans either continue up the Médoc to the Pointe de Grave (where there is a ferry to Royan), or else return to Bordeaux via Lesparre and the N215.

Dégustation: Stop to Taste; Stop to Buy

Visiting wine properties in the Médoc is somewhat different from in other wine regions of Bordeaux and the rest of France. In the great properties, certainly, visitors are received almost always by appointment only. It is unlikely, furthermore, that casual wine travellers and tourists will be offered wines for tasting: indeed, in many cases the wines are not even available for sale. Yet such visits give a fascinating insight into the great wine properties of the Médoc, so it is well worth taking the time and effort to write in advance (or telephone when in the region) to arrange an appointment. Furthermore, there are plenty of other opportunities for visiting, tasting, and purchasing wines at the properties listed below as well as at many others.

Vintages

Most properties in Bordeaux, as well as throughout France, generally offer only their current or recent vintages for sale direct to the consumer, rather than stocks of mature wines. The publication of general vintage charts is therefore of limited use. Moreover, such charts can be misleading, for the implication is that in lesser years, or poor vintages, the wines are 'bad'. Certainly, bad wines can be made in poor years, but no château worth its name would wish to release them under its label. On the other hand, bad or less good wines can also be made by individual properties in fine years, due to particular circumstances which don't correspond with the general chart.

Generally, so-called poor years indicate vintages which are not suitable for lengthy conservation. Such wines, though lacking the necessary concentration and high tannin levels which would enable them to mature for a decade or more, are often, on the other hand, suitable for drinking while young, and as such may be of more interest to the buyer who wishes to drink it immediately or within the space, of say, months, not years. The way to tell if a wine is bad is not by slavishly consulting a chart but by tasting and forming your own opinion.

1

Barton & Guestier
Château du Déhez
53, rue du Déhez
33290 Blanquefort
tel: (56) 35 03 07
Hours: By appointment only for customers and wine professionals.
Barton & Guestier is an important *négociant-éleveur* with an operation which covers not only the fine wines of Bordeaux, but a further 45 *appellations* throughout France.
English spoken.

2

Château Moulin à Vent
33480 Moulis-en-Médoc
tel: (56) 58 15 79
Hours: Mon–Fri 9–12h; 14–18h.

BORDEAUX

Château Moulin à Vent AOC Moulis-en-Médoc *Crus Bourgeois*. Visits to the *chais* and vineyard and wine available for tasting and purchase. English spoken.

3 Château Prieuré-Lichine
Cantenac
33460 Margaux
tel: (56) 88 36 28
Hours: Open every day of the year 9–19h.
Château Prieuré-Lichine AOC Margaux (fourth growth), Château de Clairfont AOC Margaux (second wine).
One of the most welcoming of all properties in the Médoc with knowledgeable tri-lingual hostesses who show visitors the *chais* and explain the wine making and ageing process in detail. Wines, books, and other accessories can be purchased in the shop. Charge for *dégustation*.
English spoken.

4 Château d'Angludet
Cantenac
33460 Margaux
tel: (56) 88 71 41
Hours: Mon–Fri 9–12h; 14h30–17h. Appointment preferred.
Château d'Angludet AOC Margaux *Cru Exceptionnel*.
This highly regarded property is owned by Peter Sichel, of Maison Sichel, fine shippers of Bordeaux.
English spoken.

5 Château Margaux
33460 Margaux
tel: (56) 88 70 28
Hours: By appointment, as far in advance as possible.
Château Margaux AOC Margaux (first growth); Château Pavillon Rouge AOC Margaux (second wine); Château Pavillon Blanc AOC Bordeaux.
One of the great properties of the Médoc which every visitor should make the effort to see. The first-year *chais* is magnificent, and there is a full-time *tonnelier* who makes about a third of the new oak barrels required by Margaux each year. Château Margaux is almost unique among the great properties in making a fine and highly regarded white wine as well as its elegant and long-lived red.
English spoken.

6 Château Beychevelle
St-Julien Beychevelle
33250 Pauillac
tel: (56) 59 23 00
Hours: Mon–Fri 9h30–11h30; 14–17h30. Appointment necessary.

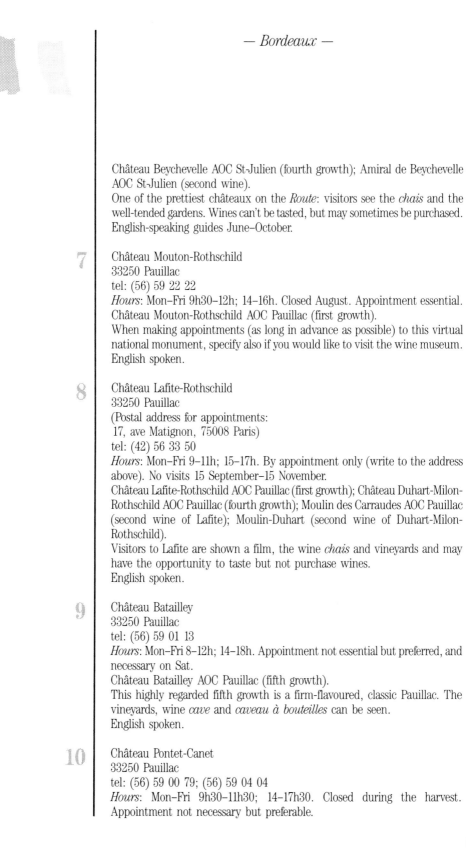

Château Beychevelle AOC St-Julien (fourth growth); Amiral de Beychevelle AOC St-Julien (second wine).
One of the prettiest châteaux on the *Route*: visitors see the *chais* and the well-tended gardens. Wines can't be tasted, but may sometimes be purchased. English-speaking guides June–October.

7

Château Mouton-Rothschild
33250 Pauillac
tel: (56) 59 22 22
Hours: Mon–Fri 9h30–12h; 14–16h. Closed August. Appointment essential.
Château Mouton-Rothschild AOC Pauillac (first growth).
When making appointments (as long in advance as possible) to this virtual national monument, specify also if you would like to visit the wine museum. English spoken.

8

Château Lafite-Rothschild
33250 Pauillac
(Postal address for appointments:
17, ave Matignon, 75008 Paris)
tel: (42) 56 33 50
Hours: Mon–Fri 9–11h; 15–17h. By appointment only (write to the address above). No visits 15 September–15 November.
Château Lafite-Rothschild AOC Pauillac (first growth); Château Duhart-Milon-Rothschild AOC Pauillac (fourth growth); Moulin des Carraudes AOC Pauillac (second wine of Lafite); Moulin-Duhart (second wine of Duhart-Milon-Rothschild).
Visitors to Lafite are shown a film, the wine *chais* and vineyards and may have the opportunity to taste but not purchase wines.
English spoken.

9

Château Batailley
33250 Pauillac
tel: (56) 59 01 13
Hours: Mon–Fri 8–12h; 14–18h. Appointment not essential but preferred, and necessary on Sat.
Château Batailley AOC Pauillac (fifth growth).
This highly regarded fifth growth is a firm-flavoured, classic Pauillac. The vineyards, wine *cave* and *caveau à bouteilles* can be seen.
English spoken.

10

Château Pontet-Canet
33250 Pauillac
tel: (56) 59 00 79; (56) 59 04 04
Hours: Mon–Fri 9h30–11h30; 14–17h30. Closed during the harvest. Appointment not necessary but preferable.

Château Pontet-Canet AOC Pauillac (fifth growth); Château Les Hauts de Pontet AOC Pauillac (second wine).
Château Pontet-Canet is one of the largest classed estates in the Médoc, and a neighbour of Mouton-Rothschild. The property is owned by the Tesseron family who also own Château Lafon-Rochet and Château Malescasse. Visitors are shown the wine *chais* and vineyards and the wines can be tasted for a small charge.
English spoken.

11 Château La Rose Pauillac
33250 Pauillac
tel: (56) 59 01 04
Hours: Mon–Sat 9–12h; 14–17h for tasting and purchase.
Château La Rose AOC Pauillac.
A visit to this local *cave coopérative* provides a necessary and fascinating contrast to the grand châteaux of the Médoc; the wine is sound and reasonably priced.

12 Château Cos d'Estournel
St-Estèphe
33250 Pauillac
tel: (56) 44 11 37
Hours: By appointment only.
Château Cos d'Estournel AOC St-Estèphe (second growth); Château de Marbuzet AOC St-Estèphe.
Visitors are shown an audio-visual presentation, as well as the vineyards and wine *chais*, and the wines can be tasted 'by appointment' as well as purchased.

13 Château Montrose
St-Estèphe
33250 Pauillac
tel: (56) 59 30 12
Hours: Mon–Fri 10–12h; 14–17h (except during the *vendange*). Appointment necessary.
Château Montrose AOC St-Estèphe (second growth).
Traditional property owned by the Charmolüe family since 1896; visitors may see the wine *chais*, *cuverie*, and vineyards, and the wines may be tasted and purchased.

14 Château Cos-Labory
St-Estèphe
33250 Pauillac
tel: (56) 59 30 32
Hours: Weekdays by appointment.
Château Cos-Labory AOC St-Estèphe (fifth growth); Château Andron-Blanquet AOC St-Estèphe (*Cru Grand Bourgeois Exceptionnel*).
The vineyards of Cos-Labory and Andron-Blanquet adjoin in some parts. Both

wines are made by the Audoy family and can be tasted and purchased. English spoken.

15 Château Phélan Ségur
St-Estèphe
33250 Pauillac
tel: (56) 59 30 09
Hours: Mon–Fri 8–12h; 14–18h. Appointment necessary.
Château Phélan Ségur AOC St-Estèphe; Château Fonpetite AOC St-Estéphe. The wine *chais* and vineyards can be visited and wines are available for tasting, though purchases should be made at the *Maison du Vin* in St-Estèphe. English spoken.

16 Cave Coopérative Marquis de St-Estèphe
St-Estèphe
33250 Pauillac
tel: (56) 59 35 83
Hours: Mon–Sat 9–12h; 14h30–17h30.
Over 200 local *vignerons* are members of this important communal *cave coopérative* located along the D2. The well-made wines can be tasted and purchased.

17 Château Loudenne
Gilbey de Loudenne
33340 St-Yzans-de-Médoc
tel: (56) 09 05 03
Hours: Mon–Fri 9–12h; 14–18h. Appointment preferable but not essential.
Château Loudenne AOC Médoc (*Cru Bourgeois*); Château Loudenne Blanc AOC Bordeaux; Château de Pez AOC St-Estèphe (*Cru Bourgeois Supérieur*); Château Giscours AOC Margaux (third growth).
This pretty pink estate was bought by the Gilbey brothers in 1875 and today remains the centre of a vast international wine operation. Unfortunately, the fine wine museum burnt down in a recent fire, but visitors are still very welcome here. If given sufficient advance notice (at least one week) visitors may have the opportunity to have lunch at the château. English spoken.

18 Château St-Christoly
St-Christoly-Médoc
33340 Lesparre
tel: (56) 41 52 95
Hours: Mon–Fri 9–12h; 14–18h. Appointment necessary.
Château St-Christoly AOC Médoc.
Visits to the *chais* and vineyard, and wine available for tasting and purchase. English spoken 'by appointment'.

BORDEAUX

Graves.

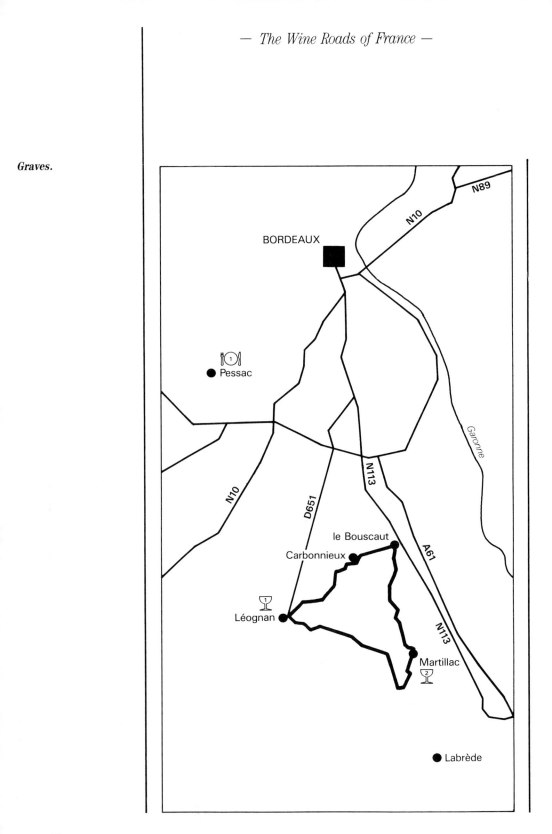

GRAVES:
Circuit Touristique des Crus Classés de Graves

In Brief   The vineyards of Graves extend from the very suburbs of Bordeaux to south of Langon, encompassing along the way the sweet wine enclaves of Cérons, Barsac, and Sauternes. Though Graves is often thought of mainly as a white wine, the wine growers here produce just as much red and it is equally highly regarded. Both the finest red and white wines were classified in the 1950s. The Graves vineyard is a rather large and sprawling area, by no means as exclusively devoted to the vine as is, say, the Haut-Médoc. However, the finest and most distinctive vineyards of Graves can be easily toured in a half day from Bordeaux, or else dipped into *en route* to Sauternes.

In the 1855 classification of the wines of the Gironde, three properties from the Haut-Médoc (Lafite, Latour, and Margaux) were classified as *Premiers Grands Crus Classés* as was one property from Graves: Château Haut-Brion. Today this famous property whose wines were enjoyed by Samuel Pepys in the seventeenth century lies virtually within Bordeaux itself, in the suburb of Pessac. A number of excellent properties which have appended the magic Haut-Brion name are also located here, including Château La Mission Haut-Brion and Château Laville-Haut-Brion, both of which today are owned, together with Haut-Brion itself, by the American-based Domaine Clarence Dillon. Unfortunately, these historic properties cannot be visited except by customers or trade professionals. Further out along the road to Arcachon lies Château Pape Clément, one of the oldest vineyards in Bordeaux, for it was the personal estate of Pope Clément V, formerly Archbishop of Bordeaux (see p.376).

The brief circular *Circuit Touristique des Crus Classés de Graves* begins and ends at Léognan, a fine little town and one of the principal centres for Graves, reached from Bordeaux by way of the D651. In Léognan, follow the wine road signs on to the D111 which immediately leads into the heart of the vineyard. Château Haut-Bailly is the first of the classed growths that is encountered; if you haven't made an appointment, take pot luck and knock on the door, advises M. Sanders, the proprietor. The classic red wines of Haut-Bailly are considered among the very finest that the Graves vineyard produces.

Notice how much wilder, less ordered, and single-minded the Graves vineyard seems compared with the Médoc. This is relatively little-visited wine country: though the wines produced are as fine and prestigious as those from the Médoc, the properties themselves on the whole have a more rural, less grand feeling about them. Château Carbonnieux, further up the road, is another famous property of Graves, and a producer of both classed white and red wines (though presumably it was the white Carbonnieux which previously

BORDEAUX

used to be shipped to Muslim Turkey as *eau mineral*). The soil at Carbonnieux demonstrates how the region was named, for it is made up not of the large pebbles and gravel of the Médoc but of a deep layer of small-to-fine aggregate, a remarkable sight.

After Carbonnieux, continue on to Le Bouscaut, then turn right on the little E4 to Martillac. This small road continues through woods and vineyards, passing classed properties such as Château Smith-Haut-Lafite. Martillac itself is a pretty little village; just outside the town, Château La Tour Martillac, is off to the left. This highly regarded property produces classed red and white Graves and can be visited.

The wine circuit continues on towards Labrède, then circles back on the D109 to Léognan. On entering Léognan, a few more classed properties of Graves can be viewed by first turning left, past Château Malartic-Lagravière, Château de Fieuzal, and others, then back around to Léognan.

Dégustation: Stop to Taste; Stop to Buy

This brief tour follows a circuit through the classed vineyards of Graves, but the vineyard extends well beyond this favoured and exclusive enclave. We have included two addresses for classed properties on the route, but there may be others offering *dégustation-vente*. Additionally, throughout the vast Graves vineyards there are châteaux producing sound red and white wines which are still relatively good value.

1 Château Haut-Bailly
33850 Léognan
tel: (56) 21 75 11; (56) 27 16 07
Hours: Mon–Fri, working hours. Appointment not essential but preferred if possible.
Château Haut-Bailly *Grand Cru Classé* AOC Graves; La Parde de Haut-Bailly AOC Graves (second wine).
M. Sanders is the *propriétaire* of this property, as well as the Château du Mayne in Barsac and the Château de Courbon in Toulenne. Because of work commitments, he is, therefore, often not at Château Haut-Bailly, but seriously interested visitors are welcome to stop during working hours: if convenient, visitors will be shown the *chais*, given the opportunity to taste the wines and receive explanations about their production.

2 Château La Tour Martillac
Société Civile Fermière des Domaines Kressmann
Martillac
33650 Labrède
tel: (56) 72 71 21
Hours: Mon–Sat by appointment.

Château La Tour Martillac is one of only seven properties which produces both red and white *Grand Cru Classé* AOC Graves. The property is the concern of the Kressman family. *La tour,* the tower, incidentally, dates from the twelfth century.
English spoken.

Other Graves producers

Château de Chantegrive
33720 Podensac
tel: (56) 27 17 38
Hours: Mon–Sat morning, working hours. Appointment not essential, but advisable.
Both red and white Château de Chantegrive AOC Graves are produced on this estate which is a *'Membre de l'Union des Grands Crus'.*
English spoken.

Domaine Château Millet
33640 Portets
tel: (56) 67 18 16
Hours: Mon–Fri 9–12h; 14–18h. Telephone call before coming.
Red and white Château Millet AOC Graves; Bordeaux Supérieur *rouge*. Visits to the *chais* and vineyards and wines available for tasting and purchase.
English spoken.

SAUTERNES AND BARSAC:
Circuit du Sauternais

In Brief   The vineyards of Sauternes begin about 40 km (25 miles) south of Bordeaux at Barsac: they can easily be reached either by the A62 *autoroute* (exit 2) or along the N113 which leads through the vineyards of Graves. The sign-posted *Circuit du Sauternais* extends through the five wine communes of Barsac, Bommes, Sauternes, Fargues, and Preignac, and as such it is the finest and most compact of all Bordeaux wine roads. The circuit can be completed in a half day, but it is far better to allow a full day, with visits to properties before and after lunch, probably in Sauternes itself where there is the choice of three good restaurants. Though one might expect that tasting opportunities for wines as rare as Sauternes would be hard to come by, this is not the case: *propriétaires* of famous classed properties are both welcoming and generous.

Barsac is the first of the five communes which make this unique and special

**Sauternes and
Barsac.**

vin liquoreux. It is the only one besides Sauternes itself, moreover, which is entitled to its own *appellation*, though wines from here can also be bottled as Sauternes or as Barsac-Sauternes if desired. To begin the wine circuit, drive through the small town and turn right on the D114 by the large *Circuit du Sauternais* sign (there is a tasting house here, open in season). This wine road leads immediately into the vineyards.

The only permitted grape varieties for Sauternes and Barsac are Sémillon, Sauvignon, and Muscadelle. As is the case throughout the great wine regions of Bordeaux, in the best properties the different varieties are vinified separately, parcel by parcel, then, after a rigorous selection of each of the various *cuves*, the finished wines are assembled at a later date

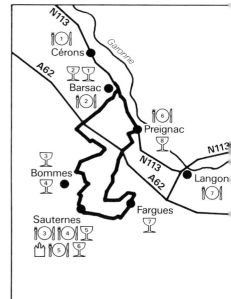

and then further aged either in oak or in stainless steel (depending on the property). It is a fascinating exercise to taste the individual varietals from the vat before this process has been completed. Sémillon generally has the most weight, concentration of mineral elements, and botyritized residual sugar, for indeed it is the variety most susceptible to *pourriture noble*. Sauvignon, though still rich, has its characteristic intense grassy pungency and a nervous vigour which keeps the wine from cloying. Muscadelle is the least complex: very fragrant and flowery, with little acid. These distinct component wines, varying of course from vineyard to vineyard and year to year, together knit into the most complex and concentrated white wine made anywhere in the world.

The wines of Sauternes and Barsac were the only others to be classified in 1855: one property, the great and legendary Château d'Yquem, was placed in a class of its own *Grand Premier Cru* or first great growth. A further 23 of the best were classified as either first growths or second growths. No fewer than nine are located in the surrounds of Barsac, and this wine road leads past or near some of the finest and most famous, all of which are noted on the sign-posts: Château Coutet and Château Climens (both first growths); Château Caillou, Châteaux Doisy-Daëne (second growths), and others. Notice the flatness and the rich, red earth at Coutet and other properties here, a contrast to the hillier, gravel vineyards of Sauternes. The wines of Barsac are generally considered to be somewhat lighter, and less sweet, than Sauternes, with a characteristic lemony tang which comes from a slightly higher level of acidity.

The *Circuit* next crosses the *autoroute* then bears left on the D109 (signposted Preignac), and leads to the single most important natural feature of the land which distinguishes these wines from others in the surrounding Graves vineyard. The little Ciron river is but a stream: as you cross over its two branches which flow so serenely on and into the nearby Garonne, consider for a moment the role it plays in autumn, when damp mists rise from its banks in the morning and settle over the surrounding vineyards. Then, when hot Indian summer afternoons dispel the moisture, the conditions for the formation of *pourriture noble* are as near to perfect as can ever be achieved for something so fickle and seemingly arbitrary.

Ciron river near Sauternes.

Continue following the *Circuit* sign-posts, bearing right now towards Bommes and Sauternes, through vineyards and past numerous wine châteaux, some of which really are fine mansions but others of which seem no more than rambling farms. The wine road continues towards Bommes, then bears left, bypassing that small and unassuming wine town. Château Sigalas Rabaud, a rather imposing fortress, is a first growth estate, as is the Clos Haut Peyraguey, further on, which offers *dégustation-vente*. These vineyards here and further towards Sauternes are quite hilly, and there are some fine views of the surrounding countryside, with the tall steeples of the wine towns just peeking through.

It always comes as a surprise, finally, to visit a wine village as famous as Sauternes, for the village whose name has been stolen and which is known throughout the world is but an unassuming and modest little wine town with not much more to it than the homes of wine growers, a church, and a few good restaurants.

Château Filhot lies outside Sauternes, one of the finest stately homes of the region, set amidst its wooded parkland of 300 hectares. The 60-hectare vineyard, though classified a second growth, was admired as one of the greatest wines of Bordeaux as long ago as the eighteenth century by the American President Thomas Jefferson.

The *Circuit* actually passes through the estate of Filhot, then returns to Sauternes, and leaves the village on the D125 towards Fargues. The wine road continues straight to Fargues, but first make a detour to Château Guiraud, a fine property producing first growth Sauternes which is regarded among the very finest. There is a well-organized tasting salon here and the wine *chais* can be visited. Château Guiraud, in common with many other Sauternes properties, also makes a dry white wine, 'G', primarily from the Sauvignon.

A carved stone pillar marks the great Château Yquem.

Return to the wine road and continue on to Fargues, pass through the small, quiet town and circle back left towards Sauternes. Château Rieussec, another famous first growth, is the great property of Fargues.

At the crossroads beyond Rieussec, turn right to arrive finally at the great vineyards of Yquem, with the château itself just visible high atop the hill. The wine which once graced the tables of tsars has been made by the Lur-Saluces family for over 200 years; indeed the Lur-Saluces can rightly claim to be the most experienced and foremost producers of *vins liquoreux* in the world, for, in addition to Yquem, they once owned Château Filhot, Château Coutet, and Château de Malle (and still hold Château de Fargues), a prestigious *monopole* of holdings by any standards. Château d'Yquem today remains the standard-bearer for the whole Sauternes and Barsac vineyard: undoubtedly and without reservation one of the greatest wines of the world. No other wine is made with more meticulous care and attention to past traditions. In other great Sauternes properties, for example, the vineyards might be harvested as many as five or six times, a necessary but extremely costly operation: but at Yquem such hand care and selection goes into the making of this great wine that the vineyard is often picked over no fewer than 10 or more times. Unfortunately, though perhaps not surprisingly, Château d'Yquem is not open to passing and thirsty wine travellers.

Château Suduiraut, beyond Yquem, is the great property of the wine commune of Preignac, capable in certain years of producing wines that can be compared even with Yquem itself. Continue on the D8 towards Preignac, then, after crossing the *autoroute* once more, either complete the circuit at Preignac, or follow the signs to the Château de Malle. The wine is a classified second growth, but the château itself is an actual classified historical monument which is open to the public.

Dégustation: Stop to Taste; Stop to Buy

Sauternes dégustation: stop to taste; stop to buy.

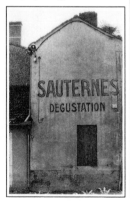

Considering that they are so rare and difficult to make, and that in the top classed properties, a vine yields just a single glass of wine, Sauternes and Barsac remain one of the relative bargain wines of France. *Propriétaires*, anxious, we sense, to demonstrate to a doubting public weaned on dry wines how very special and unique Sauternes and Barsac can be, are extremely welcoming and generous in offering samples to serious and interested wine travellers. For those wishing to purchase wines to bring home, Sauternes and Barsac are one of the few white wines which are vinified to be conserved for very long periods: the best will continue to improve and develop for decades or even more.

1   Château Coutet
Barsac
33720 Podensac
tel: (56) 27 15 46
Hours: Mon–Fri 14–18h.
Château Coutet AOC Barsac *Premier Cru*; dry white Château Coutet AOC
Graves.
Château Coutet is one of the oldest properties in the Sauternais, dating back
to the thirteenth century. The property, long considered one of the finest in
Barsac, was purchased by M. Baly in 1977.
Charge for *dégustation*.
English spoken.

2   Château Caillou
Barsac
33720 Podensac
tel: (56) 27 16 38
Hours: Mon–Fri 9–12h; 14–18h. Appointment necessary.
Château Caillou AOC Sauternes-Barsac (second growth); dry white and red
Château Caillou AOC Graves.
Traditional family exploitation, and a large stock of old wines.
Tasting free for purchasers.
English spoken.

3   Château Clos Haut Peyrauguey
Bommes
33210 Langon
tel: (56) 63 61 53
Hours: Daily 8–12h; 14–18h.
Château Clos Haut Peyrauguey AOC Sauternes *Premier Cru*; Château Haut-
Bommes AOC Sauternes.
The estate, located on a hill looking across to Yquem, is most welcoming; visitors
are shown the vineyards and *cave* and the wines can be tasted and purchased.

4   École de Viticulture et d'Oenologie
Château La Tour Blanche
Bommes
33210 Langon
tel: (56) 63 61 55
Hours: Mon–Fri 9–11h30; 15–17h.
Château La Tour Blanche AOC Sauternes *Premier Cru*.
This state-owned property is a school of viticulture and wine making, where
theory is put into practice with the production of a fine first growth Sauternes
which can be tasted and purchased.

BORDEAUX

5

Château Filhot
Sauternes
33210 Langon
tel: (56) 63 61 09
Hours: Daily by appointment.
Château Filhot AOC Sauternes (second growth).
One of the grandest and most famous properties of Sauternes: the *Circuit* actually passes through the wooded parkland, but in order to ensure the opportunity to visit, taste and purchase wines, it is necessary to telephone for an appointment. The Comte de Vaucelles is a most knowledgeable host who will delight in explaining not only his own wines but the fascinating history of the region as well.
English spoken.

6

Château Guiraud
Guiraud
Sauternes
33210 Langon
tel: (56) 63 61 01
Hours: Daily 9–12h; 14–18h. Appointment preferred.
Château Guiraud AOC Sauternes *Premier Cru*; 'G' AOC Bordeaux (dry white). Another great property of Sauternes, with good facilities for receiving visitors. The *caves* can be visited and the wines tasted for a charge.
English spoken.

7

Château Rieussec
Fargues
33210 Langon
tel: (42) 56 33 50
Hours: Mon–Fri 9–11h; 15–17h expect 15 September–15 November. Written appointment essential: c/o 17, ave Matignon, 75008 Paris.
Château Rieussec AOC Sauternes *Premier Cru*; 'R' de Rieussec AOC Bordeaux (dry white).
Château Rieussec, the great growth of Fargues, is owned by the Rothschilds of Lafite. Visitors are welcome, though it is necessary to write for an appointment as far in advance as possible; the wines may be tasted but are not available for purchase.
English spoken.

8

Château de Malle
Preignac
33210 Langon
tel: (56) 63 28 67
Hours: Daily except Wed, 15–19h. July and August 10–19h.
Château de Malle AOC Sauternes (second growth); Château de Cardaillan AOC Graves (red); Chevalier de Malle AOC Bordeaux (dry white).

Though the Château de Malle dates from the early seventeenth century the vineyard has been in the same family for some 500 years, a possibly unique situation in Bordeaux. Both the Sauternes and Graves vineyards are straddled, enabling the property to produce *vin liquoreux* as well as red Graves and dry white Bordeaux. Visits can be made to the château itself and the Italianate gardens at the hours shown above. However, visits to the vineyards and *caves*, together with wine tastings, are available only by appointment.

ST-EMILION AND POMEROL

In Brief   The wine country of the right bank of the Dordogne is best explored either from Libourne (an important and historic river port) or from St-Emilion. At least a day should be set aside to explore and enjoy St-Emilion itself, for we consider it one of the finest and most picturesque medieval wine capitals in the country. Though the wine region of St-Emilion proudly calls itself 'the land of a 1000 châteaux', there is not, as yet, a sign-posted wine road through the vineyards which extend over the undulating chalky hills to the east, known as the Côtes, as well as over the flatter gravelly Graves vineyards that continue on into Pomerol. If the St-Emilion vineyard is difficult to follow in any ordered fashion, the vineyard of Pomerol is equally elusive. However, no wine traveller will wish to miss visiting these prestigious vineyards.

The origins of St-Emilion date at least to Roman times: the Gallo-Roman poet Ausonius reputedly had a vine-surrounded villa here, and indeed one of St-Emilion's finest and most famous properties is named after him. The town itself is named after St. Emilion, a hermit monk who apparently settled in an underground limestone cave. Indeed, the town's unique Église Monolithe — a magnificent sight, not to be missed — was actually hollowed out of the same soft limestone, and numerous natural and artifical caves still serve as excellent cellars for the wine growers of the town.

Today, St-Emilion, with its steep cobbled streets and mellow ochre houses with tiled roofs, remains without doubt the most enjoyable of all Bordeaux wine towns. Come here to watch the lively little market which sprawls through the streets below the church; to taste wine in any number of specialist shops; to enjoy such self-consciously regional specialities as *lamproie à la bordelaise* (lamprey stewed in claret); or to wander up to the ruined, overgrown Couvent des Cordeliers to sit in the shade amidst the ruins of the former cloisters and eat macaroons and sip not St-Emilion wine but refreshing, locally made 'bubbly'. The *Maison du Vin* here is one of the region's best organized and most helpful: not only is there much useful literature available, appointments can be made to visit wine properties and there is also an extensive selection of wines from various vintages and prices which are displayed 'supermarket' style for purchase.

BORDEAUX

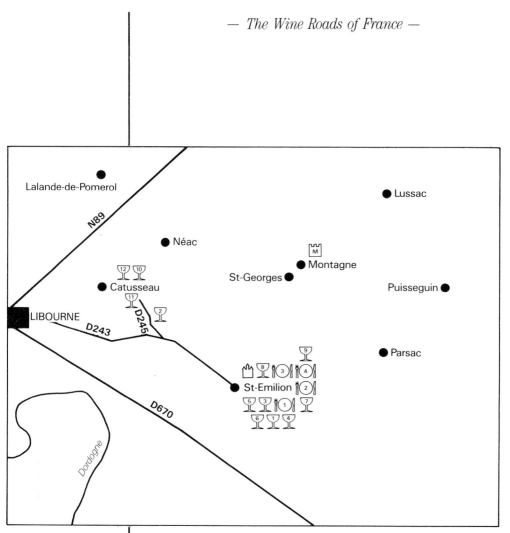

St-Emilion and Pomerol.

Monsieur Delbeck draws a sample of new wine at Château Ausone.

The vineyards of St-Emilion begin at the very edge of the town. Indeed, along its southern flank, the town is perched on the edge of a steep, precipitous cliff which drops down to the river plain of the Dordogne. Vines are grown on this well-exposed limestone slope, and there is a cluster here of some of the town's most famous and finest properties.

When the wines of St-Emilion were classified in 1955, Château Ausone together with Château Cheval Blanc (located to the north-west of town) were placed in a class of their own above the other designated *Premier Grands Crus Classés*. Ausone, certainly, remains one of the finest properties in Bordeaux, producing red wine which is comparable in quality and price to the great 'firsts' of the Médoc. Yet the contrast between Ausone and, say, Margaux or Mouton is incredible: the well-exposed amphitheatre of vines at Ausone which extends around the historic south-facing flank is less than a tenth of the size of the productive vineyards at either of those imposing properties, a mere 7 hectares in total, planted with 50 per cent Merlot and 50 per cent Cabernet Franc, old gnarled vines as thick as a man's leg with an average age of 45 years.

The wine press is miniscule, and the seven oak fermentation vats are also surprisingly small. The essential French principle of quality wine making is followed whereby individual parcels are vinified separately, then assembled after a process of rigorous selection (there is no second wine at Ausone — rejected wines are sent down to the village *cave coopérative*). This, explains *régisseur* Pascal Delbeck, enables critical quality control at every stage. The impression without doubt is of a hand-made, an *artisan*-made product, necessarily on a very small scale. Even the great limestone cellars at Ausone are a striking contrast to the cool, low-lying first-year *chais* of the Médoc: this indeed is a real wine *cave*: dark, cobwebbed, damp, and atmospheric.

M. Delbeck is also in charge of the adjoining Château Belair. Though its vineyards are virtually contiguous with those of Ausone, the wine produced has its own distinct and somewhat lighter character. Other great wine properties of this Côtes vineyard include Château La Gaffelière, Château Magdelaine, Clos Fourtet, Château Beauséjour-Becot, Château Beauséjour-Duffau-Lagarrosse, Château Pavie, and Château Trottevieille, all classified *Premiers Grands Crus Classés*.

After the great properties of the Côtes, the other principal region of St-Emilion extends over the flatter plateau to the west and north of the town known as the Graves (not to be confused, of course, with that separate *appellation*.) From St-Emilion take the D243 towards Libourne, then branch right on the D245. These surrounding vineyards are the heart of the Graves, a striking contrast with the Côtes due to the flatness of the terrain and the richer, darker soil, full of gravel and pebbles. Château Figeac (*Premier Grand Crus Classé*), Petit Figeac, La Dominique, La Tour du Pin Figeac, and La Tour Figeac (*Grands Crus Classés*) are all highly regarded properties producing ripe concentrated wines.

Just along the road, virtually on the edge of the Pomerol vineyard, lies Château Cheval Blanc, the great property of the Graves, an imposing farmhouse approached up a long drive. The vineyard here is planted unusually with a very high proportion of Cabernet Franc: nowhere else does this *cépage* produce wine of such incredible depth and almost jammy ripeness.

There is something of this same profound mouth-filling richness, ripeness, almost sweetness, about the wines of Pomerol. For from Cheval Blanc, the heart of the Pomerol vineyard is but a pebble-throw away. Château La Conseillante, Cheval Blanc's immediate neighbour, is a highly regarded Pomerol estate, as are nearby Petit Village and L'Evangile.

The wines of Pomerol, perhaps rather surprisingly, have never been classified: indeed, until relatively recently they were not considered on equal status with the greats from the Médoc or St-Emilion. Yet crossing over the road leads to a clutch of vineyards which today are ranked, by wine lovers at least, as equal peers: first Vieux Château Certan, then Château Pétrus itself, and Château Le Gay, Château La Fleur, Château La Fleur Pétrus, and others.

Pétrus, incredibly, is just a simple farmhouse, little to suggest that from its surrounding vineyards which appear superficially little different from those around it, comes possibly the most expensive and sought after wine in the

BORDEAUX

world, rivalled only, perhaps, by the wines of the Domaine de la Romanée-Conti in the Côte d'Or. These wines, great though they undoubtedly are, fetch prices which seem to have little basis with reality: such are the supply-and-demand economics of scarcity and prestige in the world of millionaire drinkers. Pomerol, as a whole, is an *appellation* which is highly prized but there are still many more wines which are accessible to all; moreover, the wines are more accessible from a drinker's point of view, for the predominance of Merlot results in ripe, simply delicious wines that are ready to drink far earlier than the more austere principally Cabernet wines of the Médoc.

Circle around to little Pomerol, hardly more than a church and school surrounded by some treasured vineyards: Château l'Église Clinet, Domaine de l'Église, Clos l'Église, Château Clinet, and others. Then continue across the flat vineyards to the larger N89 and further explore this fascinating vineyard or else carry on to Libourne, Bordeaux, or back to St-Emilion.

Both Pomerol and St-Emilion have their hinterland wine country where similar, if less distinguished, wines are produced in abundance. The vineyards of Lalande-de-Pomerol extend mainly to the north of the commune of Pomerol, while those of St-Emilion extend over five so-called satellite communes: St-Georges, Montagne, Lussac, Puisseguin and Parsac. While there are well-known châteaux located here, producing wines that fetch prices not far below those of the finest properties of Pomerol and St-Emilion, on the whole there are scores of lesser bargain discoveries to be made at small farms and estates dotted throughout these somewhat hillier, wilder, and less-travelled regions. Simply knock on the door of any offering *dégustation-vente*. The wine museum at Montagne is particularly worth a visit.

One other area on the right bank should be mentioned: the vineyards of Fronsac and Canon Fronsac, just north-west of Libourne. Good, undervalued wines are produced here and the regions deserve further exploration in their own right.

Wine Museum

L'Ecomusée du Paysan Vigneron en Libournais
Montagne
33330 St-Emilion
tel: (57) 51 01 75
Hours: Mon–Fri 10–12h; 14–18h. Sat and Sun afternoons only.
Montagne is located some 4 km (2½ miles) from St-Emilion: this excellent little wine museum traces not only the history of viticulture in the region but also the social life and times of the *vignerons* of the Libournais through a collection of well-presented exhibits.

Dégustation: Stop to Taste; Stop to Buy

We include visiting information for some of the most famous and greatest estates in St-Emilion, as well as for other classed properties in St-Emilion and for three highly regarded properties in Pomerol. However, this is a concentrated wine region in every sense, and tasting opportunities abound. Do explore the wine regions and find your own list of favourites, not only in Pomerol and St-Emilion, but also in the rich hinterlands of Lalande-de-Pomerol, the St-Emilion satellites, and nearby Fronsac. To locate the properties ask for a detailed map at the *Maison du Vin* in St-Emilion, or telephone for directions.

1

Château Ausone
33330 St-Emilion
tel: (57) 24 70 94
Hours: By appointment only: telephone M. Delbeck on the above number.
Château Ausone AOC St-Emilion *Premier Grand Cru Classé A.*
Château Ausone is an historic and famous property: provided he receives a telephone call in advance, M. Delbeck is pleased to show serious visitors the deeply hewn limestone *cave* as well as the vineyard itself, though usually this rare wine can neither be tasted nor purchased.
English spoken.

2

Château Cheval Blanc
33330 St-Emilion
tel: (57) 24 70 70
Hours: Mon–Fri 9–11h; 14–17h. Appointment essential.
Château Cheval Blanc AOC St-Emilion *Premier Grand Cru Classé A.*
Château Cheval Blanc, one of the greatest wines of Bordeaux, is located on the flatter Graves plateau of St-Emilion and provides a contrast to Ausone. Visitors see the concrete fermentation vats, and first-year wine *chais*.
English spoken.

3

Château Belair
33330 St-Emilion
tel: (57) 74 41 97 or (57) 24 70 94
Hours: By appointment.
Château Belair AOC St-Emilion *Premier Grand Cru Classé.*
Telephone M. Delbeck at Ausone to arrange a visit to this prestigious neighbour. The vast carved *caves* of Belair, hewn out of limestone, are said to be the largest in St-Emilion. The wines can be both tasted and purchased.
English spoken.

4

Château Pavie
33330 St-Emilion
tel: (57) 24 72 02
Hours: Mon–Fri 9h30–12h; 14h30–17h30. Appointment preferred.
Château Pavie AOC St-Emilion *Premier Grand Cru Classé.*
Château Pavie is another highly regarded Côtes estate with long-established vineyards and a *cave* carved out of the rock. This *cave* was once an ancient

BORDEAUX

limestone quarry. The wines may be tasted, but not purchased.
English spoken.

5

Château Beauséjour-Becot
33330 St-Emilion
tel: (57) 74 46 87
Hours: Daily by appointment.
Château Beauséjour-Becot AOC St-Emilion *Premier Grand Cru Classé*.
Visitors see the underground *galeries* where over 300,000 bottles lie ageing.
Charge for *dégustation*; wines available for purchase.
English spoken.

6

Château La Gaffelière
33330 St-Emilion
tel: (57) 24 72 15
Hours: Mon–Fri 8–12h; 14–18h. Appointment preferred.
Château La Gaffelière AOC St-Emilion *Premier Grand Cru Classé*.
An outstanding Côtes château located at the bottom of the slope below St-Emilion off the D122. Charge for *dégustation*; wines available for purchase.
English spoken.

7

Château Troplong-Mondot
33330 St-Emilion
tel: (57) 24 70 72
Hours: Daily, working hours. Appointment preferred.
Château Troplong-Mondot AOC St-Emilion *Grand Cru Classé*.
30-hectare vineyard on the plateau east of St-Emilion, above Château Pavie.
Wine can be tasted and purchased.
English spoken.

8

Château Le Chatelet
33330 St-Emilion
tel: (57) 24 70 97
Hours: Daily, 9–20h from 15 June to 30 October.
Château Le Chatelet AOC St-Emilion *Grand Cru Classé*.
The vineyard and *cave* can be visited and tastings are free for purchasers of a minimum of three bottles.
English spoken.

9

Château Soutard
33330 St-Emilion
tel: (57) 24 72 23
Hours: Mon–Fri, working hours. Appointment necessary.
Château Soutard AOC St-Emilion *Grand Cru Classé*.
Visits to the *cave* and possibility of tasting but not purchase.
English spoken.

10 Société Civile du Vieux Château Certan
Pomerol
33500 Libourne
tel: (57) 51 17 33
Hours: Mon–Fri 8–12h; 14–18h. Appointment essential.
Vieux Château Certan AOC Pomerol; La Gravette de Certan AOC Pomerol (second wine).
One of the most highly regarded of all Pomerol estates: visitors are welcome by appointment, but the wines cannot be purchased.
English spoken.

11 Château Petit Village
Pomerol
33500 Libourne
tel: (56) 44 11 37
Hours: By appointment.
Château Petit Village AOC Pomerol.
This long-established vineyard estate, located in the Pétrus nucleus, is now owned by the Prat family, who also own the great St-Estèphe estate of Cos d'Estournel. Visits for serious wine amateurs by appointment. The wine can neither be purchased nor tasted.

12 Château La Croix
Pomerol
33500 Libourne
tel: (57) 24 74 87
Hours: Mon–Fri 9–12h; 14–18h. Appointment essential.
Château La Croix AOC Pomerol.
Located just outside Catusseau on the plateau of Pomerol near Petit Village, this 10-hectare estate is owned by the Janoueix family, who also own Château Haut-Sarpe in St-Emilion and the neighbouring Pomerol Château La Croix St-Georges. The Janoueixs are happy to receive serious wine amateurs by appointment; the wines can be tasted and purchased.

OTHER BORDEAUX WINE TOURS

Premières Côtes de Bordeaux; Loupiac, Cadillac and Ste-Croix-du-Mont

The vineyards of the Premières Côtes de Bordeaux extend in a long band along the right bank of the Garonne, from Bordeaux south to St-Macaire, encompassing the sweet wine enclaves entitled to their own *appellations*: Cadillac, Loupiac, and Ste-Croix-du-Mont. The Premières Côtes produces a full range of wines, including red, dry white, and sweet white. The region, moreover, is little travelled compared with the great and famous vineyards above. From Bordeaux, cross to the right bank and follow the river road D10 south to Cadillac, taking time, if desired, simply to explore the smaller towns and villages.

Cadillac is a fine medieval town and former *bastide* which rises dramatically above the Garonne opposite Cérons. Much of its fourteenth-century fortifications are intact. The Château des Ducs d'Eperon dates mainly from the seventeenth century and has been extensively restored. It houses the *Maison du Vin*, an organization that promotes not only the wines of the right bank, but also those from the vineyards of Sauternes and Barsac across the river. Loupiac is a particularly pleasant small wine village, located just off the main road. Vineyards seem to grow everywhere: on the surrounding fields and hills, in back gardens, even around the church. The wines of Loupiac have been celebrated for millennia: Ausonius reputedly had a second villa here to retreat to from St-Emilion.

Between Loupiac and Ste-Croix-du-Mont there are some grand properties along the main road, offering *dégustation-vente*: the sweet wines of Loupiac and Ste-Croix-du-Mont must be sampled on the spot, for they are little-known, undervalued, and particularly delicious: nowhere near as unctuous, complex, and concentrated as the great Sauternes across the river, yet because of their lighter, slightly less sweet character (not to mention their considerably lighter price) they are wines that can be enjoyed simply with *pâtisseries*, with *pâté* on a picnic (a rich combination that, surprisingly, works), or as an *apéritif*.

Ste-Croix-du-Mont is a steep, picturesque hill town: climb up here, passing wine producers along the way, then relax by the church square and take in a splendid view over the town's vineyards and across the Entre-Deux-Mers countryside. Surprisingly, considering the height of the town above the Garonne, the sub-soil here is riddled with fossilized oysters, and there are numerous grottoes and wine *caves* carved out of the soft, shell-ridden rock. Just below the church, in one such grotto, there is a pleasant tasting *cave* open in summer where Ste-Croix-du-Mont can be enjoyed by the glass or bottle together with simple snacks.

The lovely wine country continues between Ste-Croix-du-Mont and Verdelais, where the artist Toulouse-Lautrec is buried, down to little St-Macaire, a fine, old fortified village which is pleasant to wander through. The vineyards around and beyond St-Macaire produce similar sweet wines which are entitled to their own *appellation*: Côtes de Bordeaux St-Macaire.

Entre-Deux-Mers

The Entre-Deux-Mers vineyards extend over a vast triangle formed by the converging Dordogne and Garonne rivers: they lie literally '*entre deux mers*' and are themselves at times (especially between La Réole and Créon) a virtual sea of vines as far as the eye can see. A tour of this rather wild, less tamed wine country that produces such vast quantities of good everyday dry white

Premières Côtes de Bordeaux; Loupiac, Cadillac and Ste-Croix-du-Mont; Entre-Deux-Mers; Bourg and Blaye.

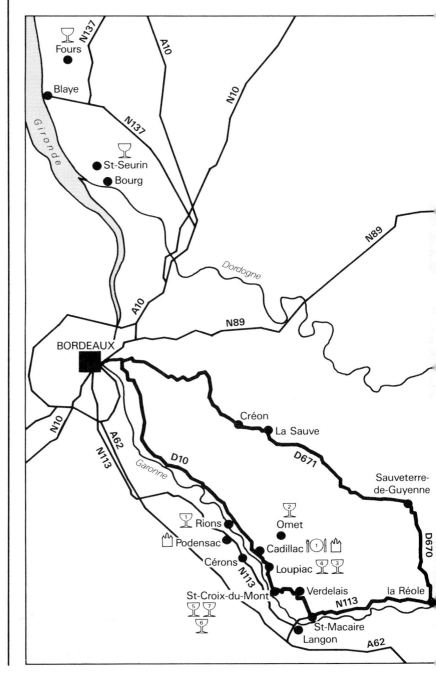

wine, particularly from the Sauvignon grape, can be made from Langon, after visiting Sauternes or Ste-Croix-du-Mont, on the return to Bordeaux, or during the transition across to the vineyards of St-Emilion.

La Réole, up-river from St-Macaire, is another fine fortified town, its winding steep streets lined with old houses that lead up to the twelfth-century town hall, one of the oldest in France. From there, head inland across to Sauveterre-de-Guyenne, an isolated historic *bastide* with entrance *portes* to the town that are still intact. It is strange to recall that these quiet towns between Bordeaux and Castillon were once strategic strongholds when this area was under English domination.

From Sauveterre, either cut up to St-Emilion and Libourne, or continue on towards Bordeaux on the D671. Though the country across this way is dominated by the vine, trained high on wires with ample space between the rows to allow for mechanization (a striking contrast with the vineyards of the Médoc), there are surprisingly few opportunities for visiting and tasting. This is because much of the wine of Entre-Deux-Mers is produced by some 40 *caves coopératives*.

At La Sauve, stop to visit the former Benedictine Abbey: once grandiose and an important stop for pilgrims *en route* to Santiago de Compostela, but now a roofless ruin, with birds flying through the glassless windows. At Créon, continue on to Bordeaux or across to Libourne.

Bourg and Blaye

Bourg and Blaye, on the right bank of the Gironde opposite the Médoc, are rather cut off from the rest of the Bordeaux vineyard due to their geographical position, virtually continuous with the vineyards of Cognac and the Charentes. We are told that these extensive vineyards were once more highly valued than those of the Médoc: today, although they are not exactly neglected, nevertheless they receive only a fraction of the attention that their more famous neighbours across the river attract. Yet if these large and undervalued wine areas, which together produce the full Bordeaux range of red, rosé, dry white, and sweet white wines were in any area other than Bordeaux, they would be hailed important wine regions in their own right. As such, they provide fruitful exploration for intrepid wine travellers.

The town of Blaye, with its immense citadel, stands opposite the Fort Médoc (there is a convenient ferry across the Gironde here, useful for those who may have stopped in the Médoc on their return journey north). Blaye thus makes a useful starting point for exploring these little-visited vineyards, known primarily for their white wines. In the past, light, sweet wines from the classic blend of Sémillon, Sauvignon, and Muscadelle accounted for the main production; though such wines continue to be made, in recent years, as tastes have swung more towards dry wines, there has been an increase in plantation of Sauvignon, thus resulting in some fine, fruity dry whites.

Bourg, further up-river towards Bordeaux itself, is the smaller of the two areas, and its châteaux are particularly worthy of further exploration. The best, whose vineyards lie generally in proximity to the Gironde, are capable of producing classic clarets in the style of the Médoc. The *appellation* Côtes de Bourg can apply both to such clarets and to smaller amounts of dry whites.

Le Bordeaux des Petits Châteaux

The classic regions of Bordeaux — the Médoc, St-Emilion and Pomerol, Graves, and Sauternes and Barsac — together contribute less than a third of the vast annual production of Bordeaux wines. Although the very grandest and most famous châteaux undoubtedly and deservedly have the highest profiles, the great wines produced on such estates are beyond the means of most of us, except perhaps on special occasions. But Bordeaux is the greatest vineyard in the world, we think, not simply because of its greatest wines, but also because of the huge quantities of well-made everyday reds, and dry and sweet whites which remain within reach of us all.

Thus, throughout the vast superficial area of the Bordeaux vineyard, over half of the wine produced is classified simply as Bordeaux AOC or Bordeaux Supèrieur AOC. This is the Bordeaux of the petits châteaux, those wine growers who often work holdings of less than 5 hectares. Such properties — no more than small farms in many cases, although they call themselves 'châteaux' — are usually more than happy to receive visitors, to offer their wines for tasting and direct sales.

Dégustation: Stop to Taste; Stop to Buy

We include a handful of addresses for wine producers in Loupiac, Ste-Croix-du-Mont, Entre-Deux-Mers, and Côtes de Bourge and Blaye. Do not confine yourselves to these suggestions only however: these areas remain, on the whole, uncharted wine country which should be explored. There are literally countless other opportunities for finding good, sound, and still inexpensive red, rosé, dry and sweet white wines. Though appointments are not often necessary, a telephone call in advance always ensures that someone is in to receive you; also telephone for detailed directions.

Château Jourdan
33410 Rions
tel: (56) 62 60 88
Hours: Mon–Sat, working hours.
Château Jourdan AOC Premières Côtes de Bordeaux (red); Château Jourdan AOC Bordeaux (dry white); Château Deylet AOC Bordeaux Clairet.
Rions is located just 4 km (2½ miles) north of Cadillac, and is considered

an important centre for the Premières Côtes de Bordeaux.
English spoken.

2

Vignobles Henri Gillet
Omet
33410 Cadillac
tel: (56) 62 97 16
Hours: Telephone for an appointment and directions.
The Gillet family offer an impressive range of wines from the right bank: Château
Grand Peyruchet AOC Loupiac; Château La Bertrande AOC Cadillac; Domaine
de Camelon AOC Bordeaux (dry white Sauvignon); Château La Bertrande
AOC Bordeaux (red); Domaine du Moulin AOC Premières Côtes de Bordeaux
(red); Chevalier de Reignac AOC Bordeaux Rosé.
A little English spoken.

3

Clos Jean
33410 Loupiac
tel: (56) 62 99 84
Hours: Daily except Sun afternoon. Telephone call appreciated.
Clos Jean AOC Loupiac; Château Rondillon AOC Loupiac; also red, rosé, and
dry white Bordeaux and Bordeaux Supérieur.
Finely sited vineyard producing excellent Loupiac.
Traditional *chais* and wines available for tasting and purchase.
English spoken.

4

Château du Cros
D10
33410 Loupiac
tel: (56) 62 99 31
Hours: Mon–Fri 8–12h; 14–18h. Weekends by appointment.
Château du Cros AOC Loupiac; Château de Lucques AOC Barsac; Château
Haut-Mayne AOC Graves.
The Château du Cros was fortified in the fourteenth century and commands
a superb position over the Garonne valley. Visitors may be able to taste and
purchase wine from the above properties, all owned by the Boyer family.
English spoken.

5

Les Grottes
Dégustation-Vente
33410 Ste-Croix-du-Mont
tel: (56) 62 01 54
Hours: In summer daily 10–19h30. Other times by appointment.
This tasting grotto is located below the church in a cave hollowed out of a
bank of oyster fossils. A good selection of the wines of Ste-Croix-du-Mont can
be tasted and purchased or else drunk on the spot with simple snacks.

6

Château La Rame
33410 Ste-Croix-du-Mont
tel: (56) 62 01 50; (56) 62 04 09
Hours: Mon–Sat, working hours.
Château La Rame AOC Ste-Croix-du-Mont; also dry white, rosé, and red Bordeaux.
Visitors can see the *caves* and vineyards and the wines can be tasted and purchased.

7

Château du Mont
33410 Ste-Croix-du-Mont
tel: (56) 62 01 72
Hours: Daily, working hours.
Château du Mont AOC Ste-Croix-du-Mont; also dry white Sauvignon and red AOC Bordeaux.
Wines can be tasted and purchased.
A little English spoken.

8

Château Les Chaumes
Fours
33390 Blaye
tel: (57) 42 18 44
Hours: Weekdays, telephone call in advance preferred.
Château Les Chaumes AOC Premières Côtes de Blaye.
English spoken.

9

Château Tayac
St-Seurin-de-Bourg
33710 Bourg
tel: (57) 68 40 60
Hours: Mon–Fri 9h30–12h; 14h30–20h.
Château Tayac AOC Côtes de Bourg (dry white and red).
The Château Tayac has a fine panorama over the Gironde; wines can be tasted and purchased, but telephone in advance for visits to the *caves* and vineyard.
A little English spoken.

Regional Gastronomy

In spite of the grandness of her châteaux and the aristocratic reputation of her most famous wines, the cuisine of Bordeaux remains foremost simple and down-to-earth. Though the region has no shortage of fine and expensive *grands restaurants*, in small country *auberges*, in the dining rooms of the wine châteaux, and in private homes, the foods that are most enjoyed are primarily just simple homely dishes which best show off the local produce and products, *à la Bordelaise*, of course.

Naturally it helps when the 'local ingredients' which you start with are

BORDEAUX

as fine as they are in the Gironde. The region is blessed with an abundance of good things to eat from sea, river, and land. The Gironde estuary may yield the fine, salmon-like fish known as *alose* (shad), a particular local favourite, but equally popular are the great catches of small-fry, caught in the enormous fine nets of the fishing boats of the Médoc or by enterprising anglers who set up hand versions, clamped stoutly to the rails of bridges and lowered with winches. The Bassin d'Arcachon is, of course, a famous source of *huîtres* — oysters — but the Bordelais don't make a song and dance about these (to us) luxury foodstuffs: they down them by the dozens, ice-cold and raw, followed by bites of piping hot spicy sausages — *lou kencous* — then gulps of chilled, fresh Entre-Deux-Mers.

This is a land where you need never feel hesitant to *faire le chabrot* — that is, add a half-glass of wine to the remains of your *garbure* (hearty bean and vegetable soup) or *tourin* (Bordelais onion soup), swill it around in the bowl, then drink it or mop up the soupy wine with good fresh bread.

The vineyard of Bordeaux naturally influences the cooking of the region in many ways. Snails, the classic vineyard pest, here become a rustic centrepiece of a meal, *escargots à la Bordelaise*, a substantial stew made with pork, bacon, wine, and shallots. Open fires of cut vine shoots and wine-impregnated staves from discarded casks are used to cook steaks or shad *aux sarments*, the smoky, winey flavour contributing its inimitable character. And, of course, wine finds its way into the cooking pot: in thick, wine-dark *daubes* or in richly flavoured specialities such as *lamproie à la Bordelaise*: lamprey from the Gironde, stewed in red wine with leeks.

Lamproie, in its dark winey sauce, is perfectly accompanied by ripe, richly flavoured St-Emilion. In the Médoc, there is no better accompaniment to those great clarets than *pre-salé* lamb, raised on the salt-marshes of Pauillac. This is simply roasted, French-style, on a *mirepoix* of chopped vegetables and wine, and always served pink. It is delicious and uncomplicated, a food which enhances wine but does not detract from it.

For in truth, Bordeaux is not really a great region for complicated local specialities. If its wines are dominant, it follows that they need only the simplest foods to set them off. An *entrecôte à la Bordelaise*, that is a good-quality steak served with a sauce of chopped shallots, bone marrow, and wine, is another classic foil to good or great claret. Some might say that even the sauce is an unnecessary encumbrance. *Cèpes*, the finest of all wild mushrooms, are another food served simply and with little fuss, sautéed with plenty of shallots and parsley. They too are superlative when accompanied by a good red Bordeaux, their earthy, autumnal flavour highlighting the warmth and depth of the wine.

Sauternes is often referred to as a dessert or pudding wine, but that is not how the Sauternais themselves think of it. Indeed, here Sauternes is often drunk as an *apéritif*. A classic combination also encountered is Sauternes with *foie gras* from the Landes (*mi-cuit* preferably), the unctuous smoothness of the rich goose or duck liver an amazing companion to the almost oily texture, and enormous flavour of the wine. Sauternes, too, is considered the finest accompaniment to the great blue cheese of the south-west, Roquefort. And, of course, it can be drunk with desserts, *pâtisseries*, or just on its own after a meal.

Spécialité Régionale:
Stop to Taste; Stop to Buy

Pêcherie-Poissonerie
Paul Heraud
11, quai Leon-Perrier
33250 Pauillac
After touring the wine country and châteaux come to the waterfront at Pauillac and purchase paper-wrapped parcels of little brown *crevettes*. These delicious shrimps, piping hot and straight out of the boiler are so sweet and fresh that you can eat them whole (except for the heads and tails) while strolling along the *quai*.

Le Pique-Nique

Jambon de Bayonne The finest *jambon cru* — raw Parma-style ham — comes from the south-west around Bayonne and is found throughout the region.

Huîtres d'Arcachon Arcachon oysters, mainly the Portuguese variety as well as some native *plates* are sold in markets and roadside stands.

Foie gras de Landes The Landes is one of the major *départements* for the production of *foie gras*, a luxury picnic food enjoyed together with chilled bottles of Sauternes or Ste-Croix-du-Mont.

Macarons de St-Emilion Macaroons, the speciality of St-Emilion.

Canele de Bordeaux An *appellation d'origine contrôlée* type of *brioche* baked in a copper mould until quite crunchy on the outside but melting on the inside.

Fromages Though the Gironde is not a great region for cheese, undoubtedly the wines of Bordeaux, especially claret, are delicious when accompanied by it. A Dutch Edam-style cheese is popular locally (emphasizing links between Holland and Bordeaux). Similarly, English style cheeses (such as French 'Cheddar') are equally suitable favourites. Roquefort, the great blue cheese of France, is the classic accompaniment to fine Sauternes.

BORDEAUX

Restaurants

Médoc (Map p.59)

1

Hostellerie des Criquets
130 ave du XI Novembre
33290 Blanquefort
tel: (56) 35 09 24
This well-equipped hotel-restaurant has a restaurant serving traditional cuisine and a choice of 180 different château-bottled wines. Recommended by Barton & Guestier.
Moderate to Expensive

2

Relais de Margaux
rte de l'Ile Vincent
33460 Margaux
tel: (56) 88 38 30
Fine hotel-restaurant highly recommended by the local wine growers: imaginative cuisine and an excellent selection of over 500 wines. In summer, meals are served on a terrace overlooking the vineyards and the 55-hectare domaine. Recommended by Château Prieuré-Lichine and others.
Moderate to Expensive

3

Le Lion d'Or
place de la République
Arcins
33460 Margaux
tel: (56) 58 96 79
Closed Mon and holiday evenings.
This friendly restaurant serves simple seasonal foods in a country *auberge* style. Selection of Médoc and Graves wines, though M. Barbier does not mind if you bring your own bottle or bottles purchased at surrounding estates. Recommended by Château d'Angludet.
Inexpensive

4

Le Relais du Médoc
Lamarque
33460 Margaux
tel: (56) 58 92 27
Closed Mon.
Favourite family-style restaurant serving **Inexpensive to Moderate** *menus* with such regional dishes as *escargots* and *entrecôte à la Bordelaise, confit,* and *magret de canard.* Near the car ferry to Blaye. Recommended by Château Beychevelle.

5

Hôtel de France
33480 Listrac

tel: (56) 58 23 68
This small family hotel has a good **Inexpensive** restaurant serving local dishes such as *grillades aux sarments* and *confit de canard*. Recommended by Château Moulin à Vent.

6

Restaurant La Renaissance
33112 St-Laurent-et-Benon
tel: (56) 59 40 29
Simple foods, reasonable prices, and excellent quality, say the local *vignerons*. Recommended by Château Phélan Ségur and Château Batailley.
Inexpensive to Moderate

7

Le Relais du Manoir
rte de la Shell
33250 Pauillac
tel: (56) 59 05 47
Closed Sun eve, Mon out of season.
This modest family-style hotel-restaurant just outside Pauillac offers good home cooking. Every weekend there is a *menu de la mer et fruits de mer.*
Inexpensive

Graves (Map p.70)

1

La Réserve
74, ave du Bourgailh
33600 Pessac
tel: (56) 07 13 28
This member of the *Relais et Châteaux* chain is close to Merignac airport and has superb facilities as well as a highly regarded **Expensive** restaurant. Recommended by Château Haut-Brion.

Sauternes and Barsac (Map p.74)

1

Hôtel-Restaurant 'Grillobois'
RN113
33720 Cérons
tel: (56) 27 11 50
Closed Sun eve, Mon.
Regional specialities and *grillades au feu de bois* in this enterprising hotel-restaurant which has a wine museum and offers wine tastings. In summer, meals can be taken in the garden. Recommended by Clos Jean.
Inexpensive

2

Hostellerie du Château de Rolland
RN113
33720 Barsac

BORDEAUX

tel: (56) 27 15 75
Amidst the vineyards of Barsac, this *château-auberge* is located in a fifteenth-century Carthusian monastery. Elegant stately setting and traditionally prepared foods. Recommended by Château Caillou.
Moderate to Expensive

Auberge 'Les Vignes'
place de l'Église
33210 Sauternes
tel: (56) 63 60 06
Closed Mon.
This old favourite is a charming rustic *auberge* in the centre of little Sauternes. Meats and *alose* are grilled over an open fire of *sarments des vignes* in the huge chimney in the dining room. Sauternes by the glass or bottle. Recommended by Château Coutet and others.
Inexpensive

Le Sauternais
33210 Sauternes
tel: (56) 63 67 13
Closed Mon.
Owned by Château Guiraud, this elegant old stone house is the best place to come for the classic combination of *foie gras mi-cuit* together with *Grands Crus Classés* Sauternes by the bottle or glass. Recommended by Château Rieussec, Clos Haut Peyraguey, and others.
Moderate

Hôtel-Restaurant Château de Commarque
33210 Sauternes
tel: (56) 63 65 94
Closed February.
This English-owned hotel-restaurant serves specialities of the Pays Basque: *chiperons dans leur encre, gambas à la plancha, coques salza verde,* and other fish and shellfish dishes. The pleasant dining room is located in the former wine *chais,* while the formerly neglected Sauternes vineyard is currently being replanted and restored. Recommended by Château Filhot.
Inexpensive to Moderate

Restaurant du Cap
33210 Preignac
tel: (56) 63 27 38
Closed Mon.
Specialities include *entrecôte, lamproie, cèpes,* and *tripes aux Sauternes* in this simple rustic restaurant with a terrace beside the Garonne. Recommended by Château Simon.
Inexpensive to Moderate

Choucroute.

Left *Château Mouton-Rothschild wine* chai.
Above Huîtres *stand near Arcachon.*
Right Tonnelier *at Château Margaux.*

Overleaf:
Main picture *Fuissé.*
Inset *Burgundian* charcuterie.

Left *Meursault.*
This page *Moët et Chandon's Orangery.*

*Poppies grow on the former
battlefields of Champagne.*

Left *Gathering oysters at La Cayenne.*
This page *The vieille ville of Cognac.*

The Charente river at Jarnac.

7

Hôtel-Restaurant Claude Darroze
95, cours du Général Leclerc
33210 Langon
tel: (56) 63 00 48
One of the great restaurants of the region, serving *cuisine du marché*: fish, shellfish and game in season, *foie gras des Landes chaud ou froid*, and a fine selection of Bordeaux wines, particularly Graves and Sauternes. Recommended by Château de Malle and others.
Expensive

St-Emilion (Map p.80)

1

Hostellerie de Plaisance
place du Clocher
33330 St-Emilion
tel: (57) 24 72 32
Old favourite located in the square above the Église Monolithe overlooking the town and its vineyards. Regional specialities served in an elegant dining room, together with a fine selection of Bordeaux *crus*. Recommended by Château Cheval Blanc and others.
Moderate

2

Chez 'Germaine'
place du Clocher
33330 St-Emilion
tel: (57) 24 70 88
Closed Sun eve, Mon.
Another wine producers' favourite in this central location: *lamproie, magret de canard grillé sur sarments de vigne*, and other regional dishes. Recommended by Château Soutard and others.
Inexpensive to Moderate

3

Le Restaurant Francis Goullée
rue Guadet
33330 St-Emilion
tel: (57) 24 70 49
Closed Sun eve.
Elegant restaurant serving regional and imaginative specialities. Recommended by Château Ausone.
Moderate

4

Le Logis de la Cadene
place du Marché-aux-Bois
33330 St-Emilion
tel: (57) 24 71 40
Closed Mon. Open evenings only in July, August, and September.

Simple, unpretentious restaurant in the heart of the medieval town serving a well-liked formula of home cooking and regional food for the past 34 years. Recommended by Château Beauséjour-Becot, Château Pavie, and others.
Inexpensive to Moderate

Cadillac (Map p.87)

Porte de la Mer
18, rue Ducros
33410 Cadillac
tel: (56) 62 18 88
Traditional and imaginative specialities such as *filet de bar à l'anis* and *magret de canard rossini aux cèpes* are served with wines from the Premières Côtes de Bordeaux and Graves. Recommended by the Château Jourdan.
Moderate

Additional Information

Et pour en savoir plus . . .

Syndicat d'Initiative de Bordeaux
12, cours du XXX Juillet
33800 Bordeaux
tel: (56) 44 28 41

Syndicat d'Initiative de St-Emilion
'Le Doyenne'
place des Créneaux
33330 St-Emilion
tel: (57) 24 72 03

Maison du Vin de Bordeaux
1, cours du XXX Juillet
33000 Bordeaux
tel: (58) 52 82 82

BURGUNDY
and the Jura

Introduction

Puligny-Montrachet, an unassuming village whose vineyards produce possibly the world's greatest white wines.

*H*ow wonderful it always is to be in Burgundy! For us, there is something so warm and comforting about the region. It is smug, certainly, self-content and proud, yet there is rarely a feeling of preciousness or pretence here. Bordeaux, with her grand châteaux, may be the most aristocratic of French wine regions: Burgundy by contrast is the most democratic.

There are historical reasons why this is so. The great vineyards of Burgundy were established foremost by the monasteries and abbeys of the region, founded as early as the sixth century. Later, in the fourteenth and fifteenth centuries when, under the Dukes of Valois, a Burgundian empire extended as far as

The Château of the Clos-de-Vougeot.

Belgium and the Netherlands, the fame of the region's wines spread too, finding royal favour with the kings of France. Admittedly, the wines of Burgundy were preferred to those of Bordeaux not simply on matters of taste but also because of the political considerations of the Hundred Years' War. None the less, when the French Revolution swept through France, the ecclesiastical holdings as well as the estates of the Burgundian nobility and landed gentry — the *ancien régime* — were confiscated, and the properties broken up into small parcels, a process furthered as each generation continued to divide their lands as birthright.

Today Burgundy is a complex variegated patchwork primarily of small and even tiny parcels of land. In contrast to Bordeaux, where in the eighteenth century the new merchant class of landowners — a *nouveau* aristocracy, as it were — were able to consolidate their holdings, acquiring great vineyards surrounding their outstanding châteaux in the Médoc and elsewhere, here in Burgundy, former single vineyards such as the Clos-de-Vougeot were progressively divided and redivided so that this *Grand Cru* today has no fewer than 70 different proprietors. The Château de Pommard, a walled *clos* of some 20 hectares (this would be considered only a small-to-average estate in the Médoc), is the largest domaine in the Côte d'Or under a single owner.

Because of this 'democratization' of the vineyards, Burgundy today remains the friendliest and most welcoming of all the great wine regions. Famous growers and *négociants-éleveurs* take time off to welcome visitors heartily and in a most generous Burgundian fashion. Great cobwebbed cellars in Beaune, Nuits-St-Georges, and Meursault keep 'open house' to passing wine tourists; moreover, after a tour, the wines offered for tasting are not measured out in thimblefuls but are poured out with gusto.

An essentially warm and honest Burgundian outlook is apparent throughout the region. Burgundy is one of few areas where the true regional foods are served unselfconsciously and without fuss and pretension. *Jambon persillé*, *coq au vin*, *boeuf bourguignon*, *oeufs en meurette* really *are* what the Burgundians themselves eat here, not some '*spécialités*' put on just for passing tourists: such foods appear on the cheapest menus of humble restaurants, as well as in grander establishments. These are hearty foods, foods to accompany opulent, silky red wines made from the rich Pinot Noir grape, or full-flavoured oak-aged whites from the noble Chardonnay.

Hearty Burgundian attitudes are apparent elsewhere, too. The Chevaliers du Tastevin, who meet in splendour in the Château du Clos-de-Vougeot each year, by all accounts end their sumptuous feasts with much raucous carousing and the singing of Burgundian drinking songs into the small hours of the morning. And where else but Burgundy would the biggest annual charity auction in the world presage a three-day regional party? To the Burgundians, life is a celebration: this to us is the essence, the eternal charm, of the region.

Well beyond the Côte d'Or, beyond the wilder Côte Chalonnaise and the Mâconnais, and far from the rugged hills of Beaujolais, lies a separate and distinct vineyard area, the Jura. This mountainous eastern region forms the southern part of the Franche-Comté, a province which once came under Burgundian rule but which was allowed to retain certain autonomous privileges, thus maintaining its own distinct history and heritage. This is a land of mountain cheeses and sausages, and of unusual, little-encountered wines like the rare and costly Vin Jaune and Vin de Paille. The vineyards around Arbois, home of Louis Pasteur, are particularly fruitful areas of exploration for wine travellers.

The Monks of Cîteaux

In 1098, Dom Robert, Abbot of Molesmes, came to the forest of Cîteaux and there founded the Cistercian religious order, the aim of which was to restore the Benedictine rule to its former austerity. The monks' motto was '*Ora et Labora*' — pray and work — and one of the main tenets of Cîteaux was that the monastery should be supported by the monks' own labour. Cîteaux thus played an important role in the development of medieval agriculture, and — foremost in Burgundy — of viticulture.

For one of the earliest needs at Cîteaux was for wine to celebrate mass. Since the marshy, poor land around the abbey was unsuitable for vines, the monks thus set out one day to follow the little Vouge river upstream towards its source. Finally, about midway between Dijon and present-day Nuits-St-Georges, they came to an inauspicious slope that they deemed suitable for their task. Generous donors, in return for mere eternal salvation of their souls, granted them land here, and, over the following centuries, throughout the region. Thus, before long the Cistercians held some of the very finest vineyards in Burgundy.

The French Revolution, however, saw the dissolution of Cîteaux and the confiscation of all its lands, including the Clos-de-Vougeot. Yet even today, that first vineyard of Cîteaux, found seemingly by chance or divine guidance, remains one of the greatest of all Burgundy's *Grands Crus*.

And as for Cîteaux today? The Trappist order of Cistercians once more inhabits the famous though much diminished abbey: though it owns no vineyards, the monks of Cîteaux, following their self-imposed destiny of hard labour and self-sufficiency, today raise livestock and make a fine, pungent rind-washed cheese which is a fitting partner to the best red Burgundies (see address below).

Orientation

Burgundy lies along the main north–south axis which runs from Paris through Dijon, Beaune, Chalon-sur-Saône, Mâcon, to Lyon and the south of France. Thus, the A6 *autoroute* provides easy and quick access to the region. Auxerre, the exit for the first Burgundian vineyards of Chablis lies some 150 km (95 miles) south of Paris. Dijon is about 310 km (195 miles) from Paris, a comfortable 3½ hours' drive. Once in the wine regions, distances are not great. Dijon to Beaune is only 35 km (22 miles). Beaune to Chalon-sur-Saône via Chagny is only 30 km (19 miles). From Chalon-sur-Saône, the vineyards of the Côte Chalonnaise, Mâconnais, and Beaujolias sprawl down virtually to the outskirts of Lyon, a further 110 km (70 miles) to the south.

The vineyards of the Jura centre around the town of Arbois, located about 60 km (38 miles) due east of Beaune.

Burgundy is well served by trains since it lies along the main Paris–Marseille route, as well as on international routes that continue on to Switzerland and Italy. The principal stop for direct TEE trains is Dijon, and from Paris this journey takes as little as 2½ hours. These high-speed trains make a day trip from Paris to Burgundy a feasibility. Many trains also stop in Mâcon, while slower local connections link Beaune, Meursault, Chalon-sur-Saône, Mâcon, and Villefranche-sur-Saône. For the vineyards of the Jura there are trains from Dijon and Lyon to Dole; from Dole, take the local connection to Arbois.

Lyon Satolas is the most convenient international airport for Burgundy. Genève Cointrin is probably most convenient for the Jura.

Michelin Maps 65, 66, 69, 70, 73, 74

The Wines of Burgundy

The Burgundy vineyard extends over four *départements*: Yonne (vineyards of Chablis); Côte d'Or (Côte de Nuits and Côte de Beaune); Saône-et-Loire (Côte Chalonnaise and Mâconnais); and Rhône (Beaujolais). The regulations defining the Burgundy *appellations* are among the most detailed and complex of all the wines of France, pinpointing the exact geographical origins of a wine as precisely as possible.

Thus wines may be given general or regional *appellations* (such as Bourgogne AOC or Bourgogne Hautes-Côtes de Beaune AOC), particular village or communal *appellations* (Nuits-St-Georges AOC or Chablis AOC), or *appellations* identifying a particular parcel or plot of land in a particular village or commune. Such vineyard parcels are known in Burgundy as *climats*. In the Côte d'Or a number of such *climats* have been classified as outstanding: *Premiers Crus* are therefore entitled to use the name of the village and the *climat* as in Pommard Les Epenots AOC. Wines produced from more than one *climat* may simply indicate the name of the village or commune together with the term, for example, Aloxe-Corton *Premier Cru* AOC.

Grands Crus are even more exclusive; there is only a select handful of such very great vineyards. In these cases, the *climat* name alone stands sufficient as the *appellation* in its own right; for example, Chambertin AOC, Corton-Charlemagne AOC, Montrachet AOC, and Clos-de-Vougeot AOC.

These matters are confusing to say the least, the more so because there are literally hundreds of named *climats* in the Côte d'Or and it is difficult for the amateur and expert to master them. However, in one sense at least, such distinctions are particularly crucial because of the Burgundian practice of appending the name of each commune's most famous vineyard. There is clearly a world of difference (in taste and price) between, say, a wine bearing a simple village *appellation* such as Gevrey-Chambertin AOC and the *Grand Cru* Chambertin AOC itself. Furthermore, even such precise knowledge is no guarantee in itself in Burgundy; because the vineyards have been so divided and redivided, there may be a number of different wine growers and *négociants* offering *Premiers* and *Grands Crus* wines entitled to the same *appellations* but of widely differing styles and even quality.

General and Regional *Appellations*

Bourgogne AOC

*T*he most general Burgundy *appellation* may apply to red, rosé, and white wines produced throughout the defined vineyard region conforming

Burgundy.

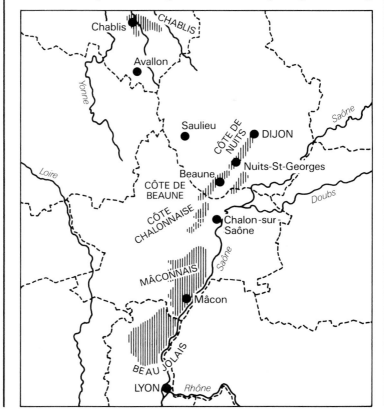

to certain regulations regarding permitted grape varieties (almost exclusively Pinot Noir for reds and Chardonnay for whites, though Gamay wines from the *crus* Beaujolais may be entitled to this *appellation*); methods of cultivation; maximum yield; and minimum alcohol content (10° for reds and rosé, and 10.5° for whites).

These basic Burgundies can be good, demonstrating the particular varietal characteristics of Pinot Noir and Chardonnay, though obviously in considerably lighter and less distinguished forms than wines bearing more specific *appellations*.

Bourgogne Aligoté AOC

*B*asic white wine produced not from noble Chardonnay but from the lesser Aligoté grape variety. High in acid, light and crisp, Bourgogne Aligoté is the classic wine to mix with *crème de cassis* for the favourite Burgundian *apéritif* Kir.

Bourgogne Hautes-Côtes-de-Beaune AOC; Bourgogne Hautes-Côtes-de-Nuits AOC

*T*he names of the 'Hautes Côtes' can be appended to the general Burgundy *appellation* for approved wines coming from vineyards located in defined areas of the higher, wilder slopes above both the Côte-de-Nuits and Côte-de-Beaune. Wines from individual producers, as well as from the outstanding Cave des Hautes-Côtes outside Beaune can be good, less expensive alternatives to more famous *appellations*.

Bourgogne Grand Ordinaire AOC

*L*ower classification of wine than 'straight' Bourgogne AOC, this *appellation* may apply to red, rosé, or white wines made to less stringent regulations and lower alcohol strength. The reds and rosé, for example, often contain Gamay as well as Pinot Noir and need only reach 9°, while the whites can be produced from Chardonnay, Pinot Blanc, Aligoté, Melon de Bourgogne, and Sacy and need only reach 9.5°.

Bourgogne Passe-Tout-Grains AOC

*W*ine produced from a blend of ⅔ Gamay and ⅓ Pinot Noir. Passe-Tout-Grains is light, fruity wine that is usually consumed while young and fresh, even slightly chilled.

Bourgogne Rosé AOC

*L*ight, pretty rosé wines produced from the Pinot Noir.

Crémant de Bourgogne AOC

*W*hite or rosé sparkling Burgundy made by the *méthode champenoise*.

Vineyards of the Yonne

Bourgogne Irancy AOC

*T*hough in the past the red and rosé wines of the Yonne were highly rated, only small amounts are made today, primarily from the Pinot Noir grape, together with smaller amounts of the César and Tressot. They should be tried when in the region.

Bourgogne Rouge AOC de Coulanges; Bourgogne Rouge AOC de Epineuil

*N*ot strictly *appellations*, but red Burgundies from these towns, like Irancy, are produced in the Yonne and are gaining recognition and favour. They are light, elegant wines that compare favourably with meatier (and more expensive) wines from the Côte d'Or.

Chablis AOC

*C*hablis is the most plagiarized *appellation* in the world. Only in the Yonne *département* is the real thing produced: a classic white Burgundy, produced from the Chardonnay grape grown at its northernmost limit for table wines. The finest Chablis are entitled to the *appellations* Chablis *Grand Cru* together with the name of one of seven such *climats*; furthermore, historically there are a further 21 Chablis *Premiers Crus* though for ease to the consumer, these have now been re-grouped into 12. While much Chablis is vinified to be drunk young, very fresh and crisp, the wine shares with the best white Burgundies an ability to age and gain in flavour and richness.

The seven *Grands Crus* of Chablis are: Vaudésir, Preuses, Les Clos, Grenouilles, Valmur, Blanchots, and Bougros.

Petit Chablis AOC

A lesser *appellation* for white wine from the delimited Chablis vineyard made to less strenuous regulations. Crisp, light, it should be drunk young, on the spot.

Sauvignon de St-Bris VDQS

*T*he Sauvignon grape, which reaches such heights in the nearby vineyards of Pouilly-sur-Loire and Sancerre, produces this fine example here in the Burgundian vineyards near Chablis.

Vineyards of the Côte d'Or

Côte de Nuits

Côte de Nuits-Villages AOC

*T*his general *appellation* may be applied only to wines from the communes of Fixin, Brochon, Prissey, Comblanchien, and Corgoloin, none of which, with the exception of Fixin, are entitled to their own village *appellations*. Wines from the extreme southern end of the vineyard, in particular at Corgoloin and Comblanchien where the Côte de Nuits blends effortlessly into the Côte de Beaune vineyards of Aloxe-Corton, can be very good indeed.

Bourgogne Rosé de Marsannay AOC

*R*osé wine produced from the Pinot Noir grape grown in the far north of the vineyard, on the virtual outskirts of Dijon. Many consider Rosé de Marsannay to be one of the finest pink wines in the world.

Chambolle-Musigny AOC

*W*ine commune between Morey-St-Denis and Vougeot prized above all for wines which combine power, delicacy, and fine scent. Chambolle has two *Grands Crus*: Les Musigny and Les Bonnes Mares (part of which lies in Morey-St-Denis), as well as 24 *Premiers Crus*.

Fixin AOC

*T*his northernmost wine commune of the Côte de Nuits (excepting Marsannay-la-Côte) produces robust, meaty red wines that are often considerably less expensive than wines from their more famous neighbours: six *climats* are classified as *Premiers Crus*.

Gevrey-Chambertin AOC

*C*lassic Burgundy from a concentration of great vineyards, including two *Grands Crus*: Chambertin and Chambertin Clos-de-Bèze, as well as a further 11 *Premiers Crus* the best five of which are entitled to append the village name after, not before, the name of the *climat*. Wines bearing the basic village *appellation* Gevrey-Chambertin are noted above all for their forceful, full-flavoured character.

The Language of the Label

Mise en Bouteille au Domaine or Mise en Bouteille à la Propriété
Bottled on the estate, Burgundy's equivalent of Bordeaux château-bottled and usually (though not always) an indication of quality.

Monopole Single owner for the entire *climat*, a relative rarity in Burgundy.

Propriétaire-récoltant Owner-grower making and (usually) selling his own wines.

Négociant-éleveur Shipper-wholesaler: in Burgundy such merchants play a particularly important role (see p.120). Many also have small or considerable vineyard holdings of their own and are thus entitled to call themselves *Négociant et Propriétaire*.

Morey-St-Denis AOC

*S*omewhat less well known than its illustrious immediate neighbours, but a wine commune of exceptional concentration and excellence — five *Grands Crus*: Les Bonnes Mares, Clos de Tart, Clos de la Roche, Clos St-Denis, and Clos de Lambrays, as well as a further 23 *Premiers Crus*.

Nuits-St-Georges AOC

*T*he heart of the Côte de Nuits, with vineyards extending around the town itself as well as the neighbouring commune of Prémeaux. While Nuits-St-Georges has no *Grands Crus* it boasts no fewer than 37 (or parts of) *Premiers Crus climats* the most famous of which is Les St-Georges. Wines from this well-known centre are often said to be 'full of stuffing': these are deep, sturdy red wines that mature well.

Vosne-Romanée AOC

'*N*o ordinary wines are to be found in Vosne', states Pierre Poupon in his classic study of the region *The Wines of Burgundy*. Indeed, this small wine commune has seven *Grands Crus*, among them the most prized and expensive wines in the world: La Romanée-Conti, Le Richebourg, La Romanée, La Tâche, La Romanée-St-Vivant, Les Grands-Echézeaux, and Les Echézeaux. There are also a further 10 *Premiers Crus*.

Vougeot AOC

*T*he tiny wine commune of Vougeot is dominated by the most famous vineyard in Burgundy (perhaps the world?), the walled *Grand Cru* Clos-de-Vougeot. There are a further four *Premiers Crus*.

The Vineyards of the Hospice de Beaune

The Hospices de Beaune, comprising the Hôtel-Dieu and the Hospices de la Charité, is one of the most important owners of vineyards in the Côte d'Or, the proprietor of 58 hectares in Beaune, Pommard, Volnay, Meursault, Aloxe-Corton, and Gevrey-Chambertin, donated to it over the centuries since its foundation in 1443. Every year (since 1859) the wines from these vineyards are auctioned to the public on the third Sunday in November, the start of the great Burgundian celebration known as '*Les Trois Glorieuses*'. The money raised at this unique sale provides an indication of prices for Burgundy in general for that year: furthermore, the income today, as in the past, is used to care for the sick and needy of Beaune, as was originally envisaged by Nicolas Rolin. Wines from the Hospices de Beaune's vineyards are entitled to a special distinctive label and usually denote the name of the donor, as in Cuvée Nicolas Rolin or Cuvée Docteur Peste. Such wines are almost always sold for a considerable premium over wines bearing comparable *appellations*.

Hôtel-Dieu, Beaune.

Côtes de Beaune

Côte de Beaune-Villages AOC

*T*his general *appellation* may apply to red wines from 16 communes in the Côte de Beaune: Auxey-Duresses, Blagny, Chassagne-Montrachet, Cheilly-lès-Maranges, Chorey-lès-Beaune, Dézize-lès-Maranges, Ladoix, Meursault, Monthélie, Pernand-Vergelesses, Puligny-Montrachet, St-Aubin, St-Romain, Sampigny-lès-Maranges, Santenay, and Saivgny. These wines can be very good value.

Aloxe-Corton AOC

*O*ne of the few wine communes of Burgundy producing both red and white wines of outstanding *Grand Cru* quality: Corton (both red and white and often followed by the name of the plot, such as Les Renardes, Le Clos du Roi, Les Bressandes, and others) and Corton-Charlemagne (white).

Auxey-Duresses AOC

*S*mall village close to Meursault, producing both red and white wines.

Beaune AOC

*T*he great wine capital of Burgundy is itself surrounded by vineyards, the largest single wine commune in the Côte d'Or, producing primarily red wines of a very high overall standard, as well as small amounts of white. Beaune has no fewer than 36 (or parts of) *Premiers Crus*, of which the best known include Les Grèves, Les Fèves, Les Marconnets, and Clos des Mouches.

Chorey-lès-Beaune AOC

*S*mall, little-known wine commune just north-east of Beaune opposite Aloxe-Corton producing both red and white wines from vineyards on the flatter plains.

Chassagne-Montrachet AOC

*C*hassagne shares with its neighbour Puligny the prestigious *Grand Cru* Montrachet, a vineyard that is said to produce possibly the most concentrated and intense white wine in the world. Criots-Bâtard and part of Bâtard-Montrachet (both *Grands Crus*) also lie in Chassagne, while the village has a further 16 *Premiers Crus* vineyards producing not only the classic rich white Burgundies that are so sought after, but also some very fine and relatively undervalued red wines.

Cheilly-lès-Maranges AOC, Dézize-lès-Maranges AOC and Sampigny-lès-Maranges AOC

*T*hree wine communes located at the southernmost point of the Côte de Beaune, just beyond Santenay, all sharing the *Premier Cru* vineyard of Lès Maranges. Cheilly has two further *Premiers Crus* while Sampigny has one. Red and white wines are produced in all three communes, though except for the classified vineyards the wines are usually sold under the Côte de Beaune-Villages *appellation*.

Côte de Beaune AOC

*T*he *appellation* does not apply to wines from the entire Côte de Beaune but only to wines from an area slightly larger than that defined for the Beaune *appellation*.

Meursault AOC	*T*he classic white wine commune of the Côte de Beaune, and the capital of the great white wines. Meursault itself has no *Grands Crus* though it does have 13 *Premiers Crus* vineyards around the town, the majority of which extend towards Puligny and Blagny. The relatively rare red Meursault is entitled to the *appellation* Volnay Santenots: it can be excellent.
Monthélie AOC	*A* tiny, modest village, lost between the famous wine commune of Volnay and Meursault producing some well-made and generally undervalued red wines: 10 *Premiers Crus*.
Pernand-Vergelesses AOC	*S*mall village located on the northern flank of the great hill of Corton: both red and white wines are produced, some of which are entitled to the superlative *appellations* Corton and Corton-Charlemagne. Another outstanding *Premier Cru* is Île de Vergelesses.
Pommard AOC	*T*he classic red wine of the Côte de Beaune; traditionally Pommard is dark, chewy, mouth-filling in contrast to the lighter, more elegant wines of Volnay. The commune has 26 *Premiers Crus* vineyards.
Puligny-Montrachet AOC	*T*he great white wine commune *par excellence*, sharing the *Grands Crus* Montrachet and Bâtard-Montrachet with Chassagne, but keeping Chevalier Montrachet and Bienvenues-Bâtard-Montrachet to itself, together with a further 11 *Premiers Crus* all capable of producing exceptional and concentrated wines from the Chardonnay grape.
St-Aubin AOC	*U*p the valley from Chassagne, this little hill town produces both red and white wines of some distinction.
St-Romain AOC	*A*nother undervalued and little-known wine commune, located beyond Auxey-Duresses, producing some fine, classic white and red Burgundies.
Santenay AOC	*T*he last wine commune of note in the Côte de Beaune, producing mainly red and some white wines. Seven *Premiers Crus* vineyards.
Savigny-lès-Beaune AOC	*W*ine commune located up the valley between the hill of Corton and the Montagne de Beaune producing mainly red wines: there are some two dozen *Premiers Crus* vineyards.
Volnay AOC	*L*ocated between Pommard and Meursault, Volnay is noted for its exceptional red wines, valued above all for their softness and delicacy: the ripe Pinot Noir at its most immediately appealing and delicious. There are some 14 *Premiers Crus* vineyards in Volnay. Just as the red wines of Meursault may be sold as Volnay, so are white wines of Volnay entitled to be sold as Meursault.

BURGUNDY and the Jura

Côte Chalonnaise

Bourgogne Aligoté AOC
de Bouzeron

Bouzeron, south of Chagny, produces one of the best Aligoté wines in Burgundy. This crisp, dry white wine is rarely encountered outside the region, so it should be tried when in the area.

Givry AOC

Mainly red wines from the centre of the Côte Chalonnaise which compare favourably with the lighter wines of the Côte de Beaune. Small amounts of white wines are also made.

Mercurey AOC

Similar red wines made exclusively from the Pinot Noir grape. Mercurey is an historic, long-standing vineyard whose best *climats* have been classified as *Premiers Crus*.

Montagny AOC

White wines from the Chardonnay grape grown around Montagny and Buxy. The best vineyards have been classified *Premiers Crus* and the name of the *climat* can be used. This full-flavoured white wine ages well and compares favourably with the more expensive white Burgundies of the Côte de Beaune.

Rully AOC

Known primarily for its white wines, though nearly equal amounts of red Rully are also produced. The best vineyards are classified as *Premiers Crus*. While white Rully is an excellent wine on its own, much of the production has traditionally been transformed into Crémant de Bourgogne.

Mâconnais

Mâcon Blanc AOC

Fresh appealing white wines are produced from the Chardonnay grape grown throughout the Mâcon vineyard. Such wines are sometimes sold as Pinot Chardonnay-Mâcon. Mâcon Blanc Supérieur must attain at least 11° alcohol.

Mâcon Rouge AOC

Large quantities of basic, everyday red wines from the Mâcon vineyard are produced from the Gamay as well as the Pinot Noir. They need only attain 9° alcohol and they are on the whole light and fruity.

Mâcon Rosé AOC

Rosé wine produced from the Gamay and Pinot Noir.

Mâcon-Villages AOC

The better white wines of the Mâconnais are entitled to the *appellation* Mâcon-Villages or Mâcon followed by the name of the permitted commune. Some of the best such communes are Mâcon-Lugny, Mâcon-Clessé, Mâcon-Igé, and Mâcon-Viré. The wines, produced mainly in large *caves coopératives*, can be very good value: approaching the character of true white Burgundy but at a fraction of the price.

Pouilly-Fuissé AOC

*O*utstanding white wine produced entirely from Chardonnay grapes grown around the communes of Fuissé, Solutré, Pouilly, Vergisson, and Chaintré. Pouilly-Fuissé is rightly considered not only the greatest wine of the Mâconnais but also one of the very best of all white Burgundies, on a par even with Meursault and Montrachet in terms of taste, quality, and (sadly) price. Vineyards classified as *Premiers Crus* must attain a degree higher alcohol, 12°, than the 'straight' versions.

Pouilly-Loché AOC and Pouilly-Vinzelles AOC

*L*ess well-known wines from the Pouilly 'satellites' are similar in style though slightly less expensive than Pouilly-Fuissé AOC.

St-Véran AOC

*T*his relatively recent *appellation* is possibly the best alternative to Pouilly-Fuissé, produced from neighbouring vineyards and in the same classic Chardonnay style, though usually considerably less expensive.

Beaujolais

Beaujolais AOC

*T*he great 'quaffing' wine *sine qua non* produced from the Gamay grape exclusively, grown in vineyards extending from the Mâconnais through the *département* of the Rhône almost to Lyon. 'Straight' Beaujolais is the epitome of youth: fruity, fresh, grapy, the sort of wine that is drunk anonymously from carafes and chipped bottles in Lyonnais *bouchons* and Parisian *cafés* alike. Most of the vast production of such wines comes from the southern Beaujolais below Villefranche-sur-Saône and should be drunk young and slightly chilled. Beaujolais Supérieur AOC indicates wines attaining the slightly higher alcohol content of 10°.

Le Beaujolais Nouveau Est Arrivé!

Every year on 15 November the most widely publicized event in the wine world takes place: the release of the 'new' Beaujolais. The races to get the first bottles or cases of wine back — to Paris originally and now anywhere in the world — are legendary, if sometimes a bit silly. But the hullaballoo is not without foundation. For each year, as we guzzle back bottle after bottle of the teeth-staining, fresh, grapy, gulpable Beaujolais *nouveau*, we join in a celebration of a minor miracle: the annual transformation of grapes — in this case, ripe, plump Gamay grapes that were still growing on the vine a mere few weeks earlier — into liquid joy.

Beaujolais Blanc AOC

*R*elatively rare white wine made from the Chardonnay grape in the northern Beaujolais vineyards of the Saône-et-Loire. The vineyard region actually overlaps that of the Mâconnais *appellation* of St-Véran so it is not unusual for *vignerons* to offer both of these similar wines, together with red Beaujolais.

Beaujolais-Villages AOC

About 40 villages in the northern half of the delimited Beaujolais vineyard are entitled to this superior *appellation*. The harder, more rugged terrain consists mainly of granite, and the Gamay grapes grown here produce wines with considerably more strength and greater depth of flavour. Such wines may be vinified in part *en primeur* for immediate drinking, but in general the *Villages* wines can improve with a few years' bottle age. The nine finest *Villages* are known as the *Crus* Beaujolais and are entitled to their own *appellations* listed below.

The Crus *Beaujolais*

Nine superior villages in the far north of the Beaujolais are all entitled to their own *appellations* for the wines they are capable of producing are a far cry from the simple, uncomplicated 'quaffing' Beaujolais of *café* fame. Such wines are considerably more full-flavoured and complex. Though they vary among themselves, from the light elegance of St-Amour to the weightier depth of Chénas or Morgon, they all benefit from some bottle ageing, after which time the fruit flavour of the Gamay mellows and even approaches the character of the great Pinot Noir: indeed the *Crus* are the only Beaujolais which are legally entitled to be sold under the Bourgogne *appellation* if desired. The nine individual *Crus appellations* are Brouilly AOC, Chénas AOC, Chiroubles AOC, Côte-de-Brouilly AOC, Fleurie AOC, Juliénas AOC, Morgon AOC, Moulin-à-Vent AOC, and St-Amour AOC.

The Wines of the Jura

Arbois AOC

The *appellation* for red, rosé, white, and Vin Jaune wines produced around this fine mountain town. Sparkling Arbois Mousseux wines are also produced here.

Arbois Pupillin AOC

Vineyards around Arbois's neighbouring village produce similar wines entitled to their own *appellation*. Rosé wines from Pupillin are particularly fine.

Château Chalon AOC

The *appellation* for the most famous Vin Jaune (see below).

Côtes du Jura AOC

Red, white, rosé, and sparkling wines produced from vineyards of the southern Jura.

L'Etoile AOC

Dry white and sparkling wine produced from vineyards around Lons-le-Saunier.

'Vin Fou'

*N*ot an *appellation* but the tradename for a sparkling wine made in Arbois that is widely available and well known.

Vin Jaune

*T*he most unique and special wine of the Jura, produced from the Savagnin grape. Once the wine has been made, it is placed in wooden barrels that are sealed: as is the case with *fino* sherry, a rare fungus known as *flor* mysteriously grows on the surface of the wine which is not racked or topped up for a minimum of 6 years. This treatment results in a wine with a particularly concentrated nutty flavour that is unique; it has, moreover, the remarkable ability to age for decades, even, it is claimed, centuries. While Vin Jaune bearing the Arbois *appellation* is very fine, the best known bears the *appellation* Château Chalon. The wines are bottled in the special squat *clavelin* which contains only 62 cl.

Barrels of Vin Jaune ageing in the cellars of Henri Maire, Arbois.

Vin de Paille

*A*nother unique speciality of the Jura, produced from grapes that have been allowed to dry out on straw mats, thus concentrating their grape sugars to produce luscious sweet liqueur-like wine. Like Vin Jaune, Vin de Paille is expensive, but both should be tried when in the region.

Other Drinks of Burgundy and the Jura

Crème de Cassis

*B*lackcurrant liqueur made in Dijon and Nuits-St-Georges and used as the basis for the cocktail 'Kir'.

Fine de Bourgogne

*B*urgundian grape brandy produced not by distilling wine but by distilling the lees, that is the barrel sediment left over after racking. The best Fines de Bourgogne are aged in oak casks for considerable periods.

Marc de Bourgogne

*M*arc is produced by distilling the residue left over after pressing the grapes: a compact, concentrated mass of skins, stems, and pips. Marc de Bourgogne is considered one of the finest of such drinks.

Marc d'Arbois

*S*imilar local spirit from Arbois.

BURGUNDY and the Jura

Macvin

*L*iqueur-like drink made from wine and spirits, macerated with herbs, spices, and other flavourings: a warming, pungent speciality of Arbois.

The Wine Roads of Burgundy

Les Routes du Vin

CHABLIS

In Brief   The vineyards of Chablis are Burgundy's northernmost, located midway between Paris and Beaune, making it a particularly convenient stop for refreshment. Lovers of this classic dry white wine will certainly wish to spend time in Chablis itself, though the less single-minded might prefer to overnight in nearby historic Vézelay, one of the finest hill towns of Burgundy.

Chablis.

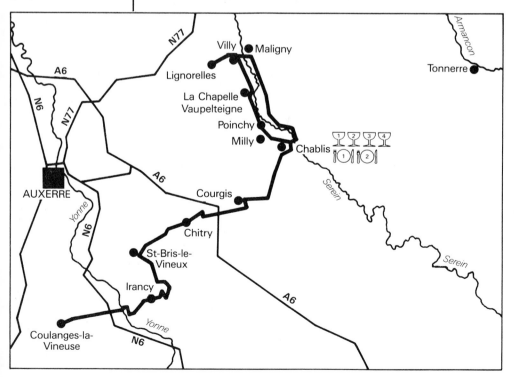

Visitors travelling from Paris or points north should exit the *autoroute* at Auxerre Sud, then find the smaller D965 to nearby Chablis itself. Little Chablis, dozing in the placid lap of the Serein valley: who would guess that this unassuming and modest town has had the name of its wine stolen shamelessly, to become one of the most imitated and plagiarized in the world. There is Californian 'Chablis', pink 'Chablis', Australian 'Chablis', probably even Chinese 'Chablis': none of which bear any resemblance whatsoever to the real Chablis, produced only from grapes grown within this compact northern Burgundian vineyard.

So famous is the word 'Chablis', that the modesty of the town itself comes as something of a surprise. For Chablis, founded by the monks of St-Martin-de-Tours in AD 867, remains today a refuge, set apart from the rest of Burgundy, indeed, almost from the rest of the world. Like many other inland French provincial towns, Chablis appears to the visitor rather self-contained and hard-working, unaware — almost — of its fame and prestige. The town and its surrounds live for and by its famous wine, and the headquarters of noted growers and *négociants-éleveurs* are located here: but don't come to Chablis in expectation of the good-natured hullaballoo of Beaune or elsewhere. *Do* come here to taste an exceptional wine and to pay homage to the *vignerons* who produce a genuine article in a world of counterfeits.

There is a sign-posted *Route du Chablis* which extends through the myriad hamlets and communes of Chablis like spokes of a wheel radiating from the central hub of the town. But it is not all that easy or necessary to follow in its entirety.

From the centre of Chablis, cross the Serein river and turn left on the D91 which leads immediately to the very finest vineyards hugging the sheltered slopes just to the north-east of the town. All seven of Chablis's *Grands Crus* lie on this distinguished south-facing slope, a ridge of deep Kimmeridgian limestone-clay riddled with a particularly high proportion of prehistoric fossils. 'It is these,' a grower told us, waving a handful of chalk-white fossilized oysters and other shells, 'which give taste and character to the wine. Where they lie, the wine is good.' As the concentration of fossils diminishes further and further from this central ridge, so does the concentration and character of the wine.

As in the rest of Burgundy, it is concentration and intensity of scent and flavour which distinguishes the Chablis *Grands Crus* from the rest: thus wines from Blanchot, Les Clos, Valmur, Grenouilles, Vaudésir, Les Preuses, and Bougros all demonstrate their own intense and unique character and identity, variations on that particular flinty, hard, and almost austere, Chardonnay flavour which is the essence of Chablis. These same general characteristics are evident in the *Premiers Crus*, especially those produced from vines grown along this same ridge: Montée de Tonnerre, Monts de Milieu, Fourchaume, and others.

The Chablis vineyard is the northernmost in Burgundy. Not only is there the danger that the grapes will not fully ripen each year, there is the further hazard of frost in spring. Thus, in the finest vineyards, you will notice an intricate system of pipes laid as sprinklers, not to irrigate the vines in summer — an anathema in French viticulture — but to spray the vines in late spring, once the sap has begun to rise. By this process, a knob of ice forms around the incipient bud, enclosing and insulating it from the damp, potentially lethal freezing conditions. Propane burners and coal braziers are also utilized to protect the vines from frost.

Of course, there are those years when the grapes do not ripen sufficiently. Even at its best, Chablis is known as a 'green' wine, that is a wine high in acidity, with that characteristic racy zing which is so loved. However, less successful vintages have traditionally been transformed into Crémant de Bourgogne, a sort of sparkling Chablis which can be very good. The Chardonnay, after all, is the classic grape of Champagne, whose vineyards lie not that far to the north.

A pleasant excursion follows the D91 further up the Serein valley towards Maligny, passing along the way the distinguished Fourchaume *climat*. At Maligny, cross the river to Villy and head out to the wine hamlet of Lignorelles or else return towards Chablis along the D131, coming first to La Chapelle Vaupelteigne, an ancient village with a fine tenth-century chapel. Poinchy, further towards Chablis, is another important wine community, as is Milly, slightly up the valley. These are the tiny enduring hamlets of Chablis, some of which have no more than a few hundred inhabitants. In all, the wines can be tasted and purchased *chez viticulteur*: just knock on the door wherever you see '*dégustation-vente*'.

Once back in Chablis, further excursions into the vineyards can be made. Head south-west on the D462/D62 to Courgis, where another clutch of *Premiers Crus* vineyards nestles along the slopes of the valley, and (passing under the *autoroute*) on to the wine community of Chitry. Though this is the limit of the Chablis vineyard, interesting excursions can be made to discover the less well-known wines of the Yonne. Continue on to St-Bris-le-Vineux, centre for pungent Sauvignon wines not dissimilar to Sancerre and Pouilly-Blanc-Fumé; to Irancy and to Coulanges-la-Vineuse, both of which produce fine, but undervalued, red Burgundies primarily from Pinot Noir.

Dégustation: Stop to Taste; Stop to Buy

Chablis may be the most widely imitated wine in the world, but the real thing still does not ever come cheap, even in the region. While the opportunity to taste *Grands* and *Premiers Crus* should not be missed, don't scorn the simpler *appellations*: 'straight' Chablis and Petit Chablis can be very good. Look out, too, for the less well-known wines of the Yonne: Sauvignon de St-Bris, and the reds of Irancy, Coulanges and Epineuil. The addresses below are all in Chablis itself, but there will be plenty of *vignerons*'s doors to knock on along the suggested vineyard route.

1

'La Chablisienne'
8, bd Pasteur
89800 Chablis
tel: (86) 42 11 24
Hours: Mon–Sat 8–12h; 14–18h.
The *Cave Coopérative 'La Chablisienne'* is an association of 250 *vignerons* from throughout the 20 villages of Chablis (⅓ of all the growers in the region), and thus accounts for an important proportion of all the Chablis wines made each year. A full range of Chablis is produced in the extremely modern and up-to-date winery, including the prestigious *Grand Cru* 'Château Grenouille', Chablis *Premier Cru* 'Fourchaume', Chablis and Petit Chablis; the wines can be tasted and are available for purchase.
English spoken.

2

Simonnet-Febvre et Fils
9, ave d'Oberwesel
rte de Tonnere
89800 Chablis
tel: (86) 42 11 73
Hours: Mon–Sat 9–11h30; 14–17h30.
Jean-Pierre Simonnet is a well-known and enthusiastic grower-*négociant* producing Chablis *Grands Crus* and *Premiers Crus*, Chablis, Petit Chablis, as well as the less well-known wines of the Yonne, Bourgogne Irancy, Coulanges, and Epineuil, and Sauvignon de St-Bris VDQS. The Simonnet family originally began the business in 1840 by specializing in sparkling Chablis and they still produce a fine Crémant de Bourgogne.
English spoken.

3

René & Vincent Dauvissat
8, rue Emile Zola
89800 Chablis
tel: (86) 42 11 58
Hours: By appointment.
One of the well-established growers of Chablis, with vineyards in some of the finest parts of the region: Chablis *Grands Crus* Les Clos and Les Preuses, as well as a number of *Premiers Crus*.

4

Guy Robin
13, rue Marcelin-Berthelot
89800 Chablis
tel: (86) 42 12 63
Hours: Daily 8–12h; 14–18h.
Guy Robin has holdings which include five Chablis *Grands Crus*: Valmur, Les Clos, Blanchot, Vaudésir, and Les Bougros, as well as a number of *Premiers Crus*. Visitors are very welcome and are shown the traditional *cave*. Charge for *dégustation*.
English spoken.

THE CÔTE D'OR

In Brief   The vineyards of the Côte d'Or are divided into two sections: the Côte de Nuits, extending virtually from the outskirts of Dijon to beyond Nuits-St-Georges, and the Côte de Beaune, continuing south from Aloxe-Corton through Beaune itself to below Santenay. It is a relatively compact region, considering the concentration of famous wines which come from these slopes, and wine travellers will certainly wish to explore its wine roads, if only to genuflect before the hallowed grounds from which emanate favourite and famous wines. However, the best opportunities for wine tasting are in Beaune itself, the capital of the region and the ideal base. Serious wine lovers should allow at least three days in the Côte d'Or: one day in Beaune itself; and one each to explore the Côte de Nuits (including a visit to the Château du Clos-de-Vougeot) and the Côte de Beaune.

Beaune: Wine Capital of Burgundy

Beaune is not only the wine capital of Burgundy, it is one of the greatest wine towns of France, and all visitors will wish to spend extended time here. Its ancient town ramparts, stone-paved streets, old Burgundian houses, and historic monuments evoke the Middle Ages, but Beaune today is a town that is very much alive, a town bubbling with excitement about all things Burgundian.

Beaune's greatest monument, the Hôtel-Dieu, a masterpiece of Gothic-Flemish architecture, is a charitable hospital whose history — past and present — remains inextricably linked to wine. It was founded in 1443 by Nicolas Rolin, Chancellor of Burgundy, and his wife Guigone de Salins, to alleviate the terrible suffering, poverty, and sickness of that age. The main 'paupers' ward', with its lines of individual wooden beds for the sick, each with a red curtain, night table, and washbasin, was still in use as late as 1948: at the end of this vast 240-foot-long hall, there is a chapel which thus allowed the sick to attend services without having to leave their beds. The kitchen, with its great fireplace and mechanical meat spit, and the restored dispensary can also be visited, while the view from the courtyard of the lacquered polychrome roof of the Hôtel-Dieu is one of the most famous in Burgundy.

The Hôtel-Dieu also houses Roger Van der Weyden's polyptych of the Last Judgement, a masterpiece that is positively frightening in its intensity! Presumably, the beatific faces of those who have been spared eternal damnation and the tortures of hell depict contemporary burghers of Beaune who donated their precious vineyards to the Hospices.

Other historical monuments in Beaune not to be missed include the Hôtel des Ducs de Bourgogne, which houses the excellent wine museum, and the

Beaune.

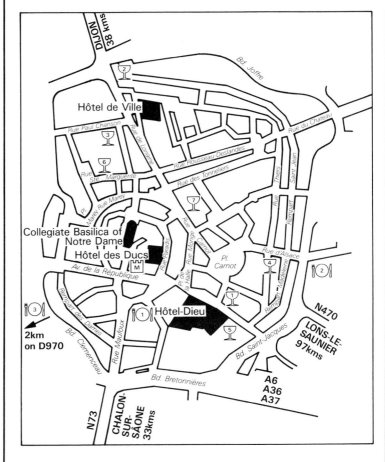

collegiate Basilica of Notre Dame, a fine twelfth-century Romanesque church with superb Flemish tapestries.

But it is wine, above all, that brings the visitor to Beaune. On approaching the town countless placards appeal to the visitor to stop and visit. Virtually every other shop in Beaune — so it seems — displays bottles of wine, glassware, silver *tastevins*, and other wine accessories. Food stores and *charcuteries* tempt with the bounty of Burgundy: green-marbled *jambon persillé*, *pâtés*, meat-filled pies, cheeses, and much else — foods that cry out to be accompanied by a good bottle of Beaune or Pommard.

Indeed, as befits France's greatest wine capital, there is no shortage of generous visiting and tasting opportunities. Beaune's famous *négociants-éleveurs* as well as some *propriétaires-récoltants* are well organized to receive visitors on an 'open house' basis. Kilometre after kilometre of dark, subterranean arched cellars can be wandered through, and tourist *caves* abound, where wines are displayed and can be tasted. Such well-publicized *caves* are undoubtedly generous and welcoming, and do much to promote not only the individual firms concerned but the region as a whole. However, long-standing amateurs of Burgundy may wish to get further behind the scenes, and away from the coachloads who only come for a 'free glass'. They will, therefore, prefer to make an appointment in advance to visit the *caves* of a favourite *négociant* or grower whose wines have been enjoyed at home: a famous name perhaps, or simply one of the dozens of small-to-average *négociants-éleveurs* whose *bureaux* and *caves* lie behind the modest brass plaques on the side streets of Beaune.

The premises of Léon Violland provides one such opportunity to meet and see a dedicated and typical Burgundian at work. M. Léon Louis-Violland is not one of Burgundy's 'superstars' but he is a highly respected grower-*négociant* who is passionate about Burgundy, its wines, and the region. His cellars are working premises, and you may have to step over hoses and filtering machines, or pick the cobwebs out of your hair. The contrast between such a Burgundian *cave* and the ordered, immaculate first-year *chais* at châteaux in the Médoc is indeed a striking one. It is here, and in similar *caves*, which extend in a complicated maze underneath the streets of Beaune, that you will see the day-to-day cellar work being carried out: the barrels being topped up, racked, fined with egg white, eventually drawn off the lees, bottled on small machines then laid down, unlabelled, to age for years or decades.

We passed one such pile of ageing bottles, no more than a couple of dozen or so, completely covered in thick black fungus, like a cloak of sable. They

The *Négociant-Éleveur*

The classic role of the Burgundian *négociant-éleveur* is to purchase wines from brokers who represent individual growers throughout the region, then, in his cellars in Beaune, Aloxe-Corton, Nuits-St-Georges, Meursault, or elsewhere, to assemble together wines of the same *appellation*, and to 'elevate' them to maturity, eventually bottling and selling them under his own label. This function is particularly important in Burgundy, with its history of micro-culture, where vineyards are divided and split into numerous tiny parcels. For by skilful selection of wines from each vintage, each village, or each *cru*, the *négociant-éleveur* may be able to produce wines which once assembled and elevated are greater than any of their individual components.

Wines from individual growers or *domaines*, it is argued on the other hand, may be able to reach higher peaks for they will be more distinctive statements about a particular *terroir*. This may be so in some cases, particularly for wines from the most famous and fastidious growers (many of whom are also *négociants-éleveurs*). However, wines from less careful growers are equally capable of delving considerably lower troughs as well.

were pre-war wines, M. Louis-Violland told us, picking one up and carrying it to the tasting room. He handled the fragile antique carefully, eased out the cork, and poured a sample. It was, he thought, a 1935 Pommard, probably a *Premier Cru*. The bouquet was intense, the colour still brilliant if somewhat brown around the edge. Though undoubtedly oxidized, the flavour was immense and mouth-filling. 'An interesting wine,' nodded M. Louis-Violland, grinning hugely, nosing the glass again, 'not great *mais pas mal* for over 50 years old.'

M. Louis-Violland, like so many of his counterparts in Beaune and throughout the Côte d'Or, clearly reflects a generous attitude that prevails, where wine is more than merely a livelihood — it is a way of life, indeed life itself — and he is eager to share his passion. This is the essence of Burgundy.

The Côte de Nuits: *Route des Grands Crus*

The Côte de Nuits begins south of Dijon and continues a further 20 km (12.5 miles) through 13 mainly east-facing wine communes ending at Corgoloin. The wines produced are almost exclusively red (with the notable exception of rosé from Marsannay-la-Côte as well as very small amounts of white); they are rightly considered to be among the greatest, most famous, and most sought-after wines in the world, prized above all for a character at once robust and vigorous, yet at the same time exceedingly elegant. To travel down the *Route des Grands Crus* is to follow one of the greatest wine roads in the world.

Though this route can be traversed from Beaune, we approach it from the north, beginning at the true capital of Burgundy, Dijon. Today the former home of the Dukes of Burgundy is a large and important regional city, a cultural capital and a great gastronomic centre in the true Burgundian sense. The vineyards of the Côte d'Or used to extend virtually into the city itself, though after the phylloxera crisis the vineyard area diminished considerably; today the expansion of Dijon ever further means that the former Côte de Dijon has virtually vanished.

Leave the city on the N74 then branch right to find the D122 at Chenôve. One relic of the former vineyards of the Côte de Dijon still remains here: an enormous thirteenth-century wine press said to be that of the Dukes of Burgundy. Marsannay-la-Côte is the first wine town encountered along the *Route des Grands Crus*, though the rosé wine produced here from the Pinot Noir — fine though it undoubtedly is — is but an *apéritif* to the great reds which shortly follow.

Fixin is the first wine commune in the Côte de Nuits proper, a picturesque little village entitled to its own *appellation*; though less well known than the villages which follow, Fixin does have a number of *Premiers Crus* vineyards, including La Perrière, Clos du Chapitre, Les Hervelets, and Clos Napoléon. The latter personage is further commemorated in the village by the statue known as the Emperor's Awakening.

Napoleon, it is said, was a great lover of Chambertin, the famous wine produced in the next wine village down this prestigious road: a man of taste,

Côte de Nuits.

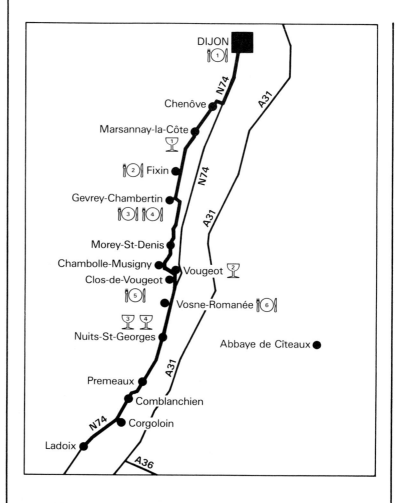

you might surmise, though history also records that the great man used to dilute it with iced water! Gevrey was the first commune in the Côte d'Or to hyphenate the name of its most famous *climat* to its own, a practice subsequently followed by nearly all others. Today, though world famous, the town itself is surprisingly simple, quiet, and sober. Chambertin AOC itself, together with Chambertin Clos de Bèze AOC are two magnificent *Grands Crus*, while six other *climats* are also entitled to append the magic name, after (*not* before) their own, an excruciatingly subtle though significant distinction: Ruchottes-Chambertin, Mazis-Chambertin, Chapelle-Chambertin, Griotte-Chambertin, Charmes-Chambertin, and Mazoyères-Chambertin.

Morey-St-Denis is as unpretentious and quiet as its neighbour. The dry-stone walls that surround Morey's best *climats* all indicate ecclesiastical origins, for indeed a nunnery was founded here in the seventh century and the devoted sisters, like their Cistercian brothers at Vougeot, furthered the cause of medieval viticulture through tending such *Grands Crus* as Clos St-Denis, Clos de Tart, Clos de la Roche, and Clos des Lambrays. I wonder, did those hard-working servants of God who lived such selfless and austere lives ever enjoy these splendid wines themselves?

The last great vineyard on the road out of Morey-St-Denis is Les Bonnes Mares, a *Grand Cru* claimed both by Morey and its neighbour village, Chambolle-Musigny. Chambolle is a particularly pretty little wine hamlet, its charm mirrored in its great wines, reputed to be the most elegant and delicate of the Côte de Nuits. These characteristics are epitomized in Le Musigny itself, a touchstone of great red Burgundy, while there are a clutch of superlative *Premiers Crus* which also number among the classics: Les Amoureuses, Les Charmes, Les Groseilles, and others.

Vougeot, of course, is dominated by its great *clos*, the walled monastic vineyard known as the Clos-de-Vougeot. So famous, so loved are the wines made from this vast 50-hectare plot that for generations passing regiments of the French Army have been ordered to stop and present arms to the vines! Today, no fewer than 70 growers or *négociants* own parcels within this prestigious plot, all making and selling Clos-de-Vougeot AOC. Undoubtedly the vineyard itself is a great one, but this is an example of where the *appellation* alone is not sufficient guarantee of quality. As always in Burgundy, it is the reputation of the individual grower or *négociant* which is the key.

Beyond Vougeot, the vineyards of Vosne-Romanée begin, a small compact commune which boasts no less than seven *Grands Crus*. The village itself is charming and unprepossessing, one of the most pleasant and modest along the *Route des Grands Crus*. Drive or walk out into the vineyards and find the great La Romanée-Conti, the vineyard which probably produces the most expensive and sought-after wine in the world. The soil here appears surprisingly rich, almost heavy and reddish, too rich and fertile, one might think, to produce great wine. Yet — and we must rely on the opinions of the experts — La Romanée-Conti is reputedly the most concentrated, perfumed, and richly flavoured of all Burgundies. Held in only slightly less esteem are the remaining *Grands Crus* of Vosne: La Tâche, Le Richebourg, Les Grands Echézeaux, Les Echézeaux, La Romanée-St-Vivant, and La Romanée. A large proportion of these great wines are produced by the prestigious Domaine de la Romanée-Conti. They are all fabulously expensive.

Nuits-St-Georges is the largest town in the Côte de Nuits, and it is the headquarters of a number of growers and *négociants-éleveurs*. Thus, there are ample tasting opportunities here. However, as a town Nuits, compared with Beaune, is somewhat sober, even a little grim; indeed, on the whole, just as we find the wines of the Côte de Nuits traditionally harder and less initially forthcoming than the sweeter, riper Côte de Beaune, so is the region itself less immediately accessible. Nuits-St-Georges has no *Grands Crus* vineyards, though a number of *Premiers Crus* extend around the town, and further south to include those of Premeaux. The communal *appellation* — evocative and easy to remember — has come to denote the archetypal red Burgundy: meaty and mouth-filling. However, as elsewhere, the *appellation* is no guarantee of quality in itself.

Beyond, the marble quarries of Premeaux, Comblanchien, and Corgoloin take over from the vineyards. Indeed, some *négociants* we have visited have had tables made from these marbles as well as from stone from Chassagne and Meursault. It is fascinating to note the strikingly different colours from each — ranging from deep purple to yellow-gold — as varied as the wines themselves. For, indeed, these underlying substrata are one factor that determines the character of the wines.

At Corgoloin, the Clos du Langres, a fine pink property surrounded by

The Château of the Clos-de-Vougeot

The Château of the Clos-de-Vougeot, an immense and grandiose building set within the walled vineyard enclosure, may seem like an overly splendid wine-making edifice for the humble and self-denying monks of Cîteaux. Yet by the sixteenth century, the wines produced by the monks not just here at Vougeot but throughout Burgundy and further afield, were held in such great esteem that it was deemed necessary to construct a fitting home for them. The oldest part of the construction, the *cuverie*, dates from the eleventh century; in this magnificent timber-roofed hall the four original gigantic wine presses together with the fermenting vats remain in place.

After the Revolution, the Château was confiscated in 1790 but, after many changes of hands, it is now, and has been since 1934, the property of the most famous wine brotherhood in the world, the *Confrérie des Chevaliers du Tastevin*. The *Confrérie* meets in splendour in the former *cellier*, a massive wine storage hall supported by monolithic pillars. The *Confrérie* also organizes the annual *Tastevinage*, a prestigious and important wine tasting where experts and dignitaries select the best wines submitted by growers and *négociants*. After undergoing rigorous anonymous selection, the chosen wines are awarded the right to use a special *Tastevinage* label. Two bottles of each selected wine are stored in the Château, to settle any disputes concerning their origin and quality. Thus, this label, whether on a 'straight' Bourgogne or a *Grand Cru* is a respected guarantee to the consumer.

No wine lover should miss visiting this historic and important monument to Burgundy and the monks of Cîteaux.

Hours: Open daily 9–12h; 14–18h.

its walled vineyard and visible from the road, marks the end of the Côte de Nuits, beyond which begin the vineyards of the Côte de Beaune.

Côte de Beaune.

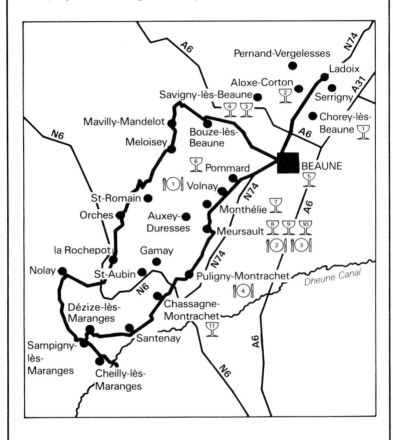

The Côte de Beaune

The Côte de Beaune is both longer and wider than the Côte de Nuits, beginning at Ladoix-Serrigny and finishing just south of Santenay. As a wine region it also has nearly twice as much area under vines as the Côte de Nuits. The Côte de Beaune is famous not only for its red wines from Pommard, Volnay, Aloxe-Corton, and elsewhere, noted above all for their elegance and ripe appeal, but also for its great white wines from Meursault, Aloxe-Corton, and the Montrachets of Chassagne and Puligny.

The first wine communes of the Côte de Beaune are located north of Beaune, and cluster around the distinctive and dominating Bois de Corton, an isolated and exceptional hill which overlooks Ladoix-Serrigny and Aloxe-Corton to the east and south-east; Savigny-lès-Beaune and Pernand-Vergelesses to the west and north; and Chorey-lès-Beaune on the flatter plains on the far side of the N74. This great broad flank is so situated that some part of it is bathed in radiant sunshine from the earliest rays at sunrise until the very end of the day: it is powerful and magnificent, an imposing rise from which one would expect great wines to come.

Indeed, Corton is exceptional for the fact that it produces both red and white *Grands Crus*; Le Corton (red and white) and Corton-Charlemagne (white). These great vineyards extend around the hill, planted primarily with Pinot Noir to the east and south, then increasingly with Chardonnay on the upper slopes, as the flank begins to curve around to the west. The communes of Ladoix-Serrigny, Aloxe-Corton and Pernand-Vergelesses all hold parts of the Corton and Corton-Charlemagne *appellations* while each has a number of further *Premiers Crus* vineyards as well.

Aloxe-Corton and Savigny-lès-Beaune both have superb châteaux where the owner-growers offer wine-tasting opportunities: the Château de Corton-André and the Château de Savigny. Pernand-Vergelesses is a lovely hill village almost hidden behind the Bois de Corton: less well known than the others, it is often overlooked. All of these wine villages north of Beaune are certainly worthy of extended exploration.

Beaune itself is the greatest single wine commune of the Côte de Beaune, for indeed, all along the broad flank of the Montagne de Beaune to the west of the town lies a great concentration of superlative *Premiers Crus* vineyards, including Les Grèves, Les Fèves, Les Bressandes, Clos des Mouches, and many others. Beaune, as well, is one of the principal areas for the vineyard holdings of the Hospices de Beaune: Cuvée Nicolas Rolin consists of wines from Les Cent-Vignes and Grèves, while Cuvée Guigone de Salins (the Chancellor's wife) comes from Bressandes and Champs Pimont.

The N74 leads to Pommard, whose wines are probably the best known and most loved of all reds of the Côte de Beaune: there is something so solid, *so* Burgundian about its very name. Indeed, the wines on the whole, especially from the *Premiers Crus* vineyards such as Les Epenots, Les Rugiens, Les Fremiers, and others, can be exceptional: dark, weighty wines with the rich characteristic overtones of the Pinot at its ripest. The Clos du Château is the *monopole* vineyard of the Château de Pommard; the property can be visited and its richly flavoured wines tasted and purchased.

Neighbouring Volnay produces red Burgundies that are considerably lighter than those of Pommard, more delicate and, at best, exceedingly elegant. The finest *climats* of Volnay include Caillerets, Clos des Chênes, Pousse d'Or, and Clos des Ducs. They are always in demand and so are correspondingly expensive. However, wines from the adjacent flanks extending up to the little hill town of Monthélie remain virtually unknown: Monthélie is an example of a less-well-known wine commune set amidst world-famous ones whose wines can be a relative bargain. The growers of Monthélie operate a tasting *caveau* located along the road to Meursault where the wines can be sampled and purchased. Nearby Auxey-Duresses and St-Romain are two other less fashionable wine communes whose wines can also be surprisingly good.

Meursault is the largest town along the wine road of the Côte de Beaune, and the centre of its greatest white wine communes. For as the valley divides, one arm heading up to Auxey-Duresses and La Rochepot, the other following the eastern flanks of the Montagne du Chatelet, the scarred remains of ancient quarries come into view, over Meursault and further on, above Chassagne. Indeed, the complex geographical make-up of the Côte de Beaune has changed here, marl giving way to a rich and deep vein of limestone, so beloved by the Chardonnay. Thus, the greatest white wines of Burgundy come from this small, compact vineyard around Meursault, Puligny-Montrachet, and Chassagne-Montrachet, concentrated, richly scented, full-bodied wines which, with age in new oak and bottle, acquire nutty, buttery, peachy, mouth-fillingly delicious flavours. Meursault itself is an excellent base from which to explore the Côte de Beaune; it is the home of some fine growers and grower-*négociants* and there are a number of tasting opportunities. A visit to the Château de Meursault should be on every wine lover's itinerary.

From Meursault, head out of town by the 'back door', past dusty, anonymous growers' houses where barrels lie in front yards: find the D113 and head out to Puligny, passing along the way the finest *Premiers Crus* of Meursault: Les Charmes, Les Perrières, Les Genevrières. Red Meursault, incidentally, is usually sold as Volnay Santenots. Puligny itself has its own rather quiet charm, with its great ship of a church, and its pleasant tree-lined square. Leave the village to continue on to Chassagne: the great Montrachet itself lies between Puligny and Chassagne, which have both hyphenated its name to their own. Indeed, set behind its imposing growers' portals, it looks every bit a *Grand Cru*, surrounded by the pretenders which many feel make wine that is only marginally less superlative: Bâtard-Montrachet, Criots-Bâtard and Les Bienvenues-Bâtard, and Chevalier-Montrachet. The wines produced from the sea of Chardonnay grapes grown here in good or great years are all heavyweights of considerable concentration *and* finesse.

One of the best places to sample the Montrachets of Chassagne is in that village's municipal *caveau*. A full and fascinating range of wines is on hand for tasting and purchase, including even Montrachet itself, as well as a number of excellent *Premiers Crus*. Chassagne-Montrachet may be noted above all for its white Burgundies, but the vineyards which surround the town are equally planted with Pinot Noir. The fine red wines of Chassagne-Montrachet are often overlooked: as a result, wines such as Clos St-Jean, Cailleret, and other *Premiers Crus* are relative bargains.

Just up the valley separating Chassagne from Puligny, lies a rather sad and overlooked village: Gamay. For indeed, this tiny hamlet gave its name to the grape which, banned from the Côte d'Or centuries ago, retired instead to splendid isolation in the rugged granite hills of Beaujolais. Beyond Gamay, St-Aubin is another often overlooked town producing both red and white wines.

Santenay is the last great wine commune of the Côte de Beaune, a spa town with thermal springs that were enjoyed by the Romans. Its vineyards produce mainly red wines as well as smaller amounts of whites. Santenay boasts a number of *Premiers Crus* vineyards, and there are also some well-respected *négociants-éleveurs* located here. Santenay lies on the border between the *départements* of the Côte d'Or and Saône-et-Loire. Three wine communes which lie in the latter have all appended the name of the finest *climat* which they all share: Cheilly-lès-Maranges, Sampigny-lès-Maranges, and Dézize-lès-Maranges. Lesser wines from these communes, though entitled to their own communal *appellations* are often sold as Côte de Beaune-Villages.

From here, either continue the wine tour to the nearby vineyards of the Côte Chalonnaise, or else, from Dézize make a pleasant return circuit to Beaune via Nolay, La Rochepot and the Hautes Côtes, passing through wilder, rugged wine villages such as Orches, Meloisey, Nantoux, Mavilly-Mandelot, and others. Apart from the wines produced, which can be surprisingly good (the best place to sample them is the Cave Coopérative des Hautes Côtes outside Beaune), the views over Meursault, Volnay, Pommard, and Beaune itself are exceptional. Descend the Montagne de Beaune via Bouze-lès-Beaune back to Beaune itself.

La Paulée de Meursault

Originally the *Paulée* was a celebration to mark the completion of the *vendange* and brought the vineyard owners and the workers together for an annual feast. Today, this great event has become considerably grander, and now forms an essential part of '*Les Trois Glorieuses*', taking place the Monday after the annual wine auction of the Hospices de Beaune. Wine growers, *négociants*, and personalities gather in the white wine capital of the world, and each brings his own bottle or bottles which are shared during the meal. A literary prize of 100 bottles of Meursault has now become a customary part of the *Paulée*.

Dégustation: Stop to Taste; Stop to Buy

There are countless opportunities to visit wine producers and *négociants-éleveurs* in the Côte d'Or. Beaune itself, as befits one of the great wine capitals of France, presents the best opportunities for organized visits without appointments. However, up and down the wine roads there will be many other chances to stop, taste, and purchase wines direct from *propriétaires-récoltants*. One of the major features of Burgundy is that growers often have acquired holdings in a number of differing vineyard areas, not just around their own *domaine*. Thus, they may be able to offer a broad range of wines — often both red and white. Search out and try the less well-known wines such as St-Aubin, St-Romain, Auxey-Duresses, and Monthélie.

On the whole, the wines available for tasting will be from recent vintages. Vintages are important in Burgundy, though here, more so than elsewhere, the skill of the grower or *négociant-éleveur* is of equal consideration; well-made wines from lesser years, on the whole, are considerably lighter and ready to drink at an earlier age. Beware 'bargain' Burgundies at knock-down prices.

Le Tastevin

e tastevin.

The *tastevin* is an indispensable tool for the wine taster in Burgundy. This small, shallow silver cup, indented with dimples and ribs and with a slightly bulging bottom and a ring for a handle, is the perfect vessel for tasting young wines from the cask in a dim, candle-lit cellar. When held to a light source, the wine's colour is reflected beautifully in the multi-faceted surface; the small cup holds just the right tasting measure; and it is easily cleaned and stored in a worker's pocket or overalls. When we taste wines today in a *salle de dégustation*, this vessel may no longer be necessary. But the *tastevin* is more than just a relic from the past: it remains an evocative instrument, a symbol of ritual and enduring tradition in Burgundy.

Beaune

Marché aux Vins
rue Nicolas-Rolin
21200 Beaune
tel: (80) 22 27 69
Hours: Open daily, 9h30–12h; 14h30–18h30. From November to March Sun and holidays open 9h30–12h; 14h30–16h.
Located nearly opposite the Hôtel-Dieu in the magnificent thirteenth- and fifteenth-century Église des Cordeliers, the *marché* is a permanent display of 40 wines of Burgundy. As such, it provides a perfect introduction to wine tasting in Beaune and should not be missed. A full range of wines is offered from 3 to 10 years old, including Bourgogne Aligoté, *Crus* Beaujolais, wines from the Hospice de Beaune, and even *Grands Crus*. The wines are displayed in the cellars and chapels of the former church and all can be tasted and purchased.
Entrance fee includes *dégustation*.

2 Reine Pédauque Exhibition Cellars
Porte St-Nicolas
21200 Beaune
tel: (80) 22 23 11
Hours: May–September daily 9–11h30; 14–18h. November–April Mon–Sat
9–11h30; 14–17h30 and Sun 10–11h30; 14–17h30. Closed 1 November, 25
December, 1 January.
Reine Pédauque are important grower-*négociants* whose wine-making
operations are located in Aloxe-Corton and Savigny-lès-Beaune; as such the
firm was the first in Burgundy to open its cellars to the public (in 1949). The
exhibition cellar, located under the ancient town ramparts at the entrance
to Beaune from Dijon, displays a full range including wines from Reine
Pédauque's own estates (Corton, Clos de Langres and others), and estates under
exclusive contract, as well as a particularly fine selection of *Premiers Crus*
Beaune. Wines can be tasted and purchased in the adjoining shop.
English guided tours possible on appointment.

3 Patriarche Père & Fils
5, rue du College
21200 Beaune
tel: (80) 22 23 20
Hours: Daily 9h30–11h30; 14–17h30. Closed 1 November; 12 December–
1 March.
One of the largest of Beaune's *négociants-éleveurs* offers tours of its extensive
cellars, parts of which date from the thirteenth, fourteenth, and seventeenth
centuries, situated in the former Ancien Couvent des Dames de la Visitation.
Extensive tasting of a range of Patriarche wines, includings *Grands* and *Premiers
Crus*.
Entrance fee includes *dégustation* and is donated to charities in Beaune. *Tastevin*
offered for use on payment of a small deposit.

4 J Calvet & Cie
6, bd Perpreuil
21200 Beaune
tel: (80) 22 06 32
Hours: Tue–Sun 9–11h30; 14–17h. Closed weekends from 1 December–1 March
and 25 December–1 January.
Calvet, one of the major wine companies of France, has extensive and historic
cellars, located in parts of the old medieval fortifications of Beaune, including
parts of the town ramparts, and fourteenth- and fifteenth-century towers.
Visits to the cellars where this important *négociant-éleveur* ages and stores
its fine wines in cask and bottle. A full range of Burgundies is shown and
wines are offered for free tasting.
English spoken.

5 Caves des Cordeliers
6, rue de l'Hôtel-Dieu
21200 Beaune
tel: (80) 22 14 25
Hours: Daily 9–12h; 14–18h.
The cellars of the ancient thirteenth-century Couvent des Cordeliers house wines from this *négociant* whose principal domaine is at Savigny-lès-Beaune. Tours of the cellars, and wine tasting for purchasers. English spoken.

6 Bouchard Aîné et Fils
36, rue Ste-Marguerite
21200 Beaune
tel: (80) 22 07 67
Hours: Mon–Fri 9–12h; 14–17h. Appointment essential.
Important *négociant-éleveur* in Beaune since 1750 offers wines from throughout Burgundy and other regions. Charge for *dégustation*. English spoken.

7 Léon Violland
13, rue de la Poste
21200 Beaune
tel: (80) 22 35 17
Hours: By appointment.
Léon Violland is a firm of grower-*négociants* in Beaune since 1844. M. Louis-Violland is an enthusiast who, if time allows, is happy to show serious visitors and customers his cellars: make an appointment direct, or through his fine wine and accessories shop: Le Vigneron, 6, rue d'Alsace, 21200 Beaune, tel: (80) 22 68 21.

Musée du Vin de Bourgogne

M Musée du Vin de Bourgogne
Hôtel des Ducs de Bourgogne
21200 Beaune
Hours: Daily 9–11h; 14–17h.
One of the best wine museums in France, explaining in detail the history of wine in Burgundy, as well as the complex geographical factors and differences in terrain, viticulture and wine-making techniques; collections of bottles, glassware, *tastevins* and other wine objects. Located in historic fourteenth-sixteenth century palace.

Côte de Nuits

1 Cave Coopérative des Grands Vins Rosés
21, rue de Mazy

21160 Marsannay-la-Côte
tel: (80) 52 15 14
Hours: Tue–Sat 9–12h; 14–18h.
There are few *coopératives* in the Côte d'Or; this one, located on the *Route des Grands Crus*, produces one of the finest rosés in France: Bourgogne Marsannay AOC.

2   La Grande Cave
21640 Vougeot
tel: (80) 61 11 23
Hours: Open daily all year 9–12h; 14–18h.
After visiting the Château du Clos-de-Vougeot, come to these fine seventeenth-century cellars, where the wines of F. Chauvenet, *négociant-éleveur* at Nuits-St-Georges can be tasted and purchased. Full range of Burgundies, including *Premiers* and *Grands Crus*.
English spoken.

3   Bourgognes Faiveley
8, rue du Tribourg
21700 Nuits-St-Georges
tel: (80) 61 04 55
Hours: Mon–Fri 9–12h; 14–16h30. Appointment necessary.
Faiveley is a grower-*négociant* with one of the most important and extensive holdings throughout the Côte de Nuits and Côte de Beaune, including numerous *Premiers* and *Grands Crus* such as Chambertin Clos de Bèze, Musigny, Echézeaux, and others. Tasting free for purchasers.
English spoken.

4   Morin Pere & Fils
Quai Fleury
21700 Nuits-St-Georges
tel: (80) 61 05 11
Hours: Daily 8–12h; 14–18h.
One of the larger *négociants-éleveurs* in Nuits-St-Georges. Visitors are shown the *caves*. Charge for *dégustation*.
English spoken.

Côte de Beaune

1   Domaine Goud de Beaupis
Château des Moutots
21200 Chorey-lès-Beaune
tel: (80) 22 20 63
Hours: Daily 9–19h.
Located between Aloxe-Corton and Beaune, the Domaine Goud de Beaupuis has a number of fine vineyard holdings at Pommard, Aloxe-Corton, Beaune,

Savigny, and Chorey-lès-Beaune. Visitors are shown the traditional cellars, and an ancient stone press weighing 7 tons which is still in use. Free *dégustation*. English spoken.

2 Château de Corton André
21920 Aloxe-Corton
tel: (80) 26 44 25
Hours: Open all year 9h30–18h.
The fine château, with its distinctive polychrome tiled roof, is a notable landmark, standing above the village at the foot of Corton. The estate produces Corton *Grand Cru*, Aloxe-Corton *Premier Cru*, Clos-de-Vougeot *Grand Cru*, and other fine wines. Visitors see the *cuverie* and *tonnellerie* and the wines can be tasted and purchased.
English spoken.

3 Château de Savigny
21420 Savigny-lès-Beaune
tel: (80) 21 55 03
Hours: Daily 9–12h; 14–18h.
Michel Pont, the proprietor of the Château de Savigny, has some 40 hectares of vineyards in Auxey-Duresses, Beaune, Monthélie, Meursault, Pommard, Volnay, and Savigny-lès-Beaune. The wines can be tasted and purchased direct at the château as well as at the Cellier Volnaysien in Volnay. The château itself is open to the public and houses a museum of motorcycles and cars.

4 Domaine Henri de Villamont
Caveau de la Métairie Langeron
rue du Docteur-Guyot
21420 Savigny-lès-Beaune
tel: (80) 21 52 13
Hours: Mon–Sat 9h30–12h30; 14h30–18h30.
Guided tours of the *caves* and tasting and sales of the wines of the domaine. The firm of Henri de Villamont is both *propriétaire* and *négociant-éleveur*. English spoken.

5 Les Caves des Hautes-Côtes
rte de Pommard
21200 Beaune
tel: (80) 24 63 12
Hours: Mon–Sat 8–12h; 14–18h.
The only major *cave coopérative* in the Côte de Beaune is located just outside Beaune on the road to Pommard. As the representative of some 105 *vignerons* who cultivate over 400 hectares of vines, it is the largest *propriétaire-récoltant* in the Côte d'Or. Its modern and large-scale wine-making facilities are a striking contrast to the dim, cobwebbed cellars of Beaune and elsewhere, but the wines produced, including 'straight' Bourgogne AOC, Hautes-Côtes-de-Nuits, and

Hautes-Côtes-de-Beaune, as well as village *appellations* are well made and excellent value. Wines can be tasted and purchased, and the lesser *appellations* are available *en vrac*.

6 Château de Pommard
21630 Pommard
tel: (80) 22 07 99
Hours: End March–3rd Sun in November daily 8h30–19h.
The Chatellenie de Pommard was founded in 1098: today the walled *clos* of vines which surrounds the château extends over 20 hectares, making it the largest single-tenanted (*monopole*) vineyard in the Côte d'Or. The eighteenth-century château and *caves* can be visited, and the meaty, full-bodied Château de Pommard wine tasted and purchased. Charge for entrance includes *dégustation*.
A little English spoken.

7 Cave de Monthélie
Monthélie
21190 Meursault
tel: (80) 21 22 18
Hours: Open daily 9–12h; 13h30–19h except during the grape harvest.
Caveau de dégustation on the main road between Volnay and Meursault, providing opportunity to sample the little-known and undervalued wines of Monthélie.

8 Château de Meursault
21190 Meursault
tel: (80) 21 22 98
Hours: Daily 9h30–11h30; 14h30–18h.
The Château de Meursault, built in 1337, has wine cellars which were dug out and built by the monks of Cîteaux, who developed a large estate in Meursault in the twelfth century. Today the Château is the *propriétaire* of some 50 hectares in Meursault, Volnay, Beaune, Pommard, Savigny-lès-Beaune, and Aloxe-Corton. A visit to this historic property is a must: after walking through the château itself and the cellars where thousands of bottles and barrels of wines lie ageing, a large selection of wines from the domaine is available for tasting and purchase, including the splendid Château de Meursault (produced from the Meursault *Premiers Crus* Charmes and Perrières) and other fine white wines, as well as a wide selection of *Premiers Crus* reds. Entrance fee includes *dégustation*; *tastevins* with the logo of the Château are loaned for a small returnable deposit or can be kept.

9 Ropiteau Frères
13, rue du 11 Novembre
21190 Meursault
tel: (80) 21 24 73
Hours: Easter–20 November open daily 8h30–19h30 except Thur.

The House of Ropiteau Frères was founded in 1848 in nearby Monthélie, and moved to the *Caves de l'Hôpital* (formerly the property of the Hospices de Beaune) in Meursault in 1920. The company is both grower and *négociant* and offers a fine range of Meursault, as well as wines from Volnay, Pommard, Beaune, Vougeot, Auxey-Duresses, and Monthélie. Visitors are shown the historic cellars and each visit, including guided tasting, is carried out by a professional of the company. Charge for visit and *dégustation*.

10

Domaine Bernard Delagrange
10, rue du 11 Novembre
21190 Meursault
tel: (80) 21 22 72
Hours: Daily 8–19h30.
The Delagrange family have been *viticulteurs* in Meursault for eight generations and today have 23 hectares of vineyards in Meursault, Volnay, Pommard, Beaune, Auxey-Duresses, St-Romain, and Savigny-lès-Beaune. Almost all of M. Delagrange's wines are sold direct to individual customers here in Meursault. Visitors are shown the fifteenth-century *caves*, and the modern *cuverie* where the wines are made. *Dégustation* for purchasers only.

11

Caveau Municipal de Chassagne-Montrachet
Centre Ville
Chassagne-Montrachet
21190 Meursault
tel: (80) 21 38 13
Hours: Daily 10h30–12h30; 14h10–19h30. Closed Sun in January.
The wines from 23 *vignerons* of Chassagne-Montrachet are on display for tasting and purchase at this welcoming municipal *caveau*. A full range from this superlative commune, from Bourgogne Aligoté to Montrachet itself, with a number of *Premiers Crus* whites as well as reds. Wines can be tasted for purchase or drunk by the glass, together with Burgundian *gougères*.

CÔTE CHALONNAISE AND MÂCONNAIS:

'Suivez la Grappe'

In Brief   The vineyards of the Côte Chalonnaise begin almost where the Côte d'Or leaves off, while those of the Mâconnais lead on effortlessly from south of Tournus to Mâcon and beyond. Thus, a tour of these important but far less visited central vineyards can be made by continuing south from the Côte d'Or. Divide the tour to allow at least a half or full day for the Côte Chalonnaise, with a lunch or overnight stop in Tournus; then continue through the Mâconnais to Mâcon itself. The prestigious vineyards of Pouilly-Fuissé are best explored from Mâcon and could be linked with a tour of the *Crus* Beaujolais. Throughout the Mâconnais, there are distinctive road signs — *'Suivez la Grappe'* — urging you to 'follow the grape-bunch' to the wine towns and tasting *caveaux*.

South of Santenay and Chagny, the ordered terrain of the Côte d'Or gives way to a wilder and more confused system of hills and valleys. Here, the vineyards are not always so dominant, interspersed with fruit orchards, meadows, forests, and uncultivated fields of thickets and grass. Yet wines from the Côte Chalonnaise, always popular with knowledgeable French drinkers, are now beginning to enjoy increasing recognition and favour as reasonably priced alternatives to the wines of the Côte d'Or. As such, coming after the splendid though rather monotonous order found in the great wine towns to the north, the region comes almost as a relief, for the wines are delicious and very similar in style, the wine roads little travelled, and the small towns welcoming.

From Chagny, first make a detour to little Bouzeron, one of the few wine communes in Burgundy where the lesser Aligoté is deemed to make superlative wine in its own right, crisp, dry, less fleshy than wines made from the Chardonnay, but a refreshing tonic none the less. Then, either find the small back road over the hill to Rully, or else return first to Chagny, and take the D981 south. Rully is no more than 15 km (9 miles) from Meursault, yet it stands a world apart: a busy little wine town, but seemingly lost in the deepest depths of rural France. Come here after you have exhausted yourself in Beaune to meander at an altogether slower pace. Both red and white Rully wines are produced, though in the past the commune was perhaps best known for its sparkling Burgundies. The vineyards lie mainly hidden around the back of the town: after stopping at a café, or picking up provisions for a picnic, drive through Rully and around its château to find a little-travelled road that extends along a broad flank not entirely dissimilar in appearance to the Côte de Beaune. The unspoiled wine road that follows this flank is one of the quietest and most beautiful in Burgundy: continue around in the direction of Aluze, but before reaching that town, turn off left to cross over the hill to Mercurey.

The vineyards of Mercurey cup the town in a broad, south-facing amphitheatre, planted almost entirely with Pinot Noir. The classic red Burgundy grape here finds the conditions more than suitable, and ripens to produce the finest reds of the Côte Chalonnaise: though on the whole they may lack the elegance and subtlety of the best of the Côte de Beaune, they none the less display the ripe, and sometimes overripe, vegetable and fruit flavours of the Pinot which are so appealing.

From Mercurey, you can easily reach the next wine town, Givry, by way of the straight D981; however, a rather tortuous though lovely route reaches the same goal by way of the Vallée des Vaux through Mellecey, St-Denis-de-Vaux, and Jambles. Throughout the vineyard areas, there are small *propriétaires-récoltants* to visit. Givry is the largest of the wine communes of the Chalonnaise; on entering the town from Jambles, there are some fine, walled vineyards which were tended in monastic times, such as the Clos Salomon. Givry, reputedly one of the favourite wines of Henri IV (along with a number of others), are almost entirely red.

The vineyards of Montagny, the final *appellation* of the Côte Chalonnaise, lie further south: take the D981 south to Buxy, then the D977 west to Montagny-les-Buxy. The Montagny *appellation* applies to white wines only, and there are a number of vineyards which have been given *Premier Cru* status. However, one should not expect such *Premiers Crus* wines to be the equivalents of their counterparts from the Côte de Beaune. Nevertheless, some fine white Burgundies are produced here, which, though perhaps lacking in delicacy, display the particular woody, nutty richness of the Chardonnay. The Cave des Vignerons de Buxy has a tasting *caveau* both here and in St-Gengoux-le-National where the wines can be sampled and purchased.

Continue south on the D981 (past the idyllic fifteenth-century Château de Sercy), then turn left on the D215 to Tournus. Tournus, a fine medieval town, situated on the banks of the Saône provides a break from wine touring: its fortified Romanesque abbey church of St-Philibert, circular town ramparts, medieval houses and narrow alleys are particularly evocative, and there are a number of artisans located here, making and selling the handicrafts of the region.

Immediately south of Tournus,

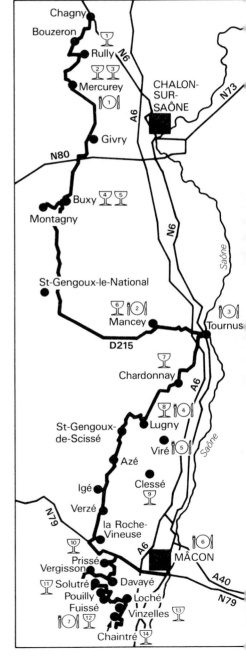

the vineyards of the Mâconnais begin. Although the famous 'superstar' Pouilly-Fuissé lies considerably further away, south of Mâcon, lesser constellations north of that city should certainly not be overlooked. After all, the finest wines of Pouilly-Fuissé now fetch prices little short of those of Meursault or Chablis. By contrast, this rather anonymous wine country produces large quantities of both white and red Mâcon that are eminently enjoyable, the closest thing to a bargain Burgundy that will ever be encountered.

The wine road signs urge you to '*Suivez la Grappe*' but in truth, they do not follow a single route but rather weave and interweave through the maze of little wine towns, all anxious to attract the wine tourist. We suggest the following route from Tournus which can either lead to Cluny, or else through the wine country and down to Mâcon — but don't hesitate to leave it and explore other wine towns that we have overlooked.

Leave Tournus on the D56 to Chardonnay, the small, totally modest village which has given its name to the great white grape of Burgundy. Then continue on to Lugny, which has one of the best-run tasting *caveaux* in the region, offering wines by the tasting measure, glass or bottle, accompanied by simple regional foods. St-Gengoux-de-Scissé and Azé are next, both of which have large *caves coopératives*: indeed these great 'wine factories' are a feature of the vast Mâconnais vineyard, a startling contrast to the small growers with their ancient cellars in the Côte d'Or. Stop in each village to purchase a bottle or two to taste and compare. The whites may be rather green and fresh, sold and drunk by the French in their year of production while still tight and very closed. As such they are light, refreshing beverages; but given even a little bottle age, they do have the capacity to open out considerably and even approach the style of the lesser Pouilly wines from further south. At Azé, either cut across to magnificent Cluny, or else continue through the vineyards and wine towns of Igé, Verzé, and La Roche-Vineuse to reach the N79, and so on to Mâcon.

Cluny should not be by-passed: though today just a skeleton of its former self, it remains one of the important and great monuments of Western civilization. Indeed, in the eleventh and twelfth centuries, Cluny was a seat of immense power, whose abbots advised kings and popes, and became popes themselves.

Mâcon is a large city and important regional market for the surrounds, including the rich hinterlands of the Bresse and Charolles. It is also a centre not only for its own Mâconnais wines, but also for those of the Beaujolais. The Maison Mâconnaise des Vins, located near the river, provides a pleasant opportunity to taste the generic wines of the region (bottled anonymously), together with good, inexpensive, simple foods.

The great vineyards of Mâcon lie to the south and west of the town. As you drive out of Mâcon west on the N79, a wide open panorama lies before you: vast slopes covered in vines, fields of golden wheat, and, to the left, the great dramatic rearing crest of Solutré, home of prehistoric man.

This magnificent landmark, together with its twin crest of Vergisson, is the salient feature of the vineyard, for it is evidence of a profound and rich layer of limestone, which — in Champagne, in Chablis, in Meursault, in Chassagne, and in Puligny — proves such fertile and beneficial ground for the Chardonnay. Indeed, lovers of white Burgundy will have an enjoyable treat in store, exploring the tiny, secret villages of Prissé, Davayé, Solutré, Pouilly, Fuissé, Loché, and Vinzelles, all nestling in this complex but compact valley, the villages extending over the hills in a pattern said to resemble '*la patte d'oie*', the foot of a goose.

Come to Prissé first, and sample St-Véran in the local *cave coopérative*. The *appellation* applies to white Chardonnay wines from a number of communes not entitled to the magic (and price boosting) name of 'Pouilly': as such, the wine is still little known and can be a relative bargain.

The five communes entitled to the *appellation* of Pouilly-Fuissé are Vergisson, Fuissé, Solutré, Chaintré, and Pouilly. Vergisson is a mere hamlet, nestling under its own magnificent, brooding spur of limestone, a virtual mirror image of the adjacent Solutré. The immense hill shelters the vines in an extremely well-exposed situation which results in some of the richest flavoured of all Pouilly-Fuissé wines.

From Vergisson, find the little track across to Solutré itself. The roads are steep and do not always lead where you expect them to, but this is great country for wine explorers, still uncharted and certainly never crowded. At Solutré, the vines grow right up the steep slopes of the great crest of rock, while hollowed underneath it there is a fine museum of prehistory explaining the Solutrean age.

Solutré itself, a small and charming hill town, is probably the most visited centre of the region. It was for this reason that the *Union des Producteurs de Pouilly-Fuissé* decided to site their tasting *caveau* here. Though the wine which can be tasted and purchased bears the special label of the *caveau*, it is very good, none the less: for each year the members of the *Union* arrange an important *dégustation* to choose a wine that is representative of what they consider to be the archetypal Pouilly-Fuissé. The chosen wine is then purchased and specially labelled for tasting and sale in the *caveau*.

It is interesting to note that although in the past Pouilly-Fuissé was generally considered a rather light and refreshing white Burgundy to be drunk while young, such has been its enormous popularity in recent years that most producers now age their wines for an initial period in new oak casks, thus imparting heavier, richer nuances to the wine which further develop with bottle age. For indeed, if not in France, then abroad certainly, Pouilly-Fuissé today is accorded almost the same reverence as the greatest white wines of the Côte de Beaune.

Pouilly and Fuissé are both mere hamlets. The latter, a village totally engulfed by its vines, is the home of one of the region's great producers, M. Vincent of the Château de Fuissé. From Fuissé, continue on to the Pouilly 'satellites' of Loché and Vinzelles. These communes are both entitled to append the name 'Pouilly' to their own, for they produce wines which, if rarely reaching

Tasting caveau, *Solutré.*

the heights that Pouilly-Fuissé is undoubtedly capable of, certainly are in a similar style (and more reasonable price, too). Chaintré, located on the flatter plains, has a large wine *coopérative* with a pleasant tasting *caveau* offering no fewer than four different Chardonnay wines: Pouilly-Fuissé, St-Véran, Mâcon-Chaintré, and Beaujolais Blanc, in addition to red Mâcon and Beaujolais. For indeed, beyond these rolling hills, the vineyards of the *Crus* Beaujolais begin almost immediately. This certainly is a confluence of great wine regions.

Dégustation: Stop to Taste; Stop to Buy

Stop to taste and buy the less well-known *appellations* of the Côte Chalonnaise which are often excellent value compared with the wines of the Côte d'Or. Few growers in this region have the facilities to keep open house as in Beaune or Meursault, but do try your luck by knocking on doors whenever you see a sign for *dégustation-vente*. In the Mâconnais, the region's *caves coopératives* produce large quantities of red and white wines that are rarely expensive. Pouilly-Fuissé is the only exception though even in this prestigious vineyard, the wines of Pouilly-Vinzelles, Pouilly-Loché, and St-Véran may be relative bargain alternatives.

Hubert Guyot-Verpiot
rue du Château
71150 Rully
tel: (85) 87 04 48
Hours: Mon–Sat working hours. Telephone call before visiting.
Red and white Rully AOC from this *propriétaire-récoltant* located near the château.

F. Protheau & Fils
Château d'Étroyes
71640 Mercurey
tel: (85) 45 25 00
Hours: Mon–Fri 8–12h; 14–18h. Appointment preferred.
The Protheaus are grower-*négociants* who produce a range of individual and highly regarded wines from some of the finest *climats* in Mercurey and Rully. English spoken.

Les Vignerons du Caveau de Mercurey
71640 Mercurey
tel: (85) 45 20 01
Hours: July–September open daily 9–12h; 14–18h. Out of season open Sat and Sun only.
The local *cave coopérative* produces Mercurey AOC, available for tasting and purchase.

4

Cave des Vignerons de Buxy
71390 Buxy
tel: (85) 42 13 72
Hours: Mon–Sat 8h15–12h; 14–17h45.
This well-regarded *cave coopérative* produces both excellent Montagny *Premier Cru* and red Bourgogne AOC, both of which spend some time in new oak. The wines are excellent value.

5

Caveau de La Tour Rouge
Dallerey Frères
71390 Buxy
tel: (85) 92 15 76
Hours: Tue–Sun 10–12h; 15–20h.
Tasting *caveau* offering Montagny, Bourgogne AOC Pinot Noir and Crémant de Bourgogne AOC. Charge for visit to *cave* and *dégustation*. The Dallerey Frères also run a restaurant serving simple foods to accompany the wines.

6

Cave des Vignerons de Mancey
71240 Mancey
tel: (85) 51 00 83
Hours: Mon–Sat 9–12h; 14–18h.
Mâcon-Mancey AOC, produced from the Gamay, as well as Mâcon white and rosé, and Bourgogne Pinot Noir and Passe-Tout-Grains can be sampled and purchased in the tasting *caveau* of the local *coopérative*.

7

Cave de Chardonnay
71700 Chardonnay
tel: (85) 40 50 49
Hours: Tue–Sat 8–12h; 14–18h. Sun 10–12h; 15–18h. Open Mon 1 May–30 September.
The *cave coopérative* was founded in 1928. Mâcon-Chardonnay AOC (white), Bourgogne AOC Pinot Noir, Mâcon Supérieur AOC and Crémant de Bourgogne AOC can be sampled and purchased.
English spoken.

8

Caveau St-Pierre
71260 Lugny
tel: (85) 33 20 27
Hours: March–October open daily except Wed 9–21h.
One of the best-organized tasting *caveaux* in Burgundy, located above the village overlooking the *lieu-dit* (named vineyard) known as St-Pierre: the excellent wines from the *Cave Coopérative de Lugny-St-Gengoux* — Mâcon-Lugny AOC Les Charmes and Cuvée Eugène Blanc (both white), Mâcon Rouge AOC, Bourgogne Pinot Noir and Passe-Tout-Grains, and Crémant de Bourgogne — are offered for tasting and purchase in a pleasant Mâconnais house with terrace. Simple foods such as *rosette, jambon cru*, or *fromage fort* are served with the wines, while full meals are also available (see Restaurants).

9 'La Vigne Blanche'
Clessé
71260 Lugny
tel: (85) 36 93 88
Hours: Mon–Sat 8–12h; 14–18h. Appointment preferred for guided visits.
Visitors see the wine-making facilities and can taste Mâcon-Clessé AOC and
Bourgogne Pinot Noir.

10 Cave Coopérative de Prissé
RN79
71960 Prissé
tel: (85) 37 88 06
Hours: Mon–Sat 9–12h; 14–18h.
This *cave coopérative* provides a good introduction to the wines of the southern
Mâconnais, and the chance to taste and compare St-Véran AOC and Pouilly-
Fuissé AOC.

11 Caveau Union des Producteurs de Pouilly-Fuissé
71960 Solutré
tel: (85) 37 80 06
Hours: Open daily including Sun and holidays 9–12h; 14–19h.
Each year the 250 *vignerons* who belong to the *Union* organize a tasting to
select a Pouilly-Fuissé that is representative of the *appellation* for tasting and
sale in this welcoming *caveau*.

12 Domaine du Château de Fuissé
71960 Fuissé
tel: (85) 35 61 44
Hours: Mon–Fri by appointment only.
M. Jean-Jacques Vincent's Château de Fuissé Pouilly-Fuissé AOC is one of
the best examples of this great white Burgundy. Other wines include St-Véran
AOC, Morgan AOC Les Charmes and Juliénas AOC. The château dates from
the fifteenth century.
English spoken.

13 Cave des Grands Crus Pouilly-Vinzelles Pouilly-Loché
71145 Vinzelles
tel: (85) 35 61 88
Hours: Mon–Fri 8–12h; 14–18h. Sat and Sun 10–13h; 15–19h30.
This *caveau* provides a good opportunity to compare the Pouilly 'satellites'
of Loché and Vinzelles with Pouilly-Fuissé AOC and the other local Chardonnay
varietals, St-Véran AOC and Beaujolais Blanc AOC.

14 Caveau du Moulin d'Or
Cave Coopérative de Chaintré
71570 Chaintré
tel: (85) 35 61 61

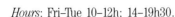

Hours: Fri–Tue 10–12h; 14–19h30.

This tasting *caveau* is located below the village of Chaintré overlooking Mâcon: Pouilly-Fuissé AOC, St-Véran AOC, Beaujolais Blanc AOC, Mâcon-Chaintré AOC (red and white), and Beaujolais AOC can all be tasted, together with simple snacks.

ROUTE DU BEAUJOLAIS

In Brief   The Beaujolais vineyard is vast, extending from south of Mâcon virtually to Lyon. This tour concentrates on the finest section, the *Crus* Beaujolais which can easily and profitably be toured from Mâcon in a single day. However, there is far more Beaujolais country, including the Beaujolais-Villages, as well as the vast southern areas producing 'straight' Beaujolais that deserves further exploration. This is eminently enjoyable wine country, which, like the wines themselves, quenches the thirst but leaves you coming back for more.

They say in Lyon that three rivers run into this great city: the Rhône, the Saône, and the Beaujolais. For the rugged hills to the north produce a veritable torrent of the world's most gulpable wine, much of which does indeed find its way to its *cafés* and *bouchons*: teeth-staining, and almost foaming with grapey freshness, the epitome of wine at its most basic and satisfying.

Indeed, Beaujolais with its rolling hills planted with free-standing, stumpy Gamay vines, though considered a part of the Burgundian vineyard, could not provide a greater contrast to the manicured, hand-tended slopes of the Côte d'Or. Likewise, the precious and richly textured reds of the Côtes de Nuits and Beaune could hardly find a more irreverent little brother than 'straight' Beaujolais, a wine meant to be enjoyed merrily within just weeks of the vintage, or else straight out of the 'fridge, or even, on a blistering summer day, with a lump or two of ice in the tumbler.

It is the Gamay grape, outlawed from the Côte d'Or (except for the lesser Passe-Tout-Grains *appellation*) that gives the wines of Beaujolais their purple youth and immediately appealing character, especially in the *primeurs* and *nouveaux* wines vinified in whole or part by *macération carbonique* (see p.381).

However, finer wines are produced in the far north of the delimited vineyard region, on the mainly granite hills south of Mâcon. These are the *Crus* Beaujolais, wines which, although they can be enjoyed while young and fruity, benefit from 2 or 3 years' bottle ageing, or even, in some cases, by as much as 10 years. Then the Gamay takes on an altogether deeper, and more elegant character which even approaches the perfumed style of the Pinot Noir wines from the north. These are not mere lightweight 'sodapop' wines, but true red Burgundies in every sense, worthy of their place among the best.

BURGUNDY and the Jura

Beaujolais.

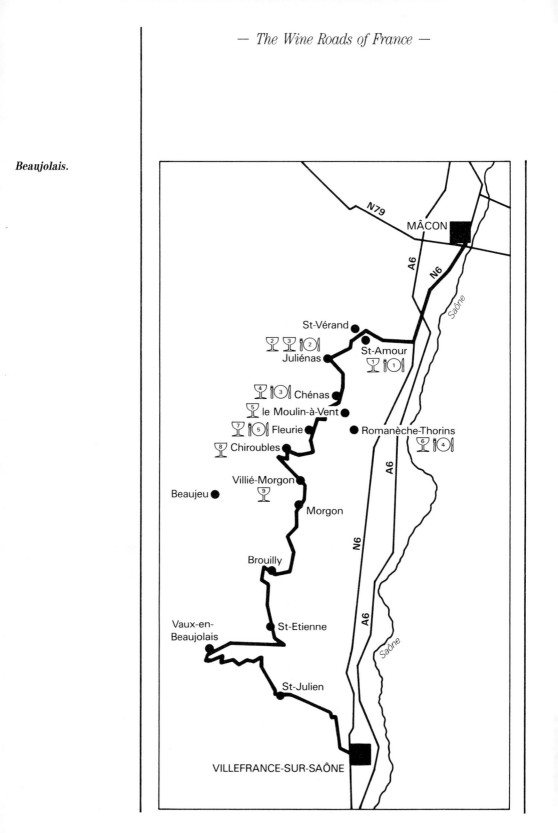

The vineyards of the *Crus* extend virtually without break from those of the southern Mâconnais. Either continue directly from Chaintré to St-Vérand and St-Amour, or else, reach this first wine town from Mâcon by heading south on the N6 and at Crêches turning west on the D31. This particular corner of the vineyard provides an overlap of wines with the *appellation* St-Véran, though here the Chardonnay grapes are often used to produce the relatively rare Beaujolais Blanc. At St-Amour, the characteristic Beaujolais terrain soon asserts itself: gnarled Gamay vines, trained '*en gobelot*' are short, stumpy, free-standing, not always even planted in straight rows, a striking contrast to the traditional and ordered Chardonnay vines of Pouilly-Fuissé. St-Amour is considered one of the lightest of the *Crus* Beaujolais.

Juliénas, the next *Cru* wine town encountered along the route produces some of the most appealing and lovely wines of the region. They can be tasted in the cool, ancient deconsecrated village church whose walls are decorated with irreverent frescoes depicting pagan bacchanalian joy.

The terrain which separates the wine towns of the northern Beaujolais is rugged and individual in the extreme: hill towns look across to one another from their lofty perches over deep plunging valleys of vines. Cross from Juliénas to Chénas (the name indicates that this area was once totally forested with oak — *les chênes*), a particularly pretty little wine hamlet with flowers and wine barrels in its church courtyard. The well-structured, deep wines can be tasted in the château above the town where great oak *cuves* and barrels full of wine lie ageing.

Within this rather confused terrain, differences in soil and microclimate change considerably from one *Cru* to another. At nearby Moulin-à-Vent, the *appellation* for vineyards north of Romanèche-Thorins, for example, great cannon-ball size lumps of black manganese are found throughout the fields. This mineral, together with other components, gives the wines of Moulin-à-Vent a particular richness and structure which make them the biggest of all the *Crus* Beaujolais and the one most capable of improving with age.

Moulin-à-Vent, Beaujolais.

These wines, it should be added, particularly those sampled from the most recent vintage at tasting *caveaux* such as that found below the armless windmill set amidst the vineyards of Moulin-à-Vent, may taste rather hard and somewhat acid, especially compared with the softer, gulpable Beaujolais wines that are so initially forthcoming. This is because the former are vinified traditionally, to extract deeper colour, more tannin, and complex flavour elements from the grape: as such, they generally need time to improve and should be tasted with this in mind.

Fleurie is the largest town among the *Crus* and as such is a minor and busy little wine centre that should not be missed. On Saturday morning, certainly, the town hums with activity and life: a small market takes place in front of the church, with vans selling *fromages de chèvres*, *andouillettes* coated in mustard and breadcrumbs and ready for grilling, yellow *poulet de Bresse*, truffled sausages, pistachioed *cervelas*, and other *charcuterie* products: the sort of hearty country foods that go so well with the local wines. Fleurie can be tasted at the *caveau* in the town centre as well as at the busy *cave coopérative* on the edge of town: its name is as pretty as the wine itself, which many consider to be the most feminine, the most elegant of all of the *Crus*.

The drive from Fleurie to Chiroubles is stunning, over rolling hills which seem almost bald, save for the vines which cover them, a vista broken only occasionally by the orange, sun-baked roof of a *vigneron's* farmhouse. Chiroubles itself is a steep hill town, whose lovely, lighter wines are almost always ready to drink earlier than the other *Crus*. Thus, they are wines which can be purchased and enjoyed on the spot for a vineyard picnic.

Villié-Morgon is the next wine town on the route, the centre for the wines known simply by the *appellation* Morgon. The town boasts the first tasting *caveau* opened in Beaujolais as long ago as 1953; today it remains one of the most welcoming, with a little wine museum of tools and glassware, and the great *fût* where the wine for the *caveau*, selected from a number of local growers, is assembled before being bottled and labelled. Morgon, in contrast to Fleurie, is a manly wine, deep in structure and richness, which needs considerable ageing to fully develop. Though it can be drunk after 2 or 3 years, wines from the best vintages can improve for a decade.

The Mont-de-Brouilly, further south, is a notable landmark rising some 500 m (1600 ft) above the plain. The great sea of vines which extends over its lower slopes and the plains around Odenas and St-Lager produce the wines of Brouilly, the largest of the *Crus appellations*. The best wines, however, come from the steeper, well-exposed south- and east-facing slopes of Mont-de-Brouilly itself. Longer-lived with more character and flavour, they are entitled to their own *appellation*: Côte-de-Brouilly. Climb up the Mont, passing *propriétaires-récoltants* along the way, to reach the summit where there is a chapel dedicated to '*Notre Dame des Vignes*' as well as fine views not just over the Saône valley, but up and down the whole of the Beaujolais, with the little hills and valleys rippling down towards Lyon in unending succession.

From the Mont-de-Brouilly, continue to explore the Beaujolais-Villages: charming little Beaujeu, St-Etienne, Vaux-en-Beaujolais, St-Julien, and others before reaching Villefranche-sur-Saône, a rather large and undistinguished town which is the centre of the region. South of Villefranche, on the lighter soils of the plateau, the same Gamay vines ripen to produce vast rivers of basic bracing Beaujolais. If the wines are less good than those from the north, the countryside of the southern Beaujolais is no less enchanting.

Dégustation: Stop to Taste; Stop to Buy

Included below are the addresses of the principal tasting *caveaux* for the *Crus* Beaujolais as well as those of a few other wine growers. While these will ensure that you will not go thirsty in the region, there are literally hundreds of other individual *propriétaires-récoltants* who offer *dégustation-vente*. The Beaujolais is a vast wine region in its own right and deserves considerable further exploration.

1

Caveau de St-Amour
71131 St-Amour
tel: (85) 36 70 70
Hours: Sat afternoon 14–19h. Sun and holidays 10–12h; 14h30–19h.
This tasting *caveau* in the centre of the village has limited opening hours, but at weekends St-Amour AOC and Beaujolais Blanc AOC wines are served by the glass, and sold by the bottle. If you telephone in advance, the *caveau*, can arrange appointments to visit *viticulteurs* direct.

2

Cave Coopérative des Grands Vins
Château du Bois de la Salle
69840 Juliénas
tel: (74) 04 42 61
Hours: Daily including Sun and holidays 9–12h; 14–18h.
The *cave coopérative* is located 1 km from the village and offers *dégustation* of Juliénas AOC, St-Amour AOC and Beaujolais-Villages AOC.

3

Cellier de la Vieille Église
Centre Ville
69840 Juliénas
Hours: Daily 9h45-12h; 14h30-18h30.
In the cool, ancient deconsecrated village church, the *Association des Producteurs du Cru Juliénas* has created a unique and memorable tasting *caveau*. Don't pass through this pretty town without stopping for a glass of Juliénas AOC.

4

Cave du Château de Chénas
Chénas
69840 Juliénas
tel: (74) 04 11 91
Hours: Mon–Sat morning 8–12h; 14–18h. Open Sat afternoon, Sun and holidays for sales only from April to December.
This serious wine *coopérative* represents some 250 growers. Visitors to the château, located above Chénas, can see the wines ageing in oak casks, and taste and purchase Chénas AOC, Moulin-à-Vent AOC, and Beaujolais-Villages AOC in bottle or *en vrac*.

5

Caveau de Dégustation
au pied du Moulin-à-Vent
71570 Romanèche-Thorins
tel: (85) 35 51 03
Hours: Open daily (except Tue) 9–12h; 14–19h. Closed 10 January–10 February.
Midway between Chénas and Romanèche-Thorins, this welcoming tasting *caveau* is located just below the famous armless windmill and offers Moulin-à-Vent AOC selected each year by the *Union des Viticulteurs du Cru 'Moulin-à-Vent'*.

6

Château des Jacques
71570 Romanèche-Thorins
tel: (85) 35 51 64
Hours: Mon–Fri 9–11h30; 14h30–17h30. Weekends by appointment.
The Thorin family produce a fine and elegant Moulin-à-Vent AOC which needs to be laid down for some years to fully mature, as well as Beaujolais Blanc AOC and a fine Marc de Bourgogne, aged in oak for at least 3 years. The vaulted wine *caves* can be visited and the wines tasted and purchased.
English spoken.

7

Caveau de Fleurie
place de l'Église
69820 Fleurie
Hours: Open daily except Sun afternoon 10–12h30; 14h30–18h30.
A pleasant tasting *caveau* for the wines of Fleurie, located just off the main square.

8

La Maison des Vignerons
Centre Ville
69115 Chiroubles
tel: (74) 04 20 47
Hours: Mon–Sat 10–11h45; 14h30–18h30. Sun and holidays 14h30–18h30.
Closed January.
Tasting *caveau* for the light, delicious wines of Chiroubles, a particularly pretty Beaujolais hill town.

9

Caveau de Morgon
69910 Villié-Morgon
tel: (74) 04 20 99
Hours: Daily including Sun and holidays 9–12h; 14–19h.
The first *caveau* in Beaujolais was opened in 1953 in the cellar of the town's seventeenth-century château. The commune has no *cave coopérative* so each year wines from individual *propriétaires-récoltants* are selected, then mixed in the great wooden *fût* of the *caveau* and eventually bottled for tasting and sale. Small wine museum of tools and glassware.

The Wine Roads of the Jura

In Brief   The wines and vineyards of the Jura are not well known or visited, but they deserve to be. This far eastern outpost of the Franche-Comté produces a fine and varied range of wines that are not only good, but also highly individual and distinctive products of this unique mountain *terroir*. Though the vineyards extend throughout almost the whole length of the Jura *département*, we concentrate only on Arbois, centre of the wine industry and home of Louis Pasteur. The rest of this beautiful wine region, however, deserves further exploration.

Arbois

Arbois, located a mere 80 km (50 miles) due east of Beaune, seems to be farther away than it is in reality, an isolated mountain outpost, centre for a remarkably varied local wine industry, and source of some of the best mountain cheeses. The small town is famous as the boyhood home of Louis Pasteur, who did so much to further the understanding of the principles of wine making.

Explore Arbois on foot, both the city centre, with its fine church of St-Just, the Maison de Pasteur, and the wine museum, as well as its tiny back streets and alleys. The Cuisance river tumbles down through the centre of the town from the mountains beyond, creating an alpine melody over the rocks which is enchanting. In front of or beside almost all of the steeply pitched houses there are stacks of wood piled high in anticipation of winter. The brown-eyed cattle which sometimes lumber in through the streets of the town wear large bells around their necks, adding further harmony to the melody of the mountains.

In the town centre, there is certainly no shortage of wine-tasting opportunities. The firm of Henri Maire dominates the Jura wine industry commercially (indeed such wines as the ubiquitous 'Vin Fou' are marketed intensively on a national scale). Henri Maire's tasting salon, 'Aux Deux Tonneaux', is certainly the most welcoming in town, offering to all visitors without appointment both tastings of a full range of wines (including the rare Vin Jaune and Vin de Paille) as well as mini-bus excursions through the vineyards to its individual estates: Domaine de la Croix d'Argis, Domaine de Montfort, Domaine du Sorbief, and Domaine de Grange-Grillard. This is the most enjoyable way to learn about the Jura vineyard.

There are a number of other individual *propriétaires-récoltants* as well

149

as the cooperative *Fruitière Vinicole* who have tasting premises near the place de la Liberté, for direct sales to passing tourists — particularly Germans, Dutch, Belgians, and Swiss — are an important outlet.

The most striking feature about the wines of the Jura is that, contrary to the current vogue for light, fruity wines that are meant to be enjoyed young, they are all without exception *vins de garde*. White wines produced from the distinctive Savagnin grape, for example, are aged in oak for considerable periods and take on a characteristic dark yellow colour, a particular nutty nose and a maderized sherry-like flavour. Such wines may be further aged in the bottle for upwards of 15 years. Even younger examples have the characteristic *goût* of the Savagnin which may seem rather odd at first, but which with the foods of the region — mountain sausage and the exceptional *poulet au Vin Jaune* — is superb. Even the Arbois rosés (almost everywhere else in the world but here, rosés are vinified to be drunk young and fruity) are similarly aged in wood, then laid down for 10 to 15 years or more. The best reds, produced from the tough local Trousseau grape, are also full-bodied and long-lived wines to be conserved, though only slightly lighter reds from the Poulsard are also enjoyed.

Undoubtedly the greatest, longest-lived and most famous wine of the Jura is the celebrated Vin Jaune. To produce Vin Jaune, the extremely ripe Savagnin grapes are pressed and fermented, then the wines are placed in oak casks which are sealed. These casks are not racked or topped up, as is usual cellar practice for other wines. In fact, they are not even opened again for a full 6 years. In the majority of casks, a type of fungus grows on the surface of the wines, thus protecting them from oxidation: if this surface covering is moved or broken then the wines turn to vinegar (this also happens to those wines which the fungus does not grow on: in some years, the entire production can fail). However, those wines which survive this unique treatment are both exceptional and virtually indestructible.

Such Vin Jaune will further mature for decades: the wine has a rather haunting bouquet and flavour — very perfumed, nutty, yet with a nervous, exciting finish that stays in the mouth for many minutes. It is always drunk *chambré*, that is at room temperature like red wine, otherwise its unique perfume would be lost. The bottle should be opened at least 2–3 hours before drinking to allow it to breathe: once opened, a bottle of Vin Jaune will last for at least 1 month. Vin Jaune is sold in a distinctive squat *clavelin* bottle which holds 62 cl: the amount left after 1 litre of wine has aged for 6 years in cask. This unique wine must be tried while in the region! It is delicious with Comté cheese.

Other wine towns to visit include little Pupillin, the neighbour village to Arbois, noted for its fine rosé wine made from the Poulsard. Château Chalon itself is a dramatically sited hill village located between Arbois and Lons-le-Saunier. L'Etoile, east of Lons-le-Saunier, is famous for its white wines which are entitled to their own *appellation*.

There is a local saying in the region:

Le Vin d'Arbois
Plus on en boit
Plus on va droit.

This translates roughly as 'Arbois wine: the more you drink, the straighter you think'. Since these and the other wines of the Jura are so rarely encountered outside the region, the only way to prove if this is true is to come here and to try them for yourselves.

Louis Pasteur and the Vine

Louis Pasteur, Arbois's famous son, is rightly regarded as the father of modern oenology. Many of his important studies on fermentation and ageing of wines — *Etudes sur le Vin* — were actually carried out in Arbois with wine made from the Pasteur family vineyard, a small plot which is still cultivated today. Pasteur was the first to identify that wine fermented through the action of micro-organic yeasts feeding on the natural grape sugars of the must. Furthermore, he also established that aceto-bacteria, in contact with oxygen, destroys wine by turning it into vinegar. Small amounts of oxygen, as absorbed through a cask or cork, on the other hand, allow wine to develop and mature. Pasteur's studies did much to make wine making a science, not a 'hit and miss' affair based on country and folk remedies and superstition. Yet Louis Pasteur, himself a connoisseur of the wines of his native Arbois, would probably be the first to agree that, after all the analysis and scientific studies, the essential and enduring mystery of wine remains.

Dégustation: Stop to Taste; Stop to Buy

In addition to the addresses below, there are other wine producers offering tastings and sales in Arbois. Though not well known, the table wines are still relatively expensive, while Vin Jaune and Vin de Paille are very expensive.

'Aux Deux Tonneaux' Henri Maire SA
place de la Liberté
39600 Arbois
tel: (84) 66 15 27
Hours: Summer 9h15–19h; Winter 9–12h; 14–18h.
Henri Maire is undoubtedly the 'big cheese' of the Jura wine producers, dominating the industry not only locally but also nationally and internationally. Visits to this welcoming tasting *caveau* are, therefore, essential for all wine lovers who come to Arbois: first a film on Louis Pasteur is shown, then visitors who wish are given a free guided tour in a mini-bus through the vineyards of Arbois, including the four estates of Henri Maire. The Domaine de Grange-

Grillard has a great and historic hall where the Pairie des Vins d'Arbois, a *confrérie* or brotherhood of Arbois wine lovers meets. The full range of Henri Maire wines is available for free tasting, including Vin Jaune and Vin de Paille; the wines can be purchased, but there is no obligation. Henri Maire also has a restaurant in the town, serving the simple mountain foods of the region (see Restaurants).

2

Caves de Bethanie
Fruitière Vinicole d'Arbois
2, rue des Fosses
39600 Arbois
tel: (84) 66 11 67
Hours: 1 July–30 September open daily 9h30–12h30; 14–19h.
While the wines from the local *fruitière vinicole* (the name here for a *cave coopérative*) can be tasted in the place de la Liberté, the *caves* and wine-making facilities can also be visited. Located just outside the centre of town, in the direction of Mesnay.

3

Fruitière Vinicole de Pupillin
Pupillin
39600 Arbois
tel: (84) 66 12 88
Hours: Mon–Fri 9–12h; 14–18h.
Little Pupillin is a tiny but intensive wine town: 45 small wine growers of the village work plots averaging less than a single hectare but still make a large range of wines in this local *fruitière vinicole*. Come here to taste the distinctive Pupillin rosé made from the Poulsard grape, as well as some interesting Chardonnay wines.

Wine Festivals

April or May	National Wine Fair	Mâcon
End of July	*Fête du Vin*	Arbois
Beginning of November	International Exhibition of Wines and Gastronomy	Dijon
3rd Sat, Sun, Mon in November	'Les Trois Glorieuses':	
Sat	Exhibition of Wines prior to the auction; Banquet for *Chevaliers du Tastevin*	Beaune; Clos-de-Vougeot
Sun	Wine Auction of the Hospices de Beaune; town festival.	Beaune
Mon	*La Paulée de Meursault*	Meursault

Regional Gastronomy

Le menu du jour.

Rich, fat Burgundy has always been considered a centre of gastronomy and good living. The Dukes of Burgundy, in their splendid palace in Dijon, built an immense and magnificent kitchen to enable them to entertain and impress their guests on a most lavish scale. But even the peasants of the region, utilizing tough cuts of meat for *boeuf bourguignon* and the vineyard pest snails for their famous *escargots* in butter, garlic, and parsley, produced a hearty regional cuisine that remains unrivalled.

Today, as in the past, the wealthy burghers (and businessmen) of Burgundy are well catered for with no shortage of fine and expensive restaurants throughout the region, serving refined *haute* and *nouvelle cuisine* alike. But the essential charm of Burgundy lies in that fact that even in the simplest and humblest *auberges* and in Burgundian homes, the true, authentic foods of the region come to the table without fuss and pretension.

For Burgundy remains, above all, a region of good, honest country cooking, utilizing the finest produce and products from its rich and well-stocked hinterland: *poulets de Bresse* (chickens which are good enough to warrant their own *appellation d'origine*); beef from the Charolles; game and hams from the Morvan and the mountains to the east; an abundance of freshwater fish and shellfish from the Saône and other rivers; fine fruits and vegetables from country gardens; *charcuterie* from the Lyonnais; and a superb selection of cheese to accompany the great red wines of the Côte d'Or.

If, in Bordeaux, that region's greatest wines are served with only simple foods in order not to distract from them, this rather intellectual approach is completely at odds with the robust Burgundian *joie de vivre*. At great banquets in the Château du Clos-de-Vougeot, at the *Paulée* in Meursault and at dinners in homes of wine growers alike, the richly flavoured and hearty foods of the region in no way take second place to even the greatest wines: *jambon persillé* (ham marbled a wonderful shade of green with a mixture of chopped parsley, garlic, and shallots), *quenelles de brochet* (pounded and sieved pike turns into a light and delicate *soufflé*), *coq au vin* (or — grandly and absurdly — *coq au Chambertin*), *pochouse* (freshwater fish, stewed in wine), and much else may be accompanied by simple Aligoté or red Bourgogne or by Montrachet or Chambertin themselves.

Wine and its by-products, naturally, finds its way into the cooking pot.

'Kir'

Burgundy's most fashionable *apéritif* 'Kir' is named after Félix Kir, a Mayor of Dijon and a hero of the Resistance. The drink, known also simply as *'vin blanc cassis'* is made by adding about a finger of *crème de cassis* to a wine glass, then topping up with well-chilled Bourgogne Aligoté. If red wine is used, the drink is called a 'Cardinal'. Crémant de Bourgogne creates a festive 'Kir Royale'.

    Crème de cassis is a sweet, concentrated blackcurrant liqueur which is a speciality of Dijon (blackcurrant bushes were planted in former vineyards after the phylloxera disaster). Nuits-St-Georges is also an important centre for such liqueurs, and delicious varieties made with other fruits include *crème de framboise* (raspberry), *crème de mûres* (blackberries), and *crème de pêche* (peach).

Slabs of ham are braised on the wine lees — the sediment left in the barrels after racking. *Oeufs en meurette* is another favourite, eggs poached in a dark, rich wine sauce. There is *fricasée de poulet au Meursault, saucisse au vin blanc, paupiettes de veau au Pernand-Vergelesses, jambon au Chablis*, to name but a few such wine-inspired dishes.

    The Jura, a part of the ancient region of Franche-Comté, has an equally rich and distinguished culinary heritage. Here the delicious and distinctive Vin Jaune is utilized to produce a particularly splendid variation of 'chicken-in-wine'. Game from the mountains, including wild boar, venison, and hare, is enjoyed in this region where hunting is still actively practised not simply as sport but as a means of providing for the table. And, of course, the mountain specialities such as cheese *fondue, saucisson*, air-dried ham and beef are all the daily staples, together with Comté and other cheeses and the plentiful local wines.

Le Pique-Nique

Jambon persillé This marbled, 'parslied' ham is sold by the *tranche* and is marvellous picnic fare.

Rosette Large *saucisson sec* from Lyon, served in wine *caves* in the Mâconnais and Beaujolais, and available at good *charcuteries*.

Arboisien sec *Saucisson sec* of Arbois.

Bresis Air-dried smoked beef fillet.

Jésus Fine air-dried *saucisson sec*.

Tourte bourguignonne Veal and pork pie, eaten hot or cold.

Gougère Choux pastry filled with Gruyère cheese: delicious hot or cold with a tumbler of Beaujolais or Bourgogne.

Pain d'épice The famous spiced gingerbread from Dijon.

Époisses Orange cheese, rind-washed with Marc de Bourgogne.

Cîteaux Cheese from the famous monastery (see address below).

Comté The great mountain cheese of the Jura, made in huge wheels, with a characteristic nutty, rather grainy taste and texture (see address below).

Bleu de Gex Blue cheese from the Jura.

Spécialités Régionales:
Stop to Taste; Stop to Buy

Abbaye Notre-Dame de Cîteaux
Cîteaux
21700 Nuits-St-Georges
tel: (80) 61 11 53
The monks of Cîteaux used to produce some of the greatest of all Burgundies at the Clos-de-Vougeot, Meursault, and elsewhere. Today, they produce one of the finest cheeses to accompany those wines; this pungent, rind-washed cheese can be purchased at the abbey direct.

'La Mère Daugier'
21190 Meursault
tel: (80) 21 23 25
Purchase superb *jambon persillé* to take away or try the famous *terrine chaude* on the spot.

Coopérative Fromagerie d'Arbois
rue des Fosses
39600 Arbois
tel: (84) 66 09 71
Hours: Daily except Sun afternoon 7–12h; 17h30–19h30.
Come here early in the morning to watch cheese being made in wooden copper-lined vats, then purchase a slab of Comté or Morbier for an excellent picnic in the vineyards. Opposite the Caves de Bethanie.

Aux Delices du Palais
39600 Arbois
tel: (84) 66 04 25
Artisan-produced *saucisson sec d'Arbois*, *bresis*, *jésus* and *morteau* to accompany the wines of Arbois.

BURGUNDY and the Jura

Restaurants

Chablis (Map p.114)

1

Hostellerie des Clos
rue Jules Rathier
89800 Chablis
tel: (86) 42 10 63
Closed Wed and Thur lunch from October to end of May.
Almost all of the *vignerons* of Chablis recommend Michel Vignaud's friendly hotel-restaurant where light, imaginative dishes are created to complement the great wines of Chablis.
Moderate to Expensive

2

Au Vrai Chablis
place du Marché
89800 Chablis
tel: (86) 42 11 43
Closed Tue eve.
This charming *bistro* serves simple regional foods such as *jambon au Chablis*, *andouilletes*, *coq au vin* together with a good list of both Chablis and the lesser wines of the Yonne.
Inexpensive

Beaune (Map p.119)

1

Relais de Saulx
6, rue Louis Very
21200 Beaune
tel: (80) 22 01 35
Closed Sun eve, Mon; 15 February–15 March; 1–10 September.
Regional and personal specialities served in an intimate, rustic Burgundian atmosphere. Recommended by Caves de Cordeliers.
Moderate

2

Rôtisserie de la Paix
47, faubourg Madeleine
21200 Beaune
tel: (80) 22 33 33
Closed Sun eve, Mon.
Personal cooking and a large wine list in this popular restaurant. Large open fire in winter; service in the gardens in summer. Recommended by Château de Pommard.
Moderate

3   Restaurant 'Au Bon Accueil'
21200 Montagne de Beaune
tel: (80) 22 08 80
Closed Mon and Tue eve, Wed.
It is worth the short journey out of Beaune to find this old favourite: a simple
but always crowded restaurant serving authentic Burgundian foods in a warm
family atmosphere. Reservations advisable. Recommended by P. Bouchard.
Inexpensive

Côte de Nuits (Map p. 122)

1   Le Vinarium
23, place Bossuet
21000 Dijon
tel: (80) 30 36 23
Closed Mon lunch; Feb.
Situated in a thirteenth-century crypt in the heart of Dijon, this atmospheric
restaurant serves the typical dishes of the region, together with a good selection
of reasonably priced wines.
Inexpensive to Moderate

2   'Chez Jeannette'
7, rue Noisot
21200 Fixin
tel: (80) 52 45 49
Closed Thur; Jan.
Situated near the start of the *Route des Grands Crus*, this simple *Logis de
France* serves traditional Burgundian foods in a friendly, rustic atmosphere.
Inexpensive to Moderate

3   Aux Vendanges de Bourgogne
47, rte de Beaune
21220 Gevrey-Chambertin
tel: (80) 34 30 24
Closed Mon; 25 January–10 March.
Simple **Inexpensive** restaurant/hotel serving regional foods and 30 different
Burgundies.

4   Rôtisserie du Chambertin
rte des Grands Crus
21220 Gevrey-Chambertin
tel: (80) 34 33 20
Closed Sun eve, Mon; first week of Aug; Feb.

This great regional restaurant in the heart of Gevrey has its dining room in atmospheric cellars dating from the twelfth and eighteenth centuries; there is a small Musée de la Tonnellerie et du Vin to visit first, before enjoying regional and classic foods accompanied by a superb selection of the wines of Gevrey-Chambertin.
Expensive

5 'Au Gastronome'
RN74
21700 Vougeot
tel: (80) 62 85 10
Closed Mon eve, Tue; 15 January–1 March.
Convenient location near the Château de Clos-de-Vougeot beside its sister establishment, the Grande Cave de Vougeot: this pleasant restaurant serves a number of **Moderate** *menus*.

6 La Toute Petite Auberge
RN74
21700 Vosne-Romanée
tel: (80) 61 02 03
Closed in winter Wed and Sun eve.
Pretty and unpretentious little restaurant in this famous wine town: Burgundian classics include *oeufs en meurette, jambon persillé, lapin aux mûres.*
Inexpensive

Côte de Beaune (Map p.125)

1 Le Cellier Volnaysien
Volnay
21190 Meursault
tel: (80) 21 61 43
Open daily for lunch, evenings Sat only.
Rustic *caveau de dégustation* serves simple **Inexpensive** regional foods: escargots, *jambon persillé, oeufs en meurette.*

2 Le Relais de la Diligence
23, rue de la Gare
21190 Meursault
tel: (80) 21 21 32
Closed Tue eve, Wed.
A lively and popular restaurant located near the railway station, serving a number of regional *menus* accompanied by a fine wine list with a particularly good selection of half bottles. Always crowded, so advisable to book. Recommended by Reine Pédauque and others.
Inexpensive

3

Hôtel-Restaurant Les Arts
4, place de l'Hôtel de Ville
21190 Meursault
tel: (80) 21 20 28
Closed Wed.
In the centre of the famous wine town, this modest *Logis de France* makes
a good base; restaurant serves well-prepared regional specialities. Recommended
by Château de Meursault.
Inexpensive

4

Hôtel-Restaurant 'Le Montrachet'
place des Marronniers
21190 Puligny-Montrachet
tel: (80) 21 30 06
Closed Wed.
A lovely Burgundian hotel-restaurant in the chestnut-lined square of Puligny:
restaurant serves fine Burgundian foods and wines.
Moderate

Côte Chalonnaise and Mâconnais (Map p.137)

1

Hôtellerie du Val d'Or
Grande Rue
71640 Mercurey
tel: (85) 45 13 70
Closed Mon, Tue lunch.
Situated in the heart of the rural Côte Chalonnaise, this fine country inn makes
a convenient base for touring this often overlooked region. Regional foods and
the wines of Rully and Mercurey. Recommended by F. Protheau.
Moderate

2

Auberge du Col des Chèvres
71240 Mancey
tel: (85) 51 06 38
Closed Wed.
Inexpensive *auberge* serving regional specialities and *fromage frais de chèvres*
accompanied by the wines of Mâcon-Mancey. Recommended by Cave des
Vignerons de Mancey.

3

Hôtel-Restaurant de la Paix
9, rue Jean-Jaurès
71700 Tournus
tel: (85) 51 01 85

Winter closed Tue, Wed lunch.
Pleasant *Logis de France* in this historic *ville* serving *quenelles de brochet*, *poulet de Bresse*, and other local foods.
Inexpensive to Moderate

4   Caveau St-Pierre
71260 Lugny
tel: (85) 33 20 27
Closed Wed; 15 November–1 March.
The tasting *caveau* and restaurant serve simple snacks and *'cuisine au vin'*: *coq au Crémant de Bourgogne, truite au Mâcon-Lugny, oeufs en meurette*, and cheeses to accompany the red and white wines of Lugny.
Inexpensive

5   Relais de Montmartre
71260 Viré
tel: (85) 33 10 72
Closed Mon.
Rustic restaurant in the heart of the Mâconnais wine country. *Grenouilles fraîches, terrines maisons, volailles de Bresse* and the wine of Mâcon-Viré. Recommended by 'La Vigne Blanche'.
Moderate

6   Maison Mâconnaise des Vins
484, ave de Lattre de Tassigny (RN 6)
71000 Mâcon
tel: (85) 38 36 70
Open daily 8–21h.
Simple Mâconnais foods are served in this large house near the river, which promotes the wines of Saône-et-Loire: Côte Chalonnaise, Mâconnais, and Beaujolais. Generic wines are served in 33 cl carafes or bottles together with *rosette, petit salé chaud ou froid, fromage fort*. Meals and wine tasting on the terrace in summer.
Inexpensive

7   Restaurant 'Au Pouilly-Fuissé'
71960 Fuissé
tel: (85) 35 60 68
Closed Tue eve, Wed.
This comfortable family-run restaurant in little Fuissé serves a simple but good *menu* to accompany the wines of Pouilly-Fuissé, St-Véran, and Beaujolais: *saucisson chaud sauce vin blanc, poulet sauce vin blanc, faux filet charollais*. Pleasant shaded terrace in summer. Recommended by Château de Fuissé.
Inexpensive

Beaujolais (Map p.144)

1 | Auberge du Paradis
71131 St-Amour
tel: (85) 37 10 26
Closed Mon eve, Thur.
Typical rustic *auberge* in this quiet Beaujolais wine town serving regional
menus. Recommended by the Caveau de St-Amour.
Inexpensive

2 | Restaurant-Bar-Hôtel 'Coq au Vin'
place du Marché
69840 Juliénas
tel: (74) 04 41 98
Open daily.
Welcoming restaurant serves *coq au vin* (of course), *andouillette au Mâconnais*,
and other local foods, accompanied by the *Crus* Beaujolais. Recommended
by Cave Coopérative des Grands Vins.
Inexpensive

3 | Restaurant Daniel Robin
'Les Deschamps'
69840 Chénas
tel: (85) 36 72 67
Closed Tue eve, Wed, Thur.
Fine restaurant serving local and personal specialities and own-produced Chénas
wines in a typical house amidst the vineyards. Meals served on the terrace
in summer. Recommended by Château des Jacques.
Moderate to Expensive

4 | Hôtel-Restaurant Les Maritonnes
71570 Romanèche-Thorins
tel: (85) 35 51 70
*Closed Sun eve, Mon in winter; Mon, Tue lunch in summer; 15 December–1
February.*
Convenient hotel-restaurant not far off the *autoroute* in the heart of the wine
country, serving regional and classic foods together with own-produced Chénas
and other Beaujolais and Burgundies.
Moderate

5 | Auberge du Cep
place de l'Église
69820 Fleurie
tel: (74) 04 10 77
Closed Sun eve, Mon.
On the central square of this pretty wine town, this elegant yet not overly

formal restaurant serves *cuisine au marché*: utilizing the freshest produce and products from the Beaujolais, Bresse, and Burgundy in a light and imaginative fashion.
Expensive

Jura (Map p.149)

'La Finette' Taverne d'Arbois
22, ave Pasteur
39600 Arbois
tel: (84) 66 06 78
Simple rustic tavern was originally a cellar for the production of Marc d'Arbois: Henri Maire then began using it for wine tastings, offering his range of wines in an informal setting of up-turned barrels accompanied by simple drinking snacks: some bits of cheese or local sausage. From this humble beginning, it has become a hugely popular wine tavern, serving mountain specialities such as *saucisson, pot de rilles, fondue,* Comté cheese together with a good selection of local wines. Located near the Maison Pasteur.
Inexpensive

Additional Information

Et pour en savoir plus . . .

Comité Interprofessionnel de la Côte d'Or et de l'Yonne
   pour les Vins AOC Bourgogne
rue Henri Dunant
21200 Beaune
tel: (80) 22 21 35

Comité Interprofessionnel des Vins de Bourgogne et Mâcon
Maison du Tourisme
ave du Mar de Lattre-de-Tassigny
71000 Mâcon
tel: (85) 38 20 15

Union Interprofessionnelle des Vins du Beaujolais
210, bd Vermorel
69400 Villefranche-sur-Saône
tel: (74) 65 45 55

Office de Tourisme
rue de l'Hôtel-Dieu
21200 Beaune
tel: (80) 22 24 51

Office de Tourisme
Hôtel de Ville
39600 Arbois
tel: (84) 66 07 45

Société de Viticulture du Jura
ave du 44e Régiment d'Infanterie
39016 Lons-le-Saunier
tel: (84) 24 21 07

BURGUNDY and the Jura

CHAMPAGNE

Introduction

Reims Cathedral.

*L*a Champagne, the region which gives the world its most elegant and exuberant wine, is itself quiet and modest, an old French province located north of Paris on the natural crossroads between Paris and Lorraine, the Ardennes and Burgundy. The word signifies open field as opposed to forested land; indeed, the vast Champagne plain was once the basin of a prehistoric inland sea which scoured the land and left behind vast, deep chalk deposits, embedded with fossils of oysters and other rudimentary forms of marine life.

Today the vineyards of Champagne cover only a very small part of the former province, extending mainly over the slight ridge of hills, optimistically named the Montagne de Reims, between Reims and Épernay, along the valley of the Marne, and south of Épernay on an area known as the Côte des Blancs because of the predominance there of the white grape Chardonnay. Beyond the vineyards, extensive fields of wheat give way to verdant pasturelands, reminding us that the region remains both an important breadbasket for France and a source of fine cheeses.

Julius Caesar and his Roman legions came to Champagne in the first century BC; indeed it was the Romans who dug the *crayères* — hundreds of great conical limestone quarries in Reims and the surrounds, a source for the soft buff-white stones which have been the building blocks of the region since that era. Over the centuries, a succession of invaders marched over this strategic plain; and time and time again the people of Champagne were forced to take refuge underground, underserved victims of wars they wanted no part of. Épernay, it has been said, has been pillaged and burnt no fewer than two dozen times since Clovis granted the town and its surrounding vineyards to St-Remi. During World War I, Reims and its great cathedral were badly damaged;

the entire region suffered profoundly both in this war and in World War II.

Champagne today, perhaps because of its grim history, presents a rather closed and introverted aspect to the world. Wine villages such as St-Imoges, Bouzy, Avize, and Damery, located along the sign-posted *Routes du Champagne,* are quiet, almost silent, for life, one senses, goes on behind walls and closed doors, not outside them as it does, say, in Provence. These wine towns are hard-working and self-contained: the wine produced from the grapes they grow may bring great joy to the world, but the towns themselves have seemingly little to offer to the outside visitor.

Reims and Épernay, though, are both lively and sophisticated urban areas, a striking contrast to those quiet wine villages. Reims has been a centre for the entire region since the Middle Ages when its famous fairs and markets attracted people from far and wide. As capitals of the most exhilarating and extrovert wine in the world, they are fitting hosts indeed: nowhere else in France will you find a warmer, more gracious and generous welcome than at the premises of the famous *grandes maisons* whose wines are household names.

Historically, Champagne has been a region to pass through. Certainly, many thousands of visitors *en route* to points east or south stop to enjoy the refreshment and hospitality which is freely given to all. Canny Parisians come to the region for the weekend, stopping in fine country hotels or in little rustic *auberges,* then purchasing Champagne to take back home with them, not from the *grandes marques* but from individual *récoltants-manipulants —* growers who make and sell their own Champagnes, often at a third or half the price of the top firms.

Reims and the Kings of France

When the barbarian Clovis, the Merovingian, succeeded his father as King of the Franks, he vowed during one of his many battles that if victorious, he would become a Christian, the religion of his wife Clotilda. After routing the Alemanni, Clovis and many hundreds of his fierce warriors came to Reims on Christmas Day in 496 to be baptized by the Archbishop Remigius, later St-Remi. Thus began a tradition whereby all the kings of France, almost without exception, came to Reims to be crowned and consecrated. 'Kings of France,' said Jeanne d'Arc to the young Dauphin, later to be crowned Charles VII, during their historic meeting at Chinon, 'are made at Reims.' Over the centuries, the great chalk cathedral of Notre-Dame, built in the thirteenth century and a masterpiece of Gothic architecture, was the splendid scene of great processions and magnificent ceremony. Reims and the entire region undoubtedly benefited from these events: coronations, after all, are powerful excuses for celebrations. And what better wine to toast the health and long life of the new monarch than Champagne?

CHAMPAGNE

Champagne, the region and its people, may not be the most immediately forthcoming of France's varied wine lands, but the essential contrast of a rustic northern country producing the world's most elegant and radiant wine is fascinating and perhaps fitting. Life *has* been harsh in Champagne: as one Champenois told us, 'We need something gay and sparkling here to lighten the skies.'

Orientation

The Champagne region is within easy reach of Paris: it is only 125 km (80 miles) to Reims and by car, via the A4 *autoroute*, this distance can easily be covered in not much more than an hour or two. As a staging post to points south from northern Europe and Channel ports, Reims or Épernay make convenient breaks to the journey.

There are frequent trains from Paris-Est to Épernay and Reims, the fastest trains completing the journey to Épernay in less than an hour. Thus, day trips to Champagne from Paris are both feasible and enjoyable.

There is not an international airport in Reims. However, Paris Charles de Gaulle connects relatively conveniently with the A4 *autoroute* via Meaux.

Michelin maps 56, 61.

Le Champagne: The Wine

Champagne

*C*hampagne (the word alone suffices and does not need to be followed on the label by AOC) is rightly regarded as the finest sparkling wine in the world, indeed the touchstone by which all others are measured, produced only in the old French province which has given it its name, La Champagne. The *appellation* is unique in that it defines the wines of Champagne both by their delimited geographical vineyard area (about 25,000 hectares are currently under cultivation in 250 communes), together with stringent regulations relating to permitted grape varieties, yield, methods of cultivation, methods of pressing and other such factors, and also by an essential and critical process of secondary fermentation in the bottle by which means the subsequent still wines are transformed into sparkling. This process is known as the *méthode champenoise*.

The permitted grape varieties for Champagne are Pinot Noir and Pinot Meunier (both black) and Chardonnay (white). The defined vineyard areas extend primarily within the *département* of the Marne over three distinct areas: the Montagne de Reims (between Reims and Épernay), the Vallée de la Marne (mainly on hills overlooking the Marne east and west of Épernay), and the Côte des Blancs (vineyards south of Épernay, planted almost exclusively with Chardonnay). There are also small and relatively less important vineyards throughout the *département* of the Aube.

While some single vineyard *monocru* Champagnes are made by *récoltants-manipulants* (the name for grower-producers who make Champagne from their own harvest), most of the Champagnes produced by the *grandes maisons* are assembled from a number of wines made from grapes (both black and white) grown in various parts of the Champagne vineyard, each contributing its own subtle characteristics and balance to the final *cuvée*. This concept of Champagne as a blended wine is crucial, for it is by this means that it is able to achieve its consistent high quality and house styles. Few, if any, of the *grandes maisons* have sufficient vineyard holdings to satisfy their own enormous requirements, so these houses must therefore purchase grapes from individual growers.

This relationship between the growers and the *grandes maisons* is an important part of the structure of the Champagne industry. Many growers are under contract to particular houses; others sell only a proportion of their grapes, and then make some 'grower's' Champagne themselves. The price which is paid for grapes per kilogram is determined each year by the *Comité Interprofessionnel du Vin de Champagne* (CIVC). The finest vineyards of Champagne are classified as *Grands Crus* and those so rated receive 100 per cent of the set price; *Premiers Crus* vineyards are rated between 99 and 90 per cent, the growers receiving the appropriate percentage. Other vineyards are all given values down to 77 per cent. For a wine to be called '*Grand Cru*' or '*Premier Cru*' it must be produced entirely from grapes with those respective ratings.

The concept of blending a *cuvée* from different wines to create a more harmonious and balanced whole has been essential to Champagne since the seventeenth century. Not only are wines from different vineyards used for this purpose, also — in most cases — wines from different vintages may be blended. For only through making use of old reserves, can the *grandes maisons* produce the consistent high quality Champagne which is unique to each house, year after year. To achieve this high level of excellence calls not only for great skill on the part of the *chef du cave* but also for considerable reserves of older wines.

Vintage Champagne is only produced in exceptional years, when the excellence of the harvest deems it possible to produce superlative and individual wines from grapes from that year only. Such village wines must age for considerably longer periods than non-vintage.

Champagne by its nature is essentially a rather sharp and acid wine — these characteristics give the wine its freshness and 'zip' which is so uplifting. However, as virtually all the residual sugar in the still wines has been utilized in the process of secondary fermentation, such *nature* wines left on their own are bone dry and austere. Thus, after *dégorgement* the wines are given a *dosage* of varying proportions of pure cane sugar and old reserve wine which determines the style of the Champagne. The most popular by far is the driest: *brut* (given only the smallest amount of additional sweetening to result in a very dry wine) though the other styles of Champagne should not be overlooked: *extra-sec* (dry), *sec* (slightly sweet), *demi-sec* (sweet), and *doux* or *rich* (very sweet, though this denotation can be misleading: such Champagnes from the best houses are not sugary in a dessert sense but rather voluptuous, luscious and full-bodied).

'Blanc des Blancs' | *L*iterally 'white wine from white grapes', i.e. Champagne that is produced entirely from Chardonnay grapes with no addition of either Pinot Noir or Meunier in the *cuvée*. Such Champagnes are noted for their lightness and extreme elegance.

Crémant | *A* style of Champagne which is less fizzy than normal, produced by using a smaller amount of *liqueur* to create the secondary fermentation.

Deluxe Champagnes | *M*any of the *grandes maisons* produce deluxe champagnes, that is, vintage or non-vintage Champagnes made from *cuvées* utilizing some of their oldest and most rare wines, or from particularly superlative years or vineyards. Such wines, often sold in distinctively dressed and shaped bottles, are always very expensive.

Rosé Champagne | *P*ink Champagne, the best of which is produced like other rosés, by allowing colour from the black grapes to 'bleed' into the white juice, thus tinting it just the required hue. Alternatively a small amount of red wine is mixed with white before the secondary fermentation.

Coteaux Champenois AOC | *T*his *appellation* applies to the still wines of Champagne. Both red and white wines are produced, and they should be tried in the region since they are rarely exported. The best Coteaux Champenois AOC wines come from the Côte des Blancs; red wine from Bouzy is also particularly well known and favoured. Such wines even in the region are relatively expensive since they are produced from the same grapes used to make Champagne itself.

Rosé des Riceys AOC | *S*till rosé wine made from Pinot Noir grapes grown around Riceys in the Aube *département*. Rarely encountered outside the region, this wine has benefited from its own AOC since 1947.

Other Drinks

Ratafia | *A* local *apéritif* made from unfermented juice of the Champagne grapes mixed with brandy, then allowed to age in casks for at least a year. Similar to Pineau des Charentes. Drink well chilled.

Marc de Champagne | *L*ocal spirit distilled from the grape skins, pips, and residue left after the grape pressing. This pungent and powerful spirit is one of the better versions, for those who like such drinks. Also used extensively in the kitchens of Champagne.

Fine Marne   *G*rape brandy distilled from local wine then aged in oak casks.

La Méthode Champenoise

Champagne does not need to include the descriptive term *'méthode champenoise'* on its label, for it is a prerequisite that all wine entitled to this exclusive *appellation* is made sparkling by this unique method. However, these words may be seen on the bottles of sparkling wines from other regions and even from different countries, for the 'champagne method' has come to be widely accepted as the finest for rendering still wines sparkling.

The *méthode champenoise* denotes secondary fermentation in the bottle. In Champagne, the basic process proceeds as follows. After the still wines have been made, fined, and assembled into the *cuvée*, a small amount of *liqueur de tirage* (pure cane sugar and natural yeasts dissolved in still wine) is added to it, and then the wines are bottled. While in the far distant past, Dom Pérignon and the other pioneers of Champagne tied down these first corks with string (and suffered a large proportion of bottles bursting under the unpredictable pressure), it is usual these days for the bottles to be sealed with a crown cork similar to that used on a bottle of pop. The yeast feeds on the sugar in the wine, causing a slow secondary fermentation that produces as a by-product carbon dioxide which dissolves in the wine, giving Champagne its sparkle.

…ght Champagne corks were …iginally tied down with string.

…r right A skilled remueur at …rk.

The bottles must remain resting on their sides to allow this slow process to be fully completed for a legal minimum of 1 year; however, as this lengthy period of ageing prior to *dégorgement* is critical for quality, many of the large

CHAMPAGNE

Bottles resting 'sur les pointes'.

firms allow even their non-vintage wines to age for a minimum of 3 years and often longer, and their vintage Champagnes to age for over 5 or 6 years.

If fine bubbles are the desired aim of this process, one undesired element remains: a fine, sludgy sediment of dead yeast cells and other solid matter which must be removed in order to render the wine crystal-clear. The nature of this sediment is such that it will not simply collect in the top of the bottle if turned upside down: rather an elaborate and intricate process known as *remuage* must be carried out whereby the bottles are placed in slanted racks known as *pupitres*. Then, over a period of months, skilled *remueurs* give each bottle a daily sharp turn and gradual twist, moving them from an initial near horizontal position to an almost vertical one. The fine deposit is thus urged to slide and slip inevitably into the neck of the bottle, until it rests there on the base of the crown cork.

Once the sediment has been directed into the necks of the bottles, they are then laid to rest *'sur les pointes'*, that is, upside down in great stacks, their necks each resting on the punt, or indentation, in the bottom of the bottle below. Vintage and deluxe wines might be left to further age in this fashion for periods of some years.

Before the wines can be drunk, however, the sediment must be removed. This process is known as *dégorgement*. The method used by most houses today involves placing the necks of the bottles in a freezing solution, thus trapping the sediment in a block of frozen wine. The bottles are then mechanically uncorked; a small hammer gives them a tap; and the pressure in the wine expels the block of ice, and with it the stubborn sediment. Then the wines are topped up with their selected *dosage*, recorked, this time with a dense, high-quality cork that is wired down with a muzzle, and dressed with the elegant foil neck capsule and label.

La Champagne: The Region

While Champagne has sign-posted wine roads which extend through the region's principal vineyards, the structure of the Champagne industry revolves primarily around the large and famous *grandes maisons* who mainly have their premises in the region's two wine capitals, Reims and Épernay. Both of these cities provide the best opportunities for visiting producers and have much to offer in their own right.

Reims

Champagne's largest city, bombed severely during World War I, is today a busy and modern metropolis. With its vast sprawling industrial areas, its hectic university, and modern downtown shopping areas, one could be forgiven for thinking that Reims was just another large provincial capital. Certainly, the city has been razed to the ground repeatedly, and rebuilt time and again from its own rubble but monuments from the past still give an impression of the magnitude and importance of the *ville-sainte* — the sacred city — which legitimized the kings of France.

The greatest monument, of course, is the Cathédrale de Notre-Dame, constructed out of the soft limestone which is the region's great heritage. The superbly decorated west front, with its 'gallery of kings' — statues of great personages lined above the rose window — the hundreds of other carved figures surrounding the portals, and the great twin towers added in the fifteenth century, is monumental to say the least. Inside, the vast, cool gallery is befitting of royal ceremony, void of overly fussy decoration, but majestic in its grandeur. It is amazing to realize that the Cathedral was set ablaze by Germans in World War I, then almost completely rebuilt and restored over the next 20 years. Fortunately, though much of Reims was damaged in World War II, this great monument escaped almost unscathed.

Reims's magnificent monument of chalk is, of course, the outward manifestation of those other underground 'cathedrals', the vast galleries and hundreds of miles of corridors that open on to great naves, chapels, and sanctuaries to wine. For indeed, under the busy streets of Reims, away from the noise and bustle and traffic fumes of the modern world, lies another

Syndicat des Grandes Marques de Champagne

When we refer to the *grandes maisons* or the *grandes marques* of Champagne it is to denote those famous firms whose wines are enjoyed and known throughout the world and which have created the aura and prestige which Champagne undoubtedly enjoys. In truth, though, there is no official list of such firms. Certain houses which we in Britain or in North America might consider *grandes marques* could be hardly known in other export markets, for example. However, the *Syndicat des Grandes Marques* is a non-exclusive group of large firms who jointly defend the interests of Champagne both in France and abroad. The following *grands noms* are members:

Ayala	Heidsieck & Co.	Masse Père & Fils	Pol Roger & Co.
Billecart Salmon	Monopole	Mercier	Pommery & Greno
J. Bollinger	Charles Heidsieck	Moët & Chandon	C. H. & A. Prieur
Canard Duchêne	Henriot	Montebello	Louis Roederer
Vve Clicquot	Irroy	G. H. Mumm	Ruinart Père &
Ponsardin	Krug	Perrier Jouët	Fils
Deutz &	Lanson	Joseph Perrier	A. Salon & Co.
Gelderman	Laurent Perrier	Piper Heidsieck	Taittinger

CHAMPAGNE

quieter realm, where work continues on the production of this most traditional wine in ways which have changed little over the centuries.

The sight of the skilled *remueurs* at work underground is a particularly wondrous one: these men with over-size hands move silently up and down the rows of *pupitres* in single galleries sometimes a kilometre or more in length. This skill of *remuage* is indeed a traditional manual art; where in the future will the Champenois find a new generation to replace those 'old hands', for what modern youngster would be prepared to spend his or her entire working life carrying out such an utterly monotonous though essential subterranean task?

It is such dedication to tradition which ultimately results in great wine: for it is this and other factors — beginning in the vineyard and ending on the bottling line — which allow Champagne to retain its rightful place head and shoulders above all other sparkling wines. Indeed, once the laborious process of making Champagne has been witnessed at first hand, then few will ever begrudge paying the premium which this luxury wine deserves.

Above ground once more, don't miss visiting Reims's Palais du Tau; this ancient residence of the Archbishop of Reims, where the kings stayed during their investiture, is another particularly important historical monument: its Gothic Salle de Tau, built in the fifteenth century, was the scene of royal

Champagne.

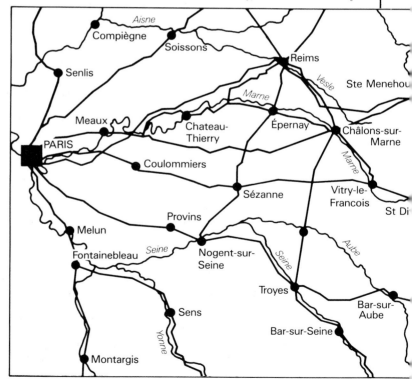

172

festivities following the ceremony. Today the cathedral museum is housed in the palace, a treasure trove including such relics as the bejewelled coronation chalice touched by the lips of no fewer than 20 kings, and Charlemagne's talisman, containing a tiny bit of the 'True Cross'. There is also a fine collection of statues from the cathedral, as well as medieval tapestries depicting historical events. Reims has been an important historic centre for centuries, and other remains of its colourful past are still in evidence: ruins of the Gallo-Roman occupation, notably the Porte de Mars, a grand third-century triumphal arch, as well as the underground *crayères;* fine medieval houses such as the Gothic Maison des Comtes de Champagne; the Renaissance Hôtel de la Salle built in 1545 and the eighteenth-century Hôtel de la Ville.

Épernay

Reims is the capital of La Champagne, the region; Épernay, on the other hand, may claim the title of capital of Le Champagne, the wine. Reims certainly may have as many of the great Champagne houses as Épernay, but they are only one aspect of a busy and modern regional city: Épernay, on the other hand, in common with other great capitals of the grape, such as Beaune, Cognac, and St-Emilion, is a town which lives and breathes almost wholly for and by its wine, in this case, Champagne.

The region may have a long history, dating back thousands of years, but Champagne, the wine as we know it today, is rather more recent. Indeed, the era of wealth and prosperity which its popularity brought to the region is nowhere more evident than along the wide, splendid avenue de Champagne, lined with eighteenth- and nineteenth-century mansions. Who would guess that below these rather pompous stately homes lies a maze of nearly a hundred miles of twisting, intertwining corridors and galleries, where literally millions of bottles of wine lie ageing, waiting to be released?

Come to Épernay for no other reason than to enjoy Champagne: to visit as many of the *grandes maisons* as you care to, discovering the unique story of each; to go to the Musée de Champagne which teaches about the region and the history of the wine; to drink Champagne by the *flûte* in city *cafés* or on a vineyard picnic while travelling any of the three sign-posted Champagne routes which all start from here; or to luxuriate in the choice of fine country hotels where the wines of Champagne are matched in elegance by the cuisine.

Dégustation:

Stop to Visit; Stop to Taste; Stop to Buy

The wine tourist to Champagne is fortunate for the *grandes maisons* offer fascinating and extremely well-organized visits, many open to the public without appointment. Each is unique and Champagne lovers will wish to visit more than one. Most tours conclude with a *flûte* of Champagne, and many also provide the opportunity to purchase not only Champagne, but also

CHAMPAGNE

ice buckets, Champagne stoppers, and other souvenirs. The latter are usually bargains (they are, after all, forms of advertising): but do check the prices of the wines and make sure that they aren't cheaper in the local *hypermarché*.

Reims

1

Ruinart Père et Fils
4, rue des Crayères
51100 Reims
tel: (26) 85 40 29

Hours: Mon–Fri 9–11h30; 14–16h30. Appointment necessary. Ruinart is the oldest firm in Champagne, founded by Nicolas Ruinart in 1729. Nicolas was the nephew to Dom Ruinart, a contemporary of Dom Pierre Pérignon at the Abbey of Hautvillers, and, thus, he may have had access to the early findings of the monks. The *caves* of Ruinart are some of the most impressive in the region, designated Historic Monuments, formed from a series of *crayères*, the Gallo-Roman chalk pits which were dug to a depth of nearly 40 m (130 ft) over no less than 8 km (5 miles). In addition to its non-vintage and vintage 'R' de Ruinart Champagnes, the firm also produces an outstanding vintage deluxe *cuvée* Dom Ruinart Blanc de Blancs. Free *dégustation* and opportunity to purchase wines.

English spoken.

Reims.

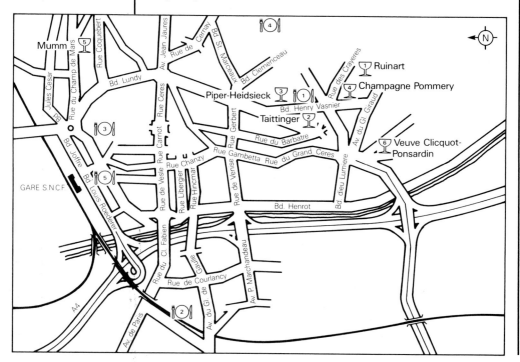

Champagne Taittinger
9, place St-Nicaise
51100 Reims
tel: (26) 85 45 35
Hours: 1 March–30 November daily 9–11h; 14–17h. 1 Dec–28 Feb closed weekends.
Though the most ancient parts of Taittinger's Champagne cellars are Gallo-Roman *crayères* from the fourth century, the most remarkable section was enlarged by the monks of the abbey of St-Nicaise, who stored their wines here in magnificent vaulted galleries, like an underground Romanesque chapel dedicated to the worship of wine. Taittinger stores some 8 million bottles of Champagne, including their prestigious deluxe Comtes de Champagne, produced in exceptional years only with the first pressing of wines from the Côtes des Blancs. Audio-visual presention followed by a guided tour of the cellars. English spoken.

Piper-Heidsieck
51, bd Henri-Vasnier
51100 Reims
tel: (26) 85 01 94
Hours: Open year round Mon–Fri 9–11h30; 14–17h30. Also open weekends and holidays from Easter to 11 November.
Another great and well-known *grande maison* founded in 1785. Piper-Heidsieck has over 15 km (9.5 miles) of galleries, so it is convenient that the guided visits are in electric trains. Piper-Heidsieck Brut Sauvage is an exceptional wine, made with no *dosage* at all; Piper-Heidsieck 'Rare' is a vintage deluxe *cuvée*. Charge for *dégustation* by the *flûte* or bottle. English spoken.

Pommery & Greno
5, place Général-Gouraud
51100 Reims
tel: (26) 05 05 01
Hours: Mon–Fri 9–11h; 14–17h. Weekends and holidays visits at 10h, 11h, 14h30, 15h30, 16h30.

Champagne Bottles

In addition to quarter, half, and normal (75 cl) bottles, the following are still in use in the region:

Magnum (2 bottles)	Salmanazar (12 bottles)
Jeroboam (4 bottles)	Balthazar (16 bottles)
Mathusalem (8 bottles)	Nebuchadnezzar (20 bottles)

CHAMPAGNE

The *maison* of Pommery & Greno was founded in 1836, and towards the end of the century became famous as one of the first great firms to produce mainly dry or *Brut* Champagnes (before this time most Champagne was relatively or even very sweet). The firm has most impressive *caves* decorated with chalk carvings depicting Champenois scenes. Visits begin with a short audio-visual presentation. No *dégustation* but possibility of purchasing wines. English spoken.

5

Champagne G. H. Mumm
34, rue du Champ de Mars
51100 Reims
tel: (26) 88 29 27
Hours: Mon–Fri 9–11h; 14–17h. Appointment necessary.
G. H. Mumm 'Cordon Rouge' is one of the best-known and loved Champagnes. Over 9 million bottles of wine age in this great firm's considerable galleries, including the delicious Crémant de Cramant, and the deluxe vintage *cuvée* MUMM Président Lalou. Visitors are shown a film, and after the guided visit there is a small wine museum to see as well as free *dégustation*. English spoken.

6

Champagne Vve Clicquot Ponsardin
1, place des Droits-de-l'Homme
51100 Reims
tel: (26) 85 24 08
Hours: 1 May–31 July and 1 September–31 October Mon–Fri 9–11h15; 14–17h; Sat, Sun and holidays 14–17h.
The Widow Clicquot took over her husband's business at the age of only 28, and built it up into one of the great Champagne firms. Madame Clicquot is credited with the perfection of the technique of *remuage:* she was undoubtedly one of the *'grandes dames'* of the region, a fact acknowledged by the firm's deluxe *cuvée* La Grande Dame, produced from select parcels of the Widow's own best vineyards which have remained in the company's possession for over 200 years. It is a wine of both exceptional full body and considerable finesse. English spoken.

Épernay

1

Champagne Moët & Chandon
18, ave de Champagne
51200 Épernay
tel: (26) 54 71 11
Hours: Open year round Mon–Fri 9h30–12h30; 14–17h30. 1 April–31 October open weekends 9h30–12h; 14–16h30.
The famous firm of Moët was founded in 1743 by Claude Moët, a wine grower who lived at Cumières. His grandson, Jean-Remy Moët, a personal friend of the Emperor Napoléon (the firm displays one of the great man's hats, a souvenir

of a visit), further built up the business which today holds some 500 hectares of vineyards throughout the region. One prized concentration of vineyards lies around Cumières and Hautvillers, where Moët also owns the Abbaye de Hautvillers, *'berceau de Champagne'.* Moët et Chandon is the most visited house in the region, and also has the most extensive galleries (28 km/17.5 miles). After the guided visit a complimentary *flûte* of Champagne is offered to all and there is the opportunity to purchase.

English spoken.

2 Champagne Mercier
73, ave de Champagne
51200 Épernay
tel: (26) 54 71 11

Hours: Mon–Sat 9h30–12h; 14–17h30. Sun and holidays closed 16h30.

After Moët & Chandon, Mercier is the most visited in Champagne. Founded in 1858 by Eugène Mercier, the *caves* extend for some 18 km (11 miles); the Galerie de Pekin, a single corridor over 1.5 km (1 mile) long, is decorated with chalk carvings which illustrate the history of Mercier and of Champagne. Also on view is the giant Mercier cask, which took 20 years to build, and which was transported from Hungary by a team of 24 oxen for the Paris Exhibition of 1889. Visits are conducted through the *caves* in electric trains and conclude with a *flûte* of Mercier NV. Other wines produced include the deluxe Mercier Réserve de l'Empereur.

English spoken.

Épernay.

CHAMPAGNE

3 Champagne Perrier-Jouët
26, ave de Champagne
51200 Épernay
tel: (26) 55 20 53
Hours: Mon–Fri 8–12h; 14–17h. Appointment necessary.
No other house so exudes the exuberant and gay image of Champagne as does Perrier-Jouët, the *maison* founded in 1811 and famous for its deluxe *cuvée* 'Belle Époque', a fine, elegant wine sold in its distinctive, pretty, enamelled bottle. Guided visits and free *flûte* of Champagne. Wines can be purchased. English spoken.

4 Champagne Pol Roger
1, rue Henri Lelarge
51206 Épernay
tel: (26) 55 41 95
Hours: Mon–Fri 9h30–11h30; 14–16h. Appointment necessary.
Pol Roger is famous as the preferred Champagne of Winston Churchill who named one of his favourite race horses after it. Maurice Pol Roger, Mayor of Épernay during World War I, was a local hero who ensured that the vineyards were tended and the wines continued to be made, thus enabling life to continue, in a fashion, even during those terrible times. The visits are personally guided and conclude with a tasting.
English spoken.

The Wine Roads of Champagne *Les Routes du Champagne*

The sign-posted Route du Champagne.

In Brief   There are three sign-posted *Routes du Champagne* which extend through the region's finest vineyards: the Blue Route (Montagne de Reims), the Red Route (Vallée de la Marne), and the Green Route (Côte des Blancs). They provide excursions into the unique Champagne country. The wine towns encountered are, on the whole, quiet and modest, and as such provide a fascinating contrast to the great *grandes maisons* in Reims and Épernay. In all, there will always be a most welcome *flûte* of Champagne to be tasted or purchased direct from a *récoltant-manipulant* — these highly individual growers' Champagnes are themselves an equal contrast to the elegance of the *grandes marques*.

South of the main Champagne vineyard lie the vineyards of the Aube, around the grape-growing centres of Bar-sur-Aube and Bar-sur-Seine. Troyes itself is a fascinating old town and is perhaps the best base for visiting these often overlooked southern wine towns.

THE BLUE ROUTE — Montagne de Reims

The gentle plateau of the Montagne de Reims, part of the great Île-de-France cliff wall, extends in a broad horseshoe around from Reims to Épernay. For those with a few hours to spare it provides a most pleasant journey between these two great wine capitals.

Leave Reims on the N31 (direction of Soissons), then soon branch left on to the D26 which climbs the flank of this *petite montagne*. As the road climbs, we are soon amidst the well-tended vines: primarily Pinot Noir, together with lesser amounts of Pinot Meunier. Pinot Noir, of course, is the great grape of red Burgundy: it is fascinating that the same *cépage* that produces those marvellous, deep, silky red wines, here in these northern vineyards produces elegant, crystal clear and effervescent Champagne.

Simply meander along the pleasant sign-posted route, through Vrigny and Jouy-lès-Reims, then up to the perched village of Villedommange; a detour

Champagne.

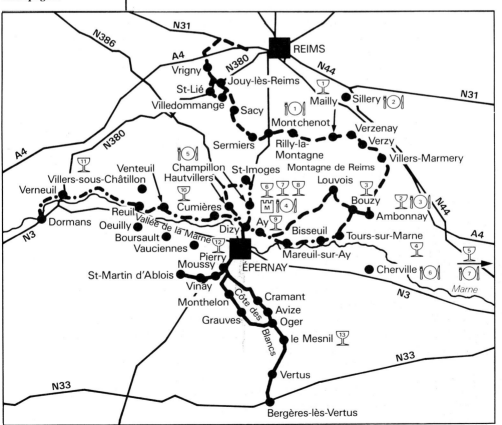

to St-Lié, with its fifteenth-century chapel, provides a splendid view across the Champagne plain. This looks down on the route used by the Gauls, linking the north of France with the corridor of the Rhône that leads to the Mediterranean and southern Europe. Indeed, when Caesar founded Reims in the first century BC (he called it Durocortorum), it was not sited for its natural position beside a river (as was usually the case) but for its strategic position astride no fewer than eight thoroughfares across Europe.

The great routes from northern Europe to the south still pass through the region, though up here in wine towns such as Sacy, Sermiers, and Montchenot it is surprisingly quiet — as if the turbulent events which have often shaken the region over the last two millennia have been forgotten or put aside in the peace of the present. Montchenot straddles the N51, the direct road to Épernay for those in a hurry.

Rilly-la-Montagne is somewhat larger than its neighbouring wine towns, a popular watering hole within easy reach for the people of Reims to come out to on summer evenings, to enjoy sipping *flûtes* of growers' Champagne while watching the lights of the city below. This is the *coeur* — the heart of the Montagne de Reims — and vineyards around villages such as Rilly, Mailly, and Verzenay proudly proclaim their élite status: for they are rated *Grands Crus* and *Premiers Crus* in recognition of the consistent superiority of the quality of their grapes, highly prized by the *grandes maisons* for the character that they add to the finished *cuvées*.

The wine growers' task throughout Champagne often ends at the harvest (except for those *récoltants-manipulants* who make and market their own wine). For so critical is every aspect of the production of Champagne, that once the grapes have been harvested, the great firms who purchase them from the growers immediately take over and oversee their care. Because Champagne is a white wine produced mainly from black grapes it is essential that they are handled with extreme care and speed to ensure that the colouring pigments from the skins are not allowed to bleed into the juice. Many firms have large press houses actually located in the vineyards. These Champagne presses are based on traditional designs which have been used through the ages: large, circular direct presses made from wood (usually) which exert gentle pressure over a broad surface area and allow the juice to percolate through quickly.

The free run grape must, or juice, which percolates through of its own accord is stored separately, as is the must from the first pressing. Two further pressings are allowed by law, with the mass of *marc* — grape skins, seeds, and stems — being broken up between operations. However, the musts from these subsequent pressings, known as the *première* and *deuxième tailles*, are correspondingly inferior — harsher and less delicate — and will be used judiciously by the best houses. These musts are then transported (usually by tanker) to the cellars of the firms in Reims, Épernay, or elsewhere, where the first fermentation is carried out.

Verzenay, incidentally, has a notable landmark, a windmill which was used as an observation post during World War I. At Verzy, take a break from the vineyards to witness a freak of nature — the so-called *Faux de Verzy*, a forest of weird, stunted beech trees, some of which are 500 years old. Nearby, the highest point of the Montagne de Reims is the site of the Observatory of Mt-Sinai.

Continue on the wine road (D26) as it turns south and makes its way towards Épernay. Ambonnay is a fine, pretty little *ville fleurie*, while along the D19 Bouzy (what a marvellous name for a wine town!) is famous for its still red wine, popular in the region's restaurants and used extensively in the kitchen for dishes such as *canard au Bouzy*. Bouzy and other red Coteaux Champenois wines can be particularly fragrant and perfumed, though they will, of course, never have the body or depth of Pinot Noir wines from further south. Nevertheless, they should certainly be tried when in the region.

In Bouzy, the Blue Route splits, and heads down to the river and the wine town of Tours-sur-Marne (with its ancient priory), or else continues on to Épernay via Louvois, which has a twelfth-century church and a château once owned by Michel de Tellier, a chancellor in the seventeenth century.

THE RED ROUTE —
La Vallée de la Marne

The Red Route extends along the Vallée de la Marne east and west of Épernay, with a brief excursion into the wooded hills to St-Imoges and Hautvillers. For travellers returning to Paris, the Red Route can be followed west: at Dormans continue on to the A5 *autoroute* at Château-Thierry.

Épernay is probably the chosen starting point for this tour (though it can also be followed as a continuation of the Blue Route at Tours-sur-Marne). From Épernay, cross the Marne to Ay-Champagne, a large and important wine town, and the home of some famous *grandes maisons* such as Bollinger, Ayala, Deutz, and others, as well as of numerous smaller or small-to-average houses which are not known internationally, but which all have their devotees, and their loyal customers who come from Paris or further afield to stock up direct with their favourite wine. Ay is an historic town whose wines have been appreciated for centuries — witness Henry IV's proud proclamation of himself simply as Lord of Ay. Though many of its old houses were destroyed in the last war, one ancient half-timbered *maison* claims to have been that Lord's *'pressoir'* — press house. Ay also has a small Museum of Champagne.

From Ay, either continue east to Tours-sur-Marne via the wine towns of Mareuil-sur-Ay and Bisseuil, or else west, first to Dizy, then into the hills and forests of the Montagne de Reims (direction of Reims), through Champillon. Just above Champillon, at Bellevue, there is a fine view of the Marne valley and the vineyards of the Côte des Blancs. Continue on the N51, then turn off on the tiny D71 to St-Imoges, a typical wine hamlet, insular, silent, and self-contained. From St-Imoges, the route carries on through the dense forest until it reaches the D386, and there turns left to Hautvillers.

Hautvillers is one of the most famous of all Champagne towns, for it was

The kitchen at the Abbey of Hautvillers.

here in the Benedictine abbey that Dom Pierre Pérignon perfected the methods still used today for the production of Champagne. The abbey itself, owned by the firm of Moët et Chandon, has been wonderfully restored, particularly the kitchens and cellars. As such, it is an important monument to wine and should be seen (apply to Moët et Chandon for visits).

From Hautvillers, the Red Route descends to meet the D1 once more; turn right to Cumières (another important wine town) and Damery, where Henry IV used to come to escape the tribulations of war and internal religious dissent: presumably, it was the still wines of Ay which he enjoyed here with Anne de Puy, for the sparkle in Champagne had not yet been perfected.

Continue along the D1 through Venteuil and Reuil, passing vineyards as well as peaceful fields of wheat interspersed with clusters of wild poppies. Châtillon-sur-Marne was the birthplace of Pope Urban II (there is a large statue of this severe man who instigated the first Crusade in 1095). From Châtillon, the Red Route carries on through Verneuil to Dormans (on the opposite bank of the river). Dormans commemorates the fierce fighting of the two Battles of the Marne. The first, in 1914, took place during the harvest, which was carried out by old men, women, and children, since the men of the region were fighting and dying. Military cemeteries here and elsewhere, their rows of uniform white crosses sprouting hideously from the same chalk soil which nourishes the vines, remind us of the recent horrors which Champagne suffered.

At Dormans, either continue on to Château-Thierry to find the *autoroute*

Dom Pierre Pérignon.

Dom Pierre Pérignon

Dom Pierre Pérignon is universally regarded as the 'father of Champagne' for, as cellar-master of the Benedictine Abbey of Hautvillers at the end of the seventeenth century, he perfected the methods of making Champagne which are still in use today. Prior to this age it had often been observed that the wines of Champagne had the curious tendency to re-ferment in the spring following the vintage. To keep the bubbles in the wine, Dom Pérignon utilized corks (a recent innovation at that time) tied down with string. If the glass bottles did not burst, then the carbon dioxide became dissolved in the wines, rendering them sparkling. 'Brothers!,' the blind cellar-master was said to have cried upon opening a successful bottle, 'Brothers, come quickly. I am drinking stars.' Whether or not Dom Pérignon was the very first to produce sparkling wine may be open to debate (the producers of Blanquette de Limoux claim it as the oldest sparkling wine in the world). What is beyond question is that he contributed profoundly to further knowledge of viticultural and wine-making techniques. Dom Pérignon's greatest contribution, it is universally agreed, was in perfecting the art of marrying wines from a great number of different vineyards to produce the balanced *cuvée* which remains the essence of Champagne today.

to Paris or else return to Épernay on the quicker N3, or through the slower, quiet wine towns of Oeuilly, Boursault, and Vauciennes.

THE GREEN ROUTE — Côte des Blancs

South of Épernay, the horseshoe curve of vineyards of the Montagne de Reims is virtually mirrored by the vineyards of the Côte des Blancs. It is here, on the deep Kimmeridgian chalk slopes, that the noble Chardonnay reigns supreme. Indeed, it is this same, or similar, subsoil in Chablis, in Meursault and the Montrachets of the Côte d'Or, and in Pouilly-Fuissé which gives such finesse and complex structure to those other great varietal wines. Here, the Chardonnay wines from the Côte des Blancs are prized above all for the supreme delicacy, lightness and elegance that they contribute to the *cuvée*.

Indeed, these Chardonnay wines are so fine in their own right that some Champagnes (including some of the prestigious deluxe *cuvées*) are produced entirely from them, 'Blanc des Blancs' Champagnes made with no addition of Pinot Noir or Pinot Meunier in the *cuvée*. Wines such as Dom Ruinart (a vintage Blanc des Blancs produced in exceptional years only) or Taittinger's Comtes de Champagne (produced in exceptional years from the first pressing only of wines of the Côte des Blancs) are prized above all for their extreme finesse and elegance.

Moreover, it is arguable that even wines produced by small *récoltants-manipulants* in towns along this Green Route with vineyards rated 100 per cent, such as Cramant, Avize, Le Mesnil, and Vertus, are among the best of such 'growers' Champagnes, or they can approach the lightness and delicacy (if rarely the profound and complex structure) of wines from the *grandes maisons*. Those growers located in the Vallée de la Marne or the Montagne de Reims who must utilize their own harvest of mainly or wholly black grapes may produce Champagnes that are more full-bodied and gutsy — fine wines certainly but often lacking the critical balance which is the hallmark of Champagne. It is entirely possible to produce a 'Blanc des Noirs' with sound oenological techniques: it is not necessarily wholly desirable.

The Green Route is the shortest of the three sign-posted wine roads, passing through more open, lower-lying country, presenting vast panoramas of the great Champagne plain. Head south from Épernay on the N51 to Pierry, Moussy, and Vinay, virtual wine suburbs on the outskirts of the city (as is St-Martin d'Ablois, further out on the D11). Return to Pierry (where the Château de Pierry, a fine eighteenth-century mansion and the estate of a Champagne grower can be visited), then find the D10 which leads through the heart of the vineyards, and the exceptional wine towns of Cramant, Avize, Oger, Le Mesnil, and (on the D9) Vertus. Vertus is a particularly fine, ancient fortified village. The nearby cliffs of Falloises are a favourite venue for rock climbers, while at the *Cave des Falloises* there is an old chalk quarry that provided much of the building material of Épernay and Reims.

The route continues to Bergères-lès-Vertus; along this brief stretch of vineyards black grapes are also grown, though virtually nowhere else in the Côte des Blancs. From here either continue south to the vineyards of the Aube and the medieval town of Troyes, or else retrace the journey to Épernay, but at Oger branch off into the slopes on the D240 to see the wine towns and vineyards of Grauves, Monthelon, and so back to Moussy and Pierry.

VINEYARDS OF THE AUBE

Far from the elegant mansions of Reims and Épernay, and the élite vineyards of the Marne, lie relatively small, but none the less important, areas where vines are cultivated: to the south of Sézanne and around Bar-sur-Seine and Bar-sur-Aube. The grapes from these vineyards, produced at the limits of the designated Champagne region, may carry lower ratings reflecting their somewhat coarser, country style, yet the wines produced from them are entitled to the prestigious *appellation* Champagne none the less. Only the most dedicated wine tourists will choose to visit these vineyards in their own right (since there is so much to visit in the heart of the region). But for those who are travelling south to Burgundy, or who come to Troyes or the surrounding countryside, an excursion into these little-visited vineyards can be rewarding.

From Épernay, take the N51 to Sézanne. There are pockets of vineyards both to the north and south of the town, as well as further south around Villenauxe-la-Grande, an important market town, better known for its ceramics, china and pottery than for its Champagnes. North of the village, lie the ruins of the Abbey of Nesle-la-Reposte, founded by Clovis in 501. From Villenauxe, cut across on the N19 to Troyes.

Troyes is an important historical centre of the region, acquired by the Counts of Champagne in the tenth century, and made the region's capital. As such, it became an important political, commercial, and cultural city, and a centre for trade, with its strategic location about midway between the north of the country and the Mediterranean. The great medieval Fairs of Troyes were, by all accounts, great and important events, attended by dealers and traders from throughout the Christian world. Troyes was destroyed by fire on a number of occasions: the town was rebuilt in the sixteenth century, a masterpiece of Renaissance domestic architecture, with numerous half-timbered and gabled houses, fine stone work and carvings, and mazes of tiny cobbled streets. This old quarter remains mainly intact and is well worth exploring. The Cathédrale de St-Pierre-et-St-Paul is one of the great monuments of Champagne.

To reach the wine country, head south-east from Troyes on the N71 to Bar-sur-Seine, a small town situated between cliff and river. Bar was once dominated by the Counts of Bar, whose château overlooked the town from atop the cliff. Numerous sieges and fire have left only the Tour d'Horloge (clock tower), but there are fine views from here of the town and the surrounding countryside.

The vineyards of Bar-sur-Seine lie mainly to the south, east, and west of the town. From Bar-sur-Seine, a short detour on the D443 leads to Chaource, nestling in the heart of the Chaource forest. This town is perhaps most famous for its excellent farm cheese of the same name.

From Chaource, the D17 leads to Riceys, a town whose position historically between the County of Champagne and the Duchy of Burgundy made it much fought over. Today the vineyards produce neither Champagne nor Burgundy, but a much appreciated local wine entitled to its own *appellation:* Rosé des Riceys. Purchase a bottle of this rarely encountered wine for a fine country picnic, together with a slab of Chaource cheese and a freshly baked *baguette.* Continue on the D17 to Mussy-sur-Seine, an historic town nestling in a bend of the river. There is an interesting Museum of the Renaissance here. Then return once more to Bar-sur-Seine.

The vineyards of Bar-sur-Aube centre around that town, located east of Bar-sur-Seine (meander cross-country on the D4). Bar-sur-Aube, like Troyes, was one of the venues for the great Fairs of Champagne. This medieval era is recalled by the town's church of St-Pierre, which has on one side a fourteenth-century *'halloy'* — a covered wooden arcade which housed some of the traders' stalls. Today Bar-sur-Aube is a small but attractive holiday resort, convenient for excursions into the Parc Regional de Fôret d'Orient. The pockets of vineyards around the town are by no means extensive or all-pervasive. But the wines produced — both Champagne and still Coteaux Champenois — should be tried when in the region. In summer, there is a tasting *chalet* located on the N19. Return to Troyes along this road.

Dégustation: Stop to Taste; Stop to Buy

We'll let you into a secret: the French, who are by far the largest consumers of Champagne in the world, popping open bottles not only on special occasions but simply for a weekday treat or a favoured *apéritif,* come to the region *en masse* to buy their favourite wine not at the *grandes maisons* (where prices may not be much better than in the *hypermarché*) but direct *chez viticulteur.* In addition to the *grandes marques* in Ay-Champagne, Tours-sur-Marne, and Châlon-sur-Marne, we therefore include addresses for *récoltants-manipulants* as well as for two *coopératives* of growers. But there are scores of others who will be encountered along the wine roads.

Les Récoltants-Manipulants

The *récoltant-manipulant* is a wine grower in Champagne who in addition to, or instead of, selling all his grapes to the *grandes maisons* prefers instead to vinify the wines, submit them to the laborious *méthode champenoise,* and then market them himself, *chez viticulteur.* The number who do this is relatively small, and the amount of wine so produced almost pales into insignificance compared with the many millions of bottles of Champagne sold by the great houses. Furthermore, the excellence of Champagne undoubtedly lies in the skilful blending of the *cuvée,* made possible only through utilizing wines from a number of different vineyards, as well as from stocks of old reserves, a prerogative only of the large houses.

While growers undoubtedly benefit from the prestige, reputation and aura of Champagne which has been created by the *grandes maisons,* those who are located in the best classified vineyard areas (*Grands* and *Premiers Crus*) can, nevertheless, produce Champagne which, though rarely, if ever, reaching the consistent heights of the *grandes marques,* can be very good indeed. Others who are less successful may produce Champagnes which have a decidedly coarse, almost country character, or whose bubbles are insufficiently long-lasting.

Montagne de Reims

Champagne Mailly-Champagne
rue de la Libération
51500 Mailly
tel: (26) 49 41 10
Hours: End of April–end of September Mon–Fri 9–12h; 14–17h. Sat 9–12h; 15–17h. Sun 15–17h.
This *coopérative* society of growers, all with vineyards rated 100 per cent in the heart of the Montagne de Reims, carries out all aspects of production, ageing and marketing of its fine and highly regarded Champagnes. Therefore, its role is similar to that of the *grandes marques,* though a visit to these workmanlike premises provides a fascinating contrast. A full range of Champagnes is produced, including non-vintage, vintage, rosé, and a deluxe *cuvée.* The wines can be purchased for consumption on the spot, or to take-away.
English spoken 'by appointment'.

Jean-Baptiste Rodez
11, rue du Clos des Vignes
51150 Ambonnay
tel: (26) 57 08 76
Hours: Mon–Sat working hours. Telephone weekends.
Non-vintage, vintage, and rosé Champagne, and Coteaux Champenois wines produced by traditional family methods. Charge for *dégustation.*
A little English spoken.

Paul Bara
4, rue Yvonnet
51150 Bouzy
tel: (26) 57 00 50
Hours: Mon–Fri 9–12h; 14–17h30. Telephone before coming.

The Bara family have been *vignerons* in this region since 1833. In addition to non-vintage, vintage, and rosé Champagne, the family produces a fine Coteaux Champenois Bouzy *rouge*. Guided visits last about 1½ hours.

Champagne Vve Laurent-Perrier & Co.
3, ave de Champagne
51150 Tours-sur-Marne
tel: (26) 58 91 22
Hours: Mon–Fri 8h30–11h; 14–15h30. Appointment necessary.
The House of Laurent-Perrier is a *grande marque* founded in 1812 in Tours-sur-Marne, midway between Épernay and Châlon, in the heart of all three renowned vineyard regions. Laurent-Perrier offers 'personalized non-tourist visits' showing every aspect of production. In addition to the non-vintage Champagne, Laurent-Perrier produces an excellent Cuvée Rosé Brut, Cuvée Ultra Brut (no *dosage*), and the prestigious deluxe Cuvée Grand Siècle. The company is also one of the larger producers of still Coteaux Champenois wines, both red and white. Visits include free *dégustation* and the opportunity to purchase.
English spoken.

Champagne Joseph Perrier Fils & Cie
69, ave de Paris
51000 Châlons-sur-Marne
tel: (26) 68 29 51
Hours: Mon–Thur 9–12h; 14–17h. Fri 9–12h; 14–16h. Appointment necessary.
Joseph Perrier, another prestigious and well-known *grande marque,* has extensive vineyard holdings mainly in Cumières, Damery, and Hautvillers, but the *caves* are located in Roman *crayères* in Châlons-sur-Marne, another important and large wine town not far off the wine route. Visitors are received in the timbererd '*haute époque*' reception gallery, and are shown the *caves* and offered a *flûte* of Champagne.
English spoken 'by appointment'.

La Vallée de la Marne

Champagne Bollinger
16, rue Lobet
51160 Ay-Champagne
tel: (26) 55 21 31
Hours: By appointment.
One of the smaller *grandes marques* though the fame of the wines of Bollinger are world-wide. Bollinger 'RD' is a rare, highly prized deluxe wine which gains its particular complex and full flavour from extensive ageing on the bottle sediment (the initials stand for '*récemment dégorgé*'). Tasting and opportunity to purchase.
English spoken.

CHAMPAGNE

7 Champagne Ayala
2, bd du Nord
51160 Ay-Champagne
tel: (26) 55 15 44
Hours: Mon–Fri 9–11h; 14–17h. Appointment necessary.
Another small but well-known *grande marque*, in Ay since 1860. Wines can be tasted and purchased.
English spoken.

8 Champagne Collery
4, rue Anatole France
51160 Ay-Champagne
tel: (26) 54 01 20
Hours: Mon–Sat 9–12h; 14–17h. Closed August.
This small family firm produces Champagne Collery mainly from its own vineyards. Visitors are shown an audio-visual presentation before touring the cellars. Charge for *dégustation*.
English spoken 'by appointment'.

9 Association Coopérative de Viticulteurs de
    Premiers Crus de la Marne
1 & 5, rue de la Brèche
51160 Ay-Champagne
tel: (26) 55 44 05
Hours: Mon–Fri 9–12h; 14–17h.
This *coopérative* association produces wines for individual growers to be sold under their own individual labels, as well as under the *coopérative* label Champagne 'Sélection de Premiers Crus'. Visits include an audio-visual presentation in English and tasting.

10 Champagne Sanchez-Le Guedard
106, rue Gaston Poittevin
51200 Cumières
tel: (26) 51 66 39
Hours: Daily, working hours.
M. and Mme Sanchez-Le Guedard are a charming young couple who produce their own Grande Réserve Brut, aged for at least 2 years prior to being sold.

11 Jacky Charpentier
rue de Reuil
Villers-sous-Châtillon
51700 Dormans
tel: (26) 58 05 78
Hours: Daily, working hours. Appointment preferred.
Jacky Charpentier produces a fine grower's Champagne, as well as *'spécialités champenoises'.* The visit and the first *coupe* of Champagne are free, but

subsequent *coupes* are charged for.
A little English spoken.

Côte des Blancs

12

Champagne Paul Gobillard
Château de Pierry
51200 Épernay
tel: (26) 54 05 11
Hours: Mon–Sat 10–11h30; 14–17h. Appointment necessary.
The Château de Pierry is a stately landmark on the Green Route: the Gobillard family, which has been making wine here since the eighteenth century, has been one of the region's most active *récoltants-manipulants,* though expansion and success of the *marque* has led the family to purchase grapes to supplement their own production. A full range of Champagnes is produced which can be tasted and purchased.
A little English spoken.

13

Bernard Launois
3, rue de la République
51190 Le Mesnil-sur-Oger
tel: (26) 57 50 15; (26) 57 57 33
Hours: Daily, working hours. Telephone before coming.
Small wine museum of ancient instruments, tools and eighteenth-century grower's press, and fine Blanc des Blancs Champagne produced from 100 per cent classified vineyards, as well as Crémant de Champagne and white Coteaux Champenois.
A little English spoken.

Wine Museums

Musée du Vin de Champagne et de la Préhistoire
13, ave de Champagne
51200 Épernay
Hours: Daily 1 March–20 November except Tue and holidays 9–12h; 14–17h.

Le Musée Champenois d'Ay
4, rue Anatole-France
51600 Ay-Champagne
Hours: Daily 10–12h; 14–17h.

Wine Festivals

22 January	Festival of St-Vincent	Ambonnay and other villages throughout the region
24 June or nearest Sat	Festival of St-Jean	Épernay, Reims, Cumières, Hautvillers, and elsewhere
2nd Sun in August	Fair of the Wines of Champagne	Bar-sur-Aube

Wine festival in Hautvillers.

Regional Gastronomy

The essential and fascinating contrast between Champagne the rustic country region and Champagne the most elegant wine in the world is apparent in the contrast between the true country foods of the region and its *vin de pays*. In every other wine region in France, we counsel that the local foods are most naturally partnered by their local vinous counterparts, but who, on the other hand, could really suggest that Champagne is a suitable accompaniment to *pieds de porc à la Ste-Ménéhould* (pig's trotters, poached, boned, rolled in breadcrumbs then grilled) or *andouillette de Troyes* (a characteristic and strongly flavoured chitterling sausage)? Certainly it is not impossible to drink Champagne with such foods; but most would agree that in this case wine and food are mismatched in terms of occasion not to mention style and taste.

Champagne *is* an elegant wine and, for most of us certainly, a luxury commodity not drunk nearly often enough. True, one of the great advantages of being in its region of production is the chance to drink this very special *vin de pays* as frequently as possible: a bottle purchased direct from a grower along one of the *Routes du Champagne* enjoyed for a vineyard picnic; a half-bottle in the hotel bath; a *flûte* before dinner . . . or after dinner. But more often than not, for most of us anyway, Champagne is reserved for rather more special occasions, not least because of its relative expense.

Here in the region, many fine and elegant restaurants have developed a refined *haute cuisine champenoise* which has evolved not necessarily from the regional or local culinary heritage, but which is certainly a fitting partner to Champagne, and the mood that only it creates. Fish such as sole and turbot are served in exquisite sauces made from fresh cream and Champagne, while the pale pink flesh of sea trout and salmon are matched by delicate sauces made from rosé Champagne. Bass is braised in Champagne, while pike and char make excellent Champagne *matelotes*. Oysters, crayfish and lobsters are simmered in Champagne, its lightness and finesse enhancing the delicacy of those shellfish. And traditional favourites such as *coq au vin* are given new significance when the wine used in their preparation is Champagne. *Foie gras*, quails' eggs or *poularde de Bresse* are set in amber, shimmering Champagne aspics.

And of course, fruit such as wild strawberries or raspberries are steeped in Champagne; pears are poached in Champagne; and *sorbets* made with Champagne or Marc de Champagne are served throughout the region.

...op-front, Troyes.

Le Pique-Nique

Jambonneau de Reims Small 'hocks' of ham, breaded or enclosed in pastry. Usually eaten cold.

Jambon d'Ardenne Country-cured ham from the Ardennes, often smoked.

Fromage de tête Head 'cheese', purchased in slices and eaten cold with *cornichons.*

Pâtés Boar (*sanglier*), pheasant (*faisan*), and hare (*lièvre*) *pâtés* are found throughout the region.

Chaource Small, cylindrical semi-soft cheese.

Brie One of the great cheeses of France, produced around Meaux, Coulommiers, Melun, and elsewhere in the region. The best are *'fermiers'* produced from unpasteurized milk (*lait cru*).

Maroille Slab-shaped strong-smelling and strong-flavoured cheese from the abbey of the same name.

Coulommiers Smaller than brie, but a similar, rind-ripened white cheese, usually produced *fermier.*

Using Champagne for cooking might seem like the height of extravagance (exceeded only by such absurdities as Beau Brummel's apparent use of Champagne in his recipe for boot blacking; or the use of the ladies of the 'Belle Époque' of special Champagne *'pour le bain'*). Certainly, in the kitchen, precious bubbles painstakingly coaxed into the wine through years of care and attention are lost the second they hit the pan. Yet Champagne, even without its bubbles, is an exceedingly fine and delicate wine. Thus, sauces prepared with Champagne will be correspondingly delicate, with the unique character that comes from the result of blending a number of wines to produce the desired *cuvée*. Moreover, our enjoyment of meals is undoubtedly heightened by anticipation: dishes labelled *'au Champagne'* cannot help but whet the appetite.

However, for our part, enjoyable as such meals certainly are — particularly when accompanied by Champagne throughout — we confess that we still prefer the simpler, rustic, authentic foods of Champagne: a plate of dandelion greens, dressed in hot, fried *lardons*, a *jambonneau de Reims*, or slab of *fromage de tête* to begin with, then perhaps a hearty Champenois rabbit stew, or that rib-sticking one-pot meal, *potée champenoise* (a cauldron containing pork, sausage, cabbage, and potatoes).

Certainly these are the foods which are still eaten in homes throughout the region, and which can be encountered in some restaurants as well. The

CHAMPAGNE

vignerons in the Montagne de Reims, Vallée de la Marne, or the Côte des Blancs may be able to drive a Mercedes-Benz (for Champagne is undoubtedly one of the most prosperous of all wine regions), but the simple foods of the land still satisfy best.

It may seem paradoxical to eat such dishes with Champagne — if so, then why bother? Drink the still Coteaux Champenois wines, or a carafe of *réserve du patron* instead and save the bubbly for breakfast.

Restaurants

Reims (Map p.174)

1 Boyer 'Les Crayères'
64, bd Henry-Vasnier
51100 Reims
tel: (26) 82 80 80
Restaurant closed Mon; Tue lunch.
Gérard and Elyane Boyer's 'Les Crayères' is one of the great restaurants of France, serving classic *haute cuisine* — *l'escalope de foie gras chaud, le panache de poissons grillés au beurre de truffes, le suprême de canard Rouennais* — in a truly elegant setting of a grand château set within its own grounds of 7 hectares. Hotel has 16 rooms.
Recommended by Pommery & Greno and others.
Very Expensive

2 Le Chardonnay
184 ave d'Épernay
51100 Reims
tel: (26) 06 08 60
Closed Sat eve; Sun.
Elegant restaurant serving *haute cuisine à base de Champagne*. Good selection of fish and extensive list of Champagnes and reasonably priced Coteaux Champenois.
Recommended by Piper-Heidsieck and others.
Expensive

3 Le Florence
43, bd Foch
51100 Reims
tel: (26) 47 12 70
Closed Sun eve.
This Louis XV-decorated restaurant is conveniently located by the A4 *autoroute* (exit Reims-Centre). Cuisine based on seasonal produce and primarily fish and shellfish.
Recommended by Champagne Taittinger.
Moderate to Expensive

Le Vigneron
place Paul Jamot
51100 Reims
tel: (26) 47 00 71
Closed Sat midday; Sun.
Authentic traditional foods of Champagne in this favourite restaurant with
small Champagne museum. *Salade aux lardons, andouillette de Troyes,* and
other regional foods, and a superb selection of local cheeses. Champagne,
Coteaux Champenois, and Rosé des Riceys.
Moderate

Hôtel-Restaurant Le Continental
95, place d'Erlon
51100 Reims
tel: (26) 47 01 47
Classic and imaginative light cuisine, including *ris de veau au Ratafia, caneton
au vin de Bouzy,* and reasonably priced house Champagne.
Inexpensive to Moderate

Épernay (Map p.177)

Hôtel-Restaurant Les Berceaux
13, rue des Berceaux
51200 Épernay
tel: (26) 55 28 84
Restaurant closed Sun night.
This friendly restaurant-hotel under French–English ownership has now added
a wine bar where meals are served to piano music on Thur, Fri, and Sat evenings.
Restaurant serves fine classic cuisine, with many dishes prepared *'au
Champagne'.*
Recommended by Champagne Pol Roger.
Moderate to Expensive

Les Routes du Champagne (Map p.179)

Auberge du Grand Cerf
rte d'Épernay (N51)
51500 Montchenot
tel: (26) 97 60 07
Closed Wed.
Comfortable country *auberge* located along the Blue Route in the heart of
the wine country. Inventive light cuisine based on seasonal products: seafood
and game.
Recommended by Ruinart Père & Fils.
Expensive

2

Le Relais de Sillery
3, rue de la Gare
51500 Sillery
tel: (26) 49 10 11
Closed Sun eve; Mon.
Chef Jeannine Adin proposes *foie gras au Ratafia, filet petits gris au Marc de Champagne,* and other dishes based on regional products. Wines include Sillery *rouge* and other Coteaux Champenois.
Recommended by Champagne Mailly Champagne.
Inexpensive to Moderate

3

Auberge St-Vincent
1, rue St-Vincent
51150 Ambonnay
tel: (26) 57 01 98
Closed Mon.
Authentic Champenois country cooking at this pleasant *Logis de France.* Ambonnay, in the heart of the wine country between Épernay, Reims, and Châlons, is a pretty *ville fleurie.*
Recommended by Jean-Baptiste Rodez.
Inexpensive to Moderate

4

Au Vieux Pressoir
2, rue Roger Sondag
51160 Ay-Champagne
tel: (26) 55 43 31
Closed Sun eve; Mon eve; Tue eve.
This pleasant restaurant is owned by M. and Mme Collery of Champagne Collery. Regional foods — *cassolette d'escargots* and meats and fish in Champagne sauces — are served at candlelit tables and outside in summer.
Moderate

5

Royal Champagne
'Bellevue'
Champillon
51160 Ay-Champagne
tel: (26) 51 11 51
Closed January.
This seventeenth-century coaching inn located along the Red Route (N51) about 10 km (6 miles) from Épernay is a member of the *Relais & Châteaux* group and serves elegant *haute cuisine* in a magnificent setting at the foot of the Montagne de Reims. Dining room and bedrooms overlook the vineyards.
Recommended by Moët & Chandon.
Very Expensive

6

Le Relais de Cherville
1, rue de l'Église

51150 Cherville
tel: (26) 69 10 78
Closed Sun; Mon.
Located south of Tours-sur-Marne, this ancient restored farmhouse has a
comfortable rustic ambiance, with a large open fire in winter and service outside
in summer. Inventive and classic foods are prepared according to the season.
Recommended by Laurent Perrier.
Moderate

Restaurant Les Ardennes
34, place de la République
51000 Châlons-sur-Marne
tel: (26) 68 21 42
Closed Sun eve; Mon eve; first three weeks of August.
This sixteenth-century *maison* serves the foods of the Ardennes in its 'rustic'
dining room: *cochonnailles Ardennaises, boudin blanc maison, escalope de
veau Champardenne.* Coteaux Champenois wines, as well as an extensive
list of Champagne.
Recommended by Joseph Perrier.
Inexpensive to Moderate

Additional Information

Et pour en savoir plus . . .

Comité Interprofessionnel du Vin de Champagne
5, rue Henri-Martin
51204 Épernay
tel: (26) 51 40 47

Comité Régional de Tourisme Champagne-Ardenne
5, rue de Jéricho
51000 Châlons-sur-Marne
tel: (26) 64 35 92

Office de Tourisme
1, rue Jadart
51100 Reims
tel: (26) 47 25 69

Office de Tourisme
7, ave de Champagne
51200 Épernay
tel: (26) 55 33 00

COGNAC

Introduction

Cellar in Cognac.

*T*he Charentes, the region which gives the world its most celebrated distillation of the vine, is rural France *par excellence*. The town of Cognac itself nestles on the banks of the slow wide Charente river, a somewhat sleepy *ville,* content within its alcoholic miasma, the result of thousands of oak barrels of ageing *eau-de-vie* yielding a quite fantastic amount of liquor through evaporation, *la part des anges*: the share, as they say here, reserved for the angels. Jarnac, further up-river towards Angoulême, and the region's second town for *eau-de-vie*, is even more charming, a sort of French version of Henley-on-Thames, with the wide, pleasantly lazy river winding through the town, where pleasure boats and river cruisers are tied up alongside the *quai* and fishermen dangle lines from the stone bridge. Rowers skim over the easy waters, while the grand château of Courvoisier stands in lieu of the blackened stacks of Henley's Brakspear Brewery, the sweet marzipany smell of ageing Cognac replacing the stinging, bitter aroma of English hops.

If today Cognac appears somewhat somnolent, the town certainly enjoyed a heyday in the fifteenth century during the reign of the Valois. Having survived and endured the upheavals and changes of fortune brought by the Hundred Years' War, Cognac prospered under Count Jean, and in 1494, saw the birth of a future King of France, François 1er. Cognac at this time was a busy trading centre, for the Charente river was then one of the great avenues of commerce, carrying goods, particularly salt and wine, from inland France to the sea, and from there eventually to the countries of Northern Europe.

It must be said, however, that the wines of the Charentes were never really all that fine: in fact, by all accounts, they were thin, acidic, and weak. However, in the sixteenth century a knight from a manor near Segonzac (a small but still important wine village in the Grande Champagne area) experimented with 'burning' the wine, then 'burning' it again in an effort to discover — and capture — the quintessence of the grape. This knight, Jacques de la Croix Maron, is credited with the discovery of double distillation and the creation of the first Cognac brandies. Is it surprising that a man of arms perfected this civilized art? Not at all, for the process of distillation itself was undoubtedly brought back by Crusaders from the Holy Lands (words such as *alambic* and *alcool* point to its Arabic derivation).

As a consequence, in the seventeenth and eighteenth centuries, the merchants of Cognac began eventually to distill the unstable wines of the Charentes before shipping them in wooden barrels to the Low Countries and to Great Britain. This was achieved not simply for matters of taste but out of hard commercial considerations as well: duty was charged on volume, thus the concentrated 'burnt' wines attracted less tax. It was almost a secondary benefit that in the process the brandies, after time spent in wood, acquired a mellowness and finesse which remains unrivalled. Such were the beginnings of a great trade whose product, Cognac, was soon renowned throughout the world. By the beginning of the twentieth century there were over 100 Cognac houses situated in the eponymous town alone.

Today Cognac is one of the great wine capitals of France, and like others such as Reims and Épernay in Champagne and Beaune in Burgundy, the famous and grand *maisons* who are household names worldwide are well-organized and gracious hosts. Firms such as Hennessy, Martell, Otard, and others in Cognac offer excellent, informative and imaginative tours to all, without appointments, together with free tastings and opportunities to purchase. In Jarnac, the great firm of Courvoisier offers an audio-visual programme in an ageing *chais*, and has a fine little museum (its prize exhibit being a hat and greatcoat of the Emperor Napoléon). Furthermore, throughout the designated Cognac region there are literally hundreds of small *propriétaires-récoltants,* wine growers who actually have pot stills on their premises and who distil and age their own unique Cognacs.

The designated Cognac vineyard is vast, extending throughout the *départements* of Charente and Charente-Maritime, west to the coast and to islands such as the Ile de Ré (off La Rochelle) and the Ile d'Oléron. The vineyards which produce the finest wines for distillation lie closer to Cognac itself in areas south of the Charentes known as Grande and Petite Champagne.

The region as a whole, however, deserves further exploration. Certainly La Rochelle and the beaches to the north have always proved popular destinations and deservedly so. Less well known are sea towns such as Royan (located at the mouth of the Gironde opposite the Médoc), Ronce-les-Bains, and Marennes, where some of the finest oysters in the world are cultivated in ancient salt marshes known as *claires*. The Marais Poitevin, an area of marshy fenland west of Niort, is a strange, inward-looking land of canals and houses on stilts, where people move about as easily by boat as by car. To the south, Saintes has been an important town since Roman days at least; later, in the Middle Ages, it was a stop on the pilgrim route to Santiago de Compostela.

COGNAC

It has given its name to the region, the Saintonge, as well as to its unique style of Romanesque architecture. Angoulême is another ancient and important Charentais town, fortified on a well-positioned limestone spur overlooking the river.

Cognac, the beverage, is a fabulous essence: the region which produces it is no less a fascinating distillation of many and varied elements.

Orientation

The Cognac vineyard, covering a vast area of approximately 95,000 hectares (235,000 acres), extends over the *départements* of Charente and Charente-Maritime, as well as into small areas of the Deux-Sèvres and Dordogne. Cognac is about 475 km (300 miles) from Paris and is reached via the A10 *autoroute* which passes through Orléans, Tours, and Poitiers before continuing on to Bordeaux. Exit at Saintes and continue to Cognac on the N141. Angoulême is on the main railway line between Paris and Bordeaux. The journey from Paris takes about 4 hours. From Angoulême there are frequent local trains to Cognac which complete the journey in about 45 minutes. Bordeaux Merignac is probably the most convenient international airport.

La Rochelle is a principal coastal town and resort, located within the Cognac vineyard area known as Bois Ordinaires. While the region itself is a fine holiday destination, traditionally the town of Cognac has benefited from tourists who pass through the vineyards and the town *en route* to somewhere else. Indeed, no one passing near Cognac should miss the opportunity of enjoying the hospitality of the great Cognac firms as well as of visiting smaller producers in outlying areas.

There are convenient ferries across the Gironde to the Médoc at Royan and at Blaye.

Michelin Maps 71, 72

Cognac, Pineau des Charentes, and Table Wines

Cognac AOC

Cognac is an *appellation d'origine* brandy or *eau-de-vie* produced by a process of double distillation of wine, following strict laws based on long-standing local customs and methods. These relate to the specific delimited vineyard area, the types of grapes cultivated, and the methods of distillation and ageing. While brandy can be produced wherever wine is made (the word itself is a corruption of the Dutch *brandewijn* meaning simply 'burnt wine'), Cognac stands head and shoulders above all others, rightly regarded as the finest distillation of the grape in the world.

The Cognac vineyard region is vast, but it is divided into seven growths, or sub-regions, based on the characteristics and quality of the *eaux-de-vie* obtained from the wines produced from each area's grapes. The finest vineyard area lies to the south of the Charente river on a slightly rolling, hilly area of deep, soft chalk. It may be coincidence that this area is known as Grande Champagne (*champagne* from the old French meaning open countryside as opposed to *bois* — woodlands), but like that other great region which produces the world's finest sparkling wines, here a similar deep chalky subsoil gives the distilled wines a particular finesse, elegance, and sheer class that cannot be rivalled or duplicated. The little, unassuming town of Segonzac is considered the 'capital' of Grande Champagne.

Petite Champagne, the next finest vineyard area, extends around and mainly to the south of Grande Champagne. The soil make-up here is also primarily chalk and the resulting *eau-de-vie* is valued for a character at once flavoursome yet rather soft and fine. The market town of Barbezieux is the centre of Petite Champagne. Just to the north of Cognac lies another vineyard area known as Borderies. *Eau-de-vie* from here is said to have a subtle but

---

By Boat Through the Vineyards of Cognac

The Charente river historically was — and remains to a certain extent today — a main and active thoroughfare for the region, giving remote inland areas access to the sea. Today the commercial barges have mainly been replaced by pleasure cruisers. One of the nicest ways to view the Cognac countryside is on board one of the many pleasure cruisers which ply up and down the river. Agences Croisières, for example, offer excursions from Cognac to Rouffiac and back with a stop for a lunch of regional *saintongeaise* specialities. Charentes Plaisance offers an excursion from Cognac to St-Brice in just under 2 hours. There are many other excursions of varying length and to different destinations.

Further details from:

    Charente Plaisance
    1, place du Solençon
    16100 Cognac
    tel: (45) 82 79 71

    Agences Croisières
    c/o Office de Tourisme
    16, rue du XIV Julliet
    16100 Cognac
    tel: (56) 82 10 71

COGNAC

distinct flavour of violets. These three areas, together making up no more than a quarter of the delimited vineyard area, produce the finest Cognacs.

Further and further from the heartland of Cognac itself lie the vineyards known as Fins Bois, Bons Bois, Bois Ordinaires, and Bois à Terroir. As the chalky subsoil of the Champagne areas decreases, giving way to marly clay and sand, so does the quality of wines and subsequent *eaux-de-vie* decrease. However, that is not to say that the more rustic Cognacs produced in outlying areas do not have their place: for a start they contribute character, flavour, and aroma in the assembled blends of the great *maisons*. On their own, purchased direct from *propriétaires-récoltants,* they can be excellent, lacking certainly the finesse and elegance of Fine Champagne Cognac (a term which can be applied only to Cognac produced from a mixture of Grande and Petite Champagne, with not less than 50 per cent of the former) but making up for this in individuality.

The principal *cépage*, or grape variety, in the Cognac region is the Ugni Blanc, known locally as the St-Emilion. It makes up some 98 per cent of the vineyard, the remaining areas being planted with Colombard and Folle Blanche. The harvest per hectare is not limited by law as it is in regions that produce quality table wines. Thus the vines yield huge quantities of grapes which make wines that by drinking standards would be considered pretty poor and thin.

Yet once these poor wines of the Charentes are distilled and aged, they are transformed into Cognac! Many wine growers here actually distil their own wines on their own premises, and this is one of the most fascinating aspects of the region. Indeed, it is wonderful to view the splendid-looking *alambic Charentais* (Charentes pot still) in a small grower's outbuilding or warehouse, even if the shiny copper onion-shaped dome, the brick furnace and the gleaming brass taps are silent and redundant out of season, used now only to prop up a windsurfer or bicycle.

The transformation, or distillation, of common wine into ethereal *eau-de-vie* takes place over winter, and must, by law, be completed by the end of March. Thus, visitors to the region in spring, summer, and autumn will not see the *alambic* in action; in truth even visitors over winter may never see the distilleries in full flight for at this busiest period there may be little time for tours.

The process of distillation is a basic and simple one. The newly fermented wines are added unfiltered to the *alambic*. A direct fire underneath brings the wines to boiling point and the alcohol vaporizes and rises into the head (*chapiteau*). From here it passes through the elegantly-shaped swan neck (*col de cygne*), and finally into the cool, coiled worm (*serpentin*), where it condenses back into liquid which can be collected. This first distillation is known as *brouillis*: it is low in strength, cloudy, and still contains impurities which render it not potable. It must, therefore, undergo the same process of distillation one more time.

The second distillation is known as *la bonne chauffe*. The first initial vapours which rise are still particularly high in impurities, thus these 'heads' must be separated; the vapours from the end of the run, the 'tails', are similarly undesirable: only the middle cut, the 'heart' of the run is kept, for it alone contains those inimitable flavouring elements and aroma which with time will become Cognac.

Time: this is the final factor which contributes to the unique character of Cognac, for the young colourless spirits, when aged in new oak casks made with wood only from the Limousin or Tronçais forests, gradually acquire a superb mellow flavour, a fine amber colour and a most distinctive perfume. Thus, in merchants' warehouses in Cognac and Jarnac, as well as throughout the region, many thousands of barrels of young as well as very old reserves lie ageing: so great is the level of evaporation that each year the equivalent of no less than 20 million bottles literally disappears into the atmosphere, to the delight of those happy angels.

Cognacs from single years are almost unheard of (unlike vintage Armagnac *millésimes*); almost all Cognac on the market is a blend not only of *eaux-de-vie* of different ages but also of differing characteristics which marry together into a harmonious and glorious whole.

Cognac has finesse, an underlying exciting flavour and aroma which really is the essence of the grape: it truly is the finest brandy in the world.

Pineau des Charentes AOC

*P*ineau des Charentes, which benefits from an *appellation d'origine contrôlée*, is a *mistelle*, that is, a drink produced by mixing fresh grape juice with young Cognac brandy; the grape juice is prevented from fermenting by the high alcohol level of the Cognac, thus resulting in a sweet, fruity *apéritif* that combines the freshness of grape juice with the strength and backbone of Cognac. Pineau was born, legend says, by chance, when in the sixteenth century a *vigneron* made the mistake of topping up a cask containing Cognac with pure grape juice. To his surprise, the grape juice did not ferment. Thinking no more of it, he set the cask aside for some years, and when he returned to it, he discovered a beverage that was excellent: fruity and delicately perfumed and flavoured.

here are numerous opportunities taste Pineau des Charentes as ell as Cognac.

Whether or not this is the exact provenance of Pineau des Charentes, the story is not wholly improbable; indeed similar drinks are made in other grape-growing areas (Ratafia in Champagne and Floc in Armagnac). It is entirely likely, furthermore, that the Charentais, faced with the bleak prospect day in and day out of having only their thin, acid wine to drink, devised this sweeter, fruitier beverage for special occasions and local festivals.

Pineau des Charentes has only been produced commercially since 1930; however, today it is an important product of the region, and visitors will encounter numerous opportunities to taste it and to buy it.

Two types of Pineau des Charentes are produced: white Pineau des Charentes, made from the grape varieties Ugni Blanc (St-Emilion), Folle Blanche, Colombard, and others; and Pineau des Charentes rosé, produced from Cabernet

COGNAC

201

Franc, Cabernet Sauvignon, and Merlot. The yield on the vines, unlike that for Cognac itself, is limited to only 50 hectolitres per hectare (hl/ha) and this results in grape juice that is rich in natural sugars with a potential alcohol content of at least 10°. But this grape juice is not allowed to ferment. It is muted by being mixed with Cognac that has a minimum age of 1 year. The ratio of grape must to Cognac is appropriately 3 to 1, resulting in a drink with an alcohol content of between 16° and 20°. Pineau des Charentes must then be aged in oak casks for at least 1 year before it is sold; the finer Pineaus may spend up to 2 or 3 years beyond this legal minimum.

Pineau has a fresh, fruity character and aroma and its considerable sweetness is balanced by a relatively high alcohol content. The French prefer

Cognac: The Quality Factor

Cognac is a blend of reserves of varying ages and from different zones of production. On the whole, the greater the percentage of older reserves in the final blend, the finer and smoother the final product. The official laws set down the minimum age of the youngest Cognacs that can be utilized in each of the following categories.

★★★; **VS** Three-Star or Very Special designations indicate a good quality 'house' Cognac. The youngest brandies in the blend must have aged for at least 2½ years in oak but in practice, the average age of such a blend from the better houses will be about 4 to 5 years.

VSOP; VO; Réserve Very Superior Old Pale, Very Old or Reserve Cognacs have a minimum age for the youngest brandies contained in the blend of 4½ years. In practice, however, this is a high quality accolade, and thus many such Cognacs will often contain certain percentages of reserves that are 10, 15 or 20 years or more in age.

Napoléon The great Emperor has long been associated with Cognac, and the term 'Napoléon' has come to imply greater than normal age. However, the term on its own has no legal standing and should not be taken as a sole guarantee of quality.

XO; Vieille Réserve; Grande Réserve These terms may be applied to Cognacs of even older age: the exact ages of Cognacs contained in the final blends will vary from house to house, but many will have an average of at least 15 or 20 years, with percentages of even older reserves added for extra smoothness and character.

Fine Champagne Cognac can be designated 'Fine Champagne' if it contains Cognacs only from the Grande and Petite Champagne zones of production, with at least 50 per cent from the former.

it as an *apéritif*, but we think it is delicious as a dessert wine, served with the wonderful fruit — especially melons and strawberries — of the Charentes.

Vin de Pays Charentais

$\mathcal{S}$ince 1981, still white, red, and rosé table wines have been produced from grapes grown in the Cognac region. Such wines, conforming to certain standards and conditions, may be entitled to the classification Vin de Pays Charentais.

The obvious question must be asked: if for centuries previously the wines of the Charentes were poor, thin, and acid — wines which, it was said, only the people of the Charentes could stomach — why is it now possible to produce good quality table wines? The answer, quite simply — and the proof is to be found in the quality of the wines themselves — is that techniques in both viticulture and wine making have improved considerably in recent years. Commercial reasons dictated the necessity for the production of still wines, too, for the market for Cognac and Pineau has actually decreased in recent years and thus can no longer absorb the entire potential grape crop.

The majority of Vin de Pays Charentais is white, produced, like Cognac, mainly from the Ugni Blanc. But while the yield per hectare for the production of Cognac is not limited, it is for the production of Vin de Pays; this factor undoubtedly results in higher quality grapes with richer flavour and higher sugar levels. For the production of white wine, a long, slow fermentation at low temperatures preserves the inherent flavours and aroma of the fruit. Thus, a clean, fruity, and crisp wine is produced that is meant to be drunk young in the same year as its production. Still very inexpensive, it is an excellent accompaniment to the fine oysters and other shellfish which the Charente-Maritime yields. Some producers are making individual single *cépage* wines from the Sauvignon and Colombard grape varieties. Such rarities are well worth seeking and trying.

Le Blanc Marine

'Blanc Marine' is the collective trademark for white Vin de Pays Charentais. The visitor to the region is fortunate that the *vignerons* here have started producing this appetizing, fresh white wine, for neither Cognac nor Pineau des Charentes are appropriate partners to the feast of shellfish and especially *fines de claires* oysters for which this region is so famous. Today there are still only about 100 producers (most of whom also make Cognac and Pineau des Charentes) as well as ten *caves coopératives* for the production of 'Blanc Marine', but it is probable that this number will increase to meet the insatiable thirst of holidaymakers at La Rochelle, Royan, and elsewhere. The symbol of this uncomplicated holiday wine is a traditional cutter-rig fishing boat, while the name 'Blanc Marine' is a guarantee that the wines are quality Vin de Pays Charentais.

COGNAC

The red and rosé Vin de Pays Charentais come from those same grapes cultivated for the production of Pineau des Charentes rosé: Cabernet Franc, Cabernet Sauvignon, and Merlot. It is not mere coincidence that these are the classic Bordeaux varieties. The Bordeaux vineyard, after all, adjoins the vineyards of Cognac, on the north bank of the Gironde around Blaye and Bourg. These red table wines from the Charentes can sometimes compare favourably with the lesser wines of Bordeaux, both in terms of price and of quality.

Cognac

and the 'Route du Cognac'

In Brief   Every wine traveller passing anywhere near Cognac will wish to break his/her journey with a visit to this great capital of the grape which lives for and by its famous distillation. Those with more time to spare, as well as serious connoisseurs of Cognac, will also wish to spend time exploring the vineyards. Thus, we have also devised a suggested '*Route du Cognac*' which leads from Cognac to Jarnac, then strikes out into the heart of the finest vineyard region, Grande Champagne. This suggested route can be completed in a half or full day: those with only a few hours to spare may wish only to visit Jarnac and Segonzac.

COGNAC

The lover of Cognac anxious to discover this fascinating essence could do no better than simply follow his nose to the town of Cognac itself where the tell-tale aroma of evaporating alcohol, the fungus-blackened walls and tiled roofs of low-lying *chais* indicate the homes of the famous Cognac merchants, the *grandes maisons* known throughout the world. Jarnac, too, is a town which exhales Cognac through its very pores: the visitor wandering through the old streets by the river is apt to get intoxicated simply by breathing in the marzipany fumes which hang in the atmosphere like fine Irish mist.

Cognac today is a rather quiet inland town, spread out on both sides of the Charente river. While now mainly pleasure boats full of tourists chug up and down the slow waters, in the past this great avenue to the sea was a busy thoroughfare for trading barges loaded with wine, salt, and, from the seventeenth century, brandy.

It was the latter, of course, which made the town a household name throughout the world, and it is Cognac brandy itself which still dominates the town today. Not only is Cognac the home of a number of great and famous firms, furthermore, the industry has led to the development of important

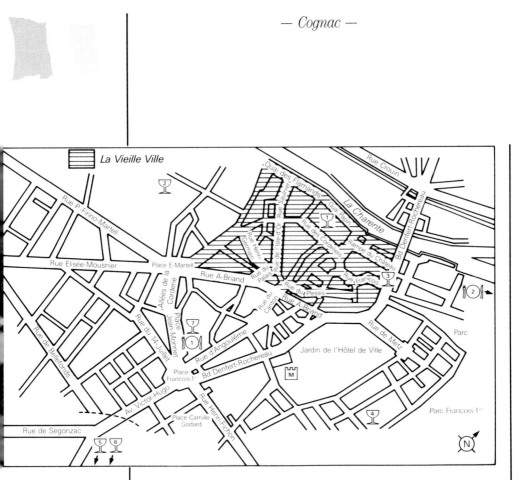

La Vieille Ville

Town of Cognac.

parallel trades. The St-Gobain glassworks, for example, is located just outside the town and is one of the largest and most modern of such factories in all of Europe. There are also two major *tonnelleries* (cooperages) here where the many thousands of oak barrels are made and repaired. Even great monuments from the past are linked today with that product which has brought such prosperity and fame to the town: the Château de Cognac, where Francois 1er was born in 1494, is now the home of the Cognac firm of Otard.

La Vieille Ville

Park along the *quai* for a walking tour of the *vieille ville*, the medieval quarter of Cognac. The Porte St-Jacques, built in 1499, is all that remains today of the town's ramparts but its twin, machiolated towers are still imposing. Pass through this entrance to the old town to arrive at the Fontaine François 1er at the back of the Château de Cognac; turn left and follow the château wall around to its entrance.

The earliest part of the château dates from the ninth century; it was undoubtedly a substantial fortress when Philip, son of Richard the Lionheart, married Amelia de Cognac, thus bringing the town under the dominion of the Dukes of Aquitaine. Over the course of the Hundred Years' War the château changed hands a number of times: the Black Prince, made it one of his favourite retreats from battle while later Bertrand du Guesclin, one of

COGNAC

France's most brilliant military leaders, recaptured it from the English in 1375. But it was under the Valois that Cognac, and its château, prospered; thus much of what remains dates from the fifteenth century. In 1795, Baron Otard, a Scotsman, followed King James II into exile, purchased the château and, like other self-imposed exiles such as Richard Hennessy and Jean Martell, immediately began to trade in Cognac. The Cognac House of Otard remains in the château today.

From the Château de Cognac, continue a walking tour of the old town, along and up rue François 1er, rue St-Caprais, and rue du Plessis, noticing the traditional Charentais houses with their faded painted shutters and old doors. The Hôtel de la Lieutenance, at the top of the rue Grande, is a particularly fine half-timbered building with some charming wood carvings on the support-beams. Turn right down the stone-paved rue Magdeleine to the place des Cordeliers, then left along the rue des Cordeliers. These grey and sombre buildings with blackened walls and roofs, the result of alcohol-hungry fungi which feed on the fumes, are the quiet back streets of an old, still-working town. They may not appear overly picturesque, but if you believe in the romance of grape juice being turned into an ethereal essence then you will appreciate breathing in the rarefied atmosphere.

The entrance to the Maison Hennessy is just off this road, on the rue de la Richonne. Founded by the Irish mercenary, Richard Hennessy, in 1765, Cognac Hennessy has today grown into one of the largest and most important of all Cognac firms. A visit to the ageing *chais* (Hennessy cellars house about 150,000 barrels) and fine cooperage museum is a must for all visitors.

From Hennessy, follow the rue de l'Isle d'Or, which leads up to the Église St-Léger, a beautiful twelfth-century Romanesque church. From here, carry on along the rue Aristide Briand to visit the *chais* of Martell, the oldest of the great Cognac firms, founded by Jean Martell, an expatriate from the Channel Islands, in 1715.

Fungus-blackened walls in the vieille ville *of Cognac.*

Musée du Cognac

Musée du Cognac
48, bd Denfert-Rochereau
16100 Cognac
tel: (45) 32 07 25
Hours: June–30 September daily except Tue 10–12h; 14–18h. October–31 May daily except Tue 14–17h30.
The basement of this municipal museum houses a fine and informative collection which explains the origins of the Cognac vineyard; viticulture and phylloxera; transformation of the wines of the Charentes into *eaux-de-vie*; methods of traditional distillation in the Charentais pot still; cooperage; the rise of the Cognac merchants; and bottles and labels. Other parts of the museum are devoted to prehistoric fossils and archaeology; domestic furniture; collections of ceramics; and a particularly fine bottle collection. Claude Boucher, a native

of Cognac, is credited with the invention of the modern glass-blowing bottle machine (previously all bottles had to be blown by hand).

Dégustation:

Stop to Visit; Stop to Taste; Stop to Buy

Cognac, like Reims and Épernay, is one of the best towns for the casual visitor, for its *grandes maisons* are well organized to receive visitors. The traditional ageing *chais* are shown, processes explained, and tasting or miniature bottles offered to all. Though there are usually opportunities to purchase, do ascertain if prices are better than in the *hypermarché* or 'duty free' shop.

Société Jas Hennessy & Co.
1, rue de la Richonne
16101 Cognac
tel: (45) 82 52 22
Hours: January–end of May and October–end of December Mon–Fri 8h30–11h; 1h45–16h30.
June–end of September Mon–Sat 8h30–17h.

By riverboat across the Charente to the ageing chais *of Hennessy.*

Richard Hennessy, an Irish soldier of fortune, settled in Cognac and in 1765 began shipping a few casks of the local brandy back to his native country; by the nineteenth century Hennessy Cognac was enjoyed as far away as South America and the Far East. Today the seventh generation of the family keeps a watchful eye over this vast empire: linked, since 1970, with the great Champagne firm of Moët & Chandon, Hennessy is an essential part of one of the most influential companies in France.

Visitors' tours begin in the small private museum with an introductory commentary by Peter Ustinov. Then they are taken across the river by boat to tour the vast ageing *chais*. Finally the bottling line is shown, as well as the fine Hennessy cooperage museum. No tasting but a miniature bottle is given to every visitor. Hennessy Cognacs can be purchased in the shop at reasonable prices.
English spoken.

Société Martell & Co.
BP 21
place Edouard Martell
16101 Cognac

COGNAC

tel: (45) 82 44 44
Hours: October–May Mon–Thur 8h30–11h; 14–17h. Fri 8h30–11h.
June and September Mon–Fri 8h30–11h; 14–17h. July and August Mon–Sat 8h30–11h; 14–17h.
Martell is the oldest of the *grandes maisons,* founded in 1715 by Jean Martell, who came to the town from his native Channel Islands. This vast company has considerable vineyard holdings in Grande and Petite Champagne, as well as elsewhere, but it still depends on growers under contract to supply the bulk of its enormous requirements of wine and brandy.

Visitors are shown the ageing *chais,* blending room, and bottling plant and there is also an audio-visual presentation. Afterwards, the tour concludes with a tasting and the opportunity to purchase the full range of Martell Cognacs. English spoken.

3

Cognac Otard SA
Château de Cognac
16100 Cognac
tel: (45) 82 40 00
Hours: 1 October–31 March Mon–Fri 10–17h.
1 April–30 September daily including Sun and holidays 9h30–17h30.
In July and August tours start every half hour.
The Château de Cognac is an important and historic landmark which should not be missed. Otard's enjoyable tour gives interesting information about the town of Cognac and the history of the Valois, as well as about the production of its Cognac brandies. Free tasting and opportunity to purchase.
English leaflet explains the commentary.

4

Camus 'La Grande Marque' SA
29, rue Marguerite de Navarre
16100 Cognac
tel: (45) 32 28 28
Hours: June–September Mon–Thur 14h15 and 15h45.
Out of season by appointment.
This family *maison* is proud of its independence and specializes in high-quality Cognac and Pineau des Charentes. In addition to the ageing warehouses, visitors are shown a private collection of Limoges porcelain and Baccarat crystal. Free tasting and the opportunity to purchase.
English spoken.

5

Cognac Prince Hubert de Polignac
Pavillon du Laubaret
RN 141
Gensac
16100 Cognac
tel: (45) 32 13 85
Hours: April–30 June 10–12h; 14h30–18h. July–15 September daily including

holidays 9–13h; 14–19h. Guided visits 10h; 11h; 14h, 15h; 16h; 17h.

There are 3,500 members of the *Union Coopérative de Viticulteurs Charentais*, the largest group of producers in the Cognac region. A visit to the Pavillon du Laubaret makes a most instructive contrast to the *grandes maisons*. In its modern ageing warehouses barrels are stacked in steel racks which can be moved by fork lift, a striking contrast to the traditional ageing *chais*. Cognac Prince Hubert de Polignac as well as a full range of Reynac Pineau des Charentes are produced and can be tasted and purchased.

English spoken.

6   Courvoisier SA
16200 Jarnac
tel: (45) 35 55 55
Hours: May–October Mon–Sat 9h30–11h30; 14–16h45. Other times by appointment.

In season, Courvoisier offers regular tours of its Cognac museum (the most notable exhibits are one of Napoléon's hats and a greatcoat, as well as a cross-section of the deep chalky soil of Grande Champagne). Visitors are shown an audio-visual 'globe' in an ageing warehouse. Miniature bottles and opportunity to purchase.

English spoken.

Cognac Shop

7   La Cognathèque
10, place Jean Monnet
16100 Cognac
tel: (45) 82 43 31

This centrally located shop has one of the best selections of a full gamut of Cognacs from the *grandes maisons* as well as small growers alike, together with a large selection of Pineau des Charentes.

'LA ROUTE DU COGNAC'

As already mentioned, there is no sign-posted wine road here, but our suggested route leads from Cognac through the Fins Bois vineyards to Jarnac, then into the heart of the Cognac vineyard, La Grande Champagne, with suggested stops at *propriétaires-récoltants* recommended by the *Bureau National Interprofessionnel Cognac*.

From the centre of Cognac, at place François 1er, turn on to rue Henri Fichon (sign-posted 'Camping') which leads over the Charente river. Find the D156 to Boutiers; immediately we are in the midst of the Cognac vineyard, the largest single delimited vineyard in Europe, with no fewer than 20,000 *viticulteurs* located throughout. Stop here to visit one of them: Jacques Brard-

COGNAC

Blanchard, whose hard-working industry is typical of the Charentais *propriétaire-récoltant* who must be grape grower, wine maker (wines for distillation as well as Vin de Pays Charentais), Cognac distiller, master blender for the production of Cognac as well as Pineau des Charentes, and sales agent (both wholesale to the Cognac merchants as well as to his own customers direct).

From Boutiers, the route continues through the Fins Bois vineyards via the D402 through silent little towns like St-Trojan, La Roche, and St-Brice, where there is a large private château. The Romanesque church beside it creates a curious impression of a fuedal hamlet that has changed little since medieval days. Follow signs to Bourg-Charente noticing the particularly rich, fertile brown earth of the Fins Bois vineyards.

After passing a golf course descend down to the river once more. The

'Route du Cognac'.

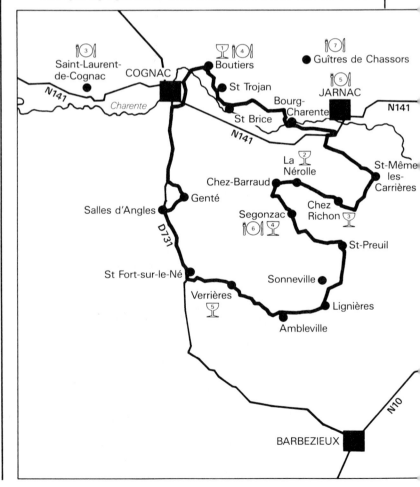

Coopers and Cognac

The simple oak barrel has been an important container for carrying liquid and dry ingredients for two millennia at least. However, for the ageing of Cognac as well as fine wines, its role is far more than merely that of a vessel. In the warehouses of the great Cognac firms, many thousands of barrels — all traditionally made by hand and containing millions of litres of Cognac — lie ageing. The barrels allow the Cognacs to breathe and in the process they gradually absorb the tannin of the wood, lose some of their initial raw fire and acquire in its place the characteristic colour, fine bouquet, and rounded flavours which make Cognac unique.

In the case of Cognac, only oak from the forests of the Limousin and the Tronçais is able to impart these desired characteristics. Thus, from mere planks of seasoned wood, the skilled *tonnelier* (cooper) must fashion a round, bulging and liquid-tight vessel. He uses about 30 staves to make each barrel, shaped and formed exactly by tools — planes, gimlets, and adzes — which have scarcely altered for centuries. Held in place with iron hoops, the hard wood is coaxed into shape by heating the barrel from within with an open fire, then gradually drawing together the bottom planks by tightening a rope. More iron hoops eventually ring the top of the barrel and the whole is made water-tight with strips of reed.

There are currently about 80 *tonneliers* employed in France, half of them in the Cognac region. Two large *tonnelleries* in Cognac give work to the majority of them. In summer, it may be possible to arrange a visit to one of these fascinating and ageless craft workshops through the Office du Tourisme. Also the Cooper's Museum at Maison Hennessy should not be missed.

Château de Bourg is a vast and impressive fortification, still privately owned. Cross over here to reach the little village of Bourg-Charente. This stretch is particularly pleasant and makes a good place to stop for a picnic and a riverside stroll (there is also a restaurant here). Next continue past Bourg's twelfth-century church and through the vineyards again to reach the town of Jarnac.

As you cross the river into this second capital of *eau-de-vie*, you cannot miss the grand riverside façade of Courvoisier, one of the great firms of Cognac. Napoléon I himself actually visited Courvoisier in 1811; today the company maintains this long-standing tradition of hospitality, offering visits and miniature bottles to all. However, the other great firms in Jarnac — Hine, Bisquit, Delemain, and others — are not organized to receive casual visitors. No matter: come to Jarnac anyway, simply to wander through the little *rues*, enjoying the heady aroma of evaporating alcohol. Come here, too, to visit the pleasant covered market to gather the ingredients for an excellent vineyard picnic: *rillettes de canard*, *grillons*, *pâtés*, cheeses, rustic country breads and Vin de Pays Charentais.

COGNAC

Once suitably provisioned, take the main N141 back towards Cognac, then find the D736 to Segonzac which leads soon into the vineyards of Grande Champagne. Now find the smaller D10 to St-Même-les-Carrières. Notice the immediate difference in soil compared with that across the river in the Fins Bois: here great pieces of white chalk are evident even amidst the loose, lighter topsoil. Drainage ditches beside the road reveal an even more profound substratum. It is this layer of chalk above all else which, as in Champagne, as in Chablis, as in Jerez de la Frontera, gives the wines (and in this case its subsequent distillations) such elegance, class, and finesse.

The terrain in Grande Champagne is hilly and open. As such it is a particularly pleasant vineyard region simply to meander through. There are numerous signs throughout for *dégustation* of growers' Cognacs and Pineaus: stop to taste and buy at any of them in addition to those whom we have listed. St-Même-les-Carrières, like virtually all the villages in the region, has its twelfth-century Saintonge Romanesque church. The town was inhabited long before this time, as a prehistoric dolmen testifies. Furthermore, the limestone quarries (*les carrières*) here have been exploited continuously since Gallo-Roman times.

Turn right on to the D90 towards St-Preuil. Even here, in the heart of the finest vineyards, fields of vines are interspersed with wheat. It is not simply a question of one parcel being better suited to vines than another, it is also a question of safeguarding one's livelihood. For after the devastation of phylloxera, when the wine growers lost everything, many of the vineyards were replanted with wheat. Even today *viticulteurs* are still wary about putting all their eggs in one basket.

The roads here are quite a maze, criss-crossing one another in a fashion that at times defies logic. Find the D95 to the little hamlet of Chez-Richon. M. Forgeron, a fine producer of Cognac and Pineau, is located on the right upon entering the town. His house is unmistakable, as grand and as white as the fabled chalky subsoil of Grande Champagne.

Continue on the D95 to the little commune of La Nérolle. Upon entering La Nérolle, one is immediately aware of the tell-tale black fungus, the sweet heady aroma of evaporating alcohol. Indeed, there is a large collective distillery for the *Coopérative Viticulteurs Réunis* located here: a building striking in its grim, functional façade. The last house in the village belongs to M. Seguinot, another fine *propriétaire-récoltant* where visitors are very welcome: the vineyards, distillery, and *chais* can be visited, while an audio-visual presentation is shown in the tasing room of the large, typical Charentais farmhouse.

From La Nérolle, follow the road on to Chez-Barraud, then turn left to Segonzac, capital of the Grande Champagne. There are numerous Cognac producers here as well as just outside this busy town including Cognac Frapin, which has the largest vineyard holding in Grande Champagne. In Segonzac, notice the curious domes on the corners of the twelfth-century Saintonge Romanesque church — they seem to us to resemble the shape of the *alambic Charentais*.

Leave Segonzac on the D1 in the direction of Barbezieux, the capital of Petite Champagne, then turn left on the little C7 to St-Preuil. The terrain is hillier now and less single-mindedly cultivated. St-Preuil itself is a pretty village. The vines carry on right up to the very edge of the church. The walls of the church appear blackened with the tell-tale fungus — could there be a pot still or barrels of old Cognac ageing inside this house of God?

Continue through this mixed agricultural terrain to Lignières Sonneville, then, via the D699 to Ambleville. From Ambleville, find the D44 to Verrières. Here M. Geffard (located down a lane to the left before entering the village) is always pleased to welcome visitors. On leaving the village, take the left fork to St-Fort-sur-le-Né, then return to Cognac on the D731 via Salles d'Angles and Genté.

Les Propriétaires-Récoltants

Within the designated Cognac region there are over 32,000 wine growers. Out of this vast number only about 3,000 distill their own wines into *eau-de-vie*. Most of them sell this raw young brandy to the *grandes maisons* but more and more are keeping some or all of it to age into Cognacs which they will eventually sell direct. Such Cognacs from *propriétaires-récoltants* rarely reach the consistent heights of the famous names simply because none could ever hold the enormous reserves which are the prerogative of the great firms: moreover the art of making Cognac, like Champagne, is one of marrying together disparate elements to create a whole that is more harmonious than any of its single components. None the less, growers' Cognacs which can be tasted and purchased direct are certainly not lacking in individuality and character; the best, from Grande Champagne, are capable of considerable finesse in their own right.

A visit to a *propriétaire-récoltant* provides a fascinating contrast to the great houses, as well as an essential insight into the make-up of the Cognac industry. The Charentais farmhouses may seem somewhat severe, built behind large walls and arranged around a central *coeur*, but be assured, the welcome you will receive, the Cognacs and Pineaus which will be offered for tasting, are most generous.

Dégustation: Stop to Taste; Stop to Buy

Jacques Brard-Blanchard
Chemin de Routreau
Boutiers
16100 Cognac
tel: (45) 32 19 58

Hours: working hours on weekdays and by appointment on weekends.
The Brard-Blanchards have recently installed a new *alambic Charentais* which they fire with wood gathered from the farm. Most of the Cognac goes into the production of their fine Pineau des Charentes. In addition to Cognac and Pineau, the Brard-Blanchards also produce Vin de Pays Charentais, *vin mousseux*, and pure grape juice, all from grapes which have been grown organically (*culture biologique* — see p.239).
A little English spoken.

2 Gerard Seguinot
La Nérolle
16130 Segonzac
tel: (45) 83 41 73
Hours: Mon–Fri 9–12h; 14–17h. Telephone call in advance preferred.
Gerard Seguinot is well organized to receive visitors. The vineyards lie literally right behind the house; grapes are pressed and the wine made in the well-equipped winery; and in an adjoining room, the shining *alambic Charentais* stands ready for the transformation of wine into *eau-de-vie*. In another warehouse, both young and reserve Cognacs lie ageing in oak barrels. These are blended in small quantities, and bottled and labelled on a hand machine. A true artisanal product. Audio-visual programme and tasting and purchase of Cognac and Pineau des Charentes.
English spoken.

3 Michel Forgeron
Chez Richon
16130 Segonzac
tel: (45) 83 43 05
Hours: Daily, working hours. Telephone call preferred but not essential.
Monsieur Forgeron is most happy to receive individual visitors and shows them the press house, *alambic Charentais*, ageing *chai*, and vineyards. He is interested in explaining not only the process of making Grande Fine Champagne Cognac but also the history and traditions of the region. The visit lasts about 1½ hours and ends with a *dégustation* of Cognac and Pineau. There is the possibility of purchase, but M. Forgeron says, *'sans obligation'*.
English spoken.

4 Cognac Frapin
rue Pierre Frapin
16130 Segonzac
tel: (45) 83 40 03
Hours: Mon–Fri 8–12h; 14–17h. Appointment preferred.
In the past, the Frapin family's Cognac from its 137-hectare vineyard holdings was sold almost entirely to the *grandes maisons* to be used in their blends. Now they are blending and bottling their own range of 'estate' Cognacs, including the distinctive single-vineyard Château de Fontpinot. Cognacs are offered for

tasting and purchase.
English spoken.

5   Henri Geffard
La Chambre
Verrières
16130 Segonzac
tel: (45) 83 74 90
Hours: Daily without appointment.
This lovely isolated farmhouse in the Grande Champagne offers guided visits
by the *viticulteur* himself. Visitors can see the vineyards, winery, distillery,
and ageing warehouse. In addition to Cognac, M. Geffard produces Pineau
des Charentes, sparkling wine by the *méthode champenoise*, and *chocolats
au Pineau*. All the products can be tasted and purchased.

Other producers not on the suggested *'Route du Cognac'*

Château de Didonne
Semussac
17120 Cozes
tel: (46) 05 05 91
Hours: Daily 9–10h; 14–18h. July and August 8–20h.
The present-day Château de Didonne was built from the ruins of the fortified
château of St-Georges-de-Didonne. From 1930 to 1960 it was run as a model
agricultural village that was totally self-sufficient. Today the 41-hectare domaine
is owned by coopérative *viticulteurs* from the surrounding communes of Cozes,
Saujon, and Royan; it serves as a centre for the documentation of nineteenth-
century agricultural life as well as the marketing operation for their products:
Pineau des Charentes, Cognac, and Vin de Pays Charentais. There is a
permanent wine museum and a restaurant open in summer. The Château
de Didonne is convenient for holidaymakers at Royan or Marennes or for those
crossing to or from the Mèdoc.

Coopérative Vinicole de l'Ile de Ré
17580 Le Bois Plage en Ré
tel: (46) 09 23 09
Hours: July and August 10h30 and 15h30. Other times by appointment.
It may seem surprising that the delimited Cognac vineyard extends even on
to off-shore islands such as the Ile de Ré. Holidaymakers to this popular and
pretty *île* should come here to purchase their Vin de Pays Charentais direct,
as well as to view a traditional Charentais distillery where Cognac and Pineau
des Charentes are also produced.
English spoken.

Robert Hauselmann & Fils
Société Civile Agricole Domaine de la Chauvillière
Sablonceaux
17600 Saujon
tel: (46) 94 70 17
Hours: Working hours for tasting and direct sales.
Robert Hauselmann is a traditional Charentais *viticulteur* who, in addition
to growing grapes for the production of Cognac and Pineau des Charentes,
has increasingly concentrated on the production of fine table wines that bear
the designation Vin de Pays Charentais 'Blanc Marine'. As well as the traditional
Cognac *cépage* Ugni Blanc, he also produces a varietal Chardonnay wine.
English spoken.

Durand Père & Fils
Le Maine Giraud
16250 Blanzac
tel: (45) 64 04 49
Hours: Daily 9–12h; 14–19h.
Cognac, Pineau des Charentes, and Vin de Pays Charentais are produced in
the domaine which was the home of the poet Alfred de Vigny from 1797 to 1863.
A local museum traces his life.

Regional Gastronomy

The Charentes, extending south from La Rochelle to the northern banks of
the Gironde, east from the Atlantic into the centre of France, is a vast and
rich bread basket yielding a wealth of fine foodstuffs. Yet, like all basically
agricultural lands with no great urban base, the *cuisine* here remains simple,
almost rustic, utilizing the bounties of sea, river, and land in ways which have
not changed over the generations.

For visitors as well as locals, seafood dominates above all else: even in
little towns far inland, there is always a van from Marennes which brings the
freshest and finest *huîtres* — oysters — to market. There is always also a
poissonnerie with iced marble slabs displaying a full array of Atlantic fish.
A typical Charentais lunchtime preparation is *chaudrée*: a magnificent stewy
cauldron containing all the local catch of that day simmered in white wine
and plenty of good sweet butter. Little flat fish such as *plie* are delicious
simply coated in flour and pan-fried. During the lengthy July-to-August
vacances the Charentais might head to the beach, the highlight of the day
being the construction and consumption of an *eclade*: first a mountain of
mussels is collected, then they are pressed into a mound of sand point up,
covered with kindling, pine needles and leaves, and finally the whole lot is
set on fire. (Given sufficient notice this unique speciality can be enjoyed at
the Oyster Museum at La Cayenne near Marennes.)

In the marshlands known as the Marais Poitevin, eels are a particular local favourite, cooked in a stew known as *matelote d'anguilles à la Charentaise*. On the surrounding salt pastures of these same marshlands *pre-salé* lamb is raised, prized for its exquisite delicate, almost iodiney flavour. Elsewhere, great tracts of wheat have replaced former vineyards, together with large waving fields of green pastureland. The Charentes is now considered by many to be the foremost butter-producing region in France, surpassing even Normandy: the peculiar Gallic passion for classification has resulted in the granting of three '*grands crus*' butter *appellations*: Charente, Charentes-Poitou, and Deux-Sèvres.

uîtres — oysters — for a classic icnic in the Charentes.

A Charentais style of cooking has emerged which combines this rich sweet butter with the great product of the local vineyard, here and in fine

Le Pique-Nique

Huîtres The first thing any visitor to the Charentes should buy is an oyster knife: then these marvellous bi-valves can be enjoyed by the dozen for picnic breakfast, lunch, or dinner (or all three). *Fines de claires* and *spéciales de claires* are the finest (see below). Though they can be eaten throughout the year, in summer months oysters tend to be somewhat milky and lose a little of that sea-fresh tang which is so exhilarating. The Charentais like to accompany their oysters with hot *saucisses au vin blanc*: first eat an oyster, then take a morsel of buttered bread, then a bite of hot sausage, and finally a swallow of Vin de Pays Charentais. The combination is an incredible sensory experience.

Jambon du pays Local ham, cured in Cognac and spices: delicious.

Grillons Similar to the *rillons* of Tours but less fatty and with more meat, cooked until caramelized and crunchy.

Torteau fromage Round cake made with fresh goats' cheese, baked in a very hot oven until the crust turns jet-black.

Chabichou Small creamy-white goats' cheese found throughout the region. Most of the cheese from the Charentes is goats', and comes in a variety of shapes: round, cylinder, or pyramid.

Pigouille True *pigouille* is made from goats' milk, but cow and ewe versions of this creamy cheese are also sometimes encountered.

Petit Semussac *Fromage blanc* from near Royan.

COGNAC

and flamboyant restaurants everywhere: everything from *tournedos* to kidneys to *crêpes* are sautéed or cooked in butter then flambéed in Cognac. Cognac is also used less ostentatiously to macerate and flavour ingredients and casseroles. Local hams are even cured in Cognac.

Life is slow and quiet in the Charentes: so slow that the Charentais themselves are affectionately known as *cagouillardes*, after the snails (*petis gris*) which used to munch their way through the vineyards with such slow but effective thoroughness. Indeed, this gastropod remains a favourite here, cooked *à la Charentaise*, that is in a casserole together with pork, shallots, garlic, and white wine.

The Charentes, of course, is the home of one of the sweetest, most perfumed and delicious of all melons: indeed there is no better finish to a meal than a whole Charentais melon, with the seeds scooped out and the interior filled with a generous measure of Pineau des Charentes. Other fine local fruits — cherries, plums, apricots, strawberries — are macerated in Cognac and sold in bottles: potent and delicious.

Cognac — in spite of the Bureau National's attempt to wean younger generations on to the concept of using it for cocktails — remains the foremost after-dinner drink in the region itself as well as throughout the world.

Restaurants (Maps pp.205 and 210)

Restaurant Le Terroir
12, rue des Remparts
16100 Cognac
tel: (45) 82 22 94
Closed Sun and Mon.
This good local restaurant is centrally located just off the place Francois 1er. Regional specialities include *petis gris à la Charentaise* (local snails), *huîtres farcies à la Marennaise, cassolette de St-Jacques*. Good selection of Vins de Pays Charentais.
Inexpensive to Moderate

La Courtine
parc François 1er
16100 Cognac
tel: (45) 82 07 93
Closed Mon.
Lovely position in the park alongside the river. In summer, local and classic dishes are served outdoors on a terrace. Recommended by Cognac Camus.
Moderate

Le Logis de Beaulieu
Saint-Laurent de Cognac
16100 Cognac
tel: (45) 82 30 50

Les Huîtres

One of the glories of the French table — and to us one of the quintessential experiences of being in France — is a plate of a dozen *huîtres* accompanied by no more than a basket of bread and a bottle of ice-cold wine. The oysters, tinged with green on their shimmering half-shell, smell of iodine, salt, and clean, fresh goodness: their sensuous flavour is the very concentrated essence of the sea.

Like wine regions, oyster regions are more than a little special. Here, not more than an hour's leisurely drive from Cognac itself (actually within the designated Cognac vineyard region) lies an area of rare beauty and unspoiled tranquillity: the Bassin de Marennes. Some 60 per cent of all oysters consumed in France come from here; the very best, the *fines de claires* and *spéciales de claires*, gain their renowned green colour and intense flavour from finishing in ancient salt marshes known as *claires* which extend like a complex patchwork on either side of the Seudre estuary from the central town of Marennes.

Come to Marennes to wander along quiet and tiny lanes, to enjoy the splendid isolated atmosphere of an area which is a designated wildfowl reserve, to meet producers and purchase from them direct, and to visit this little family-run museum at La Cayenne. The Sonnette family are one of only two who live permanently on this isolated spit of land and their well-presented display explains the whole process of *l'élevage des huîtres*. You can enjoy their *fines de claires* on the spot while actually overlooking the

The Bassin de Marennes.

claires, together with a sharp, refreshing bottle (or several) of Vin de Pays Charentais.

Musée Artisanal Ostreicole
rte du Port
La Cayenne
17320 Marennes
tel: (46) 85 01 06
Open 1 April–30 September daily from 8h.

Closed December 23–31.

This lovely Charentais house located 5 km (3 miles) outside Cognac in the midst of the vineyards (just off the N141 to Saintes) is a most pleasant hotel-restaurant. *Mouclade, escargots, melon au Pineau des Charentes*, and a fabulous collection of old and rare Cognacs.
Moderate

4

Auberge de Châtenay
rte de Ste-Sévère
Boutiers
16100 Cognac
tel: (45) 32 41 40
Closed Mon.
On the banks of the Charente, this little *auberge* serves traditional specialities such as *cagouilles farcies* and *noix de St-Jacques au Pineau*. Recommended by Jacques Brard-Blanchard.
Inexpensive

5

Restaurant du Château
15, place du Château
16200 Jarnac
tel: (45) 81 07 17
Closed Sat lunch; Sun eve; Mon.
On the main square in Jarnac opposite Courvoisier Cognac, this fine little restaurant specializes in Charentes seafood: *huîtres, saumon, soupe au poisson, cassolette des fruits de mers*. Recommended by Courvoisier.
Inexpensive to Moderate

6

La Cagouillarde
rue Gaston Briand
16130 Segonzac
tel: (45) 83 40 51
Closed Sat lunch; Sun eve.
This charming little *bistro* serves *cagouilles* (of course!) and *grillades au feu de bois*. Recommended by Gerard Seguinot.
Inexpensive to Moderate

Le Terminus
rte du Port
17560 Bourcefranc-le-Chapus
tel: (46) 85 02 42
Closed October; Mon out of season.
Near Marennes, this very simple, unpretentious waterfront restaurant overlooks the Ile d'Oléron and serves local shellfish, fish, and oysters from the surrounding *claires*.
Inexpensive

Table d'Hôte

7

Guy et Paulette Duquerroy
Domaine de la Cadois
Guîtres de Chassors
16200 Jarnac
tel: (45) 81 07 07
Lovely simple old Charentais farmhouse in the heart of the wine country.
Madame Duquerroy's *civet de lapin* is legendary.
Telephone in advance for rooms or meals.

Wine Festivals

End of July	Fête Ostreicole	Port de la Cayenne
Mid-July	Fête du Vin de Pays Charentais	Gemozac
24 August	Foire aux Melons	St-Georges-des-Coteaux
11–20 September	Foire Exposition de Cognac	Cognac
3–4 October	Fête de la Vendange	Cognac

Additional Information

Et pour en savoir plus . . .

Office du Tourisme
16, rue du XIV Juillet
16100 Cognac
tel: (45) 82 10 71

Bureau National Interprofessionnel du Cognac
3, allées de la Corderie
16101 Cognac
tel: (45) 82 66 70

Comité National du Pineau des Charentes
112, ave Victor-Hugo
16100 Cognac
tel: (45) 32 09 27

COGNAC

DORDOGNE
and GASCONY

Introduction

Saturday market at Sarlat.

*T*he hinterland of Bordeaux, extending inland in a wedge greater than that formed by the diverging Dordogne and Garonne rivers, encompasses a vast area of splendid natural beauty, rich in history, prehistory, and gastronomy. The Dordogne and Lot valleys, their rugged slopes covered with vines, heavy forest, or topped with rocky eyries on which cling the remains of medieval castles, resemble not so much the manicured tedium of the Médoc as a scene from Germany's romantic Rhineland. Further south, the unspoiled countryside of Gascony, with its numerous fortified *bastides*, still appears to be the land from which hailed Dumas's musketeer d'Artagnan, still *is* the land which gives the world a spirit at once full of fire yet exceedingly smooth, Armagnac.

From the fertile plains of Aquitaine across to the edge of the great Massif Central, we pass through three ancient regions: Périgord, Quercy, and Gascony. A full range of wines and spirits comes from varied vineyards, including rich meaty reds; fragrant dry whites; unctuous sweet whites; everyday reds and rosés; as well as Armagnac, one of only two brandies entitled to its own *appellation d'origine contrôlée*, and Floc d'Armagnac, a *mistelle* made from mixing unfermented grape juice with young Armagnac. These lands form an essential part of the backbone of rural France and visitors here find that food, as a matter of course, is also overwhelmingly generous: rich truffle-perfumed *foie gras*, *confits de canard*, stews simmered with *cèpes*, coarse country *pâtés*, and much else.

The vineyards of the Dordogne, on the southern edge of Périgord, are actually contiguous with those of Bordeaux, continuing from St-Emilion and Castillon-la-Bataille up the river valley to Bergerac and beyond. Indeed, it is the proximity to the great Bordeaux vineyard which caused the wines of Bergerac to suffer in the past, for as long ago as the thirteenth century, restrictions were placed on the transport of wines from Bergerac down to

Libourne and the Gironde. It was not until 1520, following the defeat of the English in the Hundred Years' War, that François 1er, King of France, authorized the free movement of wines along the Dordogne at all times of the year. The quayside at Bergerac, once lined with hundreds of barrels waiting to be loaded on to flat-bottomed river barges, today is a car park, but this fascinating old town is still an atmospheric and worthy centre for the region.

While vineyards are concentrated on both sides of the river around Bergerac, as well as further to the west in the direction of Bordeaux, the Dordogne valley is possibly even more majestic to the east. Here are charming medieval towns such as Sarlat, with its lively Saturday market; centres of prehistory at Les Eyzies (home of Cro-Magnon man) and Lascaux; and important strategic fortresses like Rocamadour, which stands some 500 ft above the sheer wall of the Alzou canyon. Here, too, are simple relaxing villages, peaceful river scenery, unpretentious restaurants and family hotels: no wonder the region is as popular as it is.

If the charms of the Dordogne are well known — and rightly so — those of the valley of the Lot, to the south, remain a far better kept secret. Indeed, the scenery here is even wilder, grander, still more remote. The Lot river follows a winding and tortuous course, as it flows from its source high in the Cevennes massif to empty into the Garonne north of Agen. East of Cahors, sheer cliffs of limestone rise from the very edge of the water, while the views of the valley from hill towns such as St-Cirq-Lapopie are quite breathtaking. To the west, from Cahors to the Château de Bonaguil, the ancient border between Périgord and Quercy, lie the vineyards of Cahors, which have been cultivated for at least 2,000 years.

Orientation

The Dordogne is considered the hinterland of Bordeaux and, indeed, its vineyards are but a continuation of the vineyards of St-Emilion and the Côtes de Castillon. From Bordeaux, take the N89 to Libourne, then follow the Dordogne river valley via the D936 to Bergerac, centre of the Dordogne wine trade. From Paris, the region is reached either by the A10 *autoroute* to Bordeaux, or by following the secondary N20 via Orléans and Limoges. At Limoges, either take the N21 to Bergerac via Périgueux, or, if travelling to the Lot valley, continue on to Cahors. Gascony is reached by following the N21 from Bergerac to Agen, then finding the smaller D931 to Condom.

The principal train route for the region is the main Paris–Toulouse line. Cahors is actually located on this main line, but it is necessary to change at Limoges for Bergerac. Condom, Eauze, and Auch are best reached via local connections at Montauban and Agen. The most convenient international airports are Bordeaux Merignac and Toulouse Blagnac.

Michelin Maps 75, 79, 82

It is hot and parched here in summer, and there is the unmistakable anticipation of the approach to the south of France. Move down a river valley or two into Gascony and that transition has been completed: in little towns such as Condom young and old seem happy to lounge all day at the outdoor tables which line the streets.

Gascony remains a land primarily of small farmers and farming communities; even Auch, its capital, retains the charm of a large provincial town. Herein lies the region's everlasting appeal. Bordered by the Pyrénées to the south, equidistant from the Atlantic and the Mediterranean, it remains an ancient land in splendid isolation: rich, self-content, and with one of the best regional tables in all of France.

Throughout these hinterlands, on or off the tourist track, meandering through vineyards or exploring old towns, the lover of fine countryside, good, honest country wines, pungent Armagnacs purchased direct from the farm, and good eating and living, can scarcely make a wrong turn.

The Wines and Armagnacs of the Dordogne and Gascony

The Wines of Bergerac

Bergerac AOC; Bergerac Rosé AOC; Bergerac Sec AOC

*T*he broadest *appellation* encompasses wines from 93 communes throughout the Bergerac vineyard. Red Bergerac, produced from Merlot, Cabernet Sauvignon, Cabernet Franc, and Malbec (also known as Cot or Auxerrois) must have a minimum alcohol content of 10°; on the whole it is a soft, supple wine vinified to be drunk young. Bergerac Sec is the *appellation* for dry white wines produced mainly from the Sémillon, Sauvignon, and Muscadelle grapes. The Sauvignon grape in particular makes attractive, crisp wines with that varietal's characteristic pungent, grass-fresh aroma. Improved wine-making technique, especially slow fermentation at low temperatures, has resulted in white wines with fruitier and fresher aromas. Bergerac Rosé is made in small quantities only.

Côtes de Bergerac AOC; Côtes de Bergerac Moelleux AOC; Côtes de Bergerac–Côtes de Saussignac AOC

*T*he Côtes de Bergerac *appellation* applies to red wines made from the Bergerac vineyard with a minimum alcohol content of 11°. The wines are, therefore, more full-bodied, vigorous, and robust than straight Bergerac and often improve with a little bottle age. Côtes de Bergerac Moelleux is the *appellation* for traditional sweet white Bergerac which formerly made up the bulk of the white wine production before popular taste changed primarily to drier wines. The vineyards of the Côtes de Saussignac extend around that small town west of the Monbazillac vineyard. Sweet wines are produced from the traditional varieties Sémillon, Sauvignon, and Muscadelle and are

The central square at Fourcès.

Bastides

One of the outstanding features of the Périgord, Quercy, and Gascony countryside are the feudal *bastides*, unique villages built to virtually identical plans in the thirteenth century by both the French and the English. Reflections of ordered medieval urban planning, the *bastides* brought the people from the countryside into towns or villages that were based on a regular plan, usually a rectangular grid extending in right angles from a central square surrounded by covered arcades. Life under the feudal system in the *bastides* ensured that the inhabitants were guaranteed protection as well as certain other rights. At the outbreak of the Hundred Years' War, many *bastides*, already built in strategic positions on rivers or hilltops, took on a further militaristic aspect when they were fortified with town walls and moats but this was not sufficient to stop many of them changing hands back and forth in the course of that long struggle.

Some *bastides* in or near the wine regions worth visiting include: Ste-Foy-la-Grande, Lalinde, and Beaumont (Dordogne); Villeneuve-sur-Lot (Quercy); Labastide d'Armagnac, Fourcès, and Montréal (Gascony).

lighter in body than their more famous neighbour but they can be fragrant and delicious, particularly with *pâtisseries* and fruits.

Monbazillac AOC

*I*n the Middle Ages, the vineyards of Bergerac lay mainly on the north side of the river, but planting by monks on southern slopes led to the discovery that a combination of heavy morning mist combined with warm autumn afternoons encouraged the formation of *Botrytis cinerea*, the 'noble rot' which concentrates grape sugars, aromas and flavours to make the finest, honeyed sweet wines (see p.53). Monbazillac is, without doubt, one of the great *vin liquoreux* of France. In the best years, as elsewhere, it is essential that the vineyard is harvested several times to ensure that only the ripest, virtually raisin-like, grapes are collected: this results in a minute yield of concentrated, honeyed wine with an alcohol content of at least 12°. Monbazillac improves with age; the best gains a deep amber colour after 3 or 4 years and will continue to develop for up to 30 years or more.

Montravel AOC;
Côtes de Montravel AOC;
Haut Montravel AOC

*T*he vineyards of Montravel are virtual extensions of those of the Bordeaux vineyards of the Côtes de Castillon. In the past, however, the land-owners of Montravel owed obeisance to the feudal seigneurs of Bergerac, and thus the wines came under their jurisdiction. Dry, *demi-sec*, and sweet white wines come from this gentle hill country where Montaigne was born in 1533. The Côtes de Montravel and Haut Montravel *appellations* apply to sweet whites from select communes in the hillsides above the flatter plains of the Dordogne, produced from Sémillon, Sauvignon, and Muscadelle. The dry Montravels, which can benefit from the addition of up to 25 per cent Ugni Blanc, are fresh, fruity, and crisp. They are bottled within 3 months of the vintage and should be drunk young. The sweet wines are bottled after 1 to 1½ years and may improve with some bottle age.

Pécharmant AOC

*P*écharmant is the finest red wine of the Périgord, produced from a small vineyard which extends mainly to the east and north of Bergerac. The traditional Bordeaux grape varieties are cultivated here, but a higher proportion of Malbec adds particular richness and backbone to the blend. The soil is a mixture of sand, gravel, and granite washed down from the Massif Central: this harsh terrain produces wines which are considerably deeper, richer, and harder than those bearing the straight Bergerac *appellation*. Pécharmant is best after 3 or 4 years of bottle age.

Rosette AOC

*T*his sweet white wine used to come from the same vineyards near Bergerac that produce Pécharmant but today the production is minimal.

Côtes de Duras AOC

*N*ot part of the Bergerac vineyard, but located south of the Dordogne adjacent to the Bordeaux vineyard of Entre-Deux-Mers. Dry white wines, primarily from the Sauvignon, are produced together with red, mainly from Cabernet Sauvignon and Merlot. The reds can be either light and fruity when vinified in part by *macération carbonique*, or else vinified traditionally to be fuller-bodied and longer-lived.

Côtes du Marmandais VDQS

*T*he hilly countryside to the north and south of the Garonne around the town of Marmande beyond the Bordeaux vineyards of Entre-Deux-Mers and Graves make up the Vin Délimité Qualité Supérieur region known as Côtes du Marmandais. These fruity reds and dry whites are little known and therefore good value.

Vin de Pays de la Dordogne

*L*ight reds, dry whites and rosé table wines.

The Wines of Cahors and the Lot

Cahors AOC

*T*he Lot valley is one of the most ancient vineyards in France, and indeed the wines of Cahors have been celebrated since Roman days at least. François 1er was an advocate of the wine of Cahors, while the Tsar Peter the Great also preferred it above all others (and even named a Russian vineyard after Cahors: Caorskoie, near Azerbaidjan). In common with other wines from the inland *haut pays*, however, Cahors suffered from restrictions placed upon its transport by the merchants of Bordeaux, anxious to protect their local interests. In spite of this, Cahors has long been drunk and appreciated for its robust and immense flavour and colour that is little short of black when young.

The main grape variety here is the Malbec (known locally as the Auxerrois) and it must account for at least 70 per cent of the total, the remaining blend being made up of the softer Merlot, as well as the Tannat and Jurançon Noir. In spite of its harsh and daunting robe, not all Cahors needs great bottle age to mellow and develop. Wines from the river-valley vineyards mature more quickly than those from the limestone plateaux to the north. It is also a question of vinification: wines vinified traditionally, with lengthy maceration to extract full colour and tannin, can be laid down to improve for upwards of 15 years. Cahors must have a minimum of 10.5° alcohol.

This robust heavyweight red is one of the finest country wines of the south-west and it is a superb accompaniment to the rich *confits*, *cassoulets*, duck and goose liver of the region. For a classic, it is still remarkably inexpensive.

Côtes de Buzet AOC

*T*he Lot river empties into the greater Garonne at Aiguillon, north-west of Agen. Along the left bank of the Garonne lie the vineyards of the Côtes de Buzet, producing primarily red wine from the classic Bordeaux varieties: Cabernet Sauvignon, Cabernet Franc, and Merlot. A high proportion of the wine is produced by the excellent and well-regarded *cave coopérative* at Buzet-sur-Baïse.

Vin de Pays Coteaux de Quercy

*R*ed and rosé table wines from vineyards on the Lot around and south of Cahors.

Vin de Pays de l'Agenais

*S*ubstantial red table wine from Thezac-Perricard known also as 'Vin du Tsar' since it was reputedly enjoyed by Nicholas II.

Gascony: Armagnac, Floc d'Armagnac and Table Wines

Armagnac AOC

*A*rmagnac, the world's second *appellation d'origine contrôlée* brandy, may still be far less well known than its famous brother Cognac, but its history extends back even further, for Armagnac has been distilled in the rugged Gascony countryside since at least the fifteenth century. However, while Cognac profited from a ready *entrée* into the English market through the port of La Rochelle and by way of the expatriate English and Irish merchants who settled in that famous brandy town along the Charente, the geography of inland Gascony kept Armagnac a relatively well-kept secret to the rest of the world until only recently. Furthermore, the structure of the industry here, unlike Cognac with its numerous and great merchant houses, is primarily one of small farmers who traditionally have produced only enough brandy for their own consumption as well as a little surplus to sell locally and to passers-by. Even today some nine bottles of Cognac are drunk to every one of Armagnac.

But Armagnac is different, very different, from Cognac and should be viewed as such. The principle grape varieties cultivated are basically the same, St-Emilion (Ugni Blanc), Colombard, and Folle Blanche, with the further small

A farmhouse alambic Armagnaçais *still in use today.*

An old alambic ambulante *which used to travel from farm to farm today displayed at the House of Janneau.*

additions of Picquepoul, Jurançon, Blanquette, Baco, and others, but the climate is more continental in Gascony, resulting in grapes that are riper and more richly flavoured. The terrain, extending throughout the *département* of the Gers and into parts of the Lot-et-Garonne and Landes, is made up of three sub-regions of production: Bas-Armagnac, considered the finest area, extending mainly to the west and south of Eauze; Ténarèze, which has the town of Condom as its centre; and Haut-Armagnac, the largest superficial area but the least important and smallest under vines.

The earthy wines which these vineyards yield are fermented only for a few weeks before being distilled on the lees in the traditional *alambic Armagnaçais*. In the past, itinerant distillers travelled through the countryside from farm to farm, trailing with them their horse-drawn Armagnac stills, wonderful Heath Robinson contraptions which, one imagines, were fired up and given a good strong kick and an oath or a curse to coax a dribble of young pungent brandy out of a quantity of cloudy, coarse, almost undrinkable, wine. Today there are still some 20 or so travelling stills which go from farm to farm, though they are a little more modern, if less picturesque, carried on the backs of big lorries. Many farmers have their own stills, while others send their wines away to be transformed into *eau-de-vie* by large collective distilleries.

The traditional Armagnac still differs considerably from the *alambic Charentais* or pot still which by law must be used in Cognac. The former works by a continuous process, that is to say, it must not be cleaned and recharged after each batch as is the case with the pot still. The wine instead flows continuously from vat to still through an ingenious design by which the incoming wine acts as a cooling agent, causing the rising alcoholic vapours to condense. The vapour furthermore absorbs some of the characteristics and flavouring elements of the incoming wine, while the wine itself is heated up in the process, until it too vaporizes. This vapour, condensed by more incoming wine, results in a spirit which has retained more of the individual and original character of the wine itself.

As is the case with Cognac (and other fine spirits such as malt whisky), the young, raw, colourless brandy needs to be aged in wood to mellow, acquire its dark amber colour and unique aromas. Here, traditionally, casks made from the black, sappy oak from the forest of Monlezun have been used for the ageing of Armagnac, and this wood lends a special earthy character which is distinct. But one only has to drive through this once densely forested area of the Bas-Armagnac to realize that the woodlands have been severely depleted over the years and can no longer supply the demands of the entire region; producers are thus having to turn elsewhere for a source of oak. Will this eventually alter the special character of Armagnac?

Armagnac, like Cognac, is usually a blend of many brandies from different years, and there are legal minimums which apply to the youngest in the blend: thus, a bottle labelled ★★★ must consist of Armagnacs which have all aged for a minimum of 1 year in wood; VO, VSOP or Réserve must have a minimum age of at least 4 years; Extra, Napoléon, XO or Vieille Réserve must contain only Armagnacs which have spent at least 5 years in wood. Many of the larger firms use brandies in their blends which are considerably older than these legal minimums as well as brandies from the three different vineyard regions.

Much Armagnac on the market today, however, is produced and sold by the growers themselves, so there is consequently a great range of individual styles and qualities. Furthermore, many *propriétaires-récoltants* age, bottle, and sometimes sell single-year vintage Armagnacs: it is not uncommon for Armagnacs that are 30 or 40 years old, or even older, to be unearthed from the depths of cellars. They are rare and wonderful essences indeed.

Armagnac is often described as coarse and rustic, a sort of uncouth country cousin to elegant Fine Champagne Cognac. This does neither spirit justice for they are both unique. Armagnac undoubtedly has a character that is more pungent and full of flavour though it does lack that certain nervous energy of great Cognac; but both at their best are exceedingly smooth and fine.

Floc de Gascogne AOC

Floc de Gascogne is to Armagnac what Pineau des Charentes is to Cognac: a sweet *mistelle* made by mixing pure unfermented grape juice with young local *eau-de-vie*. This beverage has been made and enjoyed locally for centuries but it was only in 1977 that the *vignerons* decided to begin producing and selling Floc on a commercial scale. Both red and white Floc is produced from the same grapes permitted for the production of Armagnac. Ripe, pure fruit juice has its fermentation muted by the addition of young Armagnac, bringing the total alcohol content up to 16°–18°. The Floc is then aged in wood for between 2 and 3 years. Floc is best drunk well-chilled as an *apéritif*, or, some say, with foie gras or desserts such as the exquisite *croustade*.

Madiran AOC

In the far south of the Armagnac vineyard, there is an overlap with the vineyard of Madiran, which extends beyond the *département* of the Gers into the Hautes-Pyrénées and Pyrénées-Atlantiques. This fine, rich red wine, produced mainly from the Tannat grape, with Cabernet Sauvignon and Cabernet Franc, is exceedingly long-lived and too powerful and tannic to be consumed young. The rich foods of the Gers, as well as the piquant cuisine of the Pays Basque finds an able partner in Madiran.

Pacherenc du Vic Bilh AOC

This oddly named white wine comes from the same vineyard region that produces Madiran. The vines, a *pot-pourri* of local varieties such as Ruffian,

---

La Pousse-Rapière

La Pousse-Rapière is the favoured cocktail and *apéritif* of Gascony, served in bars and restaurants alike. It is made by adding 1 part *liqueur d'Armagnac* (a sweet Armagnac liqueur macerated with oranges and other flavourings) to a special tall glass, and topping up with 5 parts *vin sauvage*, the local sparkling wine. It is quite refreshing.

Petit and Gros Manseng, and Courbu, are trained high above the ground on posts: local dialect translates this into '*pachets-en-ranc*' hence the name. The wine is dry or medium-dry, full-bodied and aromatic. It is well worth trying.

Côtes de St-Mont VDQS

Red and white wines from the *département* of the Gers. The reds in particular can be excellent, lighter versions of Madiran.

Vin de Pays Côtes de Gascogne

Red, dry white, and rosé table wines from the Armagnac vineyard. These Vins de Pays are gaining favour in export markets and can be very good indeed. The fragrant varietal Colombard wines are particularly worth watching out for.

The Wine Roads of Bergerac

Les Routes du Vin de Bergerac

A wine road of Bergerac.

Maison du Vin, Bergerac.

In Brief   The wine roads of Bergerac extend through this region's wine districts from Montravel in the west to Pécharmant, just to the east of Bergerac, but without doubt the finest area for wine travellers is the vineyard region south of the Dordogne around Monbazillac. This is well-travelled wine-tourist country, and in summer at least, there are numerous roadside stands where you can quench your thirst. The sign-posted circuit can be easily covered in a half day, but most visitors will wish to spend longer than this: a guided visit to the Château de Monbazillac is a must and, in addition to wine producers to visit, there is a selection of places to eat along the way.

La Route du Vin: Monbazillac

Bergerac is the centre of the wine region which bears its name: as a minor wine capital it is a worthy one. Indeed, vines have been planted in the region since as long ago as the first century AD; by the thirteenth century the wines of Bergerac were appreciated in England as well as further afield. Trade was further increased when François 1er authorized free movement on the Dordogne for the wines of Bergerac, to the not inconsiderable ire of the growers and merchants of Bordeaux. When the English were finally defeated at Castillon-la-Bataille in the Hundred Years' War, the resourceful wine growers turned their allegiance to the Dutch market; the revocation of the Edict of Nantes caused refugees to settle in Holland, and thus trading ties were further strengthened. Today, in the Dordogne, the most common visitors — more, it seems at times, than the French themselves — are the English and the Dutch, thus reinforcing the long-standing relationships.

Today Bergerac remains a most pleasant and picturesque town. The old quarter, with its once busy town *quai*, stone-paved streets, and old half-timbered houses is particularly atmospheric. The *Maison du Vin* is located here, in an ancient cloistered convent, and there is a fine wine museum which

Monbazillac.

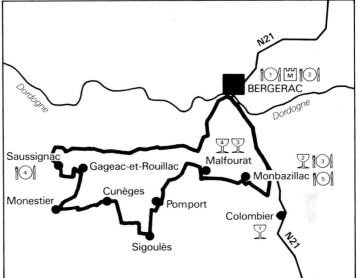

Cyrano de Bergerac.

documents not only the history of the vine but also the fascinating evolution of river trade on the Dordogne. And, of course, there is a statue (in the place de la Myrpe) to Bergerac's most famous son, the legendary Cyrano, whose monstrous nose, according to the poet and dramatist Edmond Rostand, led him to engage in over a thousand duels. Bergerac has some fine restaurants, as well as shops selling the gastronomic specialities of the Périgord: *confits, foie gras, huile de noix, arlequins de Carlux,* and much else.

To begin a circuit on the wine road of Monbazillac, leave Bergerac on the N21 (direction of Villeneuve-sur-Lot and Agen). Soon after leaving the town, the vineyards begin: in season wine growers may set up shaded stands where they offer their wines for tasting and for sale. Indeed, this compact wine region is well organized for wine tourists: some *propriétaires* even set up tables in their gardens for picnic areas. About 5 km (3 miles) out of Bergerac, look for a small road to the right (C16) to the small wine communes of La Badie and Colombier.

Notice as you climb into the hills that the vines are mainly trained high and wide, spaced in rows a full 3.5 metres (5 ft) apart. There are far fewer plants per hectare under this so-called high culture system than in traditional labour-intensive vineyards like the Médoc, and such a method is certainly not without its advantages. Fewer vines per hectare means a saving on initial capital expenditure; the wide spacing allows complete mechanization, including mechanical picking; and the vines give considerably greater yield per plant, resulting in lower costs. Some producers argue, moreover, that mechanization does not simply cut costs but also increases quality; for example, harvesting

DORDOGNE and GASCONY

231

mechanically in considerably shorter periods of time in early morning or evening when the temperatures are low can result in white wines which maintain more freshness and essential fruity aromas. On the whole, however, it is generally accepted that a high culture system, although capable of producing good and even very good wines, won't ever produce great wine.

Monbazillac, of course, is a very special wine indeed and demands considerably greater care and attention. The clay and limestone soil of these southern, well-exposed hills is perfectly suited to the traditional grape varieties, Sémillon, Sauvignon, and Muscadelle, and the microclimate which tends in autumn to follow heavy morning mist from the valley with warm afternoon sunshine allows the grapes to ripen and over-ripen, as well as, in certain years, to gain from that peculiar phenomenon known as *pourriture noble*. But such super-rich, honeyed, almost raisin-like grapes that result under such conditions cannot be picked mechanically, in one indiscriminate pass through the vineyards: the individual bunches, indeed single grapes, must be collected by hand in successive tries.

The Château de la Jaubertie is owned by Englishman Nick Ryman: it is a beautiful and historic property, the wines produced here are superb, and the welcome is a warm one. From Colombier, pass back through La Badie, then turn left to reach the little town of Monbazillac itself. There was originally a fortification on this site in the thirteenth century, but the present Château de Monbazillac dates from another three centuries later, built on the very edge of the great plateau of the Monbazillac vineyard, with a splendid view down to the Dordogne valley and the town of

Château de Monbazillac.

Bergerac. Owned by the *Cave Coopérative de Monbazillac* it has been fully restored with period furniture and tapestries. In the cellars there are the ancient kitchens as well as a small wine museum; a fraction of the *Coopérative's* vast production of Monbazillac is stored here.

The château can be toured; there is, furthermore, a tasting salon where Monbazillac, Pécharmant Château La Renaudie, and Bergerac white and red can be sampled and purchased. In season, there is a restaurant too, which serves regional foods and wines. Indeed, there is no shortage of choice for eating in this small town: in addition to the château restaurant, there is an elegant, if rather formal, starred restaurant, and also the rustic *ferme-auberge* of the Gazzinis.

Suitably fortified, the wine tour continues: from Monbazillac, find the D14e to Malfourat. Château Le Barradis, a few kilometres out of the town, is one of the most welcoming wine properties in the area: there is a well-organized salon where the *culture biologique* Monbazillacs can be tasted and there is a picnic area for any who care to relax. Carry on next to the Moulin de Malfourat to gain another splendid view over the vineyards, then continue on the *Route du Vin* until reaching the larger D933. Turn right, then soon left on the D17 and continue through small wine towns such as Pomport and Sigoulès. Outside Sigoulès, follow the *Route du Vin* signs to Cunèges, a charming little hamlet of stone houses with grand tiled roofs. This is lovely, quiet country, where the vines often give way to fields of wheat and other crops; it is a transitional area, too, between the vineyards of Monbazillac and those of less well-known Saussignac. From Cunèges, continue to Monestier, and the start of the vineyards of Saussignac. Find the road to Gageac-et-Rouillac, where there is a marvellous fortified château dating from the time of the Hundred Years' War, then turn left to Saussignac itself, a considerably more substantial yet still quiet and pleasant wine town.

There are a number of producers here and in nearby Razac-de-Saussignac who offer *dégustation* and direct sales: the wines produced are lighter than Monbazillac. Rarely encountered out of the region they should be enjoyed on the spot, well chilled with fresh fruit-filled *pâtisseries* for a special afternoon 'tea'. From Saussignac, return to Bergerac on the D14 via St-Laurent-des-Vignes.

Montravel

The vineyards of Montravel lie between the two fortified towns of Ste-Foy-la-Grande and Castillon-la-Bataille. They produce the dry white Montravel and sweet white Haut-Montravel and Côtes de Montravel. Lost somewhat between the great Bordeaux vineyards of St-Emilion and better-known vineyards of

Montravel.

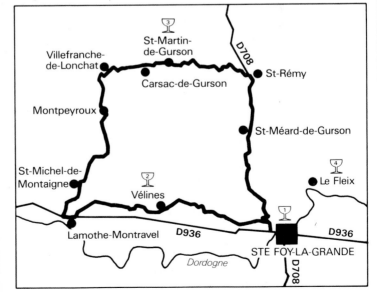

Bergerac, this remains quiet, totally unspoiled wine country. A sign-posted *Route du Vin* extends through the small region.

From Ste-Foy cross to the north bank of the Dordogne and find the small back road down-river to Vélines where the Montravel vineyards begin. Continue on to Lamothe-Montravel. Though in the midst of the vineyards, there are relatively few opportunities to visit *propriétaires-récoltants*; the reason for this is that the great majority of *viticulteurs* belong to the six *caves coopératives* found throughout this compact vineyard. Wines can usually be tasted and purchased at the *coopératives*.

From Lamothe the wine road strikes into the Montravel hills: make a circular loop through this scenic wine country, driving to St-Michel-de-Montaigne, Montpeyroux, Villefranche-de-Lonchat, Carsac-de-Gurson, St-Rémy, St-Méard-de-Gurson, and so back to either Ste-Foy or Bergerac. There are *coopérative* cellars at Lamothe, Villefranche, Ste-Foy and Carsac.

Pécharmant

Pécharmant.

The Pécharmant vineyard is a tiny one, covering only about 200 hectares (490 acres), but as it is so close to Bergerac, and as these mainly gravelly hills produce the region's finest red wines, it should not be overlooked.

To make a short circuit of the Pécharmant vineyard, leave Bergerac on the D32. The well-signposted *Route du Vin* soon begins, leading to little wine communes such as Creysse, St-Sauveur, and Lembras. The signs indicate individual *propriétaires* and many can be visited, although a large proportion of Pécharmant is produced in the fine *Cave Coopérative de Bergerac* which can also be visited. Pécharmant itself is hardly a village, more just a collection of houses amidst the vines: follow the *Route* back towards Bergerac and at Pombonne cross the N21 and find the smaller D107. The wine road sign leads towards Jaure then bears right to little Ste-Foy-des-Vignes before returning to Bergerac. From a high hilly crest there is a magnificent view looking down to Bergerac, nestling beside the Dordogne, with its red-tiled roofs and its pointed church steeple set against the ribbed vineyards of Monbazillac beyond.

An Englishman's Castle

It may well be every Englishman's dream to one day buy a château, complete with vineyard, somewhere deep in the heart of rural France: here at the Château de la Jaubertie that dream is reality. The imposing property looks every bit a Renaissance château and has a pedigree to match: the French King Henry IV installed a mistress here and made frequent amorous visits. Yet today, for Nick Ryman and his family, the château represents no mere romantic idyll; the reality is hard work and constant stimulating challenge.

When Ryman purchased the property in 1973, he knew little about wine but he did have what some might have then called a rather arrogant and presumptuous aim of making no less than the finest wines of the area. However, the prizes which he has since consistently won at the great wine fairs of Paris, Mâcon, Bordeaux, and elsewhere, speak for themselves.

Wine Museum

Musée du Vin et de la Batellerie
rue du Grand Moulin
24100 Bergerac
Hours: Tue–Fri 10–12h; 14–17h30. Sat 10–12h.
Fine wine museum and museum tracing the history of the river trade on the Dordogne.

Dégustation: Stop to Taste; Stop to Buy

The Bergerac vineyard is essentially made up of small family *propriétaires*: the average vineyard holding is only around 5 hectares. While many such growers make and sell their wine direct, a full 40 per cent of the production takes place in the nine *caves coopératives* which form the group known as UNIDOR.

Monbazillac

Château de la Jaubertie
Colombier
24560 Issigeac
tel: (53) 58 32 11
Hours: 8–12h; 14–16h. Telephone call appreciated.
The 50-hectare vineyard around the Château de la Jaubertie was acquired by the Rymans in 1973: today a full range of wines is produced in the modern winery, including excellent white Bergerac made exclusively from the

Sauvignon; white Bergerac assembled from the traditional *cépages* Sémillon, Muscadelle,and Sauvignon; light, youthful red Bergerac from the Merlot and Cabernet Sauvignon meant to be drunk young; full-bodied rosé Bergerac from the Merlot; and deeper reserve red wine made exclusively from Cabernet Sauvignon and aged in new oak Bordelais barrels. New viticultural and wine-making techniques are utilized wherever possible to ensure that the essential character of the fruit is preserved.
English spoken.

2

Château de Monbazillac
Monbazillac
24240 Sigoulès
tel: (53) 57 06 38
Hours for visiting the Château: October–April 10–12h; 14–17h. May 9h30–12h; 14–18h. June–September 9–12h30; 13h30–20h.
This classified historic monument is the property of the *Cave Coopérative de Monbazillac* which has 160 *viticulteur* members. Guided tours of the sixteenth-century Renaissance château last about ¾ of an hour. There is a tasting salon which can be visited on its own, where the *Coopérative's* Château Monbazillac as well as Pécharmant Château La Renaudie can be tasted. There is also a restaurant serving reasonably priced meals including regional specialities and wines. Visits to the working *Cave Coopérative* itself can be arranged, followed by a free tasting, weekdays in working hours.

3

M. & Mme S. Labasse-Gazzini
Château 'Le Barradis'
24240 Monbazillac
tel: (53) 58 30 01
Hours: Daily except Sun in winter 9–12h; 14–17h.
The 40-hectare vineyard of the Château 'Le Barradis' is cultivated entirely by *culture biologique* and the Monbazillac produced is superb. Visit this most informative and welcoming tasting room where a range of wines is on offer. In addition to traditional Monbazillac, Bergerac red, rosé, and white Sauvignon wines are also produced, together with a fine non-alcoholic *jus de raisin*. Unique specially commissioned glass shaped like Cyrano's nose for making 'Myrano' cocktail (*crème de myrtilles* and Monbazillac). Also a pleasant picnic area.

4

Christian & Patrick Chabrol
Château de Malfourat
24240 Monbazillac
tel: (53) 58 30 63
Hours: Daily, working hours.
Opposite the famous landmark, le Moulin de Malfourat, this family *propriétaire-récoltant* produces Monbazillac, and white, red, and rosé Bergerac. Purchase tins of *foie gras* here for a classic Périgord picnic amongst the vines.

Montravel

1

Union de Viticulteurs de Port Sainte Foy
78, rte de Bordeaux
33220 Port Sainte Foy
tel: (53) 24 75 63
Hours: Mon–Fri 9–12h; 15–18h. Appointment preferred.
Montravel AOC and Bergerac AOC.
A little English spoken.

2

Jean Itey de Peironnin
Château la Raye
24230 Vélines
tel: (53) 27 50 14
Hours: Daily, working hours. Appointment preferred.
Visits to the surrounding vineyards and *chai* where traditional Côtes de
Montravel Moelleux as well as prize-winning red Bergerac are produced and
aged.

3

'La Grappe de Gurson'
Cave Coopérative de Carsac et de
   St-Martin-de-Gurson
24610 Villefranche-de-Lonchat
Hours: Tue–Sat 8h30–12h30; 14–18h. Appointment preferred but not essential.
Bergerac AOC, Montravel AOC, Côtes de Montravel AOC, Bordeaux AOC.

4

Cave Coopérative Le Fleix
Le Fleix
24130 La Force
tel: (53) 24 64 32
Hours: Mon afternoon–Sat morning 8–12h; 13h30–17h. Appointment preferred
but not essential.
Le Fleix is located on the north bank of the Dordogne up-river from St-Foy-la-
Grande. Bergerac AOC, Montravel AOC and Bordeaux AOC.

Pécharmant

1

Cave Coopérative de Bergerac
'Domaine du Grande Boisse'
72m bd de l'Entrepôt
24100 Bergerac
tel: (53) 57 16 27
Hours: Mon–Fri, working hours.
This large *Cave Coopérative* has won numerous medals for its Pépcharmant
AOC, and white and red Bergerac AOC.

2

Domaine du Haut Pécharmant
Pécharmant
24100 Bergerac
tel: (53) 57 29 50
Hours: Daily by appointment.
Pécharmant means 'charming hill', and some consider that this fine red wine
finds its greatest expression on the higher slopes above Bergerac, such as on
those of the vineyards of the Domaine du Haut Pécharmant. Madame Roche
has been winning medals for her fine wines for many years.
A little English spoken.

3

Gilbert Dusseau
'Chartreuse de Peyelevade'
Pécharmant
24100 Bergerac
tel: (53) 57 44 27
Hours: Daily, working hours.
Another medal-winning Pécharmant AOC.

La Culture Biologique

'The way to tell if a wine is well made is to drink it until it comes out of
your ears. If it is a good wine, you will feel perfectly fine the next morning.'
So a well-known wine-maker in Alsace once told us. I think there is something
to this, for it is often, you may be reassured to know, not simply *sheer* quantity
which causes the problem but any number of invisible chemicals or additives.

There is a growing number of wine-makers who recognize this and their
concern for purer, more natural products has led to the practice of *'la culture
biologique'*, the French name for organic farming. Thus they cultivate their
vineyards without the use of any synthetic or chemical pesticides, fertilizers,
or weedkillers. All weeding is done by hand or machine, and organic fertilizers
such as seaweed and natural phosphates are used. The yeasts which form
naturally on the bloom of the grapes initiate the fermentation, and chemicals
and artificial aids are not used in the wine-making process. Sulphur, in
particular, is avoided or else used in as small doses as possible. Stabilization
is usually carried out by filtration.

There are, at present, about 150 wine growers who practice *culture
biologique* in France.

The Wine Road of Cahors

Circuit du Vin de Cahors

In Brief   The full *Circuit du Vin de Cahors* is about 120 km (75 miles) long. It is one of the loveliest and least known wine roads of France. It leaves Cahors at the dramatic Pont Valentré and extends along the Lot and into its majestic hills all the way to the ancient border of Quercy and the magnificent feudal Château de Bonaguil. The *Circuit* then returns to Cahors by way of the hillier vineyards and towns north of the Lot. Though it could be completed in a long day, a stop-over in Puy-l'Évêque is recommended. Otherwise, discover this wonderful river valley *en route* to points west. A shorter tour of the vineyards of Cahors can be made by following the *Circuit* to Luzech, then crossing to the north bank to return to Cahors via Crayssac and Mercuès.

Cahors is located on a spectacular bend in the Lot river. This natural strategic position allowed the town to gain power and influence, so that by the thirteenth century it was not only the capital of Quercy but a foremost European banking centre. So impregnable was Cahors that it alone was the only town of Quercy to resist being taken over by the English during the Hundred Years' War. However, after the Black Death had taken its toll and the town was eventually ceded, it declined into ruin, never to recover its former glory.

Even today, inland Cahors, now a quiet and rather sullen provincial backwater, presents a mainly defensive aspect: the splendid fortified Pont Valentré is a masterpiece of military architecture, while the Cathedral appears a stout, ugly fortress reminding us that it was built to serve as a retreat in times of war. The old quarter of Cahors has not been self-consciously restored

Cahors.

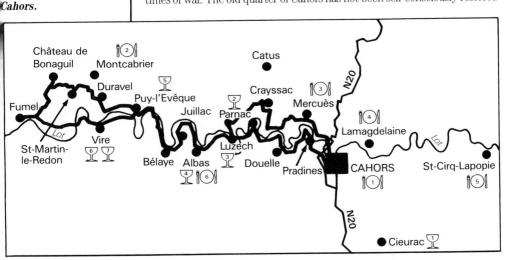

DORDOGNE and GASCONY

but still remains a place of narrow streets and crumbling houses, one foremost where people live. The position of the town, on its immense horseshoe bend, seems to create a rather odd feeling of separateness, somewhat like that found on islands.

If the banking houses of Cahors once lent money to Popes and Kings, the wines produced from the rugged slopes mainly to the west graced their tables. Cahors wine has been celebrated and appreciated for centuries. Yet these vineyards themselves remain isolated and little visited. To begin the wine tour, cross the historic Pont Valentré, immediately turn right and follow the D8 in the direction of Pradines. Outside Pradines, the road

Pont Valentré, Cahors.

climbs into the hills above the Lot where the Cahors vineyards begin. These ancient Auxerrois vines (the local name for the Cot or Malbec) are stumpy, gnarled and free-standing, traditionally trained in the old-fashioned goblet method, though in fact, extensive replanting has been taking place here in recent years, and some growers are adopting more modern viticultural methods.

This still remains an ancient and majestic land: the hills above the valley are bare rock covered with scrubby trees; grand châteaux and ample Quercyois farmhouses with their distinctive *pigeonniers* (dovecote towers) are found around every bend.

Douelle is the first little wine town of any note: the actual signs for the *Circuit* begin here and there are numerous producers who offer *dégustation* and direct sales. Watch out, too, for farm producers of *foie gras, confits de canards* and *conserves*: you can often stop to taste and buy them as well. The next concentration of vineyards and growers is at Parnac. The valley here has widened somewhat, and on the hills and flatter stretches the soil is rich with alluvial deposits. A number of producers have grouped together as part of the highly-respected *Cave Coopérative 'Les Côtes d'Olt'*; the *cave* can be visited and the wines tasted in summer.

At Luzech the Lot makes yet another of its fantastic and tortured loops, almost making an island of the little town. The isthmus is only 200 m (220 yards) wide at its narrowest point. Inhabited since Gallo-Roman times, Luzech was held by Richard the Lionheart in the twelfth century and later became the seat of one of the baronies of Quercy. Today Luzech, though quiet and unassuming, is one of the important wine communes of Cahors, and there are producers both in and outside the town.

The *Circuit* continues for quite a way further west; at this point, however, some may wish to return to Cahors: if so, follow the returning *Circuit* signs towards Catus and branch off to Crayssac and Mercuès, where there is a fine château hotel-restaurant complete with wine *cave*. Intrepid wine travellers, however, will push on to Albas, Juillac, and Bélaye. Little Bélaye was an ancient fief of the bishops of Cahors; from this hilly spur high above the Lot there is a fine viewpoint over the surrounding vineyards and the twisting river.

Puy-l'Évêque, with its ochre and gold houses clinging to the hillside above the calm, wide Lot, is one of the prettiest towns along the *Circuit*. It is also another important wine centre. Smaller neighbouring hamlets such as Vire have numerous *propriétaires-récoltants* producing fine, inky traditional wines which should be tasted at the source. For those who love such meaty red wines, Cahors remains one of the bargain country wines of France.

Château de Bonaguil.

From Puy-l'Évêque, continue on to Duravel, then climb up through the steep town and on to St-Martin-le-Redon, a tiny village with particularly lovely stone houses. We are out of the vineyards now, and pass through thick wooded hills before finally opening out onto a spectacular view of a majestic Renaissance fortified castle, the Château de Bonaguil. This beautiful fortress is still a formidable and commanding example of military might and a vivid reminder that these peaceful and isolated lands were once hotly contested. The castle can be toured, and there are restaurants and cafés offering refreshment below the castle walls.

The *Circuit* continues on to Fumel, a rather dull industrial town, then loops back to Vire before recrossing the Lot at Puy-l'Évêque and back to Cahors by way of Crayssac and Mercuès.

Dégustation: Stop to Taste; Stop to Buy

Although there is only one *appellation* produced along this wine road, there are styles and variations between different Cahors AOC, ranging from light, youthful reds which can be drunk after only a year, to immense and almost black wines which have vinified traditionally to keep and improve for 10 or 15 years or more. Try to sample both styles.

Georges Vigouroux
Château de Haute-Serre
Cieurac
46230 Lalbenque
tel: (65) 38 70 30
Hours: Mon–Sat 9–12h; 14–17h.
Not actually on the *Circuit du Vin de Cahors*, but none the less universally regarded as one of the very finest producers of traditional Cahors. Guided

visits and audio-visual.
English spoken 'by appointment'.

2 Cave Coopérative 'Les Côtes d'Olt'
46140 Parnac
tel: (65) 30 71 86
Hours: July and August Mon–Fri, working hours.
This large *coopérative* produces a fine range of Cahors of varying styles.

3 Maison Rigal & Fils SA
Château St Didier Parnac
46140 Luzech
tel: (65) 30 70 10
Hours: Mon–Sat 8–12h; 14–18h.
Parnac is considered one of the most important wine centres for Cahors; the Château St Didier Parnac is one of this commune's larger and more well-known producers.

4 GAEC du Domaine Eugénie
Jean et Claude Couture
La Rivière Haute
46140 Albas
tel: (65) 30 73 51
Hours: Mon–Sat, working hours. Appointment preferred.
The Couture family have been in the region since 1470 and have always been *vignerons*: the Domaine Eugénie, they say, formed part of the vineyard which made the wines reserved for the Tsars of Russia. Cahors AOC is sold in bottles and *en vrac*.

5 Baldes & Fils
Clos de Triguedina
46700 Puy-l'Évêque
tel: (65) 21 30 81
Hours: Mon–Fri 9–12h; 14–18h. Appointment preferred.
The Baldes family have been growing grapes for seven generations and make meaty, traditional Cahors from their 40 hectares. Two *cuvées* are offered: Clos Triguedina and the prestigious Prince Probus, made exclusively from old vines with an average age of at least 45 years.
A little English spoken.

6 Domaine de Filhol
Vire-sur-Lot
46700 Puy-l'Évêque
tel: (65) 36 52 84
Hours: Fri and Sat by appointment.
The Filhol brothers make the 55-km (35-mile) trek up to Sarlat in the Dordogne each Saturday to sell their young Cahors AOC in the lively market there.
A little English spoken.

7

V. Bernède & Fils
Clos la Coutale
Vire-sur-Lot
46700 Puy-l'Évêque
tel: (65) 36 51 47
Hours: Daily, working hours.
Traditional long-lived Cahors produced by the Bernède family in the fine little wine commune of Vire.
A little English spoken.

The 'Route d'Armagnac'

In Brief   The Armagnac vineyard extends over a vast area comprising the greater part of the Gers *département* as well as parts of the Landes and Lot-et-Garonne. There are three principal vineyards: Ténarèze, Bas-Armagnac, and Haut-Armagnac, with the best wines for distillation coming from the first two. The principal towns are Condom (Ténarèze); Eauze (Bas-Armagnac); and Auch, the capital of Gascony (Haut-Armagnac). For wine travellers, an excellent route combining vineyards, farmhouses, and distilleries with lovely historic *bastides* can be made through the countryside between Condom and Eauze. The distance is not great (48 km/30 miles) but it is most pleasant to take a full day for the journey.

There is, furthermore, a sign-posted *Circuit de l'Armagnac* through the Bas-Armagnac, but in our experience this route is almost impossible to follow (and no map of it seems to exist). Intrepid Armagnac lovers will, none the less, want to strike out into the heart of this region, so we include a suggested route from Eauze to Labastide d'Armagnac and back. Other vineyards and distilleries are found elsewhere throughout the region: major centres include Nogaro, Vic-Fézensac, Fleurance, and, of course, Auch itself.

Condom to Eauze

Little Condom is a fine old wine town. The former seat of a bishopric until the time of the Revolution, its huge sixteenth-century cathedral attests to its former importance. The low-lying *chais* of Armagnac producers and merchants lie alongside the Baïse river, whose peaceful, stone-paved *quais* were once the scene of intense activity, especially during the nineteenth century when thousands of barrels were rolled directly on to barges to be shipped down-river to the Garonne, and so on to Bordeaux. In those days, certainly, much Armagnac was never known as such, but found its way into the blending vats of the shippers at Cognac. Indeed, the brandies from this remote land-locked region have begun to receive world recognition in their own right only

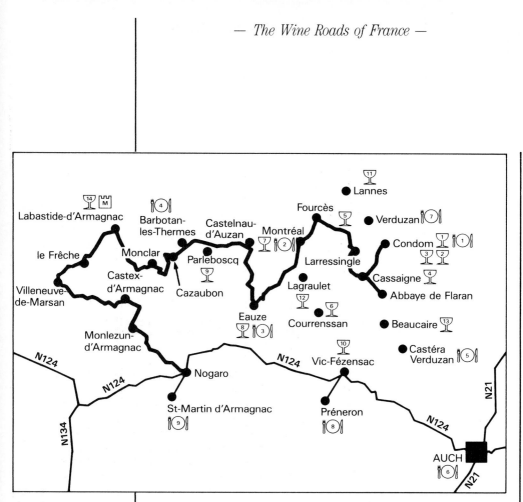

Armagnac.

relatively recently. The House of Janneau, founded in 1851 and located by the river, is one of the oldest and largest producers of Armagnac.

To begin the tour to Eauze, leave Condom on the D931 (passing the local *Cave Coopérative de Condom*) then branch off on the D208 to Cassaigne. The Château de Cassaigne dates from the thirteenth century when it was used by the Bishops of Condom as a summer country house. The nearby ancient Cistercian Abbaye de Flaran also dates from the thirteenth century. Though growing wealth eventually led the monks away from the austere rules of the order, the dormitory, gardens, and cloister still give an idea of their hard-working life of manual labour and self-sufficiency.

The wine tour continues back through Cassaigne on the D142 and on to Larressingle, a remarkable, totally intact fortified village, clustered around its ruined château. The Papelorey family own the Château de Larressingle, and the town has given its name to their range of Larressingle Armagnacs and Flocs. These can be tasted and purchased at the *Syndicat d'Initiative* at the entrance to the village.

From Larressingle, continue down to the D15 then find the smaller D278 which leads to the road to Fourcès. Before turning to Fourcès, visit the Château de Pomès Pébérère, another fine family producer of Armagnac and Floc, with interesting ageing *chais* and their own traditional *alambic*. Fourcès is another fine Gascon *bastide*, but unlike most which conform to a rigid rectangular grid, this little fortified *ville* is built around a circular central dirt plaza, with its old half-timbered houses and arched walkways extending around an outer moat. Contrast Fourcès to Montréal, for example, the next hilltop *bastide* on the route to Eauze: the latter is more typical, yet how atmospheric these ancient towns remain! From Montréal continue on to Eauze, passing through more vineyards of the Ténarèze.

Eauze to Labastide d'Armagnac

Eauze is considered the capital of the Bas-Armagnac, the vineyard region known also as 'Black Armagnac', due to its once extensive and dense forests of black Monlezun oak. This sappy oak, certainly, is one of the key factors which determines the quality and character of Armagnac, for the tannins and flavourings which it imparts to the brandies through slow absorption during ageing are totally different to those found in oak from the Limousin, itself so essential to the character of Cognac.

Although comparisons between Cognac and Armagnac are not wholly relevant since the two brandies are so different, they are, none the less inevitable. For example, if in Cognac the finest vineyards are universally acknowledged to be those of Grande Champagne, on its deep substratum of chalk, here in Armagnac the opposite is the case: the vineyards of Bas-Armagnac, which undoubtedly produce the finest Armagnacs, lie on ground which at times is as sandy as a beach. Haut-Armagnac, on the other hand, the least important vineyard area, is known also as 'White Armagnac' because its vineyards lie on chalk.

Eauze today is a busy market town, but on Thursdays the merchants no longer come here to sample pungent Armagnacs simply by rubbing a few drops in their hands and smelling. However, that is not to say that on this day the cafés and bars of the town are not full of men in bobbing Basque berets, downing tots of fiery brandy morning, noon and night.

A tour of Bas-Armagnac is certainly of interest to the amateur of Armagnac, but it should be pointed out that in itself the region is, dare we say, a little dull and single-minded. From Eauze, take the D43 to Castelnau-d'Auzan, then continue through the vineyards to Barbotan-les-Thermes, a spa town with that peculiar and unique French atmosphere where everyone is taking '*une cure*', needed, no doubt, after over-indulgence in the fine but so rich foods of the Gers: *foie gras*, *confits*, *croustade*, and much else.

From Barbotan, continue on to nearby Cazaubon, then find the D32 and the D33 to Monclar. This is the heart of the Bas-Armagnac, an area known as '*La Grande Bas-Armagnac*'. Does it really exist? Not officially, according to the *Bureau National Interprofessionnel de l'Armagnac* in Eauze, but certainly to the wine growers and Armagnac producers themselves there is no doubting their position and status. Certainly brandies from Monclar, Le Frêche, and Labastide are prized above all by the few large producer-shippers who marry together brandies from various regions to produce their harmonious blends. The Armagnac industry, though, is not so dependent on such shippers as is the case in Cognac; indeed, the majority of Armagnacs are produced and sold by individual *propriétaires-récoltants*. It is possibly for this reason that there is such great range and individuality in Armagnac.

From Monclar, follow the signs along the D154 to the *Musée du Vigneron*, an Armagnac museum located in the seventeenth-century Gascon barn of a *propriétaire-récoltant*. Continue on to Labastide-d'Armagnac itself. Labastide is another fine and characteristic *bastide*. These towns are surprisingly small, almost claustrophobic in feel, with their narrow streets and old houses all converging on to an ancient crumbling square. Wander through the cobbled back streets to gain a feel of a genuine medieval village — not overly restored or self-conscious, but one where people still must live much as they have for centuries.

Continue next to little Le Frêche and Villeneuve-de-Marsan, then return to Eauze through the heart of the vineyard, via Castex-d'Armagnac, Monlezun-d'Armagnac, and Nogaro. Nogaro itself is an important Armagnac town, and also the centre of the barrel-making industry.

Dégustation: Stop to Taste; Stop to Buy

The wine growers and Armagnac producers of the region generally offer a full range of different qualities of Armagnac. Many also produce Floc d'Armagnac, fruits steeped in Armagnac, or table wines. We have also included the addresses of a few producers who specialize in table wines.

1 Janneau Fils SA
50, ave d'Aquitaine
32100 Condom
tel: (62) 28 24 77
Hours: Mon–Sat 9–12h; 14–18h. Appointment preferred but not essential. The oldest Armagnac house and the world market leader is most welcoming to visitors: cellars can be visited, and there is a fine collection of instruments in the tasting room, including an ancient *alambic ambulante* (travelling Armagnac still).
English spoken.

2 Armagnac Larressingle
rue des Carmes
32100 Condom
tel: (62) 28 15 33
Hours: Mon–Fri 9–12h; 14–17h.
The Papelorey family has been making Armagnac in Condom for five generations. Taste their products here and in nearby Larressingle.
English spoken.

3

Cave Coopérative de Condom
ave des Mousquetaires
32100 Condom
tel: (62) 28 12 16
Hours: Mon–Fri 9–12h; 14–17h.
On the road out to Eauze, this *cave coopérative* sells Armagnac as well as
table wine *en vrac*.

4

SARL Henri Faget et ses enfants
Château de Cassaigne
Cassaigne
32100 Condom
tel: (62) 28 04 02
Hours: Daily 9–12h; 14–19h.
Constructed in 1247 by the Abbot of Condom, the Château de Cassaigne is
an interesting historic monument as well as a family Armagnac enterprise.
The ancient kitchen of the château, with its beehive brick ceiling, is particularly
fascinating, and the range of single-year vintage Armagnacs is one of the most
extensive that we have encountered.
English spoken.

5

Château de Pomès-Pébérère
32100 Condom
tel: (62) 28 11 53
Hours: Daily 9–12h; 14–17h.
This fine old Gascon farmhouse in the heart of the Ténarèze is located about
5 km (3 miles) from Condom on the D114 road to the *bastide* of Fourcès. Come
here to see a real working operation, complete with *alambic Armagnaçais*
and ageing *chais*. The Armagnacs and Flocs produced are excellent as are
the delectable *pruneaux d'Agen à l'Armagnac* (Agen prunes steeped in
Armagnac).

6

Armagnac Veuve Goudoulin
Domaine du Bigor
Courrenssan
32330 Gondrin
tel: (62) 06 35 02
Hours: Mon–Fri 9–12h; 14–19h.
Courrenssan is located off the main Condom–Eauze road, just south of Gondrin.
Visitors see the ageing *chais* and are offered a range of old Armagnacs for
tasting and purchase.

7

Société Fermière du Château de Malliac
Château de Malliac
32250 Montréal
tel: (62) 29 44 87
Hours: Mon–Fri 8h30–12h; 13–17h30. Appointment preferred but not essential.

DORDOGNE and GASCONY

247

This family firm is located in the thirteenth-century Château de Malliac and produces a full range of Armagnacs, including a rare single-vintage Armagnac distilled entirely from the traditional Folle Blanche variety. Audio-visual presentation and visits to the *chais*.
A little English spoken.

8 Marquis de Caussade
ave de l'Armagnac
32800 Eauze
tel: (62) 09 94 22
Hours: Daily 10–12h30; 15–17h30. Appointment preferred but not essential. On the route to Cazaubon. Guided visit of the *chais* and audio-visual presentation. Art and craft *exposition* in July and August.
English spoken.

9 Château de Lacaze
Parleboscq
40310 Gabarret
tel: (58) 44 33 65
Hours: Mon–Fri 9–12h; 14–17h30.
Located on the suggested route, between Castelnau-d'Auzan and Barbotan-les-Thermes, the Château de Lacaze is in the heart of the Bas-Armagnac and an historic property: it was once held by England's King Edward I, and France's most famous royal toper Henry IV came here to study as a young man. A full range of Armagnacs is distilled on the premises only from grapes grown on the vast estate. Guided visits and audio-visual presentation.
English spoken.

10 Armagnac Marcel Trépout
Château Notre Dame
22, rue Notre Dame
32190 Vic-Fézensac
tel: (62) 06 33 83
Hours: Daily 8h30–12h30; 14h30–18h.
Vic-Fézensac is another important Armagnac centre, though it is perhaps better known for its bloodless bullfights. In this ancient twelfth-century Monastère de Notre Dame, the Trépout family specialize in old Armagnacs: a range of Armagnacs *millésimes* (single vintage) are available dating back to 1904.
A little English spoken.

11 Michel Kauffer
Domaine de Cazeaux
Lannes
47170 Mezin

tel: (53) 65 73 03
Hours: Daily 10–19h.
Armagnac and Floc de Gascogne produced by the Kauffer family for the last 150 years.

Other Wine Producers

12

Michel Duffour
Domaine de St Lannes
Lagraulet
32300 Gondrin
tel: (62) 29 11 93
Hours: Working hours.
Vin de Pays Côtes de Gascogne.

13

Olivier Galabert
au Château de Pardailhan
Beaucaire
32410 Castéra-Verduzan
tel: (62) 68 15 43
Hours: Daily 9–20h.
Vin de Pays Côtes de Gascogne.

Armagnac Museum

14

Musée du Vigneron d'Armagnac
40240 Labastide-d'Armagnac
tel: (58) 44 81 08
Hours: Mon–Sat 9–12h; 14–18h. Sun and holidays 15–18h.
The museum is on the property of Armagnac producer Charles Garreau. Visits to the *chais* on Tue, Thur and Sat by appointment.

Regional Gastronomy

The cuisine of this vast south-western hinterland is rich and varied: the Périgord, Quercy, and Gascony are all great gastronomic regions. Arguably it is possible to eat better and cheaper here on true and unpretentious regional foods than almost anywhere else in France. Certainly, it is not the place to come for those who are worried about their waistlines.

Without a doubt, the cuisine centres around both the goose and the duck. Throughout the region, there are countless farms specializing in their *élevage*. Force-fed by an ancient method known as *la gavage*, both are prized above all for their unctuous livers: the *foies gras d'oie et canard* that are considered such delicacies not only in France but throughout the world. In restaurants, the finest *foie gras* comes *mi-cuit*, which means that fresh livers have been cooked delicately at a low temperature and are served still slightly pink, either cold in slices or else warm with a *salade tiède*.

While *foie gras* is undoubtedly a refined and expensive delicacy, simpler *pâtés* made from mixtures of goose or duck liver and pork are enjoyed for everyday meals. *Magret de canard* may now be found throughout the country, but nowhere else will you encounter more delicious breasts of duck, grilled and served *au point*, that is still slightly rare. *Confits* of goose and duck are another speciality encountered almost everywhere. A *confit* is an ancient method of conserving meat such as goose, duck, pork, chicken, or chicken gizzards (*gésiers*) by first salting, then cooking for slow periods in their own rendered fat. The meats, packed in earthenware pots or glass jars sealed with more fat, can be kept for considerable periods. To prepare the *confit* it is only necessary to heat it up, ensuring that the skin (of duck or goose) is well crisped without drying out the meat. When done well, a *confit de canard* can be almost as good as Chinese duck.

Though such *confits* are considered one of the great regional plates, like many others they are at heart simple peasant foods and evolved out of the need to be able to preserve meats over the long winter. Indeed, the foods of the south-west share an essential rustic character which may seem at odds with the newer trends in French cooking. Goose fat, not oil or butter, remains the primary cooking medium and no one here seems too concerned with such things as cholesterol levels: *confits*, for example, are universally served with sliced potatoes sautéed in the same fat, seasoned heavily with just salt and pepper: they are exquisite, and damn the calories!

Other simple hearty foods include Gascony's *garbure*, a one-pot stew containing different meats such as salt pork and ham, vegetables and *confit*. Another typical plate is the supremely simple *omelette aux cèpes* from Périgord: no more than the freshest farm eggs made into an omelette with sautéed fresh *cèpes*, that most delicious and prized of all mushrooms. Even the most expensive, rarest delicacy of all, the black truffle, maintains its rustic country roots: in autumn markets in Sarlat, Cahors, Lalbenque, and elsewhere, women wrapped in overcoats, wearing wool caps and fingerless gloves, display wicker baskets full of these weird, lumpy, jet-black tubers wrapped in tea cloths as if they were no more than mere baskets of eggs. While to most of us, truffles are usually only encountered in thin precious slivers — more as a garnish than anything else — here they are chopped and served in omelettes; there are truffle soups; truffles are added to sausages, pâtés, and casseroles; and they are even cooked whole, '*sous la cendre*', in the ashes of hot coals.

The great *vin liquoreux* of the region, Monbazillac, traditionally accompanies *foie gras*; odd though this combination may sound, it really is superb: richness complementing richness. We are perhaps more used to drinking Monbazillac and other such wines for dessert. Indeed, they are wonderful accompaniments to the sweet, dark strawberries of the Périgord, peaches, cherries, and apricots, all macerated in the wine itself. In Gascony, there is *croustade*, an exquisite, flaky pastry with layers of apples or plums, soaked generously in Armagnac.

Restaurants range from the simple and rustic to great starred establishments; this too is the foremost region for the unique and hospitable *fermes-auberges*: don't miss them.

Walnuts and Walnut Oil

Walnut trees abound in the lush countryside of the Dordogne, and their fruit is put to use in a variety of ways: fresh green walnuts are delicious with a glass of chilled Monbazillac; walnuts are coated with chocolate and cocoa to make the wonderful *arlequins de Carlux*; *liqueur au noix* is another speciality of the Périgord; and of course, *huile de noix* (walnut oil) is the favourite salad seasoning here. It is one of the finest flavoured of all oils and adds a particular and distinctive flavour to both salads and vegetables as well as in cooking. If you would like to visit a traditional mill this one is located near Sarlat:

> Moulin à Huile de Noix
> Moulin de la Tour
> Ste-Nathalene
> 24200 Sarlat-la-Canada
> tel: (53) 59 22 08

Le Pique-Nique

Pâtés This is the great land of *pâtés* and *terrines*: perfect picnic fare. Made from pork, duck, goose, chicken, rabbit, hare, or partridge, studded with truffles or pistachios, smooth or rough: every market, every *charcuterie* offers an incredible range, the best *fabriqué maison* of course.

Foie gras Jars of whole *foie gras au naturel* or *truffé* are sold throughout the region, which is the foremost area for their production in France. Most *foie gras* is made by small artisans who raise the poultry themselves. It is a ready-to-eat delicacy that may be expensive but which is one of the real treats of the region. Cut into slices and serve with glasses of chilled Monbazillac.

Cabecou Made from sheep's and goats' milk, this small disc of cheese is found throughout the region: good served hot, on a round of toast, melting and dribbled with walnut oil: a luxury rarebit from the Périgord.

Arlequins de Carlux Local walnuts dipped in chocolate and cocoa: the ultimate car snack.

Ferme-auberge.

La Ferme-Auberge

Eating out in restaurants in France undoubtedly can be one of the great experiences of being in the country; for us, however, tasting the real foods and meeting the people of each region is equally important. Here in the Dordogne and Gascony like-minded travellers have the opportunity to join families at their table at numerous *fermes-auberges* located throughout. The concept of the *ferme-auberge* is that visitors can join the family (often in their own dining room), eating the same local foods and produce prepared to regional recipes. 'Regional foods' here may mean such delicacies as *foie gras maison*, *omelettes aux cèpes*, *confits de canard*, *croustade*, and much else, always accompanied by the local wines, Floc or Armagnac. Though it is possible to turn up at a *ferme-auberge* unannounced, it is almost always advisable to telephone in advance. A word of warning: don't come to a *ferme-auberge* if you are, as they say, *très pressé*: the first time we visited one in Monbazillac, we sat down at the long trestle table at one o'clock and did not rise again until after five in the afternoon. Indeed, many *fermes-auberges* specialize in *grands menus* which consist of course after course after course. Our meal that day began with Jean-Louis's home-made *apéritif* which he facetiously calls 'Kyrano'.

Jean-Louis's 'Kyrano'

Take a bottle of Monbazillac and pour it into a jug. Slice a lemon, add it to the jug, and leave to macerate in a refrigerator for a day. Add half a glass of *crème de cassis* to the jug and, just before serving, a generous squeeze of fresh lemon juice. Serve in glasses with lemon slices to garnish.

Restaurants

Dordogne (Maps pp.231 and 234)

Le Cyrano
2, bd Montaigne
24100 Bergerac
tel: (53) 57 02 76
Closed Sun eve, Mon.
The classics of Périgord are handled in a decidedly lighter fashion: *escalope de foie de canard chaud, magret de canard grillé au feu de bois, salade*

à l'huile de noisette et au foie de canard confit together with a fine selection of Bergerac wines.
Moderate

2

Le Terroir
Hôtel de Bordeaux
38, place Gambetta
24100 Bergerac
tel: (53) 57 12 83
This hotel-restaurant is agreeable and meals can be taken in the garden in summer. *Foie de canard aux pommes, magret en croûte*, and Bergerac wines.
Moderate

3

La Closerie Saint-Jacques
Monbazillac
24240 Sigoulès
Closed November and January.
tel: (53) 58 37 77
A lovely, rather formal dining room in a typical Périgord house in this famous wine village: specialities include *fricassée de homard au vieux Monbazillac, escalope de foie de canard sauce raisins et Monbazillac*, accompanied by Monbazillac by the *pichet* and other wines of Bergerac.
Recommended by François Gerardin and others.
Moderate

4

Hôtel-Restaurant 'à Saussignac'
Saussignac
24240 Sigoulès
tel: (53) 27 92 08
Closed Sun eve; October–March.
Pleasant family hotel-restaurant in this quiet wine town. *Magret de canard* a speciality together with Saussignac wines.
Inexpensive

Fermes-Auberges

5

Jean-Louis & Danielle Gazzini
'La Grande Maison'
Monbazillac
24240 Sigoulès
tel: (53) 58 36 38
Daily, telephone call preferred.
Jean-Louis and Danielle Gazzini offer formidable Périgordian feasts in their thirteenth-century farmhouse: a typical meal might include all of this: *soupe, crudités, pâté de foie de canard, omelette aux cèpes, confit de canard, salade, fromage*, and fresh strawberries macerated in Monbazillac, all accompanied by Jean-Louis's own Monbazillac and red Bergerac.
Inexpensive

6 Martine Cazalet-Canaux
Faurilles
24560 Issigeac
tel: (53) 58 72 87
Evenings exclusively by reservation only.
Family atmosphere and good home cooking: everything served, including all meats, vegetables, and wine are produced by *la culture biologique*.
Inexpensive

The Lot Valley (Map p.239)

1 La Taverne
1, rue J-B Delpech
46000 Cahors
tel: (65) 35 28 66
Closed Sun eve out of season.
On the edge of the old *ville* near the Cathedral, this comfortable restaurant serves '*cuisine au marché*' based on what is available at each day's market. Typical dishes of Quercy include *la salade de truffes, cassoulet au confit de canard*.
Moderate

2 Relais de la Dolce
rte Villefranche-du-Périgord
Montcabrier
46700 Puy-l'Evêque
tel: (65) 36 53 42
Closed November–April.
North of Puy-l'Évêque not far from the Château de Bonaguil, this *Relais du Silence* would make a good base after travelling the Cahors wine circuit. Restaurant serves all the regional specialities with its own accent: *magret de canard sauce au miel, pintadeau aux baies de cassis*.
Moderate

3 Château de Mercuès
Mercuès
46090 Cahors
tel: (65) 20 00 01
Once part of the fief of the Bishops of Cahors, this historic château has been completely renovated into a luxury hotel-restaurant located north of Cahors in the heart of the vineyard. Owned by the renowned wine producer Georges Vigouroux (see above), the restaurant serves fine classic cuisine. Vinification and ageing *caves* are located under the park of the château and can be visited.
Moderate to Expensive

4 Restaurant 'Chez Marco'
Lamagdelaine

46090 Cahors
tel: (65) 35 30 64
Closed Sun eve; Mon out of season; January and February.
Local specialities together with a large selection of Cahors wines are served
in this traditional Quercyoise restaurant with attractive terrace.
Moderate

5

Auberge du Sombral
St-Cirq-Lapopie
46330 Cabrerets
tel: (65) 31 26 08
Closed Sat out of season.
Not actually on the wine route, but up-river from Cahors in one of the most
majestic sections of the Lot valley: the 'rustic' character of this little *auberge*
combines with a touch of elegance evident both in the dining room and the
food served: *truite aux vieux Cahors, gratin de cèpes, foie gras de canard
frais*. Good selection of Cahors, as well as Vin de Pays Coteaux de Quercy.
Moderate

Ferme-Auberge

6

Ferme-Auberge Imhotep
La Rivière Haute
Albas
46140 Luzech
tel: (65) 30 70 91
Closed Mon, Tue midday.
Foie gras, magret de canard, cassoulet, confit, and *couscous* (every Fri).
Inexpensive

Gascony (Map p.244)

1

La Table des Cordeliers
32100 Condom
tel: (62) 28 03 68
Closed Sun eve, Mon.
An especially striking and fine regional restaurant: one of the dining rooms
is located in the fourteenth-century chapel of the Cordeliers. The classics of
Gascony are served as well as *nouvelle cuisine* in an *ancien* setting.
Recommended by Janneau, François Faget, and others.
Moderate

2

La Gare
route d'Eauze
32250 Montréal-du-Gers
tel: (62) 28 43 37

Closed Thur eve, Fri.
Located 3 km (1.8 miles) from Montréal in a disused station house: regional foods include *garbure, magret de canard*.
Recommended by Château de Mailliac.
Inexpensive

3 Auberge de Guinlet
Guinlet
32800 Eauze
tel: (62) 09 85 99
This simple, friendly *auberge* outside Eauze is one of our favourites: excellent *menus* serving all the specialities of Gascony: *confit de canard, salmis de palombes, foie gras*, and an exquisite *croustade à l'armagnac*. Good selection of the 'little' wines of the south-west: Vin de Pays Côtes de Gascogne, Madiran, Pacherenc du Vic Bilh, Côtes de Buzet.
Inexpensive

4 La Bastide Gasconne
Barbotan-les-Thermes
32150 Cazaubon
tel: (62) 69 52 09
Closed November–April.
Many come to spa towns like Barbotan-les-Thermes to give themselves the opportunity to recover from the effects of excessive consumption of the hearty, rich foods of Gascony. Here, the classics are handled in an altogether lighter and elegant style in this fine restaurant run by the famous Guérard family.
Recommended by Château de Lacaze.
Expensive

5 Le Florida
32140 Castéra-Verduzan
tel: (62) 68 13 22
Closed Sun eve, Mon; October–May.
Regional cuisine and local wines are served on the pretty terrace in summer.
Moderate

6 Hôtel de France
Restaurant Daguin
place de la Libération
32000 Auch
tel: (62) 05 00 44
Closed Sun eve, Mon.
One of the great restaurants of France: chef André Daguin is renowned for his ability to combine the best elements of classic Gascon cuisine in a manner which is completely in harmony with modern *nouvelle* tastes. Auch is a charming town that deserves to be visited.
Expensive

Fermes-Auberges

7

Ferme-Auberge de Verduzan
Verduzan
32100 Condom
tel: (62) 28 11 77
Open daily by reservation only.
Regional specialities such as *foie gras*, *magret de canard*, *poulet farcie* served in an *ambiance familiale* together with own-produced wines.
Inexpensive

8

Ferme-Auberge 'La Baquère'
Préneron
32190 Vic-Fezenac
tel: (62) 06 42 75
Open by reservation only.
La Baquère is located just outside Vic-Fezenac in the hamlet of Préneron. Here the Barrets have created a most welcoming *ferme-auberge* serving the classics of Gascony in a decidedly lighter fashion: *confit de canard*, *foie gras de canard*, *garbure* and *pâtisseries maison*. They also offer *chambre d'hôte*, *gîte rural* and *camping à la ferme*. The Barrets raise all their own ducks, and early morning or evening visitors can see *la gavage*.
Inexpensive

9

Ferme-Auberge du 'Bergerayre'
St-Martin d'Armagnac
32110 Nogaro
tel: (62) 09 08 72
Open daily; telephone call in advance is appreciated.

Truffles

Périgord and Quercy are the major centres in France for truffles. These most highly prized black tubers are valued for their unmistakable aroma and a flavour which is somehow more a sensation than a taste. They are found by the roots of certain truffle oaks only, their presence discovered with the aid of trained pigs and dogs. To watch trained truffle dogs at work is quite a sight: the little beasts go literally mad with delight upon smelling the tuber buried in the ground below. But the truffle hunter must be quick to fetch the prize before the animals devour it! Truffles appear in the winter only, with a season lasting from about November to February. At this time throughout the Dordogne and Quercy, there are truffle markets where baskets are displayed for sale to restaurateurs and private gastronomes alike. Some of the major centres include: Sarlat, Périgueux, Sault, Cahors, and Lalbenque.

One of the best run *fermes-auberges* that we have visited, offering a cuisine as fine as that found in many starred restaurants. Home-produced *foie gras*, *grillades au feu de bois* and *confits* are all excellent, but Pierrette Sarran's *pastis gascon* (paper-thin pastry filled with Armagnac-soaked apples) is legendary. Four comfortable *chambres d'hôtes*.
Inexpensive to Moderate

Additional Information

Et pour en savoir plus . . .

Maison du Vin de Bergerac
2, place du Docteur Cayla
24100 Bergerac
tel: (53) 57 12 57

Union Interprofessionnelle
  du Vin de Cahors
ave Jean-Jaurès
46004 Cahors
tel: (65) 22 55 30

Bureau National
  Interprofessionnel de l'Armagnac
11, place Felix-Soulès
32800 Eauze
tel: (62) 09 82 33

Office de Tourisme
97, rue Neuve d'Argenson
24100 Bergerac
tel: (53) 57 03 11

Office de Tourisme
place A Briand
46000 Cahors
tel: (65) 35 09 56

Syndicat d'Initiative
à la Mairie
32800 Eauze
tel: (62) 09 85 62

Office de Tourisme
place Cathédrale
32000 Auch
tel: (62) 05 22 89

LANGUEDOC and ROUSSILLON

Introduction

THE WINES OF ROUSSILLON/
LANGUEDOC
Page 261 and Page 263

THE WINE ROADS OF
ROUSSILLON/LANGUEDOC
Page 268 and Page 276

DÉGUSTATION
Pages 273, 278, 281, 287

WINE FESTIVALS
Page 289

REGIONAL GASTRONOMY
Page 289

RESTAURANTS
Page 292

ADDITIONAL INFORMATION
Page 297

Terraced vineyards of Banyuls.

*A*s we head down through France, there comes a point when we realize that we are in the south, the Midi. The town cathedrals and churches are now made of redbrick, not stone; slate roofs have given way to terracotta tiles and solid wooden doors are replaced by waving, coloured strips of plastic; outdoor tables with Noilly Prat and Ricard umbrellas are to be found on every street corner; and in every town, even in the smallest village, there is a *cave coopérative*. Like great secular cathedrals, they stand on the outskirts, the most dominant and imposing structure in otherwise somnambulant *villes*.

Indeed, the *cave coopérative* is the focal point of the local economy, for this really is the land where the vine reigns supreme. From terraces under the shadow of the Pyrénées way down by the Spanish border, all along the sun-baked Mediterranean coast and up into its broad hinterland, a sea of vines covers the land, sometimes as far as the eye can see, from horizon to horizon. This is the largest wine-growing region in Europe, producing more than a third of all French table wines. Admittedly, sheer volume should not be considered an accolade in itself, yet simply in terms of area under vines and amounts of wine produced, Languedoc–Roussillon must clearly be considered an outstanding and important wine region.

Some of the oldest vineyards in France are to be found here, long-established even before the Romans, and still today planted mainly with the traditional old-fashioned grape varieties of the Mediterranean: Carignan, Mourvèdre, Cinsault, Grenache, Maccabéo, Malvoisie, Picpoul, and others. In the past, perhaps, the wines of the Midi have often been considered of little worth compared with the quality wines from regions to the north. True, the climate here is brutally hot and a profusion of grapes reaches a high degree of ripeness; quantity, moreover, has often been the aim of wine producers

LANGUEDOC and ROUSSILLON

at the expense of quality, resulting in vast wine lakes of simple, ordinary table wines.

But such have been the improvements in viticultural and wine-making techniques in recent years that those days are, on the whole, mainly past. Even many of the simpler table wines today are being produced to more stringent guidelines and have thus been elevated to Vin de Pays status. Furthermore, fine quality wines have always been produced here even if they have never been household names. Fitou is a hard, classic red wine that can be superb. Collioure, produced from the scorched, terraced vineyards around Banyuls is another little-known but fine, old-fashioned red. Vin Doux Naturels (VDN) such as Banyuls, Maury, Rasteau, Rivesaltes, and others, are little-known wines which have suffered, we feel, simply because sweet, fortified dessert wines are not currently fashionable exports. However, VDN Muscat wines (from Beaumes-de-Venise in the Rhône, as well as from Rivesaltes, Frontignan, and elsewhere) seem to be gaining in popularity once again so we may see a minor revival.

As wine-making techniques have improved, some of the best wines have been rewarded with elevation in status: Minervois and Corbières are both regions which now benefit from *appellations d'origine contrôlée* and they produce sound and sometimes fine wines. In this vast wine region, though, even more so than elsewhere, it is the individual wine grower that often makes the difference. Thus, even in areas with humble classifications, some growers have replaced the traditional Mediterranean *cépages* with classic grape varieties such as Cabernet Sauvignon and Merlot. The results are some exciting and fine new wines.

Historically, the Languedoc differed from the rest of France in many aspects, not least of all linguistically (*langue d'oc* means the tongue of *oc*, that is the region where *occitane* was spoken, as opposed to the *langue d'oïl*, which eventually came to predominate). Stronghold of the Cathari heretics, frontier between Spain and Provence, this timeless land still looks every bit as imposing, as rugged, and as proud as it must have done in the times of the Crusades. Carcassonne, for example, with its magnificent ramparts rising above the plain is a breathtaking sight. Fortified Aigues-Mortes, perched on the edge of the marshy Camargue, still recalls the age when St. Louis set off from here on the first of his crusades to the Holy Land in 1248.

Today, Languedoc is linked to Roussillon, but this administrative convenience really brings together areas which have little in common except their southern proximity. For Roussillon itself remains a proud and separate region with a Catalan heritage that is contiguous with the Spanish Catalan country across the border. Perpignan, the capital of Roussillon, was formerly a home of the kings of Majorca: their grand, brick former palace still dominates this fine and distinctive city. Roussillon was only annexed to France in the mid-seventeenth century.

Languedoc–Roussillon has much to offer to the visitor: timeless seaside fishing villages co-exist alongside new resort towns which seem to have appeared (almost) overnight. In the hinterlands, villages remain quiet and totally unspoiled. The cuisine of the Midi, like its wines, is nothing if not forthright and robust. This is a lazy, easy, hot land that appears sometimes, through the ever-present shimmering heat haze, more like an inland sea, a sea of vines stretching from horizon to horizon. To be where such vast quantities of wines are produced: can life ever be less than congenial?

Orientation

The region of Languedoc–Roussillon extends over about half of the French Mediterranean coast and its hinterland, west of the Rhône delta across to the Spanish border and the Pyrénées. It includes the *départements* of Pyrénées-Orientales; Aude; Hérault; Gard; Lozère; and Tarn. Major cities include Toulouse, Montpellier, and Perpignan, located from Paris respectively 700 km (440 miles), 760 km (475 miles), and 910 km (570 miles). For motorists, there are two principal routes to the south: via the A6–A7 *autoroutes* Paris–Lyon–Avignon, then the A9 *autoroute* west to Nîmes, Montpellier, Narbonne, and Perpignan; or via the A10–A62–A61 *autoroutes* Paris–Bourdeaux–Toulouse–Carcassonne–Narbonne.

There are direct train services from Paris to Toulouse, with comfortable services completing the journey in about 8 hours. From Lyon there is a direct service to Montpellier, Béziers, Narbonne, and Perpignan. The journey from Lyon to Perpignan takes about 6 hours.

The most convenient international airport is Toulouse Blagnac.

Michelin Maps 82, 83, 86

The Wines of Roussillon

Banyuls AOC;
anyuls Grand Cru *AOC*

Banyuls is considered to be one of the foremost Vins Doux Naturels (VDN), a classic of its type produced mainly from Grenache grapes grown on steeply terraced slate and shale vineyards near the Spanish border. The grapes gain a particular concentration of flavour and richness in natural sugars due to their excellent exposure and extremely low yield. The resulting wines, fortified by a process of muting (see below), may be sweet or semi-sweet, medium-dry or even dry. The finest are designated *Grands Crus* and must be aged in wood for at least 2½ years; even older wines are known as *vieux* or *rancio* and they take on a characteristic maderized flavour. Banyuls AOC is usually drunk here as an *apéritif* though it is equally suitable to serve, like port which it resembles, as an after-dinner drink.

Collioure AOC

Powerful red wine produced from the same vineyards as Banyuls, mainly from the Grenache grape. The grapes are equally rich and concentrated

The Cathari

In the late twelfth and early thirteenth centuries, the sects of the Cathars and the Albigensians gained large followings in this south-western corner of France. Both preached what they believed to be purer forms of Christianity based on the Manichaean duality of good and evil. The Church deemed these sects to be heretical and the Albigensian Crusade was launched to eradicate them. Carcassonne was attacked and captured by Simon de Montfort. Little,

isolated, Minerve, in the heart of the wine district to which it gives its name, was an important stronghold for the Cathars. In spite of its natural fortified position astride the Clesse gorge, it too was captured, and a stone marks the spot where some 180 prefects and followers were burnt at the stake in 1210. The Cathari retreated further into isolation, high in the Pyrénées, and were able to hold out at the Château de Montségur until 1244, living a life, apparently, of licentious and wild promiscuity (one reason, no doubt, for the sect's popular appeal). Finally, after a 5-month siege, the château was taken and another 250 Cathari submitted to the tortures of fire rather than recant their faith.

The strategically sited village of Minerve.

and this results in a wine high in alcohol (13°) with a deep, dark colour, lots of tannin, and warm, spicy, rich aromas. Though rather unforthcoming and harsh when young, after 4 or 5 years' ageing it gains a more mellow, rounded character. Collioure, the smallest *appellation* of Roussillon, is rarely encountered outside its region of production and should be sampled on the spot, especially with gutsy Catalan food such as Collioure *anchois* (fresh anchovies marinated in oil, parsley, and garlic) and the classic seafood medley *paella*.

Côtes du Roussillon AOC

*R*ed, white, and rosé wines produced from the traditional Mediterranean grape varieties: primarily Carignan, with the addition of varying proportions of Grenache, Mourvèdre, Cinsault, and Syrah for the reds and rosés, and solely Maccabéo and Malvoisie for the whites. Strong, robust, and full-bodied, they are made primarily in *caves coopératives* throughout the region and can be very good, inexpensive country wines.

Côtes du Roussillon-Villages AOC

*T*he finest reds of the Côtes du Roussillon gain this superior *appellation*. They come mainly from the Agly valley and have more concentrated flavour and body and a slightly higher alcohol content. Two villages only are entitled to utilize their names on the bottle: Caramany and La Tour de France, both

of which produce superlative wines available from their respective local *coopératives*.

Grand Roussillon AOC

*V*in Doux Naturel red, rosé, and white wines from the vineyards of the Côtes du Roussillon.

Maury AOC

*H*igh up in the Agly valley, the loose shale hills of Maury lend an individual and distinct character to the Grenache grapes utilized to make this renowned Vin Doux Naturel.

Muscat de Rivesaltes AOC; Rivesaltes AOC

*T*he highly perfumed Muscat de Rivesaltes AOC is one of the better-known VDNs, delicious served well chilled as a dessert wine or with Roquefort cheese or *foie gras*. The small town of Rivesaltes gives its name to the *appellation* which extends well beyond its municipal borders, throughout many of the vineyards of Roussillon. Rivesaltes AOC is the *appellation* for red and rosé VDNs made primarily from the Grenache, Maccabéo, and Malvoisie grapes produced from the same vineyard area.

Vin de Pays des Pyrénées-Orientales

*T*his *départemental* classification for the simple Vins de Pays of Roussillon covers the whole area and can apply to red, white, and rosé wines which satisfy certain conditions relating to permitted grape varieties, methods of cultivation and yield per hectare. In addition to the traditional Mediterranean grape varieties, the region has recently encouraged the plantings of Carbernet Sauvignon and Merlot, and the results so far suggest that some distinctive varietal wines will result. As well as the large *départemental* classification, there are four specific Vins de Pays from smaller designated zones: Vin de Pays Catalan (west and south of Perpignan), Vin de Pays des Côtes Catalanes (covering the Rivesaltes and La Tour de France areas), Vin de Pays Val d'Agly (Côtes du Roussillon-Villages area), and Vin de Pays Coteaux des Fenouillèdes (vineyards further east to the border of the Aude *département*).

The Wines of Languedoc

Blanquette de Limoux AOC

*M*éthode champenoise sparkling wine produced mainly from the Mauzac grape with the addition of some Chardonnay and Chenin in vineyards south of Carcassonne around the little wine town of Limoux and 42 other villages of the Aude. Blanquette de Limoux is said to be the oldest sparkling wine in the world, documented as long ago as 941. Today most of the wine is made at the *cave coopérative* of the Blanquette producers.

Clairette du Languedoc AOC

*O*ne of the three *crus* of the Coteaux du Languedoc produced in the hills above Pézenas: the white wines are dry or medium-dry and come exclusively from the Clairette grape. Older, stronger examples classify as Vins

Vins Doux Naturels

Tradition in wine has often resulted historically from economic and social need. It is no coincidence that the greatest wines of France — those with the richest and most concentrated and subtle flavours: the *Grands Crus* of Bordeaux and Burgundy; Sauternes; or Château-Chalon from the Jura — are also those wines which can be conserved for the longest periods. In distant times, long before hygienic bottling or refrigeration, before even the cork had been discovered, the need to produce wines that were capable of being conserved was indeed a pressing one.

Thus, in the thirteenth century during the time when the kings of Majorca resided in splendour at Perpignan, it was a considerable achievement when Arnau de Vilanova, in his Caves du Mas Deu at Trouillas, discovered a method of 'muting' wines with the addition of grape brandy to result in a drink that was not only highly palatable but also — particularly important in this scorching climate where underground cellars were virtually non-existent — able to last for many years and even decades.

Such wines became known as Vins Doux Naturels and are still produced by age-old methods today. Though the name translates 'sweet natural wines', they differ from Sauternes, Monbazillac, and other *vin liquoreux* which are truly produced naturally like other table wines. Vins Doux Naturels, on the other hand, undergo a process of muting by fortification with grape brandy. The wines are first produced from grapes with exceptionally high levels of ripeness and natural sugars, then they have their fermentation arrested by the addition of grape brandy. This has the result of stopping fermentation at a desired point, thus allowing the wines to retain a natural residual sweetness in varying degrees.

Today, such traditional wines are virtually the opposite to the light, crisp, dry white wines currently in vogue: yet even if they are hardly fashionable, Vins Doux Naturels are centuries-old classics and as such remain an essential part of the great spectrum of the wines of France.

de Liqueur and have that distinctive, almost woody, taste similar to aged Vins Doux Naturels. Such wines are often designated *Rancio*.

Corbières AOC

*R*ecently elevated to *appellation d'origine contrôlée* status, the wines of Corbières come from a vast and varied vineyard, extending over the rugged Corbières massif from Narbonne to Perpignan, and from Carcassonne to Limoux, encompassing some 94 wine communes in the Aude. Red, white, and rosé wines are produced, primarily from the traditional Mediterranean *cépages*: Carignan, Grenache, Mourvèdre, Maccabéo, Cinsault, Piquepoul, Clairette, Malvoisie, and others.

While some red Corbières AOC is vinified traditionally with a lengthy maceration to produce full-bodied wines that can benefit from ageing, the majority are vinified at least in part by *macération carbonique* resulting in wines that are meant to be drunk while young and fruity. White Corbières is today often vinified at low temperatures and this has brought about a great improvement in quality in recent years, resulting in wines that are clean, fresh, and aromatic. Corbières AOC is a good, inexpensive country wine which should be enjoyed on the spot. The rosés, in our experience, are not as fine as those from Provence or the Rhône, but they can be pleasant and refreshing enough in the summer heat.

Costières du Gard AOC

*W*ines produced from vineyards located between Nîmes and Arles in the *département* of the Gard have recently gained *appellation d'origine contrôlée* status. Red wines are vinified for very short periods to result in soft cherry-coloured wines that can be enjoyed almost immediately; the rosés are also attractive. Smaller amounts of white wines are made.

Coteaux du Languedoc AOC

*A*nother *appellation* which has been rewarded with enhanced status in recent years: it applies to vineyards over vast and numerous distinct areas, including three superlative *crus*: Faugères, St-Chinian, and Clairette du Languedoc, and 12 designated *terroirs*: Cabrières, La Clape, La Mejanelle, Montpeyroux, Picpoul de Pinet, Pic-St-Loup, Quatourze, St-Christol, St-Drézery, St-Saturnin, St-Georges-d'Orques, and Verargues. These wines may be presented under the general regional *appellation*, under the *appellation* together with the name of the *terroir* or locality, or, in the case of the *crus* under that name alone. Not surprisingly, a huge number and variety of wines come under this broad banner: reds, whites, rosés, and sweet wines of all different styles and qualities. As such, it is often the reputation of the individual *propriétaire-récoltant* or the local *cave coopérative* which is the most important quality factor. Some very good wines are being made by dedicated growers. In other cases, less distinguished, though on the whole sound, wines make pleasant holiday drinking.

Faugères AOC

*C*oteaux du Languedoc *cru* produced from vineyards to the north of Béziers. The red wines in particular are good robust examples of the wines of the Midi.

Fitou AOC

*C*onsidered by many to be the finest red wine of the Languedoc, Fitou was the first *appellation d'origine contrôlée* wine of the region and has benefited from this status since 1948. Produced from a minimum of 75 per cent of Carignan, a particularly tough and unforthcoming traditional *cépage*, Fitou is a deep, dark wine meant to be laid down to age for at least 4–5 years before drinking, perhaps even longer. There are two principal zones of production: the littoral, encompassing the communes near the sea of Leucate, La Palme, Caves, Treilles, and Fitou itself, and the inland region extending into the Corbières hills, around the communes of Cascastel, Villeneuve, Tuchan,

LANGUEDOC and ROUSSILLON

and Paziols. Fitou is a classic red wine, superb with the strongly flavoured foods of the region, especially *cassoulet*.

Gaillac AOC

*T*he Gaillac *appellation* applies to one of the oldest vineyards in France (planted in the first century AD), located today in the *département* of the Tarn, north-east of Toulouse on the road to the provincial capital of Albi. A wide and extremely varied range of wines comes from Gaillac. Dry and medium-dry white wines are produced mainly from the Mauzac grape; at best they are clean, aromatic, and refreshing. Red wines are made from little-known local varieties such as Duras, Braucol, Negrette, Fer, and others, with the addition of some Cabernet, Merlot, and Jurançon; when made by *macération carbonique* they can be drunk cool, while young and fruity. Some red wines are still made by traditional methods for ageing. Sparkling Gaillac Mousseux is produced from the Mauzac grape; the wines gain their sparkle either by *méthode champenoise* or else by a local method known as *méthode gaillaçoise*. Gaillac Perlé is a semi-sparkling *pétillant* wine which can be very refreshing. The wines of Gaillac are marketed in the distinctive 'Gaillaçoise' bottles, a guarantee that they have been bottled in their region of production.

Minervois AOC

*T*he Minervois vineyard was planted by the Romans and is named after the ancient city of Minerve, a remarkable fortified *ville* whose patron saint was the goddess of wisdom. The wines have thus been known and renowned for centuries, but they too have been elevated to full AOC status only since 1985. The vineyard region itself is quite large and varied, extending over the southern extremity of the Massif Central between Carcassonne, Béziers, and Narbonne, over 45 communes in the Aude and 16 in the Hérault. Red, white, and rosé Minervois AOC wines are produced from the traditional Mediterranean varieties, while there is also one Vin Doux Naturel, Muscat de St-Jean-du-Minervois VDN. Red Minervois is generally supple and fruity, meant to be drunk while young and fresh; the whites and rosés are similarly youthful and uncomplicated wines. There are, however, considerable variations in style, not only between individual producers but also from different zones within a surprisingly large region.

Muscat de Frontignan VDN;
Muscat de Lunel AOC;
Muscat de Mireval VDN

*F*ragrant Muscat wines, fortified by the process of *mutage* with grape brandy (VDN), are produced throughout Languedoc, though those from Frontignan are among the best and best known. Mireval is a neighbouring commune producing very similar wines, while Muscat de Lunel comes from vineyards east of Montpellier.

St-Chinian AOC

A cru Coteaux du Languedoc *appellation* for rather large amounts of mainly red wine from vineyards located in the hinterland above Béziers. The wines are produced mainly from Carignan, Grenache, Cinsault, and other traditional varieties; they can be both good and good value.

Phylloxera

In the second half of the last century a natural disaster occurred which was so profound that it is almost impossible to conceive of: *Phylloxera vastatrix*, a tiny little aphid, arrived in France from North America on American vine varieties which were imported and which were themselves resistant to the pest. *Phylloxera* found the vineyards of France, indeed, Europe to its extreme liking and immediately began its scourge, spreading from region to region and finally country to country. So vicious, so unbelievably deadly was this pest, that by the turn of the century virtually every vineyard in Europe — from the most humble to the most illustrious — had been destroyed. The only way to eradicate the pest was to grub up the vines, burn the stock and sterilize the soil.

This was a French national, not to mention local and personal, crisis in the extreme, for wine has always been — and always will be — not just a major agricultural product but a virtual national asset. After many years of despair, during which the agricultural face of France was altered as certain areas abandoned the vine in favour of other crops, a solution was discovered: if European vines (*Vitis vinifera*) were grafted on to aphid-resistant American root stock then they could be replanted in safety. This was done and even today this remains standard practice throughout the world. But in rare pockets ungrafted vines remain: the vineyards of the Sables du Golfe du Lion, like the vineyards of Colares, near Lisbon, are planted in deep sand, and thus the pest was never able to penetrate the rootstock.

Vin de Pays de l'Hérault

A vast catchment for the vineyards of the Languedoc: there are a further 28 specific Vin de Pays zones within the Hérault for the red, rosé, and white table wines. The largest, Vin de Pays des Collines de la Moure, produces over 10 million bottles annually. Though such wines in the past served only to help swell the proverbial EEC wine lake, the standard of production has generally risen greatly in recent years.

Vin de Pays de l'Aude

A nother vast *départemental* classification for an ocean of everyday red, rosé, and white table wines. There are a further 20 Vin de Pays zones within the Aude, some of the best being Coteaux de la Cité de Carcassonne, Côtes de Perpignan, and Vallée de Paradis. In general, the more specific the geographical designation, the more distinctive the wine, though in practice, many of these wines appear very similar.

Vin de Pays du Gard

S traightforward red, rosé, and white wines from the *département* of the Gard; the vineyard area is further classified into 12 zones.

Vin de Pays des Sables
du Golfe du Lion

*R*ed, white, rosé, and *gris* wines are produced from traditional and classic grape varieties planted in the deep sand dunes extending over the littorals of the Gard, Hérault, and Bouches-du-Rhône *départements*. One of the largest producers is Les Salins du Midi who market wines from their various estates under the trade name Listel. The wines can be very good indeed.

In all, the Vins de Pays of Languedoc and Roussillon account for a full three-quarters of all Vins de Pays produced in France.

Pétillant de Raisin

*T*his quality sparkling grape juice is produced throughout the Gaillac vineyard from the Mauzac grape. It gains its sparkle from secondary fermentation in the bottle, but this results in an alcohol content usually only of less than 1° and guaranteed to be no more than 3°. It is an excellent beverage for drivers, children, and non-drinkers. Les Salins du Midi also produces a fine *pétillant de raisin*.

The Wine Roads
of Roussillon

In Brief   The vineyard of Roussillon extends to the north and south of the region's capital Perpignan, along the east-facing coastline as well as into the hills to the west. As such, it is a vast natural amphitheatre formed by three massifs: les Corbières to the north, le Canigou to the west, and les Albères to the south. There are numerous resorts along the coast, including Le Barcarès, Canet Plage, Argelès Plage, Collioure, and Banyuls itself. Perpignan is an elegant and fascinating city and certainly one which repays exploration. Inland villages are, on the whole, tiny, unspoiled, and little visited.
      We include details of two wine tours: a brief but dramatic excursion into the terraces of Banyuls; and a slightly longer wine tour which begins in Rivesaltes and travels through the Agly valley, where the finest Côtes du Roussillon-Villages wines are produced. Along the way there are numerous 'Haltes Rivesaltes' to refresh the thirsty. Either tour could be completed in a half day, but these are not wine roads to rush along. Other Roussillon wine roads extend from Argelès into the hills of the Aspres, as well as around Perpignan itself.

The Terraces of Banyuls

The vineyard of Banyuls extends over four communes: Collioure, Port-Vendres, Banyuls-sur-Mer, and Cerbère, the last located virtually at the Spanish border. To reach the start of the *Route du Vin* drive to Collioure via the N114 from Perpignan or along the D81 coast road. At Argelès-sur-Mer, a profound change in the geology of the region is apparent as the rather dull and flatter coastal stretches give way to a beautiful and confused rocky coast and steeper hinterland which rises under the shadows of the Pyrénées. It is this marked change in terrain, allied with exceptional exposure and hours of sunshine, which defines the Banyuls vineyard.

The first wine town on this brief but exciting wine road is Collioure, which gives its name to the fine red table wine produced from these same vineyards. Collioure is a lovely old fishing village dominated by its Château Royal, a former summer residence of the kings of Majorca. The town, apparently, was 'discovered' by the artists Matisse, Derain, Dufy, and others, who came here to paint earlier in the century; even today along its little cobbled streets and alleys there is no shortage of *ateliers*. Yet the town retains its charm in spite of the crowds who come here to wander along the promenades. Lateen-rigged fishing boats still work these waters and their catch — especially the famous fresh anchovies of Collioure — finds its way to the tables of any number of waterfront restaurants. Come here, too, to enjoy the small but beautiful beaches, positioned so dramatically with the terraced vineyards of Banyuls rising steeply behind them.

Continue on the coast road to Port-Vendres, which remains very much a working port, then on to little Banyuls-sur-Mer itself. Banyuls, with its waving palm trees ringing the wide, sweeping bay, its Spanish houses, and its restaurants serving Catalan specialities such as *paella* and *gambas sur la plancha*, certainly feels closer to Barcelona than, say, to Bordeaux. And why not? Historically as well as geographically this separate Mediterranean corner *is* closer: the region of Roussillon only became a French province under the Treaty of the Pyrénées as late as 1659.

From Banyuls, either continue down to the frontier town of Cerbère or else strike out into the magnificent vineyards that tower above the town. On the way out (route du Mas Reig), stop at the 'Celliers des Templiers', where the *Groupement Interproducteurs du Cru Banyuls* have over 30,000 hectolitres of Banyuls ageing. An audio-visual presentation explains the history of the region and there is the opportunity to taste the wines. Further along the road,

Banyuls.

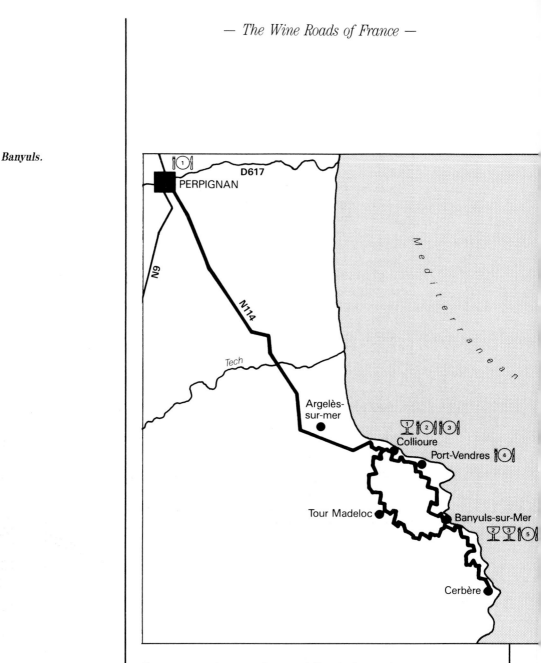

the same group has an underground 'Grande Cave du Mas Reig' where some of the oldest Banyuls *rancio* lie ageing; it too can be visited.

The vineyards themselves lie on an incredible system of criss-crossing stone terraces, with stone-paved drainage channels running vertically and diagonally down and across the slopes. They are without doubt some of the most striking and dramatic vineyards in Europe, not wholly unlike the Port vineyards of the scorched Upper Douro valley in northern Portugal (indeed, the wines themselves bear a certain similarity as well).

Naturally, these vineyards are so torturously steep that virtually no mechanization is possible. Apart from tending the vines, the constant upkeep required just to maintain the dry-stone terraces is monumentally arduous. The vineyard region is no longer as extensive as it once was (is this because the wines are no longer as popular or because there is simply too much effort involved in tending such vineyards?). One need only notice the neglected and forlorn terraces to see how quickly the land, once corsetted into ordered shapes and patterns, when freed so quickly returns to its natural and wild state.

In times past, it was difficult to transport the harvest, since no roads extended into the hills, so the grapes were pressed and vinified on the spot in small mountain huts, then transported to the villages below by way of an intricate system of terracotta channels which extended down the hills, precursors of modern pipelines! Today, as in the past, there is precious little in these hills, save the vineyards themselves: tasting opportunities do exist, but in the towns below, not up here.

Simply enjoy this dramatic vineyard road for its own sake: following the winding and narrow mountain track back around to Collioure, stopping at any number of lay-bys to view the Catalan coast extending to the north and south. Climb up to the Tour Madeloc (if you dare!) for possibly the finest view of all, then continue back down to Collioure for a glass of good, sweet Banyuls at a roadside tasting stand, or, better still, at a pleasant waterfront table.

The Agly Valley: *'Ici, Halte Rivesaltes'*

This tour of the Agly valley and the Fenouillèdes begins at the fifteenth-century military fortress known as the Château de Salses (located on the N9 Narbonne–Perpignan road). This great fortification, which can be visited, is one of the

Agly Valley.

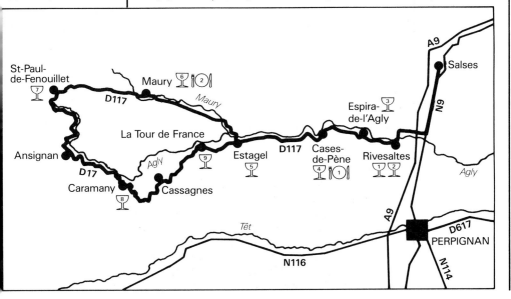

finest examples of military architecture in the region. From Salses, continue further south on the N9 then turn off to the town of Rivesaltes. Rivesaltes gives its name to an *appellation* which extends over some 86 communes in the Pyrénées-Orientales and another nine in the Aude, which all produce the distinctive Muscat de Rivesaltes and Rivesaltes Vins Doux Naturels. The town itself is rather large and pleasant enough, especially on market days, and there are a number of wine producers to visit.

People have been coming to Rivesaltes to sample the wines for centuries: Muscat de Rivesaltes has been made since at least the thirteenth century, and it is probable that pilgrims on the road to Santiago de Compostela enjoyed many a glass of this delicious and distinctive wine *en route*. It was the playwright Edmond Rostand who first used the expression '*Halte Rivesaltes*' in *Cyrano de Bergerac*: today, throughout the entire Rivesaltes vineyard region, there are countless such 'Rivesaltes stops', displaying a bright and inviting banner urging all visitors to stop and try a cool glass of the golden, perfumed nectar.

To follow the wine route, leave Rivesaltes on the little D5d to Espira de l'Agly then find the D117, which continues up the Agly valley. This is a quite spectacular route, following the little Agly river from Cases-de-Pène to Estagel, then the Maury river higher up the valley to Maury and St-Paul-de-Fenouillet. Vines grow on virtually every bit of earth and on steep dry-stone terraces, and in this protected hothouse atmosphere, the grapes, sheltered to the north by the sharp and jagged Corbières range, reach a rare degree of ripeness and concentration. It is for these factors that the wines produced in the valley are deemed superior, entitled to the *appellation* Côtes du Roussillon-Villages.

In Cases-de-Pène take time to visit the Château de Jau, an important wine domaine which also has a permanent art *exposition* open to the public and a pleasant grill-restaurant, open in season, serving Catalan specialities. The rugged terrain around Maury is particularly well suited to the Grenache grape, giving it a character that is particular and remarkable, thus Maury VDN has gained its own unique *appellation*: stop here at the *coopérative* of the *Groupement des Vignerons de Maury* to try it. St-Paul-de-Fenouillet is the centre of the Fenouillèdes, the region which extends into the Corbières hills and the valley further inland. The town *cave coopérative*, located on the main road, is a most welcoming '*Halte Rivesaltes*'.

From St-Paul, find the D619 which cuts across a wild and spectacular gorge to Ansignan: there an ancient aqueduct, set against the vines and rocky scenery, completes a timeless and beautiful picture. From Ansignan, find the smaller D9 which leads to Caramany, an isolated hill village deep in this remote wine country: one only has to drive up this high isolated gorge to appreciate why the wine from this commune receives the special accolade of being able to append its name to the Côtes du Roussillon-Villages *appellation*. Fine oak-aged wines made in the village *coopérative* can be tasted and purchased in the Caveau du Presbytère: come here to enjoy a picnic at the shaded tables set up in this pleasant tasting area, overlooking the village and its vineyards.

From Caramany, continue through this wild and unspoiled country, around to Cassagnes then descend once more back to the Agly valley. La Tour de France, today so quiet and remote, was once an important frontier town, marking the border between France and Spain. Today it is known above all for its fine wines, for it, together with Caramany, is the only other village which can append its name to the *appellation*.

From La Tour de France, return to Rivesaltes, Perpignan, or your beachside retreat at Le Barcarès, Canet or St-Cyprien-Plage.

Dégustation: Stop to Taste; Stop to Buy

Roussillon is primarily a region of *petits vignerons*, many of whom tend small parcels of vines as a supplement to other forms of farming or income. Due to the nature of the terrain as well as the economics of the region there is relatively little mechanization here, and as far as making the wines goes, many *vignerons* depend on the services of their local *caves coopératives*. Indeed, some 64 *caves coopératives* and a further 60 or so private cellars have joined forces under the marketing *groupement 'Vignerons Catalans'*. Côtes du Roussillon and Côtes du Roussillon-Villages table wines are still inexpensive bargains; Muscat de Rivesaltes is less expensive than its currently fashionable sister VDN Muscat de Beaumes-de-Venise from the Rhône.

Reno Cellier.

Banyuls

1

Reno Cellier
66190 Collioure
Located on the main road into Collioure, this tasting stand offers Banyuls, Banyuls *Grand Cru* VDN, and Collioure AOC, as well as *anchois de Collioure* and other products and specialities of the region.

2

Cellier des Templiers
rte du Mas Reig
66650 Banyuls-sur-Mer
tel: (68) 88 31 59
Hours: Daily 9–19h.
The *Groupement Interproducteurs du Cru Banyuls* is the largest producer of this famous and distinctive Vin Doux Naturel; its large-scale operation, located above the town, is most welcoming. Visitors see a film on the history of Banyuls and visit the cellars where the wines lie ageing in wooden barrels. Banyuls VDN, Banyuls *Grand Cru* VDN, and Collioure AOC can be tasted and purchased. The *Groupement* offers other visiting opportunities in Port-Vendres as well as further up the road at their 'Grande Cave du Mas Reig'.
English spoken.

3 Domaine du Mas Blanc
9, ave Général de Gaulle
66650 Banyuls-sur-Mer
tel: (68) 88 32 12
Hours: Daily by appointment.
Family producer making fine traditional Collioure AOC and Banyuls VDN.

The Agly Valley

1 Société Coopérative Vinicole de Rivesaltes
rue de la Roussillonnaise
66600 Rivesaltes
tel: (68) 64 06 63
Hours: Mon–Fri 8–12h; 14–18h. Appointment preferred.
Muscat de Rivesaltes VDN, Rivesaltes VDN, Côtes du Roussillon-Villages AOC,
Château de Vespeilles Côtes du Roussillon AOC, Vin de Pays.
English spoken.

2 Domaine Cazes Frères
4, rue Francisco Ferrer
66600 Rivesaltes
tel: (68) 64 08 26
Hours: Mon–Fri 8–12h; 14–18h. By appointment.
A full range of fine table wines and VDNs are produced by the Société Cazes
Frères.

3 A Mercier
Domaine de la Joliette
Espira de l'Agly
66600 Rivesaltes
tel: (68) 64 50 60
Hours: Mon–Sat 8–19h. Appointment preferred.
This lovely domaine, located midway between Rivesaltes and nearby Espira,
sits at the foot of the Corbières hills, with a view overlooking the sea. A full
range of wines is produced: Muscat de Rivesaltes VDN: Rivesaltes *doré* and
rancio vieux; red, white, and rosé Côtes du Roussillon AOC; and Côtes du
Roussillon-Villages AOC.
A little English spoken.

4 Château de Jau
RN117
66600 Cases-de-Pène
tel: (68) 64 11 38; (64) 54 51 67
Hours: Daily 11–19h.
The Château de Jau, domaine of the family Dauré, is an historic property
surrounded by its well-exposed vineyards and with a most modern winery.

The estate produces Château de Jau red and white (Côtes du Roussillon AOC) and Château de Jau Muscat de Rivesaltes VDN. There are art *expositions* open to the public all year long, and in summer there is a grill-restaurant serving Catalan specialities (see below).
English spoken.

5

'Aglya'
Société Coopérative Agricole de Vinification
66310 Estagel
tel: (68) 29 00 45
Hours: Daily, working hours. Visits by appointment.
Member *vignerons* work some 850 surrounding hectares of vines to produce Rivesaltes *doré* and *tuilé* VDN; Muscat de Rivesaltes VDN; Côtes du Roussillon-Villages AOC; Vin de Pays Côtes Catalanes; and pure *jus de raisin*.

6

Groupement des Vignerons de Maury
128, ave Jean Jaurès
66460 Maury
tel: (68) 59 00 95
Hours: Mon–Fri 8–12h; 14–18h. Appointment preferred.
Maury VDN; Muscat de Rivesaltes VDN; Côtes du Roussillon-Villages AOC.

7

Société Coopérative Vinicole
17, ave Jean Moulin
66220 St-Paul-de-Fenouillet
tel: (68) 59 02 39
Hours: Daily, working hours.
Rivesaltes *doré vieux* and *tuilé vieux* VDN; Muscat de Rivesaltes VDN; Côtes du Roussillon-Villages AOC 'Cuvée des Champions'; red, white, and rosé Côtes du Roussillon AOC; Vin de Pays.

8

Caveau du Presbytère
66720 Caramany
tel: (68) 84 51 42
Hours: June–August daily 14h30–19h. Out of season Sun 14h30–17h. Other times by appointment. Closed October.
In the heart of the village, this pleasant *caveau* is run on behalf of the local *cave coopérative*. Two styles of Côtes du Roussillon-Villages Caramany AOC are produced: a lighter, youthful wine made in part by *macération carbonique* and a traditional longer-lived wine aged in oak. Pleasant picnic area and permanent *exposition* of vineyard tools and barrels.

9

Les Vignerons de La Tour de France
2, ave Général de Gaulle
66720 La Tour de France
tel: (68) 29 11 12
Hours: Mon–Sat, working hours.

LANGUEDOC and ROUSSILLON

Côtes du Roussillon-Villages La Tour de France AOC; Côtes du Roussillon AOC; Muscat de Rivesaltes VDN; Vin de Pays and table wines *en vrac*.

The Wine Roads of Languedoc

In Brief   There is no way to be brief about the wine roads of Languedoc. This is such a vast vine-covered region, that virtually all roads lead to or through vineyards at some point. We therefore include brief touring details for the principal *appellations* together with addresses of some producers and *caves coopératives* to visit. While this will take the wine traveller into the main vineyard areas, and direct to the source of the generous and abundant wines of the Languedoc, the region still remains very much uncharted wine country and there are scores of discoveries to be made. No matter where the visitor stays — in coastal resorts by Montpellier, Narbonne, or Béziers, or inland in historic centres such as Carcassonne, Pézenas, or Albi — there are countless vineyards to explore and committed individual wine growers to find.

Gaillac

The Gaillac vineyard is located in the *département* of the Tarn, extending over the rolling hills above that river in the countryside between Rabastens, Gaillac, and Albi, the region's capital, as well as over the hills and up to the fine medieval *bastide* of Cordes. As such, it is a single-minded and intensive wine region which is not overly large, yet which produces a full range of types and styles of wines. The entire vineyard can easily be covered in a day or two, but this fine region is really worthy of longer stays. The high inland towns are particularly peaceful and pleasant, and there are some fine country *auberges* and restaurants serving the ample foods of the region. Albi, too, is an elegant and sophisticated provincial capital with much to offer the visitor.

Medieval bastide *of Cordes.*

     The region is reached by exiting the A62 *autoroute* on the north side of Toulouse and finding the N88 which leads eventually through the vineyards to Albi. Though today the Tarn is not officially part of the Languedoc–Roussillon region (just as Nantes is no longer officially part of Brittany — a ridiculous administrative omission), the people here certainly have no problems with their identity. There is no question, either, about the feel of villages such as Rabastens, with its brick church and immense, dirt promenade where men gather in the evenings to play *pétanque*: this *is* the Midi.

     To begin a tour of the vineyards, find the smaller D18 out of Rabastens to Gaillac, a small road that leads through the hills above the lovely Tarn valley.

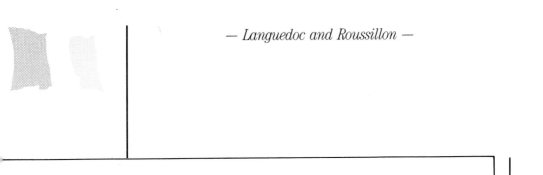

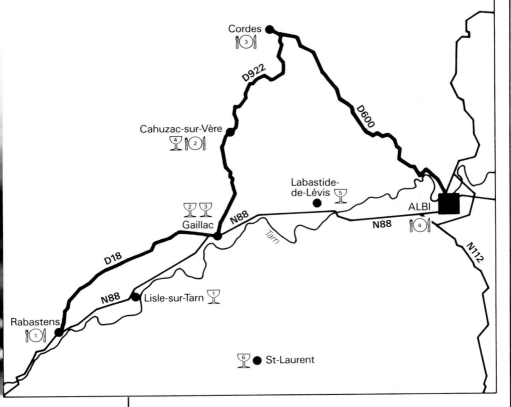

Gaillac.

These are well-tended and prosperous vineyards, not haphazard ones; this care is similarly reflected in the wines of Gaillac, which are enjoying increasing recognition as sound and well-made country wines available at reasonable prices.

Gaillac is an extremely busy little wine capital, especially on Tuesdays, Fridays, and Sunday mornings when there is a market on in the place Thiers. There is certainly no shortage of packed bars on such days where the men of the town gather to talk and down tumblers of the tasty red or white Gaillac, or the delectable semi-sparkling Gaillac Perlé: in summer there is a large tasting '*tonneau*' for visitors, set up in the centre of town.

The countryside between Gaillac and Cordes is particularly beautiful, almost Italianate in feel, with its abstract patterns made by lines of vines extending over and down the hills, and its towns or hamlets perched on top, the red-tiled roofs of the houses glowing in the sun. Cordes itself rises dramatically above this hilly landscape. Park down below and climb the winding, narrow stone streets of this thirteenth-century *bastide*, one of the most complete and attractive in France. Today, certainly, the old houses are populated with new generations of artisans — weavers, leather-workers, artists, printmakers, dress designers and the like — and one feels a lively sense of industry and enterprise. The views of the surrounding countryside from the top of the town are magnificent.

From Cordes, continue down to Albi on the D600. Albi, astride the Tarn, dominates the region with its towers and turrets. Its great ship of a cathedral, glowing pink in time-mellowed brick and cooing with pigeons, though massive and somewhat grim from the exterior, is richly imaginative inside. A visit to this important religious monument is a must for all visitors. Indeed, Albi itself deserves lengthy exploration, whether around its winding medieval quarter or in its sophisticated and stylish commercial centre.

Dégustation: Stop to Taste; Stop to Buy

Gaillac is a region of industrious *propriétaires-récoltants*, most of whom are more than happy to receive visitors for *dégustation-vente*. The wine region, though small, is compact and dense, with about 20,000 hectares under cultivation. The wines, on the whole, represent excellent value. Drivers and non-drinkers should enjoy the excellent, virtually non-alcoholic *pétillant de raisin*.

1 Boyals Etienne & Fils
Cellier Les Augustines
10, rue St Louis
81310 Lisle-sur-Tarn
tel: (63) 33 37 80
Hours: Daily, working hours.
Gaillac AOC wines from the Domaine de Mazou can be tasted and purchased.

2 René Assié
Château de Rhodes
81600 Gaillac
tel: (63) 57 06 02
Hours: Daily 8–10h. Appointment not necessary but a good precaution.
Full range of Gaillac AOC wines.

3 Robert Plageoles & Fils
Domaine des Très-Cantous
81600 Gaillac
tel: (63) 33 90 40 and (63) 33 18 08
Hours: Daily 8–12h; 14–18h. Appointment not essential but appreciated.
The Domaine des Très-Cantous is located just off the main Gaillac–Cordes road. White and red Gaillac AOC is produced and visitors are received by the

vigneron and his sons.
English spoken.

4

Vignobles Jean Cros
Château Larroze
81140 Cahuzac-sur-Vère
tel: (63) 33 92 62
Hours: Mon–Sat 9–19h; Sun 15–18h. Appointment preferred.
The full Gaillac AOC range, produced by the Cros family in hill vineyards located off the D1 Cahuzac-Cestayrols road, have received considerable praise in recent years as well as numerous awards at all the major wine fairs.
English spoken.

5

Cave Coopérative de Vinification des Coteaux de Gaillac
    et du Pays Cordais
81150 Labastide-de-Lévis
tel: (63) 55 41 83
Hours: Mon–Fri 10h and 16h.
Gaillac AOC, Vin de Pays des Côtes du Tarn, *pétillant de raisin*.
English spoken.

6

GAEC Cazottes & Fils
Domaine des Terrisses
St-Laurent
81600 Gaillac
tel: (63) 57 09 15
Hours: Mon–Sat, working hours. Appointment preferred but not essential.
A full range of Gaillac wines is produced by the Cazottes family, traditional *vignerons* in the region for generations.
A little English spoken.

Corbières, Minervois, Fitou, and Blanquette de Limoux

The principal wines of the *département* of the Aude are Corbières, Minervois (whose vineyards also straddle the Hérault), Fitou, and Blanquette de Limoux. This is an immense vineyard, extending north and south of Carcassonne across to the Mediterranean shores. Known primarily for its typical robust red wines, producers have also been making some surprisingly fresh and enjoyable white wines in recent years, as well as some decent rosés. Blanquette de Limoux claims to be the oldest sparkling wine in the world.

Fitou, the first, and for a long time the only, AOC of the Languedoc, is the smallest. The vineyards which produce this distinctive, tough red wine lie mainly on chalky soil by the salt-water *étangs* of Lapalme and Leucate, and inland on the slately scrub *garrigues* of the Corbières hills. These two areas produce wines with distinct characteristics. Seaside holidaymakers,

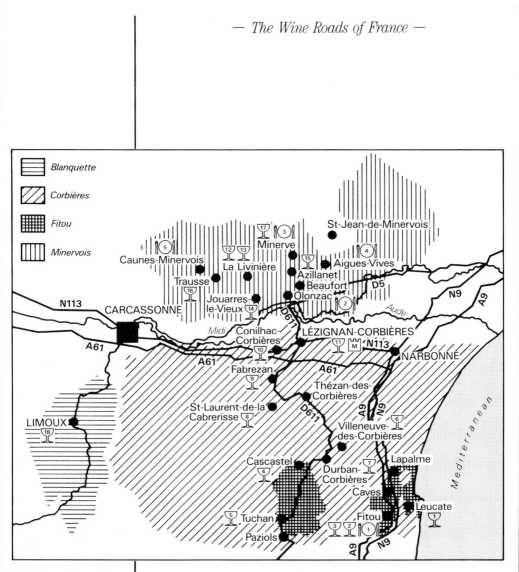

Corbières, Minervois, Fitou, and Blanquette de Limoux.

therefore, can sample the wines of the littoral at Leucate, La Palme, Caves or little Fitou itself, a fine, intensive wine town where the houses along the main road are all hollowed into the rock behind to create deep natural *caves*. The wines from the slatey and inhospitable hills beyond Fitou can be tasted by visiting the wine communes of Cascastel, Villeneuve-les-Corbières, Tuchan, and Paziols.

Fitou must be produced from at least 75 per cent Carignan, an uncompromising traditional *cépage* of the Midi which produces long-lasting and deep wines that must be aged. Corbières, on the other hand, usually has higher proportions of the more supple Grenache and the wines are often made with a fairly high (30 per cent) proportion vinified by *macération carbonique*; this method promotes fresh fruit taste and aroma to result in supple wines that can be drunk much earlier. There are 94 communes which make up this vast *appellation*, bordered in the north by the main Carcassonne–Narbonne road, to the west by the Aude river, to the south by the border with Roussillon and to the east by the Mediterranean.

Made up essentially of a multitude of little villages and hamlets which are remote within these rugged hills, there is no set wine road that leads logically or comprehensively through the region. One suggested route continues on from the vineyards of Fitou and Villeneuve-des-Corbières, across the vine-covered hill country via Durban-Corbières and Thézan-des-Corbières across to Lézignan-Corbières. Lézignan is the centre of the wine industry, poised between the vineyards of Corbières and Minervois, and thus it makes a most suitable base for serious wine travellers. The town itself is pleasant enough, and there is a fine little wine museum here which should not be missed.

Minervois, like Corbières, was elevated to AOC status in 1985; made from the same grape varieties, the wines are quite similar, and much is vinified to be drunk young, though some traditional wines are made which can improve with age. The region extends over the hill country in a triangle formed by Carcassonne, Narbonne, and Béziers. The vineyards of this region were among the most prosperous during Roman times and they were praised by Cicero and Pliny the Younger. The region, today so quiet and seemingly remote, was the scene of tragic events in the thirteenth century, for it was at little Minerve itself that the prefects of the Cathari made a bold and last-ditch stand before finally capitulating and submitting to Simon de Montfort. Today, though Minerve itself remains the historic capital of the region, Olonzac is actually the centre of the Minervois wine trade.

A circular, although by no means comprehensive, tour of the vineyards of Minervois can be made from coastal resorts such as Narbonne-Plage or Valras-Plage: first visit Lézignan-Corbières, then strike out into the vineyards of Olonzac and across to Minerve itself via the small wine villages of Beaufort and Azillanet. Minerve is a remarkably sited medieval village, astounding in its dramatic position astride the Cesse gorge: a visit here is a must. From Minerve, follow the Cesse river to Aigues-Vives and either return to the coast, or else further explore wine towns such as St-Jean-de-Minervois, famous for its luscious Muscat wine.

While improvements in wine making in recent years mean that sound, clean — if not over-exciting — white wines are being made in these vineyards of the Midi, there is one remaining vineyard area which has made white wine of renown for centuries: Limoux. Located south of Carcassonne on the D118 beside the Aude, the principal grape grown here is the Mauzac, which produces both excellent still and sparkling wine in not-far-off Gaillac. The Mauzac does indeed lend itself well to sparkling wines, as the *vignerons* of the region discovered many centuries ago: today a large proportion of this easy-to-drink and still relatively inexpensive (compared with Champagne) wine is produced by the *Société des Producteurs de Blanquette de Limoux*. If you are anywhere near Limoux, their *cave coopérative* is worth a visit.

Dégustation: Stop to Taste; Stop to Buy

The vineyards of Corbières, Fitou, and Minervois blend one into another and many producers and *caves coopératives* produce two or more *appellations* in addition, perhaps, to Muscat de Rivesaltes VDN. This gives a visitor the opportunity to try a range of wines and note the differences between them. The wines from these regions are still very inexpensive. Fitou, however, does fetch a relative premium since it was the region's first AOC, but for those who enjoy such heavyweight red wines or seek longer-lived wine to bring home to lay down for a few years or more, it is still good value.

1

Cave Coopérative 'Les Vignerons du Cap Leucate'
2, ave Francis Vals
11310 Leucate
tel: (68) 40 01 31
Hours: Daily 14–18h.
This seaside *coopérative* is handy for holidaymakers and it produces sound red, white, and rosé Corbières AOC, Fitou AOC, Muscat de Rivesaltes VDN, and Rivesaltes VDN.
A little English spoken.

2

Cellier de la Pierre
54, ave de la Mairie
11510 Fitou
tel: (68) 45 77 03
Hours: In summer daily 8–12h; 14–19h. Out of season closed Sun.
On the main street in Fitou, this *cave* has been carved out of the chalk cliff behind. The Ayrolles family own vineyards in different parts of the Fitou vineyard and thus offer the two contrasting styles, vinified precisely the same way, enabling you to taste the difference which soil makes. Rivesaltes VDN and Muscat de Rivesaltes VDN are also produced.

3

Cave Coopérative de Fitou
11510 Fitou
tel: (68) 45 71 41
Hours: Daily 8–12h; 14–19h.
Fitou AOC, Rivesaltes VDN, Muscat de Rivesaltes VDN.
English spoken.

4

Les Maîtres Vignerons de Cascastel
11360 Cascastel
tel: (68) 45 91 74
Hours: Mon–Fri 8–12h; 14–18h. Appointment not essential but preferred.
Corbières AOC, Fitou AOC, Rivesaltes VDN and Muscat de Rivesaltes VDN.

5

Paul Colomer
11350 Tuchan
tel: (68) 45 46 34
Hours: Daily 8–20h.
The small *caveau de dégustation* offers the *vigneron's* own Fitou AOC, Rivesaltes VDN and Muscat de Rivesaltes VDN.

6   Cave Pilote
11360 Villeneuve-des-Corbières
tel: (68) 45 91 59
Hours: September–June Mon–Sat 8h15–12h; 14–18h. July–August Mon–Sat
8h15–12h30; 14–19h and Sun and holidays 9–12h; 14–19h.
Red, white, and rosé Corbières AOC, Fitou AOC, Rivesaltes VDN, and Muscat
de Rivesaltes VDN.
English spoken by appointment.

7   Caves de l'Ancien Comté
11360 Durban-Corbières
tel: (68) 45 90 16
Hours: Daily 8–12h; 14–18h. Appointment preferred for visits.
Red, rosé, and white Corbières AOC.

8   de Volontat
GFA 'Les Palais'
St-Laurent-de-la-Cabrerisse
11220 Lagrasse
tel: (68) 44 01 63
Hours: Daily 8–12h; 14–18h. Appointment preferred.
Red and white 'Château Les Palais' Corbières AOC.

9   GFA Bouffet
Château Vaugelas
Fabrezan
11200 Lézignan-Corbières
tel: (68) 43 60 73
Hours: Mon–Sat morning 9–12h; 14–18h. Other times by appointment.
Located between Fabrezan and Lagrasse off the D212, the domaine has been
in the Bouffet family since 1817. Red and rosé 'Château Vaugelas' Corbières AOC.

10 Cave des Producteurs 'Roger de Connerac'
11200 Conilhac-Corbières
tel: (68) 27 08 07
Hours: Mon–Fri 8–12h; 14–18h.
Red, rosé, and white Corbières AOC and Vin de Pays.
A little English spoken.

11 D. de Girard
Château de Paraza
11200 Lézignan-Corbières
tel: (68) 43 20 76
Hours: Mon–Fri 8–18h. Closed August.
Red and rosé 'Château de Paraza' Minervois AOC.

LANGUEDOC and ROUSSILLON

12 Jacques Maris
Chemin de Parignoles
La Livinière
34210 Olonzac
tel: (68) 91 42 63
Hours: Daily, working hours. Sat afternoon, Sun morning by appointment.
White, rosé, and red Minervois AOC.
A little English spoken.

13 de Faucompret
Domaine de la Senche
La Livinière
34210 Olonzac
tel: (68) 91 42 87
Hours: Telephone in advance.
Minervois AOC.

14 Cave Coopérative 'Vins Vieux'
Jouarres-le-Vieux
11700 Azille
tel: (68) 91 22 15
Hours: Mon–Fri 8–12h; 14–18h. Open Sat July–August.
Red, rosé, and white Corbières AOC and Minervois AOC.

15 Cave Coopérative 'Les Vignerons du Haut-Minervois'
34910 Azillanet
tel: (68) 91 22 61
Hours: Mon–Fri 8–12h; 14–18h. Appointment preferred for guided visits.
Red and rosé Minervois AOC, Vin de Pays.

16 SCAV Costos Roussos
Trausse
11160 Caunes
tel: (68) 78 31 15
Hours: Mon–Fri 8–12h; 14–17h. Appointment preferred.
Red, rosé, and white Minervois AOC from this pretty village north-east of
Carcassonne.

17 Domaine Tailhades Mayranne
34210 Minerve
This tasting cellar in Minerve is located opposite the monument to the Cathars
burnt at the stake in 1210. Medal-winning Minervois AOC.

18 Société des Producteurs de Blanquette de Limoux
ave du Mauzac
11300 Limoux
tel: (68) 31 14 59
Hours: Mon–Fri 8–12h; 14–18h. Open daily in summer.

One of the most modern installations in Europe, producing this excellent, refreshing, and undervalued sparkling wine.

Wine Museum

Le Musée de la Vigne et du Vin
Caves Saury-Serres
RN113
11200 Lézignan-Corbières
tel: (68) 27 07 57
Hours: Open all year round 9–12h; 14–19h.
One of the best little wine museums in France and a thorough introduction to the life of the *viticulteur* in the Languedoc in the early part of the twentieth century: change comes slowly in such rural regions, and many wine growers still carry on their age-old art using the same tools and methods displayed even today. Exhibits of old presses, ploughs, and other machinery, and a re-creation of a vineyard kitchen and bureau. A full range of wines, including Corbières, Fitou, Minervois, and Blanquette de Limoux, can be tasted and purchased, including some very old wines 'elevated' by the Saury-Serres family. Meals of cold platters or *cassoulet* can be arranged for groups; if there is room, individuals can sometimes join in too.

The Musée de la Vigne et du Vin: young students of the subject of viticulture and wine.

Coteaux du Languedoc

The Coteaux du Languedoc *appellation* encompasses primarily the vineyards of the Hérault, from west of Nîmes in the north-east all the way across to Narbonne in the south-west. In addition to the three best *crus* which are each entitled to their own *appellation* — Faugères, St-Chinian, and Clairette du Languedoc — there are a further 12 classified areas or *terroirs* which can append their names to the general Coteaux du Languedoc *appellation*. Six sign-posted wine routes extend throughout the region. We have not traversed all of them in detail (nor will any but the most dedicated and fanatic), but we include brief information about them below. Wine travellers and holidaymakers can use this as a starting point to orient themselves within this vast vineyard — one of the largest in all of Europe — but they should not be hesitant about improvising and heading off the beaten track to make their own discoveries.

La Route Bleue covers the vineyards of Quatourze, which extend into the hinterland beyond Narbonne itself, and La Clape, those coastal vineyards between Narbonne and the Mediterranean which encircle the Montagne de la Clape. The red, white, and rosé wines of Quatourze are heavyweights: meaty full-bodied wines of the sun which go down well on the beach or with simple grilled foods. The rosés and whites of La Clape are somewhat more delicate and can even approach levels of considerable finesse. Much of the production of the former is carried out by the *Cave Coopérative des Vins du Quatourze* in Narbonne. For the wines of La Clape, leave Narbonne on the road to

LANGUEDOC and ROUSSILLON

285

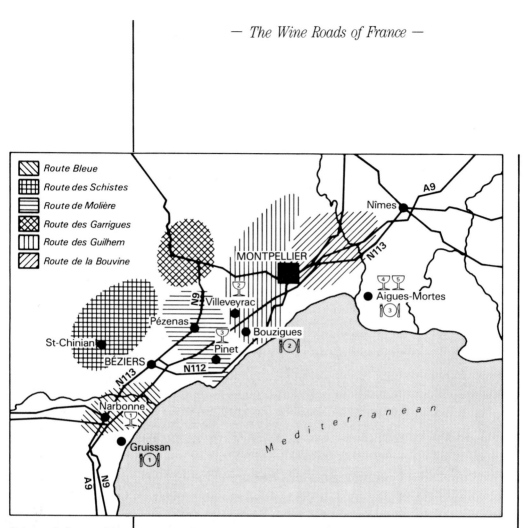

Route Bleue
Route des Schistes
Route de Molière
Route des Garrigues
Route des Guilhem
Route de la Bouvine

Coteaux du Languedoc.

Narbonne-Plage, then circle through the marshy vineyards to Gruissan, Narbonne-Plage, Fleury d'Aude, Salles d'Aude, Armissan, Vinassan, and so back to Narbonne.

La Route des Schistes covers the important *crus* of Faugères and St-Chinian, located in the hill country north of Béziers. Both are best known for their fine and robust red wines, made primarily from Carignan, with Cinsault and Grenache in varying proportions. St-Chinian itself is a pleasant enough inland town with a serious local *cave coopérative*. Other important wine towns include Murviel-lès-Béziers, St-Nazaire-de-Ladarez, Cessenon, and Causses-et-Veyran. The principal wine towns of Faugères are Faugères, Roquessels, Laurens, Cabrerolles, Lentheric, and La Liquière.

La Route de Molière covers those vineyards to the north and south of Pézenas, a particularly fine medieval town which was once the seat of the Languedoc government and the home of the seventeenth-century dramatist Molière. To the south, between Pézenas and the oyster-rich Bassin de Thau, lie the vineyards which produce Picpoul de Pinet, one of the best and most refreshing white wines of the region, and a fitting partner to a feast of local shellfish. Pinet itself, Mèze, Pomérols, Florensac, and Castelnau-de-Guers are all wine towns that grow the distinctive Picpoul grape, which also finds its way into the blending vats for that most distinctive vermouth Noilly Prat. Clairette du Languedoc is the third *cru* of the region, a dry and medium-dry white wine produced from the Clairette grape. When vinified from sugar-rich late-picked grapes, a powerful and sweet Vin Doux Naturel can also be produced. Such wines come from vineyards north of Pézenas around Aspiran, Adissan, Fontès, Péret, and Lieuran-Cabrières. The neighbouring village of Cabrières itself is noted for its fine rosés, made from grapes that grow on the steep slatey hills there.

La Route de Garrigues covers a small vineyard area in the hinterland between Béziers and Montpellier, especially around the villages of St-Saturnin and Montpeyroux. Both are *terroirs* of the Coteaux du Languedoc producing the traditional robust reds and forceful rosé wines of the region.

La Route des Guilhem is another tour of vineyards near Montpellier, to the immediate west of the vineyards of St-Georges d'Orques (red wines only), to the east for the vineyards of the Coteaux de la Mejanelle (rich, deep red wines and a little white), and to the north-east for the vineyards of Pic St-Loup (red, rosé, and white wines).

La Route de la Bouvine, the easternmost of the wine roads of the Coteaux du Languedoc, centres on the vineyards of Lunel, St-Christol, and St-Drézéry. Lunel is perhaps best known for its fragrant and distinctive Muscat de Lunel, but red and rosé table wines from this area's vineyards are classified as Coteaux de Verargues. Red wines from St-Christol and St-Drézéry are also both classified *terroirs*.

Dégustation: Stop to Taste; Stop to Buy

This enormous vineyard region is literally made up of many thousands of *propriétaires-récoltants*. The great feature of nearly every wine town or hamlet in the Languedoc is its local *cave coopérative* where a high proportion of such wines are made. Some individual growers, however, are making superb estate-bottled wines. Included below are a few addresses only: don't be hesitant in this vast vineyard to stop, visit, taste, and buy from producers encountered throughout. This is still very much uncharted wine country, and there are scores of individual discoveries to be made.

1

S. A. J. Saignes
Château de Pech Redon
11100 Narbonne
tel: (68) 90 41 22
Hours: Mon–Sat, working hours. Appointment not necessary June–September. Highly regarded red and rosé Coteaux du Languedoc La Clape AOC, Vin de Pays des Coteaux de Narbonne (*cépage* Chardonnay). Conveniently situated for holidaymakers on the coast.
A little English spoken.

2 L'Abbaye de Valmagne
Villeveyrac
34140 Mèze
tel: (67) 78 06 09
Hours: Visits to the Abbey 15 June–15 September every afternoon except Tue.
Out of season by appointment for groups.
Visits to the wine *cave* by appointment.
The Abbay de Valmagne, located near the Bassin de Thau, was founded in 1138 and grew into one of the richest in the south of France during the twelfth and thirteenth centuries. Like all the abbeys of France, Valmagne was dissolved after the Revolution, after which time its fine Gothic church became a wine store for the estate; today great vats of Russian oak rest in its arched and vaulted chambers. The de Gaudart d'Allaines family has restored the abbey, which can be visited in season. In addition to the 'Abbaye de Valmagne' Coteaux du Languedoc AOC red wine, the estate produces its 'Cuvée Cardinale' and 'Cuvée Tradition' wines which are well appreciated in France and abroad.
Charge for visits to the Abbey.
English spoken.

3 Cave Coopérative 'Les Producteurs de Vin Blanc'
34850 Pinet
Hours: Mon–Sat morning 8–12h; 14–18h.
An excellent source for the superb shellfish wine, Picpoul de Pinet AOC.

Les Sables du Golfe du Lion

4 Domaines Viticoles des Salins du Midi
Domaine de Jarras
30220 Aigues-Mortes
tel: (66) 53 63 65
Hours: Easter–1 October daily 10–17h30.
Europe's largest *propriétaire-récoltant*, Les Salins du Midi, has 1672 hectares under vines in nine domaines spread throughout the region. A full range of red, rosé, and white wines is produced, as well as the Domaine de Jarras's speciality, the distinctive *gris de gris*, made from free-run juice which has only the briefest contact with the skin, resulting in a pale pink-grey colour and more delicate flavour and bouquet. Visitors approach the Domaine up a long avenue that borders the salt works which are the main business of this great company, and mountains of pink-tinged sea salt dominate the landscape.
English spoken in season.

5 Cave Coopérative 'Les Remparts'
30220 Aigues-Mortes
Hours: Mon–Sat, working hours.
Located on the outskirts of this fine fortified *ville*, producing a full range of Vins de Pays Sables du Golfe du Lion sold in bottles or *en vrac*.

A typical Dordogne village.

Lot valley.

A local at Sarlat market.

Bergerac.

Languedoc vinescape.

Terraced vineyards of Banyuls.

Above *A farmyard in the Upper Loire.*
Right *Angers tapestry.*

Opposite *Saumur château.*

Étang de Thau, Bouzigues.

View from Port Grimaud.

Market produce at Aix-en-Provence.

Séguret.

Nyons.

Montélimar nougat.

Wine Festivals

Fête des Rivesaltes	Rivesaltes
Oyster Festival	Bouzigues
Fête des Vins	Gaillac
Fête du Vin Nouveau	Perpignan
Recontres Gourmandes de Banyuls	Banyuls and other Roussillon villages

Regional Gastronomy

The Languedoc and Roussillon make up a vast sun-drenched quarter of the country, embracing culinary influences as seemingly far apart as the goose-fed south-west, garlic-and-herb laden Provence, spicy Spanish Catalan, and the Arab flavours of North Africa. Throughout the Languedoc, food and wine share a character that is, above all, forthright and concentrated, never particularly subtle, refined, or sophisticated but void of all fuss and pretension. This, after all, is the land of *cassoulet*, a hearty bean-feast steaming with bits of pork, goose *confit* or good Toulouse sausages and sweet mutton, the likes of which would not be out of place on the Formica tables of any *relais routier* in the land. Perhaps this is the ultimate accolade for the cuisine of Languedoc: it is truck-stop food *par excellence*.

Aigues-Mortes.

Provence may have her *bouill-abaisse* — and she can keep it. How absurd to add lobsters, langoustines, and the like to an essentially humble fisherman's pot, turning it into a '*spécialité*' for which outrageous prices are charged to tourists the length and breadth of the Côte d'Azur. Here, in Sète, Béziers, or Le Grau-du-Roi, the basic catch of the day remains just that: *soupe de poisson* or *bourride*, a simple and inexpensive staple fisherman's broth, flavoured always with red-hot *rouille*, a pungent garlic-and-chilli mayonnaise.

This is the land of rich, winey *daubes*, tough old beef marinated in copious amounts of strong red wine, then pot-roasted with olives, pine nuts, and herbs until meltingly tender; of *estouffades*, collections of beans, meat, and salt pork; and of *mouton en pistache*, leg of mutton, studded with 50–100 cloves or garlic or more, and braised with vegetables and wine for hours. And, as in other great vineyard regions, those perennial pests, snails, are put to use in quite delectable ways: *cargolade à la languedocienne* snails stewed in wine together with ham, anchovies, and walnuts.

Fish is often simply grilled out-of-doors over a wood fire; in Roussillon, thick tuna steaks are eaten rare, like beef, or else braised with red peppers and olives. Rice from the Camargue is simmered with a medley of fish and shellfish in Spanish combinations up and down the coast, while fresh *anchois* from Collioure are simply filletted and marinated with olive oil, garlic, and parsley, a delicious, powerfully flavoured accompaniment to glasses of full-bodied red wine. And of course throughout the Midi, in spite of an abundance of fine, fresh Mediterranean fish, dried salt cod remains a favourite staple, boiled and served with *aïoli*, the garlic-rich 'butter' of the south, with chickpeas at Lent, or mixed into a creamy, smooth, and exquisite emulsion known as *brandade*. The Languedoc, too, has become one of the major centres of France for the raising of both *huîtres* and *moules*, mainly on the salt-water Bassin de Thau, south of Montpellier.

This certainly is a region of many influences: it has been so since the Greeks settled here centuries before Christ and even today it continues to

The yard of Noilly Prat at Marseillan.

Noilly Prat Vermouth

One of the most remarkable wine-related sights in the south of France is the yard of Noilly Prat, where many hundreds of wooden barrels filled with wine made from local Picpoul and Clairette grapes lie ageing in the open air. These barrels stay outside every day of the year, under the baking heat of the summer sun and through winter rains and even occasional snow. As the wines evaporate the sun-bleached barrels are not topped up; after a year, the wines have acquired a characteristic amber colour and a strong and complex bouquet and maderized flavour. This process of ageing wines is, we think, unique, and it is essential to the character of Noilly Prat vermouth. After this outdoor ageing process, the Picpoul and Clairette wines are blended with a *mistelle*, that is a fortified mixture of Muscat wine and grape brandy; this brings the alcohol level to about 16°. The mixture is then macerated in great oak casks with a secret blend of up to 40 different aromatic plants and herbs gathered from all over the world. The result is Noilly Prat Extra Sec, a dry, yet robust, *apéritif* wine whose complex flavours of wood and plant taste of the Midi sun.

Come to Marseillan to visit Noilly Prat, then enjoy an *apéritif* under the green-and-white umbrellas beside the *quai*, followed by a feast of local oysters and fish from the Bassin accompanied by the tart local table wine, Picpoul de Pinet.

Noilly Prat & Cie
1, rue Noilly
34340 Marseillan
tel: (67) 77 20 15
Hours: Mon–Sat 9h30–11h30; 14h30–17h30.

absorb foreign influences into a style that is its own. Only two decades ago there was another minor influx here, after Algeria gained its independence; already *couscous*, a typical North African stew of mutton or fish served on a feather-light bed of steamed semolina together with a mouth-searing chilli paste called *harissa*, has become a regional classic. As such, it fits perfectly into the gutsy, forthright *menu* of the Languedoc–Roussillon, where food and wine is nothing if not honest and full of flavour.

Le Pique-Nique

Jambon de la Montagne Noire Raw mountain ham similar to *jambon de Bayonne*.

Saucisse montagnarde Mountain-cured, air-dried sausages.

Huîtres Buy them by the dozen at Bouzigues to enjoy with ice-cold Picpoul de Pinet.

Pâté de Pézenas True mincemeat pies from Pézenas, made with diced mutton, brown sugar, and spices.

Fougasse Plaited flat bread found throughout the south. Sometimes flavoured with bits of fried meat (*grassons*), olives or anchovies.

Roquefort One of the greatest of all French cheeses: made high in the Haut-Languedoc with ewes' milk only, with a natural blue mould which forms in the moist *caves* of Roquefort-sur-Soulzon. There are many imitations of Roquefort but the real thing is protected with its own *appellation d'origine contrôlée*. Delicious with the red wines of the Languedoc, or, say many here, with a glass of Banyuls VDN or Muscat de Rivesaltes VDN.

Cassoulet

Cassoulet is another great peasant stew which has become a '*spécialité*': but it is no less delicious for all that. This great bean-feast is considered such an important part of the regional culinary heritage that certain towns argue vehemently over what constitutes the 'real' thing. *Cassoulet* from Castelnaudary, for example, claims to be the purest, consisting simply of white haricot beans, sausages, and pork and pork rind, flavoured of course with plenty of garlic, herbs, and wine; Carcassonne's version may contain mutton or even partridge; but *cassoulet* from Toulouse, the great regional capital, really is something special, made always with *confit d'oie, saucisses de Toulouse*, fresh or salted pork and mutton, the whole lot topped with a golden crust of breadcrumbs, broken once, twice, even three times argue some, back into the bubbling cauldron to create a creamy, crusty, meltingly delicious topping.

LANGUEDOC and ROUSSILLON

Spécialités Régionales:
Stop to Taste; Stop to Buy

Ste Roque
40, rue de la Democratie
66190 Collioure
tel: (68) 82 04 94
Hours: Open daily except Sat.
Come here to taste and purchase the famous Collioure *anchois* preserved in salt or oil, *crème d'anchois*, olives, and home-produced Collioure wine and Banyuls VDN. The *atelier de fabrication* where the anchovies are prepared is open to visitors Mon–Fri.

Huîtres de Bouzigues
There are countless opportunities to taste and purchase Bouzigues oysters both in that little Bassin town, as well as from numerous stands on the main road from Mèze. Don't miss a visit to the Musée de la Conchyliculture, open daily 10–12h; 14–19h.

Restaurants
Roussillon

Banyuls

(Map p.270)

1

Le Relais St Jean
place de la Cathédrale
66000 Perpignan
tel: (68) 51 22 25
Closed Sun; Mon midday.
Next to the Cathedral St Jean, this fine restaurant serves mainly fish specialities in its atmospheric twelfth-century *cave*.
Moderate

2

La Frégate
24, quai de l'Amirauté
66190 Collioure
tel: (68) 82 06 05
In season open every day.
A lovely port-side restaurant serving both regional and imaginative cuisine together with the wines of the Côtes du Roussillon.
Moderate to Expensive

3

La Bodega
6, rue de la République

66190 Collioure
tel: (68) 82 05 60
Closed Mon night, Tue out of season.
Fish and Catalan specialities served in an old dock-side *chais*.
Inexpensive to Moderate

4

Restaurant Le Chalut
8, quai François-Joly
66600 Port-Vendres
tel: (68) 82 00 91
Open every day in season.
Local seafood, *soupe de poissons* and other dishes accompanied by a large choice of Banyuls and other Roussillon wines, in this waterside restaurant.
Moderate

5

Hotel-Restaurant 'Les Elmes'
plage des Elmes
66650 Banyuls-sur-Mer
tel: (68) 88 03 12
Open March–end of October.
On the entrance into town, a popular hotel-restaurant, with tables overlooking the sea.
Inexpensive

6

Le Sardinal
4 bis, place Paul Reig
66650 Banyuls-sur-Mer
tel: (68) 88 30 07
Closed Sun night and Mon out of season.
Local seafood served on the terrace in season in this family-style restaurant on the main drag of Banyuls. Recommended by Cellier des Templiers.
Moderate

The Agly Valley

(Map p.271)

1

Grill du Château de Jau
Château de Jau
66600 Cases-de-Pène
tel: (68) 64 11 38
Open 15 June–15 September daily. Reservation advised.
This fine wine producer serves an excellent Catalan menu accompanied with own-produced wines on a pleasant outdoor terrace. Specialities include *fougasse aux gratons, jambon de pays, grillades aux sarments, Roquefort*.
Inexpensive to Moderate

2

Auberge de Quéribus
93, ave Jean-Jaurès

66460 Maury
tel: (68) 59 10 26
Closed Wed.
Local specialities such as *canard au vieux Maury* and *escargot à la Catalane* together with Maury VDN and Côtes du Roussillon-Villages wines. Recommended by Groupement des Vignerons de Maury.
Inexpensive to Moderate

Languedoc

Gaillac

(Map p.277)

1

Hôtel-Restaurant 'Le Pré-Vert'
54, promenade des Lices
81800 Rabastens
tel: (63) 33 70 51
Closed Sun night, December.
Lovely eighteenth-century house opposite the town square serving hearty foods of the Tarn in a tastefully decorated dining room. *Foie gras, magret de canard, riz de veau sauce aux cèpes*, accompanied by a good selection of Gaillac AOC and Vin de Pays Côtes du Tarn.
Inexpensive to Moderate

2

La Ferme de Roziès
Cahuzac-sur-Vère
81140 Castelnau-de-Montmiral
tel: (63) 33 90 34
Closed Mon and every evening except Fri and Sat.
Quiet, simple *ferme* restaurant serving only Gaillac wines and regional dishes such as *confit de canard, cassoulet*, and *poulet au pot*. Recommended by Château de Rhodes.
Inexpensive

3

Hostellerie du Vieux Cordes
rue de la République
81170 Cordes
tel: (63) 56 00 12
Closed Mon.
This thirteenth-century *hostellerie* has all the comforts of the twentieth century: restaurant serves regional foods and wines.
Moderate

4

'Le Jardin des Quatre Saisons'
19, bd de Strasbourg
81000 Albi

tel: (63) 60 77 76
Closed Mon; Tue midday.
Many fish specialities such as *filet de sandre du Tarn à l'infusion d'ail* and
le boudin de poisson. Recommended by Domaine des Très-Cantous.
Moderate

**Corbières,
Minervois, Fitou,
and Blanquette
de Limoux**

(Map p.280)

1

La Cave d'Agnès
11510 Fitou
tel: (68) 45 75 91
Closed Wed.
Large converted *cave* at the top of Fitou village, surrounded by vineyards.
Friendly, informal atmosphere and simple foods of the region: meats grilled
over an open fire, homemade pastries and desserts and a good selection of
the wines of Fitou, Corbières and Côtes du Roussillon. Recommended by Cave
Coopérative de Fitou.
Inexpensive

2

Restaurant du Minervois 'Bel'
ave d'Homps
34210 Olonzac
tel: (68) 91 20 73
Simple restaurant serving regional dishes and local wines. Recommended by
the Société Coopérative Les Vignerons du Haut-Minervois.
Inexpensive

3

Restaurant 'Les Aliberts'
rte d'Olonzac
Minerve
tel: (68) 91 22 95
Closed Wed.
This restaurant, with its thirteenth-century dining room, is perched
dramatically amidst the vineyards overlooking Minerve and serves simple,
authentic foods of the region: *fromage de chèvre chaud, tarte aux
champignons, caille aux raisins, coquelet au romarin* and wines of Minervois,
Corbières, Fitou, and St-Chinian.
Inexpensive

4

Auberge Minervoise
Aigues-Vives
34210 Olonzac
tel: (68) 91 23 82

A good, simple place to 'refuel': full of locals enjoying the simple midday *menu*.
Very inexpensive

5

Hôtel d'Alibert
place de la Ville
11160 Caunes-Minervois
tel: (68) 78 08 40
Closed Fri eve and Sat midday out of season.
Sixteenth-century *Logis de France* serving *languedocienne* specialities including *cassoulet* and *daube* with Minervois and Corbières wines. Recommended by SCAV Costos Roussos.
Inexpensive

Coteaux du Languedoc

(Map p.286)

1

Restaurant le Chebek
quai d'Honneur et du Levant
11430 Gruissan
tel: (68) 49 02 58
Closed Mon.
Languedocienne specialities and *produits de la mer* can be sampled together with wines from La Clape.
Inexpensive to Moderate

2

Chez Pierrot
Rive de Thau
Bouzigues
tel: (67) 78 31 83
Just off the edge of the Bassin, serving the freshest oysters and mussels in this restaurant owned by an oyster-producer. Try the hot *huîtres gratinées* with ice-cold Picpoul de Pinet.
Inexpensive

Les Sables du Golfe du Lion

3

La Camargue
19, rue de la République
30220 Aigues-Mortes
tel: (66) 51 86 88
This favourite rustic restaurant in the centre of the medieval *ville* has devised an excellent formula: *anchoïade, daube de boeuf gardienne*, or *grillades au feu de bois* and hectic gypsy and flamenco music.
Moderate

Additional Information

Et pour en savoir plus . . .

Comité Interprofessionnel des Vins Doux Naturels
19, ave de Grande-Bretagne
66000 Perpignan
tel: (68) 34 42 32

Conseil Interprofessionnel des
  Vins de Fitou, Corbières et Minervois
RN113
11200 Lézignan-Corbières
tel: (68) 27 04 35

Comité Interprofessionnel des Vins de Gaillac
Abbaye St-Michel
81600 Gaillac
tel: (63) 57 15 40

Office de Tourisme
quai de Lattre-de-Tassigny
66000 Perpignan
tel: (68) 34 29 95

Office de Tourisme
19, place Ste-Cécile
81000 Albi
tel: (63) 54 22 30

Office de Tourisme
place R Salengro
11100 Narbonne
tel: (68) 65 15 60

Office de Tourisme
place Comédie
34000 Montpellier
tel: (67) 72 54 82

THE LOIRE
VALLEY

Introduction

Château d'Ussé.

*T*he long, lazy Loire winds its way up and across a broad swath of the country, starting life surprisingly far south, high in the rugged Auvergne, then heading north slowly through the heart of the country before turning west at Orléans to empty, finally, into the cold Atlantic waters of Brittany some 960 km (600 miles) later. All along most of its way, from north of Nevers to St-Nazaire, the vine is rarely far from its shores: the Loire valley is one of the principal wine regions of France, and, in a country where far many more bottles of red wine are drunk to every bottle of white, it remains one of the most important and abundant sources of the latter.

Indeed, a full and fascinating range of wines comes from the Loire: simple white, red, and rosé Vins de Pays du Jardin de la France; sea-fresh Muscadet and Gros Plant; everyday whites and rosés from Touraine and Anjou; sparkling wines from Saumur; distinguished classic white wines such as Savennières, Pouilly Blanc Fumé, and Sancerre; some of the longest-lived and finest dessert wines from Vouvray, Montlouis, and the Coteaux du Layon; intensely perfumed strawberry reds from Chinon, Saumur-Champigny, and Bourgeuil; and many others.

The region remains deservedly one of the most popular of all tourist destinations in France. The appeal of meandering along riverside roads past grandiose châteaux and historic towns in a region which, above all, remains noted for a way of life — this land of Rabelais — which puts a premium on eating, drinking, and living well, is indeed compelling. The opportunity for wine touring and wine tasting, combined with less single-minded pursuits — sightseeing, sports, walking, eating — all amidst totally unspoiled and beautiful countryside, is possibly unsurpassed anywhere else.

It should be remembered that the Loire valley *is* a vast region: indeed, it is not one but many regions, her principal vineyard areas extending across no fewer than eight different *départements*. The contrast between the western

Atlantic Pays Nantais, historically a part of Brittany, and, say, the vineyards around Pouilly-sur-Loire in the Nièvre, far inland and culturally closer to Burgundy, is indeed a profound one. In between lie distinct but historic regions which maintain their own identities and personalities: Anjou, Touraine, Poitou, Orléanais, and the Berry.

Le Jardin de la France, as the Loire valley is also known, is indeed a bucolic and fertile land which yields its riches generously to all. There are few visitors who can resist its charms: fairy-tale castles, lazy rivers and woodlands, a classic, yet sublimely simple, regional kitchen, and (mainly) abundant uncomplicated wines that demand — above all else — to be drunk not next year, not in 10 years, but right now, immediately, in their unashamed and fresh flush of youth. The once-deep reds of the fourteenth-century tapestry at Angers may have faded to a pale limpid coral; yet this shade, when duplicated in thousands and millions of bottles of Rosé and Cabernet d'Anjou, brings vivid and immediate joy, drunk here on the spot, as well as throughout the world.

Orientation

Getting to the region depends on where along the river you wish to begin. Nantes, the centre of the Pays Nantais and the Muscadet wine country, is easily accessible from ferry ports in Brittany and Normandy. Visitors coming via Paris may wish either to head there direct via Le Mans and Angers on the A11 *autoroute*, or else travel first to Orléans (A10), then meander slowly down-river through Blois, Tours, Saumur, and Angers. The distance from Paris to Nantes is about 380 km (237 miles); Paris–Tours 235 km (147 miles); and Paris–Orléans only 130 km (81 miles). Wine travellers may wish to include visits of the Upper Loire *en route* to Burgundy. From Paris take the N7 south to Pouilly-sur-Loire (about 200 km/125 miles), then after visiting that wine town and its twin across the river, Sancerre, cut cross-country to Beaune via Autun.

There are frequent daily trains from Paris to Nantes via Angers. The journey to Nantes takes less than 3½ hours. Tours is on the main Paris–Bordeaux line: there are frequent daily trains which complete the journey in less than 2 hours.

The Loire valley is close enough to the capital to make Paris the most convenient destination for international flights. There is also an international airport at Nantes Château Bougon.

Michelin Maps 63, 64, 65, 67

THE LOIRE VALLEY

The Châteaux of the Loire

The châteaux of the Loire are one of the great wonders of France: a remarkable and overwhelming series of magnificent fortified medieval castles, Renaissance and neo-classical stately homes, lining the banks of the great river and its tributaries the Cher, Vienne, Indre, and others, from Nantes way up-river to past Orléans. As such, they form the highlight for visits to the Loire valley. Many of the finest châteaux are actually located in the wine country and thus wine and châteaux tours can easily be combined. A short-list of some of our favourite châteaux includes: Angers (thirteenth-century feudal fortress with magnificent tapestries); Chinon (twelfth century, built on a former Roman fortification high above the Vienne river — the young Jeanne d'Arc had her famous meeting with the Dauphin here); Ussé (fifteenth century, said to be the inspiration for Perrault's *Sleeping Beauty*); Azay-le-Rideau (sixteenth century, another 'fairy tale' castle); and Chenonceaux (sixteenth century, inhabited by Henry II's mistress Diane de Poitiers and later by his widow Catherine de' Medici, as well as other formidable *grandes dames*). One other great architectural marvel should not be missed: the Abbey of Fontevraud, containing the tombs of the Plantagenets and also a remarkable octagonal Romanesque kitchen which has 20 chimneys.

The Wines of the Loire

The Pays Nantais

Muscadet AOC; Muscadet des Coteaux de la Loire AOC; Muscadet de Sèvre-et-Maine AOC

*T*his popular and well-loved dry white wine comes from vineyards planted near the mouth of the Loire. Only one grape variety is permitted, the Muscadet, known also as Melon de Bourgogne. The wine is fresh, dry but never acid, an excellent partner to the shellfish and seafood of the region. Wines bottled '*sur lie*', that is, while still on their lees or barrel sediment, take on a rounder, more full-bodied flavour and have greater depth of bouquet. The largest area of production (and many say the finest) is the Sèvre-et-Maine area south-east of Nantes. The vineyards of the Coteaux de la Loire lie just further east, on the north and south banks of the river around Ancenis. 'Straight' Muscadet AOC is produced mainly to the south-west around the lake of Grand-Lieu.

Gros Plant du Pays Nantais VDQS

*V*in Délimité Qualité Supérieure wine produced from the Folle Blanche grape, known locally as Gros Plant. Gros Plant is bone dry, extremely crisp — sometimes even overly sharp — but when well made, there is no better wine to accompany oysters and other Brittany shellfish. In recent years, much more Gros Plant has been made and marketed '*sur lie*': the wines are usually somewhat rounder and slightly less lemony.

Coteaux d'Ancenis
VDQS

Red and white VDQS varietal wines produced from grapes grown in vineyards around the town of Ancenis on both sides of the Loire. The label must indicate the grape variety used: Pineau de la Loire (Chenin Blanc), Malvoisie, or Pinot-Beurot for white wines; Gamay or Cabernet Franc for red and rosé. These light and inexpensive wines are not often encountered outside the region: the Gamay *primeur* wines in particular are worth looking out for: grapey, fresh, and delicious.

Anjou

Anjou AOC

Anjou AOC is the regional *appellation* for a vast vineyard extending on both sides of the Loire around Angers down-river to Saumur. A full range of wines is produced here, including dry, medium, and sweet white wines; rosé wines; fully sparkling *mousseux*; and light red wines. In general, the finer wines bear more specific *appellations*. White and rosé wines have been the traditional mainstays of the Anjou vineyard, but in recent years the production of red wines has increased (now about 15 per cent of production).

Anjou Coteaux de la
Loire AOC

Firm and delicate dry and medium-dry to medium-sweet white wines produced in vineyards primarily to the north of the Loire, and west of Angers.

Anjou Gamay AOC

Light, supple, fruity red wine produced from the Gamay grape. While all such wines are vinified to be drunk young (as in Beaujolais, the great and foremost habitat of the Gamay), some wines are marketed within only weeks of the harvest as *primeur*.

The Loire Valley.

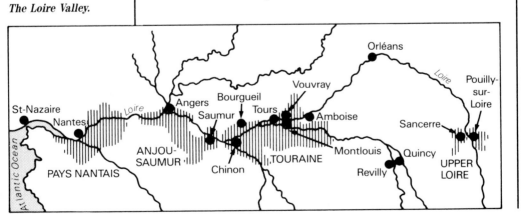

Bonnezeaux AOC

*G*reat growth of the Coteaux du Layon, Bonnezeaux is a *vin liquoreux* produced from ripe and over-ripe Chenin Blanc grapes which have been individually harvested in successive passes through the vineyard. Unctuous, highly perfumed, and concentrated, the wine manages to maintain a freshness and balance which comes from the high natural acidity of the Chenin Blanc grape. One of the great sweet wines of France, and a fascinating contrast to Sauternes or Barsac.

Cabernet d'Anjou AOC

*M*edium-dry to medium-sweet rosé wine from Anjou produced entirely from the Cabernet Franc (mainly) or Cabernet Sauvignon grape varieties. The wines must have a higher alcohol content than Rosé d'Anjou, and though they retain a residual sweetness, they are capable of considerable distinction, noted for their fine raspberry bouquet.

Coteaux de l'Aubance AOC

*T*he vineyards which centre around the town of Brissac on the Aubance river produce mainly medium-sweet white wines from the Chenin Blanc grape, as well as dry white and rosé wines.

Coteaux du Layon AOC

*T*his important *appellation* applies to the Anjou vineyard on the south side of the Loire, producing sweet white wine exclusively from the Chenin Blanc grape. Vineyards extend over 25 communes, the best of which are entitled to the superior *appellation* Coteaux du Layon combined with the name of the commune: Beaulieu-sur-Layon, Faye d'Anjou, Rablay-sur-Layon, Rochefort-sur-Loire, St-Aubin-de-Luigné, St-Lambert-du-Lattay. The greatest growths bear superior *appellations*: Coteaux du Layon Chaume, Bonnezeaux, and Quarts de Chaume.

As is the case for the production of great sweet wines from elsewhere, the grapes are harvested only when they are super-ripe, in the best years having been attacked by *pourriture noble*. Generally, the basic *appellation* Coteaux du Layon applies to wines which, though possibly retaining a high degree of residual sweetness, are somewhat lighter and less intense than the more concentrated great growths.

Quarts de Chaume AOC

*G*reat growth of the Coteaux du Layon: a luscious, honeyed wine, produced in the best years from Chenin Blanc grapes affected by *pourriture noble*.

Rosé d'Anjou AOC

*T*he *appellation* for extremely popular and plentiful medium-dry rosé wine produced in vineyards throughout Anjou, essentially to the south of Angers across to Saumur. Grape varieties include Groslot, Gamay, Pineau d'Aunis, and the Cabernets. This easy-to-drink wine accounts for half the production of Anjou.

Rosé de Loire AOC

*A*ppellation for paler, dry rosé wine from the same vineyard areas as above though made in considerably smaller quantities. The wines must utilize a minimum of 30 per cent Cabernet Franc or Cabernet Sauvignon.

Saumur AOC	Dry white and red still table wines from the vineyards of Saumur may bear this basic *appellation*.

Saumur Mousseux AOC

Saumur is best known for its fine sparkling wines produced from grapes grown in the deep chalky tufa that resembles the soil of Champagne. The Chenin Blanc, Chardonnay, and Cabernet grapes are used to produce a *cuvée* (blend of still wines) which undergoes secondary fermentation in the bottle by means of the *méthode champenoise*. The wines must age on their sediment for a minimum of 9 months before the *dégorgement*. A full range of styles (including some excellent sparkling rosé) and levels of sweetness of wines is produced by the great firms who age their wines in deep chalk caves above the banks of the Loire.

Saumur-Champigny AOC

The best red wine of Saumur is entitled to its own *appellation*. Saumur–Champigny AOC, produced primarily from the Cabernet Franc, is considered one of the finest red wines of the Loire, noted above all for its pronounced aroma of raspberries.

Savennières AOC

The *appellation* for dry white wines produced from vineyards around the commune of Savennières, west of Angers. This fragrant, full-bodied wine, produced entirely from the versatile Chenin Blanc grape, is one of the finest dry white wines of the Loire. Two great vineyards are entitled to their own *appellations*: La Coulée de Serrant and La Roche aux Moines.

Savennières-Coulée de Serrant AOC

Great dry white wine produced in minute quantities from a *monopole* vineyard in the commune of Savennières. Rather hard and closed initially, the wine takes a relatively long time to develop but after 5 years or more, it demonstrates its unusual depth of flavour.

Savennières-Roches-aux-Moines AOC

Less concentrated than the above, but a full, rich wine of considerable class none the less.

Touraine

Bourgueil AOC and St-Nicolas-de-Bourgueil AOC

Red Touraine wines produced almost exclusively from the Cabernet Franc grape (and only limited quantities of the Cabernet Sauvignon) grown on vineyards west of Tours on the north bank of the Loire. The principal communes are Bourgueil, St-Nicolas-de-Bourgueil, Restigné, Ingrandes-de-Touraine, St-Patrice, Benais, La Chapelle-sur-Loire, and Chouzé-sur-Loire. Though the two *appellations* are separate, the wines are very similar: full, rather deep in colour, and with the characteristic pronounced raspberry bouquet combined with the rather earthy scent of the Cabernet Franc. The wines of St-Nicolas-de-Bourgueil are usually somewhat lighter than Bourgueil. Though the two, considered among the best red wines of the Loire, are generally regarded as light wines to be drunk while young and fruity, some wines are vinified

THE LOIRE VALLEY

to be conserved and are capable of considerable development after 4–5 years or more.

Chinon AOC

*T*he *appellation* for red wine (as well as tiny amounts of white and rosé) from vineyards on the south bank of the Loire and over both banks of its tributary the Vienne, particularly around the beautiful medieval town of Chinon. The red wine is produced mainly from the Cabernet Franc, known locally as the Breton: it has a soft perfumed bouquet and fruity strawberry or raspberry flavours. Though usually drunk young, the best examples improve for 5 years or more. Chinon wine was much loved by the town's favourite son, Rabelais.

Crémant de Loire AOC

*T*his general Loire valley *appellation* for sparkling wines applied to wines made not just in Touraine but also in Anjou and Saumur, though the finest examples may be entitled to bear more specific *appellations* such as Saumur Mousseux AOC or Vouvray Mousseux AOC. The broader *appellation* none the less lays down strict rules regarding the production, which must be by the *méthode champenoise*.

Jasnières AOC

*D*ry white wine produced from a small vineyard area just north-east of La Chartre-sur-le-Loir around the villages of Lhomme and Jasnières. Not often encountered, the wine, made from Chenin Blanc grapes (known in Touraine as Pineau de la Loire) grown in the most northern part of the Loire (some 30 km/19 miles north of the river), can be overly acid and tart, though in hot years it is said to be very fine, almost honeyed.

Montlouis AOC

*G*reat wine commune on the opposite (south) side of the Loire from Vouvray producing dry, medium-dry, and sweet wines, as well as *pétillant* (slightly sparkling) and fully sparkling wines, all exclusively from the Chenin Blanc grape.

Touraine AOC

A vast and important general *appellation* for white, rosé, and red wines produced throughout the extensive vineyards of Touraine. For the reds and rosé wines which account for about two-fifths of production the Gamay and Cabernet grapes predominate. For the remaining white wines, the Chenin Blanc (Pineau de la Loire) still predominates, though there has been considerable increase in the planting of Sauvignon. Sauvignon de Touraine is a particularly fine, fresh dry white that has recently gained favour as a less-expensive alternative to other distinguished Sauvignon wines from further up-river. Touraine Gamay is sometimes marketed as *primeur* or *nouveau* wine, as early as 15 November after the harvest.

Touraine-Amboise AOC

*R*ed, rosé, and dry or medium-sweet white wines from vineyards on both sides of the Loire around the town of Amboise.

Touraine-Azay-le-Rideau AOC

White and rosé wine produced in vineyards along the Loire and Indre rivers, near this pretty town, famous for its lovely château.

Touraine-Mesland AOC

Excellent, undervalued red, rosé, and white wines from a fine, but little visited, wine commune north of Amboise.

Vouvray AOC

One of the great wines of Touraine praised and enjoyed since the Roman occupation. The Vouvray vineyard lies some 10 km (6 miles) from Tours and is planted exclusively with Chenin Blanc (Pineau de la Loire) on the soft tufa chalk hills which surround it and six other villages: Rochecorbon, Vernou-sur-Brenne, Parçay-Meslay, Chançay, Noisay, and Ste-Radegonde (now part of the city of Tours). A full range of wines is produced, including the luscious and long-lived *moelleux* wines made from grapes affected by *pourriture noble*, as well as *demi-doux* (medium-sweet), *demi-sec* (medium-dry), and *sec* (dry) wines, and also *pétillant* (semi-sparkling) and *mousseux* (fully sparkling) wines produced by the *méthode champenoise*.

Upper Loire

Menetou Salon AOC

White wine made from the Sauvignon grape grown in the province of Berry around Menetou Salon can resemble wine from nearby Sancerre in everything but price. A small quantity of red wine from the Pinot Noir is also made.

Pouilly-sur-Loire AOC

The wine commune located on the upper reaches of the Loire utilizes this *appellation* for lesser wines produced from the Chasselas grape.

Pouilly Blanc Fumé AOC or Blanc Fumé de Pouilly AOC

One of the great Sauvignon wines of France, produced from vineyards of the Nièvre on the east bank of the Loire opposite Sancerre. The wines can have great depth of scent and the marked flavour of this distinctive grape, with its undertones of blackcurrants and grass. The *'fumé'* term, incidentally, probably applies to the powdery bloom on the grapes before the harvest, not to some imagined flavour of 'gun flint'.

Quincy AOC

Another less well-known wine from the *département* of the Cher, produced from the aromatic Sauvignon. Quincy, together with Reuilly, is capable of considerable distinction.

Reuilly AOC

Appellation for wines produced from Sauvignon grapes grown in the Cher *département*. A small amount of red and rosé wine from the Pinot Noir is also produced.

Sancerre AOC

Well-known white (mainly) Sauvignon wine from vineyards opposite Pouilly-sur-Loire. Many consider Sancerre to be the finest example of all the Sauvignon wines produced in the Loire, noted for its pronounced

THE LOIRE VALLEY

fruity and floral character, and its light elegance and roundness which sets it in a class apart. Small amounts of rosé and, when there is enough sun, red Sancerre AOC are also produced from the Pinot Noir grape. The red, a sort of light, minor Burgundy, can be quite delicious.

St-Pourçain VDQS

*R*ed, dry white, and rosé wines produced from the vineyards further up the Loire in the *département* of the Allier. St-Pourçain can be fine, undervalued country wine worth looking for.

Vin de l'Orléanais VDQS

*R*ed, white, and rosé wines from vineyards around the town of Orléans, more famous for its *vinaigre* than its *vin*.

Vin de Haut Poitou VDQS

*R*ed, dry white, and rosé wines from vineyards south of the Loire, bordering the vineyards of the Charentes. Some quite good wines are being produced here, particularly from the Sauvignon grape.

Vin de Pays du Jardin de la France

*O*ne of the single most important of all French Vins de Pays, this regional classification applies to simple red, rosé, and white wines produced throughout the Loire valley.

The Versatile Chenin Blanc

The Chenin Blanc may not be as well known as other great classic *cépages*, but I don't think there is a single grape variety in the world that is more versatile and exciting. Within the compact vineyards of Anjou and Saumur, for example, this same grape produces an amazing range of different wines. There are vast quantities of green-apple fresh, everyday drinking wines bottled, sold, and drunk locally simply as 'Pineau de la Loire'. In Savennières, on the other hand, the Chenin Blanc ripens to an exceptional degree, especially at the prestigious *monopole* of La Coulée de Serrant, where a distinguished and forceful dry white wine is produced which is capable of ageing for considerable periods; indeed La Coulée de Serrant is considered by some experts to be one of the great dry white wines of France. Yet just across the river at Bonnezeaux and Quarts de Chaume, the Chenin Blanc takes on an altogether different character, for this remarkable grape also has the rare and highly valued ability, in certain autumnal conditions, to over-ripen and become prone to the beneficial microscopic fungus known as *pourriture noble*, thus allowing intense, honeyed, golden dessert wines to be made. Yet again, further up-river, this same grape grown on the chalk tufa of the Saumur hills, is harvested while it still maintains its essential sharp fruity acidity, thus giving a racy 'zip' to the fine sparkling wines of Saumur and elsewhere.

The Wine Roads of the Loire Valley

LA ROUTE DU MUSCADET

In Brief   The Muscadet country is located at the mouth of the Loire, mainly to the south and east of Nantes. There is a sign-posted *Route du Vin* which leads through the finest and most important Sèvre-et-Maine area which can easily be toured in a half or full day. The wine country remains relatively remote and little visited: apart from the recommended restaurants, this is fine country for vineyard picnics. Nantes, a rather grand and elegant city whose eighteenth-century prosperity was based on the profits of merchants and slave traders, makes a good base for the area, though many will visit the vineyards *en route* south to the beaches of the Vendée and Charente-Maritime.

Muscadet.

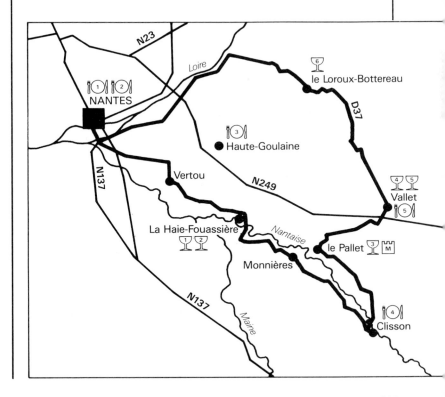

Muscadet '*sur lie*' is to white wine what Beaujolais is to red: young, youthful, quaffable, primarily a wine which is meant to be swilled back with unashamed gusto and enjoyment. That is not to say that either wine is light-weight soda-pop — not at all. But it is the way that both Muscadet and Beaujolais have conquered first Paris café society, then the rest of France, and now the world's collective wine-drinking imagination which creates this gay image.

The Muscadet vineyard where tradition dies hard.

The Muscadet region itself remains primarily stereotypical French wine country, a land of small vine growers, where work is done manually and even, in many cases, by horse-drawn machinery. The villages are unassuming yet picturesque, and in small, dark, dingy wine cellars of small *propriétaires-récoltants*, the wines are made as they have been for centuries: drawn directly out of wooden barrels while still on their lees, the thick deposit of dead yeast cells and other solid matter which is usually removed by racking. The extra time spent on the lees is supposed to give Muscadet '*sur lie*' a rounder and fuller flavour, as well as an appealing *pétillance* (a very slight sparkle), and there is certainly something to this. But it is the romantic image, above all, of wine bottled while still fresh and foaming from the barrel, tasting as close as possible to how it does in the cellar, that is most appealing. The only way to tell if this is entirely true is to come to the region and taste the wines direct from the barrel *chez viticulteur*.

To tour the Sèvre-et-Maine, from Nantes, cross to the south side of the river and leave the city in the direction of Clisson on the N149, then find the little D59 to Vertou. The vineyards of Vertou were cultivated by monks in the eleventh century, but today this town has become virtually a suburb of Nantes. Yet vines are still planted on side streets and even in back gardens here, for this is a land where everybody owns a few hectares of vines, at least to make enough wine for home consumption as well as a little surplus to sell to passing wine tourists.

Next, turn left on the D359 and continue on to La Haie-Fouassière, admiring along the way the gentle wine country with its pretty rolling vistas, such as the sight of the Byzantine-inspired steeple of St-Fiacre-sur-Maine peeping over the vines. La Haie-Fouassière is but a small and unassuming wine village, though its importance in the Muscadet country has been enhanced since the new *Maison des Vins* for the Pays Nantais recently opened here. The *Maison* is the headquarters for the *Comité Interprofessionnel des Vins d'Origine du Pays Nantais*. As such, one of its principal roles is to promote the wines of the region: thus visitors are very welcome to visit and to taste wines here, as well as to pick up leaflets and other informative literature.

Appointments, where necessary, can be made to visit wine producers. There is an interesting exhibit here of a glass-fronted barrel showing the wine resting on its lees.

From La Haie, continue through the wine country to Monnières where no less than 10 village steeples are visible peeking over the green and rolling hills. There are a number of small producers here who will happily offer you a tumbler of their sea-fresh Muscadet in the hope that you might leave with a couple of bottles tucked under your arm.

Busy Clisson nestles in a hollow formed by the confluence of the Sèvre-Nantaise and the Moine rivers. The town was razed to the ground after the French Revolution in revenge for the loyalty of the townspeople to the King. Only the covered fifteenth-century marketplace survived: a lively gathering still takes place here weekly. The town, ostracized then for being royalist, was subsequently rebuilt in a rather aristocratic Palladian style.

From Clisson, leave the town on the D763 north in the direction of Vallet but soon turn off left on the N149 to little Le Pallet. It was here, in 1079, that the ill-fated Pierre Abélard was born. The Musée Pierre Abélard is both a memorial to his life as well as a small museum depicting the folk art and traditions of the Pays Nantais vineyards. At Le Pallet there are pleasant picnic spots along the Sèvre.

Vallet, next, is one of the most important wine centres of the region and it is also the place to come to for immediate refreshment. The *Maison du Muscadet*, on the route d'Ancenis, is open every day throughout the year. This pleasant tasting room is run by 30 *vignerons* from the commune of Vallet who have a rota for sharing 'desk duties'. They are enthusiasts and are keen to demonstrate that *their* Muscadet is the best of the region and to tell you why over a glass or two . . . or three.

From Vallet, continue up to Le Loroux-Bottereau, and from there return to Nantes or else follow the Loire to Ancenis for a further tour of the regions

---

Héloïse and Abélard

Pierre Abélard, born in Le Pallet in the heart of the Muscadet country, was considered one of the keenest theologians of the twelfth century, but he and Héloïse are also remembered foremost as the star-crossed lovers who were as famous and tragic as Shakespeare's Romeo and Juliet. After the couple met and fell in love, they fled to Brittany where Héloïse bore Abélard a son (some say he was actually born in Le Pallet, like his father). Abélard and Héloïse then were married in secret. But Héloïse's uncle found out what had happened: Héloïse fled to the convent of Argenteuil, but the hapless Abélard was caught and had his manhood mutilated. Though they never met again, Héloïse and Abélard continued to correspond with each other, a poignant collection of medieval love letters.

of Muscadet des Coteaux de la Loire and the Coteaux d'Ancenis. Principal communes for these wines include, along the south bank of the Loire, Champtoceaux, and St-Florent-le Vieil, and on the north, Varades, Ancenis, Carquefou, and inland Ligné. Ancenis itself is an historic town, with the remains of a massive fifteenth-century castle which once marked the frontier between Brittany and Anjou. The small, evocatively named wine town of Le Cellier is also particularly pleasant.

For visitors *en route* to the beaches of the Vendée, a short detour into the vineyards of Muscadet and Gros Plant can be made south of Nantes by turning off the D751 to Bouaye, then left on the D164 leading to Machecoul. There are vineyards throughout this region, many planted in proximity to the Lac de Grand-Lieu. St-Philbert-de-Grand-Lieu is an important wine centre.

Dégustation: Stop to Taste; Stop to Buy

While the opportunities for organized cellar visits are few and far between in the Muscadet country, there are countless small wine growers who place signs outside their houses or bungalows offering *dégustation-vente*. Stop and knock on the door any time you see such signs. In season, too, there are numerous stands set up alongside the main roads. Muscadet is still an inexpensive country wine; Gros Plant is even more of a bargain, though it should be borne in mind that it is one local wine which definitely tastes better on the spot, preferably with a dozen oysters. The wines of the Coteaux d'Ancenis are little known and also good value.

1

Maison des Vins du Pays Nantais
'Bellevue'
44690 La Haie-Fouassière
tel: (40) 36 90 10
Hours: Mon–Fri 8h30–12h30; 13h30–17h30.
This important centre for the wines of the Pays Nantais — Muscadet AOC, Gros Plant VDQS, and Coteaux d'Ancenis VDQS — is a must for all serious wine travellers as much information on the vineyard region can be gained. The wines can be tasted and the *Maison* can help arrange any appointments for visiting producers direct, as well as supply maps and directions.

2

Maurice et Olivier Bonneteau
La Juiverie
44690 La Haie-Fouassière
tel: (40) 54 80 38
Hours: Mon–Sat 9–12h; 14–18h. Appointment preferable.
Home-produced Muscadet de Sèvre-et-Maine AOC and Gros Plant VDQS can be tasted and purchased.

3

Pierre Lusseaud
Château de la Galissonnière

Le Pallet
44330 Vallet
tel: (40) 26 42 03
Hours: Mon–Fri 8h30–12h30; 14–18h30. Appointment preferred.
Muscadet de Sèvre-et-Maine AOC *sur lie*; Gros Plant VDQS; Coteaux d'Ancenis Cabernet VDQS. An historic château producing well-known and well-regarded wines. Visit to the cellars and tasting.
A little English spoken.

4 Maison du Muscadet
rte d'Ancenis
44330 Vallet
Hours: Daily all year round 9–20h.
Muscadet de Sèvre-et-Maine AOC *sur lie*; Gros Plant VDQS. 30 *viticulteurs* from Vallet organize and run this tasting *caveau*.

5 Sauvion & Fils
Château du Cléray
BP 3
44330 Vallet
tel: (40) 36 22 55
Hours: Daily including weekends, 8–12h; 14–18h. Appointment preferred.
Muscadet de Sèvre-et-Maine AOC *sur lie*; Gros Plant VDQS. Another historic château which has a fine reputation for its family-produced Muscadets and Gros Plant. The Sauvion family is also *négociant-éleveur*. The *caves* can be visited and the wines tasted and purchased.
English spoken.

6 Caveau Communal du Loroux-Bottereau
44430 Le Loroux-Bottereau
Tasting *caveau* open every day all year, working hours.

Wine Museum

Musée Pierre-Abélard
Chapelle St-Michel
44330 Le Pallet
tel: (40) 26 40 24
Hours: May–November Sat, Sun and holidays 14–18h. Other times by appointment.
This little museum traces both the history and times of Pierre Abélard and his affair with Héloïse; the history of Pallet and the region; and the traditions and cultivation of the vine.

LES ROUTES DES VINS D'ANJOU

In Brief   The vineyards of Anjou extend from west of Angers to up-river of Saumur. This is particularly pleasant wine country to meander through, beginning in Angers itself, an important and lovely city, and ending up in Saumur. The *Conseil Interprofessionnel des Vins d'Anjou et de Saumur* has devised six separate vineyard circuits, but we have combined the best of them into a tour which could be covered in a long day. An alternative would be to tour the vineyards of Savennières and the Coteaux du Layon in a round trip from Angers, and the vineyards and sparkling-wine establishments of Saumur separately in a trip from Saumur. Tasting opportunities begin at the *Maison du Vin* in Angers and range from visits to small producers in the lovely Layon valley to highly organized guided tours of the sparkling-wine establishments.

Angers straddles the Maine river, its squat, massive château dominating everything that it overlooks. This great monument certainly, in contrast to the rather effete Renaisance châteaux further up-river, is a genuine medieval fortress, a thirteenth-century military fortification, moated and flanked by no fewer than 17 enormous circular towers. Inside the walls, however, a more serene, protected world still exists: the gardens are beautiful and vines even grow around the ramparts. The vaulted Ste-Geneviève chapel, moreover, contains some fine fifteenth-century Flemish tapestries, while the Apocalypse tapestries are displayed in a purpose-built modern gallery.

Angers itself is a fine town to explore. First visit the *Maison du Vin* just opposite the château. The *Maison* is the headquarters of the region's professional wine body, and as such it serves to publicize the wines of Anjou: glasses of wine are freely offered to all, together with maps and much other useful information and literature. The *Maison* can advise on properties to visit as well as help with appointments and directions. Then walk down from the castle to explore the old quarter of Angers, with its fascinating stone-paved and uneven streets and leaning old houses.

Leave Angers on the N23 west, then soon branch left on the D111 in the direction of Bouchemaine. The vineyards of Anjou begin before Savennières, a wine commune that gives its name to the finest dry white wines of the Loire. Savennières AOC may not be the best-known wine outside the region, but that is in part because the production is so small: much of the wine is thus enjoyed locally and in the surrounding restaurants where it is such an able partner to the many and delicious fish dishes of the Loire.

The Château de La Roche aux Moines is well sign-posted and located just before the village itself. This famous and most welcoming estate is the sole proprietor of the *monopole* vineyard La Coulée de Serrant. La Coulée

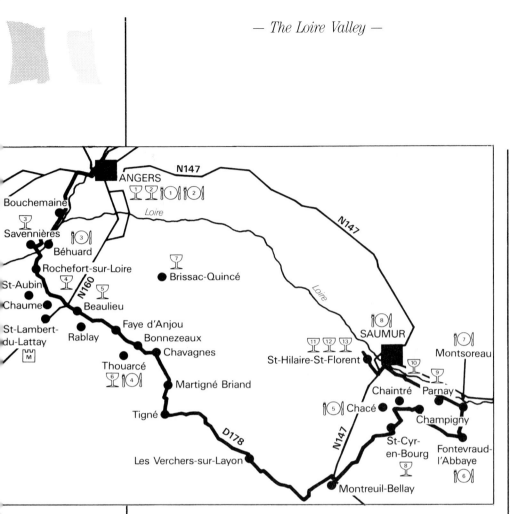

Anjou.

de Serrant was planted in the fourteenth century by monks, and it has long been considered one of the great white wines of France. Curnosky, the gourmet and writer, ranked it in the top five, alongside the illustrious Château d'Yquem, Le Montrachet, Château-Grillet in the northern Rhône, and the rare and celebrated Vin Jaune Château Chalon from the Jura. The vineyard is only 7 hectares, a steep, natural amphitheatre which benefits from remarkable exposure. The soil is loose slate, so working the vineyard calls for back-breaking manual labour. Yet the wine repays such dedication: its fullness and rich and complex flavours develop with age, and the natural high acidity of the Chenin Blanc enables this remarkable wine to be kept for upwards of 40 years. After climbing the steep inhospitable vineyard on a blistering summer day, Madame Joly, the sprightly and charming *propriétaire* told us, 'Thank goodness the wine is good — otherwise I'd keep goats.'

The other celebrated *cru* of Savennières is La Roche aux Moines, entitled, like La Coulée de Serrant, to its own *appellation*. Madame Joly owns a small parcel of this vineyard as well, though it is not a *monopole* and others also make this rich and distinctive wine, notably the Soulez brothers of Château de Chamboureau. Another celebrated vineyard of Savennières is the Clos du Papillon — I wonder, are butterflies, like bees, attracted to the honey-rich oozing Chenin grapes?

Savennières itself, with its brick and stone church beside the bridge over the Loire, is a quiet and pleasant little wine town. Cross the bridge and, mid-river, turn off to explore the agricultural island of Béhuard, with its fifteenth-century church built out of the rugged rocks that surround its base.

The Loire is wide and slow here, and the land on the other side is a considerable contrast to the forests and steep vine-covered hills at Savennières: much flatter, considerably richer, more intensely cultivated. It is this difference in soil, above all, combined with a unique microclimate as well as priorities in wine making, which results in such contrasting types of wine. For in the rolling hills of the Layon valley, the Chenin Blanc is capable of reaching an exquisite and rare degree of ripeness; furthermore, the grapes in the best years are attacked by *Botrytis cinerea*, the fungus which results in *pourriture noble*, thus concentrating their honeyed essence even further.

The wine road thus meanders along the Layon valley, on and off the D55 through the principal villages of the Coteaux du Layon, those which are entitled to append their names to the general *appellation*: Rochefort-sur-Loire, St-Aubin, Chaume, St-Lambert-du-Lattay (stop here to visit the fine wine museum), Beaulieu, Rablay, and Faye d'Anjou. This is quiet, unspoiled wine country, little visited by wine tourists and, thus, not really well organized for visits. But small *vignerons* are found throughout, offering *dégustation-vente*: don't hesitate to stop to taste and buy whenever the opportunity arises.

Most of the wines which bear the *appellation* Coteaux du Layon are *demi-sec*, medium-dry to medium-sweet wines which combine the delicious ripe flavour of Chenin with its refreshing tart acidity. As such, they are light and delightful wines to drink well chilled beside the river, with a handful of fresh walnuts, or a slab of fruit-filled *pâtisserie*. The two great growths from this region, however, must be singled out, for they produce exceptional wines in a class of their own.

Quarts de Chaume is a prestigious *cru* whose origins go back to medieval times when the *grand seigneur* of the area reserved for himself a tithe of the best quarter of wine made from the vineyards of Chaume. Today, only minute quantities of wine bear this *appellation*, but they can be among the finest sweet wines in the world. Bonnezeaux, further up the Layon valley, is but a mere hamlet along the wine road, yet its vineyards, too, produce sweet wines of incomparable depth and distinction.

These great growths are considerably different from their *vins liquoreux* counterparts in Sauternes and Barsac. For the Chenin Blanc grape is far higher in fruity acid than the mighty Sémillon: thus the great sweet wines of the Loire, though rich in honeyed, concentrated residual sugars, are able to maintain a more apparent nervous energy which comes from a balance of sugar and acid, a considerable contrast to the heavier golden, unctuous, almost oily, textures of the great sweet wines of Bordeaux. Quarts de Chaume and Bonnezeaux, though long-appreciated by connoisseurs, are not as widely popular as they should be. Thus, they remain relative bargains which should be sought.

After Bonnezeaux, the wine tour continues through the Haut Layon, through wine towns such as Chavagnes, Martigné Briand, and Tigné, whose château can be visited and wines tasted. In truth, though, the opportunities for tasting come few and far between in this part of the tour, as we next travel cross-country to Les Verchers-sur-Layon and then on to Montreuil-Bellay. For the country here is in transition, not solely devoted to viticulture by any means, as great tracts of wheat give way to a patchwork of market gardening and fruit farming, a link area between the vineyards of the Coteaux du Layon and those of Saumur.

Montreuil-Bellay, rising above the Thouet river, is a fine old Saumurois town, its limestone castle a curious combination of medieval fortress and Renaissance residence. Between Montreuil and Saumur some 8 km (5 miles) to the north, the vineyards once more command the landscape. The single feature which dominates the vineyards of Saumur is its deep vein of chalk tufa: the village houses are built from it, and there is a fine layer of chalk dust on the small network of roads which lead from wine town to wine town. St-Cyr-en-Bourg is an important centre for the wines of Saumur: the surrounding wine growers have formed an excellent *cave coopérative* located just out of town (it is well sign-posted) which can be visited. This *coopérative* makes the famous sparkling wines of Saumur, as well as some highly regarded still white and red wines.

From St-Cyr, continue to pick your way through wine villages such as Chaintré and Champigny. The latter is, of course, the centre for the production of one of the finest Loire valley reds, entitled to its own *appellation* Saumur-Champigny. The Cabernet Franc, when grown on the chalk soil of Champigny, takes on an intensely scented, fruity character which is quite delicious. This red wine is often drunk while still young, served slightly chilled, a refreshing and invigorating companion to meals. But certain wines, particularly those selected from older vines, may have the ability to gain in complexity after several years of ageing.

From Champigny, continue through the forest of Fontevraud to visit the famous abbey, with its remarkable Romanesque kitchens and its tombs of the Plantagenet kings and queens, then carry on up to the Loire at Montsoreau and take the river road D947 to Saumur. Between Montsoreau and Saumur, there are numerous wine-tasting opportunities along the main road such as the Château du Parnay at Parnay. Look out, too, for the curious troglodyte houses, intricate and fine façades of seeming mansions set in front of deep caves extending into the soft tufa.

Both this side of Saumur, as well, principally, on the other side at St-Hilaire-St-Florent, the caves extending into the cliffs at Saumur are even more extensive and impressive. For it is here that many of the numerous well-known sparkling Saumur houses are located. This concentration of *grandes maisons*, as in Champagne, is most welcoming and generous to casual visitors: many keep 'open house' and offer guided tours with English-speaking guides, followed by a tasting. No wine tour to the Loire would be complete without a visit

Abbey kitchen at Fontevraud.

315

to at least one or two.

Saumur itself, finally, is one of the loveliest of all the Loire valley towns. Its château, particularly in the light of early morning, is splendidly grand, overlooking river and town. Apart from its wine and its château, Saumur is known for its illustrious cavalry school, the Cadre Noir riding team which gives frequent displays in the town's arena.

Dégustation: Stop to Taste; Stop to Buy

The Anjou vineyard produces a varied range of wines, from the rare and expensive (La Coulée de Serrant, Quarts de Chaume and others) to plentiful and accessible everyday rosés, reds, and whites. The sparkling-wine establishments outside Saumur provide fascinating and well-organized tours, while those who wish for a respite from the grape can visit the distillery and museum of Cointreau.

Maison du Vin de l'Anjou
5 bis, place Kennedy
49000 Angers
tel: (41) 88 81 13 and (41) 87 62 57
Hours: March–30 September open daily except Tue 9–13h; 15–18h. 1 October–30 December hours as above but closed both Mon and Tue.
The full range of wines from Anjou and Saumur is on display at this welcoming *Maison* located opposite the entrance to the château. The wines are available for free tasting, together with explanations about the different styles and types made in the region. Literature and information about the wines is available, and the *Maison* is happy to help with route planning, appointments for visits, or directions to properties.
A little English spoken.

Cointreau SA
BP 654
49006 Angers
tel: (41) 43 25 21
Hours: Mon–Fri 9–17h.
Located off the N147 by St-Barthélemy-d'Anjou, this world-renowned producer of the famous orange liqueur has fine facilities for welcoming visitors: reception, museum, audio-visual theatre and bar. Charge for visit and *dégustation*.
English spoken.

Mme Joly
Château de la Roche aux Moines
49170 Savennières
tel: (41) 72 22 32
Hours: Daily except Sun and holidays, working hours without appointment.
Clos de la Coulée de Serrant, Savennières-Coulée de Serrant AOC; Château

de la Roche aux Moines, Savennières-La Roche aux Moines AOC; Château de la Roche.

This historic property is well sign-posted and extends a warm welcome to all. The vineyards are cultivated '*en méthode biodynamique*', a sort of homoeopathic approach to viticulture which utilizes the most natural methods possible in the wine-making process. The rare La Coulée de Serrant is available only in minute quantities.

English spoken.

4　Domaine des Baumard
8, rue de l'Abbaye
49190 Rochefort-sur-Loire
tel: (41) 78 70 03
Hours: Mon–Fri, working hours. Appointment essential.
Quarts de Chaume AOC; Savennières AOC; Coteaux du Layon AOC; Crémant de Loire AOC; Anjou Mousseux AOC.
Fine, highly regarded family producer of exceptional Chenin Blanc wines: dry Savennières AOC 'Clos de Papillon' and *demi-sec* Domaine des Baumard Quarts de Chaume AOC provide fascinating contrasts. Also sparkling wines, including a fine Cabernet rosé Anjou Mousseux.
English spoken 'by appointment'.

5　Jean-Pierre Chéné
Domaine d'Ambinos
Impasse des Jardins
49190 Beaulieu-sur-Layon
tel: (41) 78 48 09
Hours: Mon–Sat, working hours.
Rosé d'Anjou AOC; Rosé de Loire AOC; Cabernet d'Anjou AOC; Anjou AOC (white and red); Coteaux du Layon-Beaulieu AOC.
Visits to the domaine, *caveau*, and vineyard; wines available for tasting and purchase include Coteaux du Layon vintages extending back to 1964.
Some English spoken.

6　SCA Domaine de Terrebrune
place du Champ de Foire
49380 Thouarcé
tel: (41) 54 01 99 and (41) 54 04 05
Hours: Daily by appointment; open permanently on Sat without appointment.
Anjou AOC (Gamay and Sauvignon); Rosé de Loire AOC; Rosé d'Anjou AOC; Cabernet d'Anjou AOC; Coteaux du Layon AOC; Bonnezeaux AOC.
Three wine growers between them exploit 35 hectares of vineyards in the Coteaux du Layon, the heart of the Anjou vineyard. Alain Bouleau is in charge of the culture of the vines; Patrice Laurendeau is in charge of wine making and René Renou is in charge of commercial affairs. An impressive range of wines is made. The informative visits include personally guided *dégustations*.

Charge for visit and *dégustation*.
English spoken.

7

Les Caves de la Loire
49320 Brissac
tel: (41) 91 22 71
Hours: Mon–Fri 8–12h; 14–17h.
Rosé de Loire AOC; Rosé d'Anjou AOC; Cabernet d'Anjou AOC; Anjou AOC
(white and red); Coteaux du Layon AOC; Bonnezeaux AOC; Saumur *méthode
champenoise* AOC.
This large *cave coopérative* represents some 500 wine growers producing the
full range of Anjou wines. Wines can be tasted and purchased, but the *caves*
can be visited only by prior arrangement.
Some English spoken.

8

Cave des Vignerons de Saumur
St-Cyr-en-Bourg
49260 Montreuil-Bellay
tel: (41) 51 61 09
Hours: May–end of September Mon–Fri 9–12h; 14–17h.
Saumur AOC; Saumur-Champigny AOC; Crémant de Loire *méthode
champenoise* AOC; and other wines.
This *cave coopérative* located outside St-Cyr is rather ordinary from above
ground, but down below there is a system of *caves* so vast that visitors are
taken around in vehicles. The wines produced are generally regarded as
excellent.

9

Château de Parnay
49730 Parnay
tel: (41) 38 10 85
Hours: Mon–Sat 9–12h; 14–18h.
Saumur AOC (dry white); Saumur-Champigny AOC.
No guided visits, but visitors welcome without appointment to the *caveau
de dégustation*.

10

Gratien & Meyer
Château de Beaulieu
rte de Chinon
49410 Saumur
tel: (41) 51 01 54
Hours: Daily including Sun and holidays 9–11h30; 14h30–17h30.
Full range of white, rosé, and red *méthode champenoise* Saumur AOC, Anjou
AOC, and Crémant de Loire AOC.
The cellars of Gratien & Meyer consist of limestone tufa caves quarried into
the cliffs and extending for several miles. The *méthode champenoise* is
demonstrated as well as the process, as in Champagne, of blending *cuvées*
from both black (Cabernet and Groslot) and white (Chenin Blanc) grapes.

The well-organized tours are open to all without appointment and conclude with a tasting on a terrace overlooking the river.
English spoken.

11 Ackerman Laurance
rue Pallustre
49416 St-Hilaire-St-Florent
tel: (41) 50 25 33
Hours: 15 April–30 September 9–12h; 15–18h. Appointment preferred.
Saumur AOC and other *méthode champenoise* and still wines.
Jean Ackerman founded the *maison* in 1811 after a long spell in Champagne. Visitors are shown an audio-visual presentation and are taken on a tour of the *caves*. Free *dégustation*.
English documentation.

12 Langlois-Château
49416 St-Hilaire-St-Florent
tel: (41) 50 28 14
Hours: Mon–Fri working hours, appointment preferred.
Saumur AOC *méthode champenoise* and still wines.
Langlois-Château are one of the few producers here who make their sparkling and still wines entirely from their own grapes. Visitors see the picturesque *caves* and the vineyards.
English spoken.

13 Bouvet-Ladubay
BP 9
St-Hilaire-St-Florent
49416 Saumur
tel: (41) 50 11 12
Hours: By appointment.
Saumur AOC *méthode champenoise*.
Visits to the *caves* with the possibility of lunching in the cellars for groups. Charge for *dégustation*.

Wine Museum

M Musée de la Vigne et du Vin d'Anjou
49190 St-Lambert-du-Lattay
tel: (41) 78 42 75
Hours: April–end of October daily 10–12h; 14h30–18h30.
Fine little wine museum which explains the history of viticulture and wine making in Anjou. Audio-visual presentation as well as recorded English commentary.

THE VINEYARDS AND CHÂTEAUX OF TOURAINE

In Brief   The vineyards of Touraine extend over a vast superficial area, but the wine traveller will probably want to concentrate on the area's four great growths: Bourgueil and St-Nicolas-de-Bourgueil, Chinon, Vouvray, and Montlouis. The Bourgueils and Chinon are small vineyard areas which can easily be toured from Saumur in a day, with lunch perhaps in the fine medieval town of Chinon. Vouvray and Montlouis are best toured from Tours itself for though they are opposite one another on facing banks of the Loire, there is no convenient bridge to link them. Other significant Touraine vineyards lie around the towns of Amboise and Azay-le-Rideau, as well as around little Mesland, located between Amboise and Blois.

From Saumur, cross to the north side of the Loire and continue along the N147 until it meets the D10; turn right and you will soon encounter the vineyards of St-Nicolas-de-Bourgueil. This rather busy main road runs right through the little village while the vineyards extend on either side, up the gentle slopes as well as down the flatter plains to the Loire. These vineyards around St-Nicolas are entitled to their own separate *appellation* though in truth it is difficult for us to distinguish between the wines of St-Nicolas-de-Bourgueil and those of Bourgueil.

In addition to these two communes, the vine thrives on these gentle slopes around six other communes: Restigné, Benais, Ingrandes-de-Touraine,

Touraine.

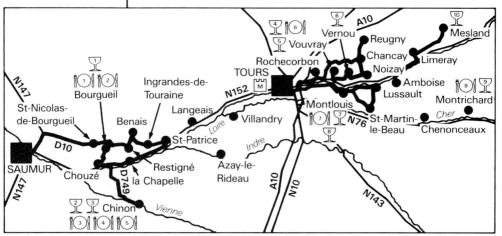

St-Patrice, La Chapelle, and Chouzé, all of which share the Bourgueil *appellation*. The only grape varieties permitted to be planted here for both *appellations* are Cabernet Franc and Cabernet Sauvignon, though it is the former, known locally as the Breton, which is predominant.

Just north of Bourgueil, the wine growers have established a most pleasant tasting *caveau* 'La Dive Bouteille' in an ancient tufa cave where visitors can come not just to sample the fruity, strawberry-scented wines of St-Nicolas and Bourgueil but also to learn about the history of viticulture in the region, and about the wines of the surrounding communes. There are some fine old fourteenth-, fifteenth-, and sixteenth-century presses here and the guides are most informative. This *caveau* is a cool respite from wine or châteaux touring and should not be missed.

Then return to Bourgueil itself to pick up the ingredients for a vineyard picnic, before further exploring these unremarkable but pleasant wine villages. Or else return to the river on the D749 and cross over, passing the monstrous Avoine-Chinon nuclear power station. The vineyards of Chinon extend along the banks of the Vienne river here, all the way to Chinon and beyond. They too are planted almost exclusively with Breton and lesser amounts of Cabernet Sauvignon. 'This excellent Breton wine is not grown in Brittany,' explained Rabelais in the sixteenth century, 'but comes from our own delightful countryside at Véron.'

François Rabelais was born just a few miles away at La Devinière where there is now a museum devoted to his life and work. A statue of the satirical author of *Gargantua* and *Pantagruel* (looking particularly well fed) presides over the main square of Chinon. Vieux Chinon, the old part of town, with its leaning brick and timber houses, probably has changed little since the stirring days when the young Jeanne d'Arc first met and recognized the Dauphin, hiding disguised amongst his courtiers in the great hall of the château. Climb the steep, cobbled streets to this magnificent medieval fortress, one of the finest and most dramatic in the Loire. The château was built originally by Henry II of England, the Plantagenet king whose mortal remains are now interred at Fontevraud; it was held later by his son Richard the Lionheart, but passed into French hands in 1205 after an 8-month-long siege.

The vineyards of Chinon extend immediately behind the château itself: one particularly well-exposed amphitheatre of vines is known as the Clos de l'Echo, for if you stand here and look towards the northern ramparts of the castle, it is possible to hear a distinct and noticeable echo. This, indeed, is one of the finest single *lieu-dits* of Chinon: the wine is deep in colour and with considerable complexity in flavour and bouquet and it can benefit from 5 years or more of ageing.

Generally, however, most of the wines of both Chinon and Bourgueil can be drunk when relatively young. The Breton vine lacks the hard tannins of its brother the Cabernet Sauvignon, and thus the wines maintain a much softer and rounder character. Because they lack excessive tannin, moreover, they can be, and often are, drunk cool, at cellar temperature or even colder here in the region. These delicious, fruit-scented wines are certainly the finest reds from Touraine.

The two other great growths of Touraine, both white, are located further up-river just beyond Tours. Between here and Montlouis and Vouvray lie three contrasting châteaux of considerable charm and beauty. The first, Azay-le-Rideau lies just south of the Loire on the Indre river. The castle certainly is a lovely and picturesque one, Gothic in outline, in appearance a *château-fort*, though in reality its stout fortifications and machiolations are purely decorative, a pastiche even when it was built in the sixteenth century. The *son-et-lumière* production in summer is another pastiche, a rather bizarre medley of lights, music, and high melodrama in the particular Gallic fashion which seems to go down so well here. Azay-le-Rideau, nevertheless, is of particular note to the wine traveller, for vineyards here along the Indre produce small amounts of white and rosé wines entitled to the *appellation* Touraine-Azay-le-Rideau which are as pretty and attractive as the château itself, usually medium-dry to medium-sweet, the perfect picnic wine.

Further towards Tours, also on the south bank of the Loire, is the Château de Villandry, which is of particular note for its fine terraced gardens, while across the river is the Château de Langeais, built by Louis XI in the fifteenth century and one of the few which did not undergo significant revisions or alterations.

Tours is a large and important provincial capital. On first glance its flat, wide boulevards, its industrial zone to the north, and the fact that it was heavily bombed in the last war and subsequently rebuilt in a rather non-descript fashion might tempt one to avoid it, especially considering the numerous smaller beauty spots which abound along this particular stretch of the Loire. Certainly, Tours could never be called a 'picture-postcard town', yet with its cathedral and medieval quarter, together with its monasteries, museums (including an excellent one devoted to wine and viticulture), and modern shops, there is more than enough to warrant spending time here.

Wine travellers next must make the difficult choice between visiting the vineyards of Vouvray or those of Montlouis. Serious amateurs of Loire wines, especially those who consider the Chenin Blanc grape in all its infinite variety to be one of the great and most fascinating of all *cépages*, will certainly want to visit both communes. But less single-minded visitors may well choose between them. Vouvray, certainly, is the better-known wine region, and an enjoyable route can be made through its valleys and wine villages. Montlouis, on the other hand, boasts an extremely welcoming tasting *caveau*, a pleasant campsite, and restaurants and wine producers located in troglodyte houses.

To reach Vouvray, cross to the north bank of the Loire, and follow the river road N152 to Rochecorbon, the first of the wine communes, nestling under the precipitous tufa slopes, where grand troglodyte mansions and seeming *petits* châteaux emerge from the cliff face, their interiors and deep, long, cool wine cellars extending far under the cliffs themselves. There are a number of producers to visit in Rochecorbon, some of whom are well-known producers

Vouvray.

of sparkling Vouvray. Indeed, in this single vineyard area alone, the Chenin Blanc displays its entire range and versatility, for Vouvray AOC can be *sec* (dry), *demi-sec* (medium-dry), *demi-doux* (medium-sweet), or *moelleux* (fully sweet, luscious, unctuous); furthermore, there is Vouvray *pétillant* (only slightly sparkling) as well as Vouvray *mousseux* (fully sparkling).

In truth, this remarkable range has its advantages for the wine growers of Vouvray: in effect, it guarantees that there are no bad years here. For the great sweet wines can only be made in exceptional years, particularly when the vineyards have been affected by *pourriture noble*. In only average years, no *moelleux* wines may be made, but there will probably be larger quantities of *demi-sec* or *sec* wines available. These wines, produced from fully ripe but not over-ripe grapes, share with their sweeter counterparts a tremendous capacity for ageing. Finally, in those years when the Chenin is not quite able to reach a state of full ripeness, the thinner and rather acid wines provide the ideal base to undergo a secondary fermentation in the bottle to result in the refreshing and much-loved sparkling wines of Vouvray.

From Rochecorbon, continue along the river road, but before reaching Vouvray, turn left up a road that leads into the Vallée Coquette, where this entire range can be sampled most informatively at the extremely welcoming *Cave Coopérative des Grands Vins de Vouvray*. Then, continue up this valley where numerous *propriétaires-récoltants* offer further opportunities for *dégustation-vente* before descending to Vouvray itself. Stop in this unassuming wine town for lunch, or else pick up picnic provisions, such as the superb *rillettes au Vouvray*, delicious with no more than a loaf of crusty bread, some fresh soft cheese, a handful of nectarines or a punnet of strawberries, and of course a chilled bottle of Vouvray *demi-sec*.

A sign-posted *Route du Vouvray* extends through the commune, into adjoining villages and vineyards and through lovely valleys such as the aforementioned Vallée Coquette, the Vallée de Vaugondy, and the Vallée de Cousse. Other principal wine towns include Noizay, Chançay, and Reugny.

Montlouis, across the river from Vouvray, produces exactly the same range of wines as its more famous counterpart. The Chenin Blanc, here as in Vouvray, is the only permitted grape variety allowed to be grown for wines destined to be Montlouis AOC. Yet in spite of the apparent similarity of their wines, in spite of the fact that they are usually written about and discussed in the same breath, the town of Montlouis, together with its small neighbouring wine communes of Lussault and St-Martin-le-Beau, comes somewhat as a contrast. Perhaps not surprisingly, the people themselves feel little affinity to their wine-growing counterparts across the river, not out of rivalry, but simply because there is no bridge over the Loire to unite the communities.

Montlouis is perfectly charming, and its *vignerons* most welcoming, possibly due to the fact that their vineyards are somewhat less visited than they deserve to be. In fact, to remedy this, a few dozen have banded together to open the *Cave Touristique du Montlouis*, located in a fine old cave on the main road below the town. This certainly is a most welcome place to sample the delicious wines: indeed, such 'tourist tasting cellars' serve a useful role, for they provide the wine growers with the means of promoting and selling their wines collectively and the visitor with a chance to taste a range of wines at the source without necessarily having to go knocking on the door of *chez viticulteur*. On the other hand, those with more time will certainly wish to explore the hills of Montlouis, and to visit dedicated producers like Christian Martin and others direct, in the hamlets around Montlouis and its surrounding communes.

We usually think of sweet *moelleux* or *vins liquoreux*, whether from Vouvray and Montlouis, or Bonnezeaux, Sauternes, Monbazillac and elsewhere, as 'dessert wines', but this designation can somewhat limit our appreciation of them. Therefore, it is worthwhile considering how the range of Chenin Blanc wines is appreciated here on the spot: the oldest, sweet Montlouis, explained M. Martin, would be drunk not at the end of the meal with pudding, but first as an *apéritif*. Then, a very dry Montlouis would accompany a first course of fish. Chicken or pork could be served with a *demi-sec* Montlouis, but with meat or cheese, M. Martin has no hesitation in stating flatly that he would drink red wine, produced from his own vineyards in Montlouis but entitled only to the general Touraine *appellation*. Finally, a medium-dry sparkling Montlouis would be offered with dessert, followed (if anyone is still standing) by an older, dry sparkling Montlouis after the meal. While we may or may not necessarily wish to follow this pattern exactly, it does once more demonstrates that when it comes to wine drinking there are no hard and fast rules.

Montlouis is a fine starting point for further châteaux tours: Chenonceaux and Montrichard lie just up the Cher river valley, while Amboise, Chaumont, and Blois beckon further up the Loire.

Two other minor vineyard areas must be mentioned: Touraine-Amboise and Touraine-Mesland. These vineyards are virtually contiguous, to the north and east of Amboise not far from the Loire itself. White wines from the Chenin Blanc, as well as red and rosé, are produced here, and any visitors to this part of the Loire will certainly wish to find favourite sources. For Touraine–Amboise, first taste a glass in the tasting cellar underneath the château of Amboise, then set out to Limeray, a heady little wine town whose streets are riddled with cellars and *caves*. The rue d'Enfer is particularly worthy of extended exploration. Mesland's vineyards extend all the way around this small, but pretty, wine village: likewise, here in the town there is no shortage whatsoever of wine producers to visit.

Dégustation: Stop to Taste; Stop to Buy

Although we have only covered the great growths of Touraine, the vineyard area extends far beyond the areas mentioned, and great quantities of simple Touraine AOC — white, red, and rosé — together with Vin du Pays du Jardin de la France are made throughout. Stop to taste and to buy these easy-drinking holiday wines whenever stocks are low or when you have the opportunity.

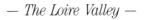
The simple Sauvignon wines of Touraine are particularly fine bargains.

La Cave Touristique de la Dive Bouteille
37140 Bourgueil
tel: (47) 97 72 01
Hours: February–30 April and October–31 November 10–12h30; 14–18h.
May–30 September 10–12h30; 14h30–19h30. Closed December and January.
This fine tasting *caveau* is located just north of Bourgueil. Cool, natural *galeries*
with displays of immense old wine presses, guided explanations of the vineyards
and wines of St-Nicolas-de-Bourgueil and Bourgueil, and tasting of wines.
Charge for entrance and *dégustation*.

Plouzeau & Fils
94, rue Haute St-Maurice
37500 Chinon
tel: (47) 93 32 11
Hours: June–October daily 9–12h; 14–18h. Rest of the year by appointment.
Chinon AOC, Bourgueil AOC, and other wines of Touraine.
Plouzeau & Fils is an established wine-growing family with vineyard holdings
which include the Domaine de la Garrelière (once owned by Cardinal Richelieu)
and the Domaine Pierre Plouzeau south of Chinon. This tasting *cave* is located
in the old quarter of Chinon, beneath the town's château.
Charge for visit and *dégustation*.

Couly-Dutheil Père et Fils
12, rue Diderot
37500 Chinon
tel: (47) 93 05 84
Hours: Mon–Fri 14–17h. Appointment necessary.
The Couly-Dutheil family is the *propriétaire* of the celebrated Clos de l'Echo,
the exceptional *lieu-dit* which produces one of the finest wines of Chinon.
Visits to the *caves* and *dégustation*.
English spoken.

Cave Coopérative des Producteurs des Grands Vins de Vouvray
38, La Vallée Coquette
37210 Vouvray
tel: (47) 52 75 03
Hours: Mon–Fri 8h30–12h; 14–18h. Weekends and holidays 9–12h; 14–19h.
Vouvray AOC.
This fine and highly regarded *cave coopérative* represents 50 wine growers
from the surrounds of Vouvray. Each makes their own wines which are then
subjected to a rigorous selection, and the best wines are then 'elevated' in
the vast galleries carved out of the soft tufa. Visitors are shown the *caves*
where still wines undergo the *méthode champenoise* process to become fully
sparkling, as well as the ageing *galeries* for the great still wines. A full range

of Vouvray may be tasted free of charge and the wines can be purchased.

5   Grands Vins de Vouvray
Manoir du Haut Lieu
37210 Vouvray
tel: (47) 52 78 87
Hours: Mon–Sat 8h30–12h; 14–18h. Appointment essential.
M. Huet is a famous Vouvray producer with three separate estates, Le Haut Lieu, Clos du Bourg, and Le Mont, comprising 32 hectares in all. A fine range of Vouvray wines is produced by traditional methods. Visits to the *caves* where three ancient presses are located in the soft chalk cellars. The Manoir du Haut Lieu is located on one of the highest plateaus above Vouvray.
English spoken 'by appointment'.

6   Gilles Champion
Vallée de Cousse
Vernou
37210 Vouvray
tel: (47) 52 02 38
Hours: Mon–Fri, working hours. Appointment preferred.
Family-produced Vouvray AOC has won a number of medals and can be tasted and purchased.

7   La Cave Touristique du Montlouis
place Abraham Courtemanche
37270 Montlouis
tel: (47) 50 82 26; (47) 45 03 42
Hours: 15 March–20 December Sat, Sun and holidays and daily from June to end of September 10–12h; 14–19h.
Full range of Montlouis AOC; red and rosé Touraine AOC.
The *Cave Touristique du Montlouis* offers a guided presentation concerning the wines of Montlouis, and the local vineyards and methods of viticulture. Free tasting of the full range of wines, produced by the 24 *vignerons* who run the *cave*. Appointments for visits to member growers can be made here. English spoken 'by appointment'.

8   Christian Martin
28, rte du St-Aignan
'La Barre'
37270 Montlouis
tel: (47) 50 82 26
Hours: Afternoons or other times by appointment. M. Martin is often in the *Cave Touristique* above.
Full range of Montlouis AOC.
M. Martin is an enthusiastic exponent of Montlouis and its wines. He is most happy to show visitors and wine tourists his own wine-making operation, and offers a tasting of a range of Montlouis of different sweetness levels and vintages.

The limestone cellars, some of which he has hollowed out with his own hands, are most impressive.
English spoken.

J. M. Monmousseau SA
71, ancienne rte de Vierzon
41400 Montrichard
tel: (54) 32 07 04
Hours: Daily 9–11h30; 14–18h from Easter to end of September. Rest of the year closed weekends.
One of the great *maisons* of the Loire, producing a full range of fine sparkling wines mainly from its own 60 hectares of vineyards. Monmousseau is also *négociant-éleveur* for still table wines from the length of the Loire: Muscadet, Montlouis, Vouvray, Touraine, Sancerre, and Pouilly Blanc Fumé. Visitors see the extensive *caves*. Charge for visit and *dégustation*.
English spoken.

Domaine de la Besnerie
rte de Mesland
41150 Monteaux
tel: (54) 70 23 75
Hours: Mon–Sat, working hours. Appointment preferred.
A full range of wines bearing the undervalued Touraine-Mesland *appellation* is produced by the Pironneau family. *Dégustation* free for purchasers.

Wine Museum

Musée des Vins de Touraine
Celliers St-Julien
16, rue Nationale
37000 Tours
tel: (47) 61 07 93
Hours: Open daily except Tue at the following hours:
2 January–31 March and 1 October–31 December 9–12h; 14–17h. 1 April–30 September 9–12h; 14–19h.
Extensive wine museum with important and fascinating exhibits which inform not only about the vineyards of Touraine, but place wine in its world historical and social perspective.

THE UPPER LOIRE

In Brief   Sancerre and Pouilly-sur-Loire lie far beyond the châteaux country of the Loire, deep inland in the heart of central France. Both vineyards have brief sign-posted wine roads. Few wine visitors to the Loire valley may make it this far up-river; better to stop here *en route* to Burgundy, perhaps, or else to come to Sancerre or Pouilly as destinations in themselves, wine pilgrimages to the source of these pungent, popular, once café-carafe wines, now, regrettably, ultra-fashionable and so no longer the bargains that they once were.

Unlike in the rest of the Loire, where on the whole the Chenin Blanc grape undoubtedly reigns supreme, here in the upper reaches of the river valley, on the Kimmeridgian clay slopes of Sancerre and the opposing hills of Pouilly, it is the Sauvignon which is dominant. The Sauvignon is one of the world's classic white grapes, grown extensively in Bordeaux, planted throughout Touraine and in New World vineyards as far apart as the Napa and Barossa valleys. But it is here alone, consider many, that the Sauvignon finds its greatest expression: combining its sometimes overly distinctive and pungent aroma — blackcurrants, spice, elderflowers — with rounder, deeper overtones which display its class and elegance.

There is no general consensus on whether the wines of Sancerre are superior to Pouilly Blanc Fumé (the *appellation* for wines from Pouilly-sur-Loire made from Sauvignon): it is a matter of taste and preference, though it is by no means an unpleasant task to try to determine for yourself.

Begin in Sancerre, a remote, fortified hill town overlooking the Loire, steep, rather self-contained in feeling, with its scores of old stone houses, its cobbled streets and massive fifteenth-century keep. The *Route du Sancerre et du Crottin de Chavignol* extends through the principal wine-making communes and vineyards, as well as through the majestic high fields where

Upper Loire.

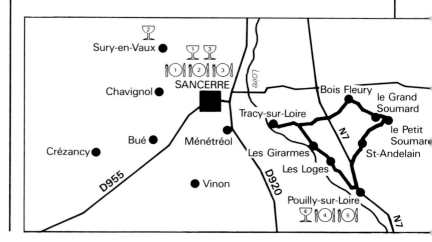

crottin de Chavignol, one of the great goats' cheeses of France.

brown-furred goats nibble the sweet grass. Their milk produces one of the great French goats' cheeses, *crottin du Chavignol*, a little round pat (the name, after all means 'dung') of cheese, either fresh and soft, or aged and hard, the most delicious accompaniment to a glass of grass-fresh Sancerre.

In truth, however, the *route* is almost impossible to follow, extending like a spider-web through tiny hamlets where the *vignerons* and their families live, such as Sury-en-Vaux, Chavignol, Ménétréol, Bué, Vinon, Crézancy, and Menetou-Râtel. Try to follow it if you must, but however far you get, don't fail to reward yourself afterwards at the *Caves de la Mignonne*, a local tasting *caveau* where you can try — what else — Sancerre and *crottin du Chavignol*.

Sancerre is most famous as a dry white wine: but the wine growers here are also fond of another classic grape, the great Pinot Noir. Though the vineyard is located rather far north for Pinot, none the less, in hot and exceptional years fruity red wine is produced, while in the remaining ones, a rather delicious rosé is made. All three types of Sancerre bear the *appellation* Sancerre AOC.

The wine communes of Pouilly-sur-Loire produce no red wine, but they do offer two types of white, the distinguished Pouilly Blanc Fumé AOC as well as the Pouilly-sur-Loire AOC, produced from the lesser Chasselas grape. The latter is an inexpensive, everyday wine to quench immediate thirst on the spot. Even the greatest Pouilly Blanc Fumés and Sancerres, however, should also be drunk while relatively young: the Sauvignon, unlike Chenin Blanc, does not have a great capacity for ageing.

Like the wine towns of Montlouis and Vouvray which, though they face each other across the Loire in Touraine, have seemingly little in common, so do Sancerre and Pouilly gaze out at the world from different points of view. If Sancerre appears to look west to the Berry and Poitou, Pouilly gazes east, for there is a definite Burgundian feel about the small town and its surrounds. A sign-posted *Route du Vin* provides a brief and pleasant (though not overly exciting) excursion into the vineyards. From Pouilly take the N7 (Paris road) north briefly, then turn off to the little river hamlets of Les Loges and Les Girarmes. Follow the gaily-painted wine road signs to Tracy-sur-Loire, then circle back and inland to Bois Fleury, Le Grand and Le Petit Soumard, and St-Andelain. The latter, a popular market town, is perched on a hill overlooking the Loire to the west and the Morvan to the east. The vineyards planted on the slopes make some of the finest wines of Pouilly.

As the Sauvignon wines of Pouilly and Sancerre have gained in popularity and price, intrepid wine merchants and amateurs have had cause to strike out in search of less expensive alternatives. Thus, the Sauvignon wines from the not too distant communes of Quincy, Reuilly, and Menetou-Salon may prove fruitful grounds for further exploration: all three are within an hour's drive of Sancerre.

Dégustation: Stop to Taste; Stop to Buy

1   Caves de la Mignonne
rte de Cosne
18300 Sancerre
tel: (48) 54 07 06
Hours: 15 March–15 November daily 9–12h; 14–18h.
The *Caves de la Mignonne* is not a Sancerre producer but a tasting *caveau*
where Sancerre AOC can be sampled by the glass or bottle together with its
classic accompaniment *crottin de Chavignol*. Throughout the year important
regional festivals and gatherings take place here.

2   Pierre Riffault
'Les Égrots'
Sury-en-Vaux
18300 Sancerre
tel: (48) 79 31 19
Hours: Mon–Sat, working hours. Telephone call preferred.
Sancerre AOC.
Pierre Riffault's elegant white Sancerre is well known in Britain, but his rosé
and red wines made from Pinot Noir also deserve attention. Typical small
family *propriétaire-récoltant*.

3   Domaine La Moussière
rue Porte César
18300 Sancerre
tel: (48) 54 07 41
Hours: Mon–Fri, working hours.
Sancerre AOC.
Not the premises of the wine-making operation itself, but a *caveau* where
you can taste and purchase Alphonse Mellot's Sancerre AOC.
English spoken.

4   Michel Redde & Fils
'La Moynerie'
58150 Pouilly-sur-Loire
tel: (86) 39 14 72
Hours: Mon–Sat, working hours.
Pouilly Blanc Fumé AOC; Sancerre AOC.
Michel Redde has vineyards in both Sancerre and Pouilly-sur-Loire, so a visit
to this producer provides the opportunity to sample and compare by the glass
the wines of both communes. Charge for *dégustation*.
A little English spoken.

Wine Festivals

Mid-January	Wine Festival	Vouvray
2nd week in January	Wine Festival	Angers
May or June	Fête du Crottin and other cheeses of France	Sancerre
2nd week in August	Wine Festival	Vouvray
Mid-August	Wine Festivals	Amboise, Montlouis, Bourgueil
Last week in October	Oyster Festival	Sancerre
Last Sun in November	Vintage Festival	Nantes

Regional Gastronomy

When Catherine de' Medici was wedded to the future Henry II of France she not only brought her own entourage of cooks with her, she also introducd to the French court a novel eating implement, the fork. Catherine, as Queen Regent, eventually came to live at Chenonceaux, having displaced her arch-rival Diane de Poitiers. By all accounts, she was a most formidable *grande dame*, credited, with introducing sophistication and refinement to the French kitchen and, in so doing, laying the foundations for *haute cuisine*. Though the days of the *ancien régime* are long past, an aristocratic and refined elegance undoubtedly remains apparent in the cuisine of the Loire valley.

In this gentle and lovely countryside, even simple foods come dressed in sophisticated robes. The most famous Loire sauce *beurre blanc* consists of no more than chopped shallots, a drop of wine or *vinaigre d'Orléans*, and good, sweet butter. Heated in a *bain-marie* then whisked vigorously, these ordinary ingredients are transformed into the most delicious, creamy emulsion, to be served with poached *brochet* (pike), *alose* (shad) or Loire salmon, a magical sauce nothing short of sublime. Other characteristic sauces of the Loire are based on sweet cream and *champignons de Paris* (the button mushrooms which are cultivated in the tufa caves about the Loire), or Chinon wine, its raspberry scent intensified with just a drop or two of *vinaigre de framboise*.

In Touraine a most unusual, almost medieval combination of fruit and meat is served: sweet, wine-soaked *pruneaux* (prunes from Touraine) and pork, cooked as a creamy *fricassée*. *Porc au pruneaux* is a classic: its sweet richness partnered most beautifully by a golden *demi-sec* Vouvray. Where else can even simple picnic foods — *pâté*, *fromages* and *pâtisserie*, creamy rillettes, white discs of *fromage de chèvre*, and colourful fruit-filled tarts — taste so delicious, *so* elegant, with just a river-cooled bottle of Clos du Papillon or Sauvignon de Touraine?

Above all, here in the Loire, it is not the individual dishes, the regional specialities which are most remarkable: rather, it is the charm of being in an area where a centuries-old history of refined good living has translated itself, down the ages, into a way of cooking, a way of living which seems to know instinctively just what is right.

Of course, the Loire is the longest river in France. There are naturally profound differences in cooking and in ingredients between, say, the Nantais and the Sancerrois. The Atlantic influence, the prevalence of *huîtres* and *moules* from Brittany and the Vendée coast provides foods which are the perfect accompaniment to Muscadet *sur lie* and tart Gros Plant. The more rugged Berry and Nièvre, where winters are that much colder, on the other hand, result in far heartier dishes — *lapin au sang* (rabbit cooked in red Sancerre and thickened with blood) or *veau au vin* (veal in wine stew). Yet throughout, the foods and wines of the Loire are reflections of their noble, proud and distinctive heritages.

Le Pique-Nique

Rillettes Creamy, stringy potted paste of pork, or sometimes of pork and goose, cooked very slowly in its own fat until it separates into strands. Each main centre claims to produce the finest: Angers, Saumur, Tours and Blois all have their own versions.

Rillons Riblets or pieces of belly pork cooked very slowly until brown, crunchy and caramelized.

Andouille de Tours Large chitterling sausage, purchased in slices to eat cold.

Crottin de Chavignol Goats' cheese from the Sancerre region, protected with its own *appellation d'origine contrôlée*.

Ste-Maure Tangy, cylindrical goats' cheese from Touraine.

Port-Salut This creamy, orange-rind cheese is available everywhere now, but originally it was made at the Trappist monastery near Le Mans.

Restaurants
The Pays Nantais (Map p.307)

La Cigale
4, place Graslin
44000 Nantes
tel: (40) 89 34 84
In the heart of old Nantes, a classic *brasserie* from the nineteenth century with tiled walls and painted ceilings. Good daily '*menu du marché*', which includes local wines by the glass, though few may be able to resist the iced platters of *huîtres*, *langoustines*, and other shellfish: delicious with house Gros Plant or Muscadet.
Moderate

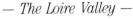

Spécialités Régionales:
Stop to Taste; Stop to Buy

SCA Séjourné-Robineau
49730 Monsoreau
tel: (41) 51 70 30
Hours: 15 June–1 September daily
except Mon morning 10–11h45;
14–18h30.

Mushroom cave and troglodyte house.
Some 70 per cent of the mushrooms
cultivated in France come from the
caves in the Saumur region. Séjourné-
Robineau is one such family enterprise. Guided tours explain the process of
cultivation, and the excellent mushrooms can be purchased.
English spoken.

Troglodyte house and mushroom cave of Séjourné-Robineau.

Charcuterie Hardouin
9, ave du Commerce
37210 Vouvray
Opposite the Maison du Vouvray on the main road, this *artisan-charcutier*
produces some of the best Loire picnic fare: *rillettes au Vouvray, rillons*, and
other *pâtés* and *saucisson*.

Le Nantais
161, rue des Hauts-Pavés
44000 Nantes
tel: (40) 76 59 54
Simple restaurant with traditional family character serving the foods of the
region: *huîtres, poisson au beurre blanc*, and *canard*.
Inexpensive

Hôtel-Restaurant 'La Lande St-Martin'
RN 149
rte de Poitiers-Clisson
44115 Haute-Goulaine
tel: (40) 06 20 06
Restaurant closed Sun eve.
Situated 7 km (4½ miles) from Nantes on the fringe of the Sèvre-et-Maine
vineyards, this is a convenient and welcoming hotel-restaurant. The restaurant
serves *matelote d'anguilles au Bourgueil, cuisses de grenouilles dorées au
Vin de Pays*, and 16 different Muscadets as well as other wines of the Loire.
Moderate

THE LOIRE VALLEY

4

La Bonne Auberge
1, rue Olivier de Clisson
44190 Clisson
tel: (40) 54 01 90
Closed Mon.
Elegant restaurant in an end-of-the-century *maison bourgeoise* in the heart
of Clisson: specialities include *blanc de turbot aux huîtres, ris de veau poêle*,
and *feuillantine de poire sabayon du caramel*. Recommended by Maurice
et Olivier Bonneteau.
Moderate

5

Restaurant Don Quichotte
35 rte de Clisson
44330 Vallet
tel: (40) 33 99 67
Closed Mon.
Huîtres chaudes au Muscadet, saumon au beurre blanc, and the wines of
the Loire in a pleasant restaurant overlooking a park and the vineyards of
Vallet. Recommended by Sauvion et Fils.
Moderate

Anjou (Map p.313)

1

Restaurant Le Toussaint
7, rue Toussaint
49100 Angers
tel: (41) 87 46 20
Closed Sun, Mon.
In old Angers not far from the château this fine eighteenth-century house
creates an atmosphere of elegance and sophistication. *Cuisine du marché*
emphasizing the best produce and products of Anjou: *foie gras au Coteaux
du Layon, poissons au beurre blanc, canard*, and a large selection of Anjou
wines, including many old *vins moelleux*. Recommended by Château de la
Roche aux Moines.
Expensive

2

Le Vert d'Eau
9, bd Gaston Dumesnil
49000 Angers
tel: (41) 48 52 31
Closed Sun eve, Mon.
Regional foods according to the seasons in this traditional restaurant. Fine
selection of over 200 Loire *millésimes*.
Inexpensive to Moderate

3

Restaurant 'Au Rocher'
Béhuard
49170 St-Georges-sur-Loire
tel: (41) 72 21 61
Closed Mon, Wed eve.
Located on the agricultural island of Béhuard, mid-stream between Savennières and Rochefort-sur-Loire, this favourite, informal restaurant serves regional Angevin cooking, especially fish, in season on the terrace opposite the chapel.
Inexpensive

4

Le Relais de Bonnezeaux
rte d'Angers
49380 Thouarcé
tel: (41) 54 08 33
Closed Wed.
Located outside Thouarcé on the road to Bonnezeaux and amidst its prestigious vineyards, this simple restaurant serves cuisine based on local products and produce. Recommended by Domaine de Terrebrune.
Inexpensive to Moderate

5

Auberge du Thouet
place de la Mairie
49400 Chacé-Saumur
tel: (41) 52 97 02
Open daily May–October. Closed weekends out of season.
Country *auberge* located just south of Saumur in the Thouet valley. The rustic restaurant serves regional foods and the wines of Saumur and Saumur-Champigny.
Inexpensive

6

Restaurant de l'Abbaye
8, ave des Roches
49590 Fontevraud l'Abbaye
tel: (41) 51 71 04
Closed Tue eve, Wed.
Bustling restaurant just around the corner from the famous abbey serves simple home cooking and foods of the Loire.
Inexpensive.

7

Hostellerie Diane de Méridor le Bussy
49730 Montsoreau
tel: (41) 51 70 18
Closed Tue.
Attractive rustic hotel-restaurant with views of the Loire and château: regional dishes include *friture de la Loire* and *sandre au beurre blanc*.
Moderate

THE LOIRE VALLEY

335

8

Restaurant 'Gambetta'
12, ave Gambetta
49400 Saumur
tel: (41) 67 66 66
Closed Sun eve, Mon.
Located on a back street of Saumur, this fine little restaurant offers a regional menu with such specialities as Loire salmon, *matelote d'anguilles*, and other fish specialities served outdoors in the garden terrace in summer. Good selection of Saumur, St-Nicolas-de-Bourgueil, and Bourgueil wines.
Moderate

Touraine (Map p.320)

1

Le Moulin Bleu
37140 Bourgueil
tel: (47) 97 71 41
Chambre d'hôte just beyond the *Cave Touristique de la Dive Bouteille* offering from April to end of September *'gouter campagnard'* at midday: simple *terrines* and *rillettes maison* and homemade *pâtisseries* together with home-produced wines, served on the terrace — weather permitting. Dinner served only to people sleeping at the Moulin Bleu.
Inexpensive

2

Restaurant Germain
rue Alain-Chartier
37140 Bourgueil
tel: (47) 97 72 22
Closed Sun eve, Mon.
Andouillette vigneronne, coq au vin and local Bourgueil, Chinon and other wines of Touraine served in a homely family atmosphere.
Inexpensive

3

Grand Hôtel de la Boule d'Or
66, quai Jeanne d'Arc
37500 Chinon
tel: (47) 93 03 13
This comfortable *logis* is located on the banks of the Cher and is noted for its regional *cuisine* together with a superb selection of Chinon and Bourgueil wines. Recommended by Plouzeau et Fils
Inexpensive

4

Hostellerie Gargantua
73, rue Voltaire
37500 Chinon
tel: (47) 93 04 71
Closed Wed out of season, November.

Historic Palais du Baillage dates from the fifteenth century and is located in the heart of the old quarter. Unique specialities include '*la fameuse omelette garganelle*', and *matelote d'anguilles Rabelaisienne*. In summer, meals are served on a terrace below the château.

Moderate

5   Auberge St-Jean
rte de Tours
37500 Chinon
tel: (47) 93 09 29
Traditional family cooking in this **Inexpensive** restaurant near the château.

6   Auberge 'La Cave Martin'
La Vallée Coquette
37210 Vouvray
tel: (47) 52 62 18
Just up the valley from the *coopérative*, this pretty little *cave* serves regional foods based on produce and products from local farms.

Inexpensive

7   Relais de Belle Roche
14, rue de la Vallée
37270 Montlouis
tel: (47) 50 82 43
Closed Tue eve, Wed, March.
Located in a former wine *cave* hollowed out of the tufa cliff, this air-conditioned restaurant serves the regional foods of Touraine together with a fine selection of Montlouis, Chinon, Bourgueil, and other wines of the Loire. Recommended by the Cave Touristique du Montlouis.

Moderate

8   Hôtel-Restaurant Le Bellevue
16, quai du Cher
41400 Montrichard
tel: (54) 32 06 17
The restaurant with panoramic dining room overlooking the Cher serves *brochet au beurre blanc, brochet au Saumur-Champigny, coq au vin*, and other regional foods and wines. Recommended by J. M. Monmousseau SA.

Moderate

Upper Loire (Map p.328)

1   Restaurant de la Tour
31, place de la Halle
18300 Sancerre
tel: (48) 54 00 81

Closed Mon out of season.
Cuisine du marché in this restaurant with its modern first-floor dining room overlooking the roofs of Sancerre to the vine-covered hills beyond. Recommended by Pierre Riffault.
Moderate

2   L'Auberge
37, rue Jacques Combes
St-Thibault-St-Satur
18300 Sancerre
tel: (48) 54 13 79
This comfortable rustic *auberge* serves the hearty foods of the Berry: *salade paysanne, coq au vin, truite au Sancerre, crottin de Chavignol grillé* together with local wines.
Inexpensive

3   Restaurant 'La Treille'
Chavignol
18300 Sancerre
tel: (48) 54 12 17
Closed Tue eve, Wed eve.
Cuisine based around this village's famous goats' cheese: dishes include *mousse de crottin chaude à la creme de ciboulette* and *faux filet sauce crottin.*
Moderate

4   Le Relais Fleuri
ave de la Tuilerie
58150 Pouilly-sur-Loire
tel: (86) 39 12 99
Charming, comfortable *petite auberge* with terrace and flowered garden on the banks of the Loire. Specialities include *soufflé de brochet au beurre blanc, sandre à l'oseille, civet de canette au Sancerre rouge.*
Inexpensive to Moderate

5   L'Esperance
17, rue René Couard
58150 Pouilly-sur-Loire
tel: (86) 39 10 68
Closed Sun eve, Mon.
This elegant **Moderate** restaurant serves classic and *nouvelle* cuisine. Outdoor dining with views over the Loire and vineyards in summer; warm rustic atmosphere in winter. Recommended by Michel Redde et Fils.

Additional Information

Et pour en savoir plus . . .

Office de Tourisme
place du Change
44000 Nantes
tel: (40) 47 04 51

Comité Interprofessionnel des
   Vins d'Origine du Pays Nantais
Maison des Vins
'Bellevue'
44690 La Haie-Fouassière
tel: (40) 36 90 10

Syndicat d'Initiative
place Kennedy
49000 Angers
tel: (41) 88 69 93

Centre d'Information des
   Vins d'Anjou et de Saumur
Maison du Vin de l'Anjou
5 bis, place Kennedy
49000 Angers
tel: (41) 88 81 13

Office du Tourisme
place du Marechal Leclerc
37000 Tours
tel: (47) 05 58 08

Comité Interprofessionnel des
   Vins de Touraine
19, square Prosper-Mérimée
37000 Tours
tel: (47) 05 40 01

Syndicat d'Initiative de Sancerre
Hôtel de Ville
18300 Sancerre
tel: (48) 54 00 26

Union Viticole-Sancerroise
Mairie de St-Satur
18300 Sancerre
tel: (48) 54 02 53

Syndicat d'Initiative de
   Pouilly-sur-Loire et de son
   Vignoble
Mairie de Pouilly
58150 Pouilly-sur-Loire
tel: (86) 39 12 55

The afternoon session of pétanque.

*P*rovence, the *Provincia Romana* of antiquity, is one of the most ancient wine regions of France. Long before even the Roman era, in the seventh century BC the Greeks came to these shores, founded the Mediterranean port of Marseille, and introduced the vine. It came, it saw, it conquered all: the wines subsequently produced for more than two and a half millennia have long been widely acclaimed: they were praised by Caesar and Pliny, enjoyed by the popes during their brief reign at Avignon, drunk by the kings of France, and applauded by such figures of *belles-lettres* as Madame de Sévigné and the Provençal poet Frédéric Mistral.

Today vines continue to flourish on slopes extending virtually to the water's edge from Marseille all the way up the coast to Nice and beyond. In the scrubby hinterland of the Maures and Esterel massifs, in the valley floor below the jagged Alpilles of Les Baux, on fine sand dunes formed on redundant salt marshes in the Bouches-du-Rhône, on the scrubby bare *garrigues* of the Provençal hinterland, the vine remains the most characteristic feature of the Mediterranean landscape, alongside the buff-leaved olive tree which was also introduced by the Greeks at the same time. Wine and olive oil, garlic and herbs; hot sun and cobalt-cool sea; whitewashed fishing villages; precariously perched hill towns; simple, vivid flavours and smells: sun-warm tomatoes and torn basil leaves, the pungent acrid aroma of meats scorched over a wood fire. Thus we return year after year from our pale northern abodes, as the poet Keats said: '. . . for a draft of vintage! . . ./Tasting of Flora and the country green,/Dance, and Provençal song, and sunburnt mirth!'

The south of France: today it remains the most popular summer destination certainly for the French themselves, as well as for literally millions of holidaymakers from Britain, Germany, Holland, Belgium, and elsewhere. In July and August you may well have to look beyond the traffic jams, the rows of tents and caravans along the beach, the tacky paintings along the waterfront, the not-so-beautiful bodies spread-eagled in the sand, the T-shirt and candy-floss stalls, to see exactly why. Yet St-Tropez, Fréjus, St-Raphaël,

Orientation

The region known as Provence is located in the south-east corner of France, and extends approximately over the *départements* of Vaucluse, Bouches-du-Rhône, Alpes-de-Haute-Provence, Var, and Alpes-Maritimes. By car, the main north–south *autoroutes* from Paris, the A6 and A7, lead down to Marseille, while the A8 branches east to Aix-en-Provence, Cannes, and Nice. The distance from Paris to Nice is 930 km (580 miles).

There are good, frequent train services to the south of France. The main Paris–Lyon–Marseille line runs several trains per day, with possible stops (depending on trains) at Avignon, Arles, Marseille, Cassis, Bandol, Les Arcs, Cannes, and Nice. High-speed trains (TGV) can travel from Paris to Nice in about 8 hours. On certain services, from Channel ports and Paris, there are motor-rail facilities for those who wish to transport their vehicles by train.

The most convenient international airports are Marseille Provence, and Nice Côte d'Azur.

Michelin Map 84

Cannes, and other such resorts, located on what must be one of the most beautiful stretches of coastline in the world, maintain their timeless appeal in spite of all.

Yet to drive away from it all, just a few miles in from the coast, up into the hinterland of Provence, is to enter another world. There could hardly be a greater contrast between the coast and towns such as Draguignan, La Garde Freinet, and little Lorgues. Aix-en-Provence, the ancient capital of Provence, today remains an elegant and very beautiful city, and an important economic and cultural centre for the region. Paul Cézanne was born in Aix and later returned to his native town to paint until his death in 1906. Arles is another fine Provençal town, an important trading centre since the days of the Greeks, and the place where Vincent Van Gogh was inspired to create some of his most famous works.

Leaving aside the great Provençal wines of the southern Rhône (covered in the Rhône chapter), it is easy, perhaps, to pass off the rest of the wines of Provence as for summer holiday drinking only: pretty pink (mainly) plonk sold in funny wobbly-shaped bottles, to drink in waterside restaurants with simple foods such as *salade niçoise* and *pissaladière*, on the campsite for an evening barbecue, or with a picnic lunch on the beach. Certainly, many wines from this sunny region are just that: uncomplicated and thirst-quenching. But there are fine, less well-known wines from Provence which will well repay a little effort on the part of the curious wine traveller to search them out: good, serious reds from Bandol, Les Baux, and the Côtes de Provence; excellent white wine from Cassis; and fine, full-bodied rosés from the Coteaux d'Aix-en-Provence and the Côtes de Provence.

Provence is a region whose appeal is eternal. How often in winter do we sit and dream of meals at outdoor tables under the dappled shade of plane trees; of a quenching, ice-cool pastis served in a chipped tumbler, turning opaque and milky as the ice melts; and of that soothing melody of the south, the nervous click-clack of metal *boules* marking the passage from afternoon into evening — 'O for a beaker full of the warm South . . .'

Street café in Aix-en-Provence.

Roman Provence

The Roman province of *Gallia Narbonensis*, which later became known simply as *Provincia* or Provence, was not only one of the most important and strategically positioned in the Empire, it was also a popular and favoured retreat for retired or exiled senators and other politicians. Provence was important strategically because it was a crossroads: the Aurelian Way led from Rome all the way to Arles, and eventually connected with other roads that led both to the Iberian peninsula and north up the Rhône corridor to Paris, Britain, and Northern Europe. Nice, Antibes, Fréjus, and Aix-en-Provence were all important trading towns along the Aurelian Way. The modern N7 roughly follows this ancient road. The finest Roman monuments still standing today include the Pont du Gard, a magnificent three-tiered aqueduct built by Agrippa in 19 BC; the ruins of the Roman city of Fréjus; the amphitheatres at Nîmes and Arles; the ruins and monuments of ancient Glanum, south of St-Rémy-de-Provence; and the great triumphal arch and theatre at Orange (southern Rhône). Perhaps the greatest Roman legacy, here as well as elsewhere, is not found simply in bricks and mortar, but lies in the values of Roman civilization which remained after the fall of the Empire and had a profound effect, not least of all on present-day Provençal attitudes to food and wine, and to easy good living.

The Wines of Provence

Côtes de Provence AOC

Rosé, red, and white wines produced from vineyards along, and in the hills and mountains above, the French Riviera, mainly in the Var *département*, as well as in part of the Bouches-du-Rhône west of Aix-en-Provence and in one commune of the Alpes-Maritimes. For the reds and rosés the typical Mediterranean grape varieties are cultivated: Cinsault, Mourvèdre, Grenache, Carignan, Tibouren, as well as some Cabernet Sauvignon and Syrah.

Rosé wines, often sold in their distinctive wobbly-shaped Provençal bottle, are the best known of the wines of the Côtes de Provence and make up a full 60 per cent of production. They can be very good indeed, relatively full-bodied and forceful, made traditionally by 'bleeding' colour from the skins during the maceration period; the best are powerful enough to stand up to great garlicky feasts and other hearty Provençal foods.

Red Côtes de Provence, accounts for some 35 per cent of production. Many red wines, like the rosés, are traditionally sold in the distinctive Provençal bottle, and such wines are generally perceived to be fruity, full-bodied, and soft, meant to be drunk young, perhaps slightly chilled in summer; they are delicious with rich *daubes* or with meats grilled over wood fires. Additionally, some of the better-known estates produce fine *vins de garde* from the traditional grape varieties as well as from varying proportions of Cabernet Sauvignon and Syrah in the *assemblage*: such domaine-bottled reds are often sold in traditional Bordeaux bottles, indicating that they require a certain amount of ageing before they are ready to drink. They are certainly not mere 'holiday' wines but serious reds which can be compared with the classic wines from better-known regions.

Only 5 per cent of the production of the Côtes de Provence *appellation* goes into making white wines, mainly from the Ugni Blanc, Sémillon, and Clairette: at their best they can be aromatic and fruity, wines to drink while still young and fresh, very cold with seafood and shellfish.

Coteaux d'Aix-en-Provence AOC

*R*ecently elevated to *appellation d'origine contrôlée* status, the designated region now encompasses the former long-established vineyards of Coteaux d'Aix-en-Provence and Coteaux des Baux-de-Provence. Red, rosé, and white wines are produced in a vast area which extends south of the Durance river from beyond Mont Ste-Victoire in the east to the range known as Les Alpilles in the west, and south around the Étang de Berre to the coast of the Mediterranean.

The same typical Mediterranean grape varieties are grown here as in Côtes de Provence, though some producers of red wine utilize a higher proportion of Cabernet Sauvignon to produce meaty reds with considerable potential for ageing. On the other hand, market demands also require the production of supple, fruity, light red wines which are meant to be drunk while young. About 40 per cent of the wines are made by *cave coopératives*. Red wines account for 60 per cent of the production.

The rosé wines of the Coteaux d'Aix-en-Provence, on the whole, may be macerated for slightly longer periods than those from the Côtes de Provence to result in forceful pink wines with plenty of body and colour. They account for about 35 per cent of production. White wines, as in the neighbouring region, account for only about 5 per cent, but improved viticultural techniques mean that even in this hot Mediterranean climate, light, clean wines with refreshing acidity can be made.

Though today the *appellation* embraces both the former VDQS areas of Coteaux d'Aix-en-Provence and Baux-de-Provence, the latter attempts to maintain its separate identity. In truth, the wines are very similar, though Les Baux benefits from a concentration of committed wine growers who produce fine wines which have received considerable attention in recent years. Les Baux, moreover, is an extremely popular tourist region, and thus the wines have always fetched a relative premium over the still undervalued wines from elsewhere in the Coteaux d'Aix-en-Provence.

PROVENCE

Cassis AOC

*T*hough red, white, and rosé wines may be produced in this tiny *appellation*, Cassis is known above all for its forceful, dry white wines made principally from Ugni Blanc, Clairette, and Marsanne. Straw-coloured, full-bodied, and high in alcohol, Cassis is the finest white wine of Provence. Undoubtedly, however, Cassis is an example of demand outstripping a rather miniscule supply: day-trippers and weekenders from nearby Marseille as well as holidaymakers from further afield seem willing to pay virtually any price for a bottle of Cassis to accompany their *bouillabaisse* at fashionable waterfront restaurants here and up and down the coast. Cassis has benefited from an *appellation d'origine* since 1936.

Bandol AOC

*T*he Bandol vineyard begins east of Cassis, extending from Les Lecques virtually to the outskirts of Toulon and into the hills beyond Bandol itself. If Cassis is the finest white of Provence, Bandol is undoubtedly among the best reds (smaller amounts of rosé and white wines are also made under the *appellation*). While the traditional Mediterranean varieties are grown here, the great vine of Bandol is the Mourvèdre, an old-fashioned variety yielding almost black, thick-skinned grapes. Red Bandol must, by law, be made with

Rosé Wine

If you cut a black grape in half, you may be surprised to find that the flesh is white. That is because all the colouring elements of the grape are contained in its skin. Thus it is entirely possible to make white wine from black grapes though to do so takes great care and skill, for the grape juice must not be allowed to come into contact with the skins after crushing (Champagne is one such example, often made primarily from the black Pinot Noir and Meunier; less well-made examples might be marketed, with characteristic New World ingenuity, as so-called 'Blush' wines). True rosé wine is made by deliberately allowing the white juice from the grapes to stay in contact with the skin for a carefully controlled period — generally a matter of hours not days — during which time only just the required amount of colour, as well as certain flavouring elements, are allowed to 'bleed' into the wine.

The finest rosés, from the southern Rhône and the Côtes de Provence, thus have a character which can be at once full-bodied and forceful, yet at the same time soft and immediately appealing, since they lack the harsher tannins necessary for conservation of red wines. Rosés are almost universally meant to be drunk while young and fresh, usually well chilled. They are extremely versatile and can accompany a broad range of foods, from grilled fish to the garlic-laden stews of Provence. Yet still, amongst many wine drinkers that we know, a certain prejudice against pink wines remains. This is difficult to understand: in summer, certainly, a well-made rosé can be one of the most refreshing and delicious drinks in the world.

at least 50 per cent Mourvèdre: many producers utilize as much as 60 to 80 per cent of this distinctive *cépage*. The wine produced is thus rich in tannins and colour, an immense traditional red wine of at least 12° which consequently requires a minimum of 18 months' ageing in oak before it can be bottled. Such red wines can be laid down for considerable periods, certainly upwards of 10 years and more.

Rosé Bandol can be very good indeed, produced like red Bandol from Mourvèdre, with the addition of Cinsault and Grenache. It too benefits from time spent in wood and is relatively full-bodied, but with good fruit and an underlying softness. Like other Provençal rosés it is an excellent partner to the simple foods of the region: salads, *tapenade, pissaladière*.

Palette AOC   *T*he Palette *appellation* applies to a tiny parcel of vineyards just east of Aix-en-Provence. Château Simone, the only major producer, makes red, rosé, and white wines from a range of traditional and old-fashioned grapes cultivated in an amphitheatre of well-exposed, terraced vineyards facing the great profile of Mont Ste-Victoire. Due to their scarcity, these wines are in great demand in the restaurants of Aix and elsewhere.

Bellet AOC   *A*nother tiny *appellation* for white, rosé, and red wines produced from grapes grown in vineyards in the mountains just behind Nice.

Coteaux Varois VDQS   *T*he majority of the vineyards for the AOC Côtes de Provence lie in the *département* of the Var: this Vin Délimité Qualité Supérieure (VDQS) *appellation* applies to wines made mainly from similar grape varieties (with some exceptions) though to less stringent requirements.

Vin de Pays   *P*rovence accounts for a full 12 per cent of the total of all Vins de Pays produced in France. The most important classifications are Vin de Pays du Var and Vin de Pays des Bouches-du-Rhône (both *départemental* classifications referring to large quantities of red, rosé, and white table wines) and Vin de Pays des Maures, Vin de Pays d'Argens, and Vin de Pays de Mont Caume (more specific zonal classifications). Such wines, on the whole, may be sound (if not exciting) and very inexpensive, usually purchased *en vrac*.

The Wine Roads of Provence

Les Routes du Vin de Provence

CÔTES DE PROVENCE

In Brief   The sign-posted *Route du Vin* of the Côtes de Provence extends over a vast and varied vineyard located both along the winding corniche of the Riviera and through the sandy isthmuses of the Maures coast into the rugged scrub hills of the massif. It is a long, circular route and few will wish to cover it in its entirety: this is a wine road to pick up and leave at leisure (or when you discover — *Mon Dieu!* — that wine supplies have been depleted once more). There are countless opportunities to taste and purchase wine direct: both simple rosé and red *en vrac* — that is, in your own jug, demi-john, cubitainer, or camp canteen — as well as fine *Cru Classé* wines in bottle. There are a number of recommended restaurants along the sign-posted *Route du Vin* but no serious wine lover will wish to miss the *Caveau de Dégustation* and excellent restaurant at the *Maison des Vins des Côtes de Provence* in Les Arcs-sur-Argens. The *Comité Interprofessionnel des Vins Côtes de Provence* is also located in this new complex, so this really is the nerve-centre of the Provence wine region and should not be missed.

The wine road can be commenced just east of Toulon; joined from resorts like Port-Grimaud, St-Tropez, Fréjus, or St-Raphaël; picked up by leaving the *autoroute* A8 at Le Luc, Le Muy, or Puget-sur-Argens; or joined off the N7. Smaller circular routes can also be made; for example, one fine day trip may leave St-Tropez to reach Les Arcs for lunch, then return through the valley of the Argens to Fréjus and back along the coast.

The *Route du Vin* actually begins just outside Toulon. Toulon itself, a large and rather grand city, is an historic port and an important naval town. The old town, with its busy market and its colourful *poissonnerie* is particularly worth exploring, but most will probably wish to get out of this busy urban sprawl into the hills or to smaller coastal villages as quickly as possible.

The wine road heads out through the hectic outskirts, first to the virtual suburb of La Valette, then, on the D29, inland to La Crau, the first real wine town on the route. From La Crau the wine road stays inland, cutting across to La Londe-les-Maures, where the vineyards grow in sight of the sea and the Iles d'Hyères, then through the Maures massif and so on to Bormes-les-Mimosas. Bormes is a fascinating hill village perched on a tortuously steep, clutch-burning slope overlooking the splendid coast. Pause here to catch your breath, to wander through the tiny twelfth-century streets or to have lunch on a cool, shaded terrace.

From Bormes-les-Mimosas, the route continues to climb out of town up the Col du Caguo-Ven until it reaches the N98, at which point it cuts east through a wooded, classic Mediterranean landscape: mixed patches of cork oaks, olive trees, and patches of vines amidst the umbrella pines. Just past La Môle, the wine road descends to the coast once more via the precarious Col du Canadel. This inland detour has not passed many wine producers, but it dramatically reveals the terrain of the Provençal vineyards, with the jagged Maures massif rising virtually from the edge of the Mediterranean. The magnificent views of the bay and Iles d'Hyères on the way down the

St-Tropez.

Col are stunning.

The corniche road continues through Le Rayol and Cavalaire-sur-Mer, then, at La Croix-Valmer, branches right on to the St-Tropez peninsula. Vineyards here often give way to secluded estates and villas, for indeed this still is one of the most exclusive resort areas in the world. Ramatuelle is a fine medieval hill village with a circular maze of stone-paved alleyways: unlike many such towns, moreover, it remains a place where people live and has not yet been wholly taken over by the boutiques and bric-a-brac *magasins*. There are vineyards around Ramatuelle and Gassin; some producers sell direct, but much wine is made in the excellent *Cave Coopérative 'Les Maîtres Vignerons de la Presqu'île de St-Tropez'* which can be visited.

St-Tropez is, of course, legendary; one can see that its typical, pale pastel coloured Provençal houses with their peeling shutters and wrought-iron balconies must once have been charming. Yet that quaint and peaceful appeal which originally attracted the *beau monde* may be difficult to find today, hidden somewhere behind the shadows of the enormous yachts that the world comes to gape at.

Nearby Port-Grimaud is an entirely new town, a lake-village designed

Côtes de Provence.

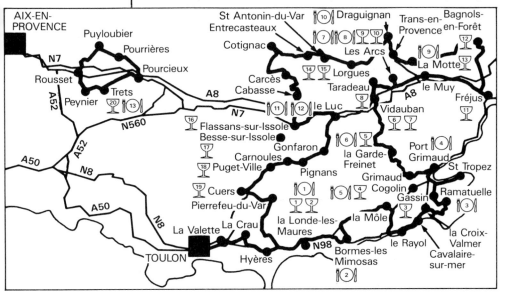

PROVENCE

Port-Grimaud.

and built by a famous town planner F. Spoerry from reclaimed marshland a mere 20 years ago. The houses, built around a system of canals, have all been designed sympathetically in the typical fashion of St-Tropez and, paradoxically, this pastiche seems to us more charming than the reality which it imitates.

From Port-Grimaud, the wine road leaves fantasy behind to strike out into the harsher landscape of inland Provence: Grimaud itself has a castle built by the Grimaldi in the eleventh century. The town is a fine, genuine, old Provençal town. The wine road continues inland through dense, wooded countryside to La Garde-Freinet, another isolated but busy and somewhat self-contained hill town. A steep, spectacular mountain pass leads to a flatter valley, where slabs of purple porphyry rocks pierce the scrubby land amidst the vines and umbrella pines. This is not a wine road that leads constantly through vineyards, but one which primarily links up wine communes such as Vidauban, a pretty, lush village further down the valley.

Les Arcs-sur-Argens should be the highlight of any tour of the *Route du Vin des Côtes de Provence*. The town itself is pleasant enough, but wine travellers will certainly wish to make their way to the new *Maison des Vins* on the outskirts. For this, without doubt, is one of the finest regional wine centres in all of France. The *Caveau de Dégustation* displays 120 different wines from individual domaines and *coopératives* and there are always 10 different wines available for free tasting and possible purchase (though there is no obligation to buy). These wines are changed every fortnight and they are also served in the adjoining restaurant, which serves authentic regional foods in a most pleasant atmosphere. The *Maison* can answer questions about the wines of the Côtes de Provence, as well as provide maps and other literature and help with any appointments.

From Les Arcs, the wine road follows the valley of the Argens through Le Muy and Puget-sur-Argens before returning to the coast once more at Fréjus, a popular resort and former Roman port which still boasts impressive ruins that are worth visiting.

The vineyards of the Côtes de Provence can be divided roughly into those near the coast and those located deeper into inland Provence. The latter towns and vineyards can be explored from Fréjus, or else by making detours off the A8 or N7 *en route* to or from Cannes or Nice. The D4 leads from Fréjus to the thickly wooded Bagnols-en-Forêt, then strikes west on the smaller D47. Vines extend over the valley floor and on the slopes, while jagged, dramatic peaks of mountains are on all sides as the road continues through a harsh and spectacular gorge to La Motte, an important wine-growing centre. At Trans-en-Provence there are some fine cascades as the Nartuby river carves its way through the steep gorge.

Draguignan is the busy centre of inland Var, and the largest town along the inland wine road. The medieval *ville* is perhaps a little shabby, with its crumbling old houses, but it is genuine. The Tour de l'Horloge is in the centre of the old *ville*: climb to the top for a fine view of the town and surrounding countryside. Draguignan has a market which takes place daily in a square just outside the old *ville*: it is a lively, colourful affair, particularly on Wednesdays and Saturdays.

From Draguignan, the wine road (D562) continues to Lorgues, a particularly pretty little wine town, then branches right on the secondary D50, through the wine villages of St-Antonin-du-Var, Entrecasteaux, and Cotignac. These little towns in high Provence all have their *caves coopératives* where wines can be tasted and purchased in bottles or *en vrac*. Equally important in many villages is the *coopérative oleicole*, where each season's pungent, green-gold olives are milled to yield their precious oil.

After Cotignac, the wine road descends, like the numerous rivers that inevitably force their way to the warm waters of the Mediterranean, towards Toulon to complete the circuit, passing *en route* through wine villages such as Carcès, Cabasse, Flassans-sur-Issole, Carnoules, Puget-Ville, and Cuers. The Lac de Carcès is a pleasant spot for a picnic before picking up the A8 *autoroute* at Brignoles, if desired.

There is one further self-contained segment of the *Route du Vin des Côtes de Provence*, a small separate *circuit* just east of Aix-en-Provence under the shadow of Mont Ste-Victoire, around the wine communes of Rousset, Puyloubier, Pourrières, Pourcieux, and, on the south side of the A8, Trets and Peynier.

Dégustation: Stop to Taste; Stop to Buy

The wines of the Côtes de Provence are considered foremost as easy holiday wines and indeed many individual *propriétaires-récoltants* and *caves coopératives* produce just this: inexpensive rosé, red, and white wines sold in bottles and *en vrac*. However, additionally there are a number of properties producing fine wines, particularly reds and rosés, that are in another class altogether. This fact was recognized as long ago as 1953 when a select number were entitled to distinguish their wines with the term *Cru Classé*: such wines are more expensive but they can be very good indeed. Drink the less-complicated, inexpensive wines when on holiday and buy the better wines to bring home.

Domaines Ott
Clos Mireille
83250 La Londe-les-Maures
tel: (94) 66 80 26
Hours: July–August 16–19h. Appointment necessary.
This great family producer has three properties in Provence, this one specializing in highly popular 'Blanc de Blancs' Côtes de Provence AOC. The property is located near the coast at Bregançon, opposite the Iles d'Hyères and about 6 km (3½ miles) from La Londe.

2
Domaine du Bastidon
83250 La Londe-les-Maures
tel: (94) 66 80 15
Hours: 8–12h; 15h30–19h30. Appointment necessary.
Côtes de Provence AOC, Vin de Pays des Maures, and *méthode champenoise*
sparkling wine produced from this seaside vineyard.
A little English spoken.

3
'Les Maîtres Vignerons de la Presqu'île de St-Tropez'
Domaine des Paris
Carrefour de La Foux
83990 Gassin
tel: (94) 56 32 04
Hours: Mon–Sat 8–12h; 14–18h.
The vineyards on the Presqu'île de St-Tropez extend over some of the most
exclusive real estate in the world: the 12 finest domaines have banded together
to form a *coopérative* that markets specially selected rosé, white and red Côtes
de Provence AOC in a distinctive and elegant bottle. These wines are especially
popular in the many waterfront restaurants of the area. The 'Cave des Maîtres
Vignerons' is located on the N98 at La Foux.
English spoken.

4
Château des Garcinières
83310 Cogolin
tel: (94) 56 02 85
Hours: Mon–Sat 8–12h; 14–18h.
Red, rosé, and white Côtes de Provence AOC. The eighteenth-century château
was constructed on the ruins of a Roman villa.

5
Domaine des Launes
83680 La Garde-Freinet
tel: (94) 60 01 95
Hours: Mon–Sat, working hours.
The red, rosé, and white Côtes de Provence AOC produced by M. and Mme
Handtmann have won many medals in recent years.
English spoken.

6
SCA Domaine des Feraud
rte de La Garde-Freinet
83550 Vidauban
tel: (94) 73 03 12
Hours: Mon–Fri 8–12h; 15–19h. Sat morning only. Telephone call preferred.
This 45-hectare domaine was established in the nineteenth century and
produces medal-winning red, rosé, and white Côtes de Provence AOC. The
white wine is produced from the Sémillon and St-Emilion grapes, while the
reds have a high proportion of Cabernet Sauvignon.
A little English spoken.

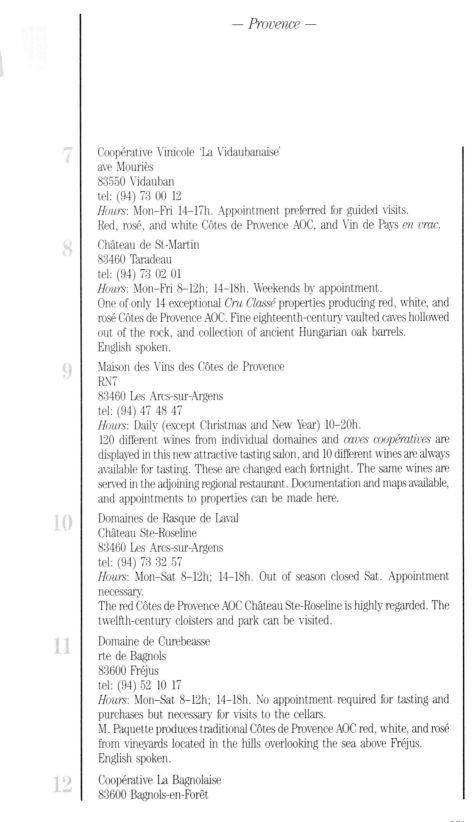

7 Coopérative Vinicole 'La Vidaubanaise'
ave Mouriès
83550 Vidauban
tel: (94) 73 00 12
Hours: Mon–Fri 14–17h. Appointment preferred for guided visits.
Red, rosé, and white Côtes de Provence AOC, and Vin de Pays *en vrac*.

8 Château de St-Martin
83460 Taradeau
tel: (94) 73 02 01
Hours: Mon–Fri 8–12h; 14–18h. Weekends by appointment.
One of only 14 exceptional *Cru Classé* properties producing red, white, and
rosé Côtes de Provence AOC. Fine eighteenth-century vaulted caves hollowed
out of the rock, and collection of ancient Hungarian oak barrels.
English spoken.

9 Maison des Vins des Côtes de Provence
RN7
83460 Les Arcs-sur-Argens
tel: (94) 47 48 47
Hours: Daily (except Christmas and New Year) 10–20h.
120 different wines from individual domaines and *caves coopératives* are
displayed in this new attractive tasting salon, and 10 different wines are always
available for tasting. These are changed each fortnight. The same wines are
served in the adjoining regional restaurant. Documentation and maps available,
and appointments to properties can be made here.

10 Domaines de Rasque de Laval
Château Ste-Roseline
83460 Les Arcs-sur-Argens
tel: (94) 73 32 57
Hours: Mon–Sat 8–12h; 14–18h. Out of season closed Sat. Appointment
necessary.
The red Côtes de Provence AOC Château Ste-Roseline is highly regarded. The
twelfth-century cloisters and park can be visited.

11 Domaine de Curebeasse
rte de Bagnols
83600 Fréjus
tel: (94) 52 10 17
Hours: Mon–Sat 8–12h; 14–18h. No appointment required for tasting and
purchases but necessary for visits to the cellars.
M. Paquette produces traditional Côtes de Provence AOC red, white, and rosé
from vineyards located in the hills overlooking the sea above Fréjus.
English spoken.

12 Coopérative La Bagnolaise
83600 Bagnols-en-Forêt

tel: (94) 40 60 13
Hours: Tue–Sat, working hours.
Red, rosé, and white Côtes de Provence AOC from this *coopérative* located
on the *Route des Vins* in the direction of La Motte. Wines sold in bottles and
en vrac.

13 Domaine du Jas-d'Esclans
rte de Callas
83920 La Motte
tel: (94) 70 27 86
Hours: Mon–Sat 8–12h; 13h30–17h30. Appointment necessary only for groups
or for personal guided visits with Mme Lorgues.
Another *Cru Classé* property producing highly regarded red, rosé, and white
Côtes de Provence AOC wines which have won numerous medals. Near the
impressive *Gorges de Pennafort*.
English spoken 'by appointment'.

14 Cave 'La Lorguaise'
rte de Draguignan
83510 Lorgues
tel: (94) 73 70 10
Hours: Mon–Fri 8–12h; 14–18h.
Local *cave coopérative* producing Côtes de Provence AOC. Wines sold in bottles
and *en vrac*.

15 Domaine Castel Roubine
N562
83150 Lorgues
tel: (94) 73 71 55
Hours: Mon–Fri 9–12h; 14–18h. Appointment necessary only for weekends
and out of season.
Wine has been produced on this estate since the thirteenth century. Classic
deep red wines, as well as rosé and white are entitled to use the term *Cru
Classé* together with the *appellation* Côtes de Provence AOC. Red and rosé
Vin de Pays d'Argens are also produced. Pleasant tasting room and modern
cellars.
English spoken.

16 Commanderie de Peyrassol
Flassans-sur-Issole
83340 Le Luc-en-Provence
tel: (94) 69 71 02
Hours: Daily 8–12h; 14–17h30. Appointment preferable weekends.
Well-known wines, widely exported to Europe and North America. The
Commanderie was founded in the early thirteenth century and there are records
of wine produced on the estate in 1256. The Rigord family acquired the property
in 1870 and the domaine is managed by Mme Françoise Rigord. Charge for

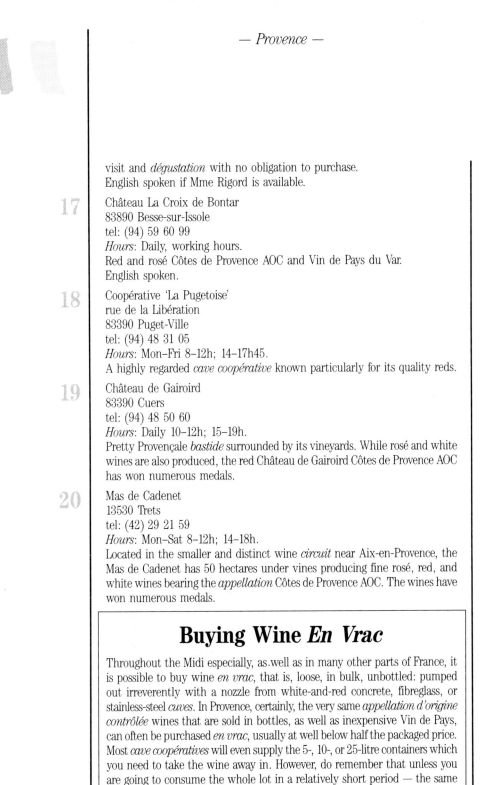

visit and *dégustation* with no obligation to purchase.
English spoken if Mme Rigord is available.

17 Château La Croix de Bontar
83890 Besse-sur-Issole
tel: (94) 59 60 99
Hours: Daily, working hours.
Red and rosé Côtes de Provence AOC and Vin de Pays du Var.
English spoken.

18 Coopérative 'La Pugetoise'
rue de la Libération
83390 Puget-Ville
tel: (94) 48 31 05
Hours: Mon–Fri 8–12h; 14–17h45.
A highly regarded *cave coopérative* known particularly for its quality reds.

19 Château de Gairoird
83390 Cuers
tel: (94) 48 50 60
Hours: Daily 10–12h; 15–19h.
Pretty Provençale *bastide* surrounded by its vineyards. While rosé and white wines are also produced, the red Château de Gairoird Côtes de Provence AOC has won numerous medals.

20 Mas de Cadenet
13530 Trets
tel: (42) 29 21 59
Hours: Mon–Sat 8–12h; 14–18h.
Located in the smaller and distinct wine *circuit* near Aix-en-Provence, the Mas de Cadenet has 50 hectares under vines producing fine rosé, red, and white wines bearing the *appellation* Côtes de Provence AOC. The wines have won numerous medals.

Buying Wine *En Vrac*

Throughout the Midi especially, as.well as in many other parts of France, it is possible to buy wine *en vrac*, that is, loose, in bulk, unbottled: pumped out irreverently with a nozzle from white-and-red concrete, fibreglass, or stainless-steel *cuves*. In Provence, certainly, the very same *appellation d'origine contrôlée* wines that are sold in bottles, as well as inexpensive Vin de Pays, can often be purchased *en vrac*, usually at well below half the packaged price. Most *cave coopératives* will even supply the 5-, 10-, or 25-litre containers which you need to take the wine away in. However, do remember that unless you are going to consume the whole lot in a relatively short period — the same day preferably — it will be necessary to bottle the wine, once broached.

PROVENCE

COTEAUX D'AIX-EN-PROVENCE

In Brief   The delimited vineyard of the Coteaux d'Aix-en-Provence is a vast one, extending from north-east of Aix all the way to Arles and from the Durance river south to the Mediterranean. It is not a particularly easy or compact wine region for exploration. However, visitors will certainly encounter no shortage of opportunities to taste and purchase wine, especially in vineyards located in the hills to the north between Aix-en-Provence and Salon-de-Provence; around the northern and eastern banks of the Étang de Berre; and in the prettiest area of all, Les Baux. Our proposed circuit concentrates on the latter area. There is a sign-posted wine road; a number of very welcoming producers who make superlative wines; good recommended restaurants: in short, all the necessary elements for happy wine touring.

Les Baux

St-Rémy-de-Provence is the true capital of this tiny little region, for the town which gives the area its name, Les Baux-de-Provence, is virtually moribund. St-Rémy, today primarily a major centre for market gardening and fruit growing, is a most pleasant town, with its shaded squares and numerous outdoor cafés. It is located to the north of the Alpilles, near the site of the important Greek town of Glanum, which was later rebuilt by the Romans. These ruins, including

Les Baux.

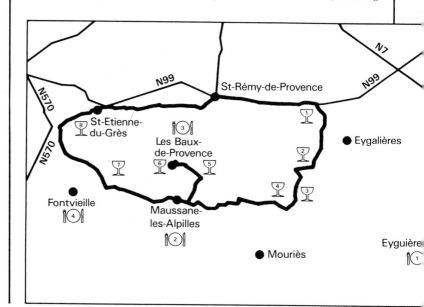

a first-century AD mausoleum, triumphal arch, temples, baths, and villas, should be visited.

The dominant feature of this small region, of course, is the impressive, jagged, white chain of limestone mountains known as the Alpilles. On the lower slopes and on the valley floor, vines and olive trees complete a particularly beautiful Provençal landscape, as the wine road leads from small village to village. The mainly circular tour begins by leaving St-Rémy on the D99 (direction of Cavaillon), then branches off right to the Domaine des Terres Blanches (direction of Mouriès). This fine property has nearly 40 hectares under vines, all grown by *culture biologique*.

Join the D24 and continue through the vineyards (the Domaine de Lauzières can be visited) then turn right on the D78 to Maussane-les-Alpilles,

*oteaux d'Aix-
n-Provence.*

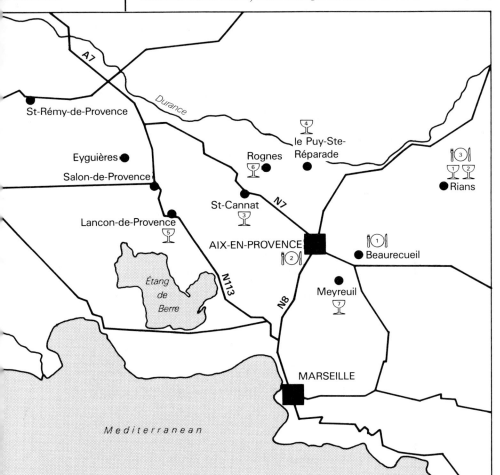

a pleasant little wine town as well as a fine centre for quality *huile d'olive* (the *coopérative oleicole* sells olive oil direct). From Mausanne, make a detour to Les Baux-de-Provence itself, passing along the way one of the better-known wine properties, the Mas de la Dame. Les Baux is situated on a mesa of sheer limestone rising dramatically some 200 m (650 ft) from the valley floor: one half of the town is known as the living village, the other half the dead.

Les Baux-de-Provence.

The living village, steep, accessible by foot only, has a number of notable medieval and Renaissance buildings (most selling tourist bric-à-brac), while the deserted village is a fine archaeological ruin consisting of the former medieval castle, ramparts and chapel. It is sometimes hard to tell where man-made walls end and nature's own fortifications take over. The views of the surrounding valley all

the way across to the Camargue are astounding. There are some notable restaurants and hotels located below Les Baux around the foot of the precipice. Also down below, there is another highly regarded wine estate, Mas Ste-Berthe.

Continue back to the D17 to rejoin the wine circuit: here, past Paradou is the Château d'Estoublon, where M. Lombrage, another serious family wine producer, makes not only excellent red and rosé wine from his 10 hectares of vines, but also a superb domaine-bottled *huile d'olive*, deep green-gold in colour, the product of 5 different types of olives all grown on the estate.

The wine road continues on the D33 to St-Etienne-du-Grès, then branches right to La Mas Veran (Domaine de Trévallon), and so back to St-Rémy.

Dégustation: Stop to Taste; Stop to Buy

In addition to the producers below, located on the circuit of the Coteaux de Baux-de-Provence, we also include other Coteaux d'Aix-en-Provence wine producers located elsewhere in the delimited vineyard region. Château Simone, located just outside Aix itself, bears the prestigious and almost exclusive *appellation* Palette.

Coteaux d'Aix-en-Provence AOC 'Les Baux'

Noël Michelin
Domaine des Terres Blanches
D99
13210 St-Rémy-de-Provence
tel: (90) 95 91 66

Hours: Mon–Sat 8–12h; 14–18h.
The 40-hectare vineyard is planted with the typical Mediterranean varieties: Grenache, Mourvèdre, Cinsault, Ugni Blanc, plus a high proportion of Cabernet Sauvignon, and is tended entirely by *culture biologique*. Red, rosé, and white Coteaux d'Aix-en-Provence AOC are produced.
English spoken.

2
Philippe Paul-Cavallier
Domaine de la Vallongue
13810 Eygalières
tel: (90) 95 91 70
Hours: Mon, Fri, Sat 9h30–12h; 14h30–18h. Appointment necessary at other times.
Coteaux d'Aix-en-Provence red and rosé can be tasted and purchased.
English spoken.

3
Domaine de Lauzières
Le Destet
13890 Mouriès
tel: (42) 04 70 39
Hours: Mon–Sat 8–12h; 14–18h.
Coteaux d'Aix-en-Provence AOC red and rosé wines can be tasted and purchased.
English spoken.

4
Nicolas Cartier
Mas de Gourgonnier
13890 Mouriès
tel: (90) 47 50 45
Hours: Mon–Sat 8–12h; 14–18h. Appointment necessary for guided visits.
Red, white, and rosé Coteaux d'Aix-en-Provence AOC.
A little English spoken.

5
M. et Mme Jacques Chatin
Mas de la Dame
Les Baux-de-Provence
13520 Maussane-les-Alpilles
tel: (90) 54 32 24
Hours: Daily year round from 8h30.
On the road up to Les Baux, a fine property producing excellent red and rosé wines, as well as estate-bottled *huile d'olive*. Van Gogh, while staying in nearby St-Rémy, came out here in 1889 and painted the 'Mas de la Dame', a landscape of vines and olives, with the Provençal farmhouse outlined against the Alpilles.
A little English spoken.

6
GFA du Mas Ste-Berthe
Les Baux-de-Provence

PROVENCE

357

13520 Maussane-les-Alpilles
tel: (90) 54 39 01
Hours: 9–12h; 14–19h. Telephone call in advance essential.
Situated at the foot of Les Baux, amidst vines and olive groves: red and rosé
Coteaux d'Aix-en-Provence AOC as well as *vin blanc de table*.
English spoken.

7 Lombrage Père et Fils
Château d'Estoublon
(off D17)
13990 Fontvieille
tel: (90) 54 64 00
Hours: Daily, working hours.
Red and rosé Coteaux d'Aix-en-Provence AOC as well as gold-medal, estate-
bottled *huile d'olive*.
A little English spoken.

8 Eloi Dürrbach
Domaine de Trevallon
13150 St-Etienne-du-Grès
tel: (90) 49 06 00
Hours: By appointment only.
Domaine de Trevallon is unusual in that the traditional Mediterranean *cépages*
are eschewed in favour only of the classic Cabernet Sauvignon and Syrah:
the wine produced is powerful and immense, with a remarkable potential for
ageing, and has rightly received considerable praise and attention.

Other Producers in the Coteaux d'Aix-en-Provence

1 Château Vignelaure
rte de Jouques
83560 Rians
tel: (94) 80 31 93
Hours: Mon–Sat 8h30–12h30; 14h30–18h30. Sun and holidays 10–12h30;
14–17h30.
M. Georges Brunet, former owner of the third-growth Bordeaux Château La
Lagune, planted his vineyard at Rians (located some 40 km (25 miles) north-
east of Aix) mainly with Cabernet Sauvignon, as well as Syrah and Grenache.
Château Vignelaure, though not inexpensive compared with others bearing
the Coteaux d'Aix-en-Provence AOC, is highly regarded and worthy of
comparison with even the very best from Bordeaux. There is an extensive
collection of modern art displayed in the château and winery. Wines can be
tasted for a charge.
English spoken.

2 SCA Domaine de Château Pigoudet
rte de Jouques

83560 Rians
tel: (94) 80 31 78
Hours: Mon–Fri, working hours.
Red and rosé Coteaux d'Aix-en-Provence AOC produced from grapes grown in 60 hectares of vineyards surrounding the château which was itself built on the ruins of a Roman villa.
English spoken.

3 Château de Beaupré
13760 St-Cannat
tel. (42) 28 23 83
Hours: Daily, including Sun, working hours. Appointment necessary for guided visits.
Classic red, white, and rosé Coteaux d'Aix-en-Provence AOC produced by the Double family for three generations.
English spoken.

4 Château La Coste
SICA Bordonado
13610 Le Puy-Ste-Réparade
tel: (42) 61 89 98
Hours: Working hours, by appointment.
Traditional producer located 12 km (7½ miles) to the north-west of Aix producing red, rosé, and white Coteaux d'Aix-en-Provence AOC grown in over 100 hectares of vineyards surrounding the seventeenth-century Palladian château. 'Rosé d'Une Nuit' is a typical speciality of the region.
English spoken.

5 Château de Calissanne
D10
13680 Lançon-de-Provence
tel: (90) 42 63 03
Hours: Mon–Fri 8–12h; 14–18h. Appointment preferred for visits. Shop open daily including Sun.
The Château de Calissanne, known since the fourth century when it was part of the *Ancienne Commanderie de l'Ordre de Malte*, is an important wine property, with over 120 hectares of vines planted in the countryside near the Étang de Berre. Traditional Coteaux d'Aix-en-Provence AOC and Vin de Pays des Bouches-du-Rhône are produced. Each year the finest *crus* are selected for the Cuvée Prestige.

6 Château de Beaulieu
13840 Rognes
tel: (42) 50 20 19
Hours: Mon–Fri, working hours.
Coteaux d'Aix-en-Provence AOC as well as a range of other Provençal wines from this union of *coopératives*.

Palette

Château Simone
13590 Meyreuil
tel: (42) 28 92 58
Hours: By appointment only, as far in advance as possible.
Château Simone is an historic vineyard, and virtually the only producer of Palette AOC red, rosé, and white. Located only minutes from the centre of Aix-en-Provence just off the N7, the vineyard position is altogether exceptional and the small quantities of wines made, assembled from traditional as well as rare Provençal grape varieties, are equally exceptional and in great demand.

CASSIS

In Brief The entire delimited vineyard area for this tiny Cassis *appellation* consists of only 150 hectares, located in the steep hills behind and around the popular fishing village. The wine road can be covered in just an hour or two, followed by lunch at the waterfront.

Cassis is a small fishing port located no more than 10 km (6½ miles) from Marseille, yet it could be another world. Here the rocky limestone coast is indented with deep, rugged *calanques* — great, steep inlets where the rocks drop almost vertically to the sea. These provide numerous sheltered harbours, as well as an abundance of rock fish: weird, strange varieties seldom encountered elsewhere — *rascasse, chapon, galinette* — fish whose names have no English equivalents, which together with sea bass, red mullet, conger-eel, and much else go into the making of that great dish of Provence, *bouillabaisse*. Today, in fancy restaurants up and down the coast, this basic fisherman's stew has become a '*spécialité*', often even including lobster! Of course, arguments rage hotly over beaded glasses of pastis as to what should and shouldn't be allowed in the pot. But one thing is clear: the best accompaniment to this gutsy festival of the sea is the fragrant, strong dry white wine of Cassis.

The geographical features which make the coast so attractive here also mean that getting in and out of Cassis can be a nightmare, especially on weekends or in summer months when, it seems, virtually all of Marseille has had the same idea. None the less, the waterfront tables overlooking the harbour are lovely, while the games of *pétanque* in the adjoining dirt square are serious to say the least (spectators have been known to come away with injured ankles, the result of over-enthusiastic *tireurs* trying to knock their opponents' *boule* out of place).

The vineyards of Cassis rise behind the town. Follow the road out in the direction of Marseille then branch right on the D41e to Carnoux. Turn right to Clos St Michel, passing a little railway station on the left. Return

Cassis.

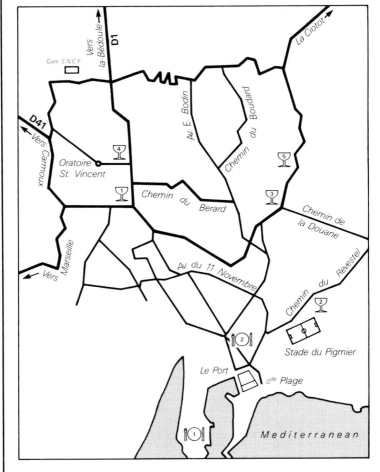

through the valley towards Cassis, passing through vineyards with the steep precipices on either side and the azure waters of the sea ahead. Other vineyards and properties are located off the road out from Cassis to La Ciotat.

Dégustation: Stop to Taste; Stop to Buy

La Ferme Blanche
BP 57
13260 Cassis
tel: (42) 01 00 74
Hours: Mon–Fri 9–12h; 14–17h30.
The first wine property on the circuit, just outside town on the road towards

PROVENCE

Marseille. In addition to the famous white Cassis AOC, some red and rosé Cassis are also made.
A little English spoken.

 2

Clos Ste-Magdeleine
ave du Revestel
13260 Cassis
tel: (42) 01 70 28
Hours: Weekdays, working hours. Appointment preferred.
20 hectares of vines grown in a spectacular setting overlooking the sea and used for the production of fine white Cassis AOC as well as a small amount of rosé.
English spoken.

3

Domaine du Paternal
rte de La Ciotat

Bandol.

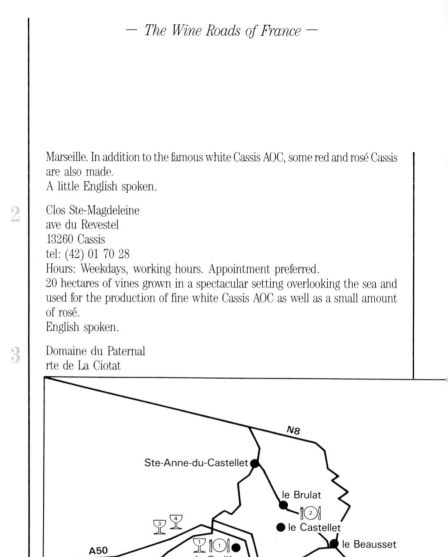

13260 Cassis
tel: (42) 01 77 03 (cellar); (42) 01 76 50 (office)
Hours: By appointment only.
The domaine is located on the incoming road to Cassis from La Ciotat. The Cassis AOC produced here is excellent.

4

Clos d'Albizzi
rte de la Gare
13260 Cassis
tel: (42) 01 11 43
Hours: Mon–Fri by appointment.
Cassis AOC white and rosé available for tasting and purchase.

5

Clos Chantecler
rte de La Ciotat
13260 Cassis
tel: (42) 01 72 66
Hours: Daily 9–12h; 14–18h.
Drop in to taste and buy white Cassis AOC as well as red and rosé from this wine grower located on the road to La Ciotat.

BANDOL

In Brief   The Bandol vineyard lies further down the coast from Cassis and extends into the hills beyond in a vast and well-exposed natural amphitheatre encircling the gulf. Though the region is five times as large as Cassis, it is still tiny. There are only about 40 producers and the vineyards can easily be explored in a half or full day.

The wine tour of Bandol begins at the resorts of Les Lecques and St-Cyr. The vines are immediately encountered along the D66 to La Cadière d'Azur, a fine, isolated, little hill town. The views across these vine-covered hills to Le Castellet are striking, for this indeed is a single-minded wine region. One of the oldest *appellations* in France, the wines have long been valued, and today Bandol is one of the few remaining old-fashioned reds: the thick-skinned Mourvèdre is macerated for lengthy periods to extract a full measure of tannin and flavour, resulting in a strong, virile wine which is rather tough and unforthcoming initially. Yet like the best reds, with time it loses some of its youthful fire and acquires more delicate nuances in bouquet and flavour.

It is worth climbing up to Le Castellet simply for the view from the medieval village of the surrounding vineyards and the sea. But be warned: although Bandol may not be well known to most of us (it remains a well-kept secret simply because most of the wine is drunk on the spot), the region itself is certainly on the well-worn track for French tourists. Le Beausset is another

PROVENCE

important wine town; from here, either head down to Bandol itself, or continue through the vineyards of Ste-Anne-d'Evenos and Ollioules until you reach the virtual outskirts of Toulon.

Don't miss the town of Bandol: a busy seaside resort with three beaches. Though it appears rather sprawling and highly developed, it is not without its charm, especially if you take time to explore its back streets. The *Maison des Vins du Bandol* on the waterfront near the *Pavillon du Tourisme*, is a good place to sample a number of different wines, on sale at the same prices as *chez viticulteur*.

Dégustation: Stop to Taste; Stop to Buy

Bandol is not an inexpensive holiday wine: the fine reds especially are among the best wines of Provence to purchase to bring home.

1

Mas de la Rouvière
Moulin des Costes
83740 La Cadière d'Azur
tel: (94) 98 72 76
Hours: Mon–Sat 8–12h; 15–18h.
Paul Bunan left the family estate in the Ain-Temouchent region of Algeria in 1961 at the time of Independence and purchased the Moulin des Costes (25 hectares) near La Cadière d'Azur. In 1969 his brother Pierre purchased the Mas de la Rouvière (20 hectares), and today they work the two vineyards as a joint operation producing Bandol AOC red, rosé, and white under both labels. The ultra-modern vinification *chais* at Moulin des Costes (located up the D559b road from Bandol before the turning to La Cadière d'Azur) belies a traditional approach, especially for the red wines which are aged for a full 2 years in oak and a further 6 months in bottle before being released. The Bunans also recently took a long-term lease on a third estate, the Domaine du Bélouvé at Le Castellet. Most of this vineyard lies within the *appellation* of Bandol but some 5 hectares, classified only as Vin de Pays du Mont Caume, have been replanted with Cabernet Sauvignon.
Some English spoken.

2

Domaines Ott
Château Romassan
D66
83330 Le Castellet
tel: (93) 34 38 91
Hours: Weekdays, working hours by appointment.
One of the larger producers in the Bandol region, producing a highly popular rosé Bandol AOC in the distinctive and elegant Ott bottle, as well as smaller amounts of red and white Bandol AOC. The Château de Romassan is located below Le Castellet on the D66 between La Cadière and Le Beausset, but the Ott family operation (which has two other domaines in La Londe-les-Maures

and Vidauban) is based in Antibes, where you must telephone to arrange visits. English spoken.

3

Château Vannières
83740 La Cadière d'Azur
tel: (94) 90 08 08
Hours: Daily in summer, Mon–Sat rest of year, working hours.
Located between St-Cyr-sur-Mer and La Cadière d'Azur, this 30-hectare property makes fine, medal-winning wines in a strictly traditional manner. The *caves*, as well as the château itself, were constructed in the sixteenth century. The wines can be tasted and purchased here, and also in the village of Le Castellet. English spoken.

4

Domaine des Salettes
83740 La Cadière d'Azur
tel: (94) 90 06 06
Hours: Daily, working hours. Appointment necessary only for English-speaking guide.
Bandol AOC red, rosé, and white medal-winning wines.

5

Domaine de la Laidière
GAEC Estienne
Ste-Anne d'Evenos
83330 Le Beausset
tel: (94) 90 37 07
Hours: Mon–Fri 8–18h.
Another medal-winning property, producing red, rosé, and white Bandol AOC as well as Vin de Pays du Mont Caume.
Located just off the N8.

6

Domaine de Terrebrune
83190 Ollioules
tel: (94) 74 01 30
Hours: Mon–Sat, working hours.
Nestling beneath the imposing Louis XIV château, this 20-hectare vineyard produces high-quality red and rosé Bandol; also own-produced goats' cheese. English spoken.

Regional Gastronomy

Provençal cuisine is based on olive oil, garlic, herbs, and all the sun-ripened produce and products of the south of France. It is one of the most direct and appealing *cuisines* in the world.

Both land and sea yield an abundance of good things as any visit to a market in Provence will aptly demonstrate. Take Saturday in Aix-en-Provence:

the place des Pêcheurs is a riot of colour and animation from early on in the morning. The profusion of fruits and vegetables brought in from the surrounding countryside is quite astounding: there are banks overflowing with shiny, near-black aubergines; crates of knobbly tomatoes; carrots with their fine green tops still on; courgettes and bright orange courgette flowers. There are deep-red peppers, pointed and sweet; bunches of thin, mild radishes; mounds of beans and fresh peas; and several types of lettuce: *batavia, mâche, romaine,* and *frisée.*

Plastic tubs are swimming with all kinds of different olives, macerated in herbs, with peppers and onions, or steeped in garlic; there are large, chestnut-brown olives from Nyons, sharp pointed ones from Nice, fat green olives, shrivelled black ones, and everything in between. Sweet, oozing melons from Cavaillon attract shoppers and honey bees; there are mounds of almost black cherries from the mountains (*brulats*), luscious nectarines (*brugnons*), fine, furry white peaches (*pêches blanches*), and baskets full of tiny, concentrated wild strawberries.

Aix may be the inland capital for a vast and rich hinterland, but Marseille and Toulon are both important centres for an essentially sea-going region. Come to the quayside at either of these two great maritime towns to see the weird profusion of fish which comes from its rocky shores. *Rascasse* (scorpion or hog fish), *congre* (conger-eel), *vive* (weever), *St-Pierre* (John Dory), *rouget grondin* (red gurnard), and many others all find their way into that classic fisherman's pot *bouillabaisse.* Though that great dish has become an expensive '*spécialité*', simpler fish broths remain everyday staples. *Bourride* is a favourite throughout the Midi, a puréed fish soup flavoured with saffron and served always with *rouille*, a chilli-hot, garlic mayonnaise.

Other fish such as *rouget* (red mullet) and *loup de mer* (sea bass) are enjoyed simply grilled over a wood fire. The latter is sometimes stuffed with fresh fennel and grilled over fennel stalks. Another great dish of Provence is *le grand aïoli*, a feast of various boiled fish, meats, and vegetables served with a pungent, garlic-rich mayonnaise, freshly made with green-gold *huile d'olive de Provence*. *Aïoli* without doubt is the 'butter' of the Midi and no visitor should miss this heady soporific treat. Considering the abundance of fresh fish available, it is perhaps curious that *brandade de morue* is another favourite staple, for this garlic and olive oil emulsion is made with air-dried salt cod.

Other typical inland dishes reflect the harsher terrain of Provence, where meat is scarce and everything must be utilized. Rabbits are hunted in the bare scrubland and upland *garrigues* and find their way into *civets* flavoured with olives and pine nuts. *Daube de boeuf* is a stew made with inexpensive cuts of beef marinated overnight in red wine and herbs, flavoured with anchovies and perhaps a piece of fragrant orange rind. *Pieds et pacquets* is another characteristic dish, turning mere mutton tripe and pig's trotter into the most delectable, little wrapped-up packets.

Above all, it is freshness and flavour which distinguishes the cuisine of

Le plateau des fruits de mer.

Provence. Everything *tastes*: those knobbly, uneven tomatoes simply have more colour and flavour; small, tight-leaved basil is incredibly pungent and peppery; scrawny, yellow-skinned chickens are somehow more 'chickeny'. Simple dishes such as *soupe au pistou* (a minestrone-type vegetable soup flavoured with *pistou*, a mixture of pounded basil, garlic, olive oil, and gruyère); *anchoïade*

Olives and *Huile d'Olive*

Everywhere you go in Provence the vine vies with the olive tree for supremacy. The products of both, wine and olive oil, are the basis of the Provençal diet. Just as virtually every town here has its own *cave coopérative* so do many also have a *coopérative oleicole* for the production of olive oil. Individual growers, too, produce their own *huiles*; some of these estate-bottled oils are to ordinary oil what estate-bottled wines are to those made in the *cave coop*.

Numerous different varieties of olives are cultivated and each has its own properties. Some olives are picked while still unripe and green, others are allowed to stay on the tree until almost jet black and fully ripe. Certain varieties are suitable only for eating or only for making oil, while others can serve both purposes. The *salonenque* and *picholine*, for example, are both harvested while green and can be eaten (after treatment in brine) as well as used for making oil; the *verdale* and *ascolana*, on the other hand, are used only for making oil. The famous, fleshy, dark chestnut *olive de Nyons* is superb both for eating and for making a prized varietal oil.

Huile d'olive is produced today as it has been for centuries. The fruit, pips and all, is crushed in a stone mill to produce a mushy pulp and the oil is then separated from the watery liquid (today a centrifuge is usually used for this purpose). There are basically three grades of cold or first-pressed olive oil: *vierge extra*, generally considered the finest, with an acidity of not more than 1 per cent; *vierge fine*, also excellent quality, with an acidity of not more than 1½ per cent; and *vierge* or *vierge semi-fine* which can have an acid level up to 3 per cent. When purchasing olive oil it is essential to determine if it is made with olives from Provence (such oils may bear the *appellation* '*Huile de Provence*') since many *coopératives* buy in olives from other countries.

Many *coopératives oleicoles*, like their vinous counterparts, are open to the public to sell their products direct. Indeed, in many, the oils are stored in concrete *cuves* not unlike those used for wine, and can be bought *en vrac*. However, out of the olive-making season (winter) they are often only open on one or two days of the week. Our favourite oil comes from the *coopérative* at Maussane-les-Alpilles.

Coopérative Oléicole de la
  Vallée des Baux
13520 Maussane-les-Alpilles
Hours: Mon–Fri 8h30–12h; Sat 14–17h.

The great variety of olives available in Provence.

(a pungent sauce of garlic, anchovies, and olive oil used as a dip for fresh raw vegetables); a rustic *tian* of baked vegetables; or the classic *salade niçoise* (salad layered with tuna, anchovies, boiled eggs, olives, and much else) become not just courses but celebrations of the sheer goodness of food, the bounty of Provence.

Le Pique-Nique

Saucisson d'Arles Only one of many local air-dried sausages (*saucisson sec*), from Arles and its surrounds. Made with beef (mainly) and pork. The genuine article is exceptional.

Pissaladière Provençal 'pizza': a flat bread dough spread with fresh tomato sauce, olive oil, anchovy fillets, and olives. Good cold or hot.

Tapenade Pounded olive, anchovy, and caper paste, delicious as a dip for raw vegetables or spread on bread. Sometimes found in *charcuteries* as a stuffing for hard-boiled eggs.

Fougasse Twisted bread made with olive oil and sometimes filled with ingredients such as walnuts, anchovies, or *lardons*. Almost a meal in itself.

Ratatouille The classic Provençal mixture of aubergines, tomatoes, courgettes, peppers, and onions stewed slowly in olive oil: often found in *charcuteries* and delicious picnic fare served at room temperature.

Fromages Provence is not known for its cheeses, but there are many local varieties made mainly from goats' and sheeps' milk. Our favourite is mature Banon. Small fresh rounds of goats' cheese are often marinated in olive oil and *herbes de Provence*.

Spécialités Régionales:
Stop to Taste; Stop to Buy

Le Fournil des Augustins
51, rue Espariat
13100 Aix-en-Provence
This traditional *boulangerie* produces a fine range of Provençal breads including *fougasse aux anchois*, *pain aux noix*, *pain aux olives*, *pain à l'ail*, and much else.

La Maison du Saucisson d'Arles
J. Mousset
13310 St-Martin-de-Crau
Located right on the N113 between Arles and Salon-de-Provence, don't pass this traditional *charcuterie* without sampling the authentic and delicious *saucisson d'Arles*.

Restaurants

Côtes de Provence (Map p.347)

1
Le Bistrot à l'Ail
plage de l'Argentière
83250 La Londe les Maures
tel: (94) 65 56 91
Closed Mon.
Provençal, Varoises, and Catalan specialities accompanied by wines of Côtes
de Provence. Recommended by Domaine du Bastidon.
Inexpensive

2
La Tonnelle des Délices
place Gambetta
83230 Bormes-les-Mimosas
tel: (94) 71 34 84
Open daily 1 April–30 September.
High up in this lovely hill town, with a glass terrace with splendid views over
the town and out to sea. Typical Provençal cuisine including *marinade de
sardines crus*, *la daube provençale*, and *feuilleté aux fruits de mer*.
Moderate

3
Auberge du Vieux Moulin
quartier des Moulins
83350 Ramatuelle
tel: (94) 97 17 22
Closed Tue and Wed out of season.
In this lovely old town, meals are served in a rustic dining room with open
fire in winter and outdoors on the terrace in summer: specialities such as
cotriade Tropezienne and *escalope de loup*.
Moderate to Expensive

4
The Salad Table
place des Artisans
83360 Port-Grimaud
tel: (94) 56 06 77
The *fruits de mer* in this English-owned restaurant are absolutely superlative,
served on a terrace overlooking the canals of Port-Grimaud. Recommended
by Les Maîtres Vignerons de la Presqu'île de St-Tropez.
Moderate

5
Au Coq Assis
place de l'Hôtel de Ville
83310 Cogolin
tel: (94) 54 57 20

Closed Wed out of season.
Simple traditional and regional cuisine in this **Inexpensive** restaurant; dining outdoors on the terrace in summer. Recommended by Château des Garcinières.

6   La Faücado
31, bd de l'Esplanade
83680 La Garde-Freinet
tel: (94) 43 60 41
Closed Tue, February.
Specialities include *civet de porcelet* and *truffes en croûte* (in season), together with a large selection of Côtes de Provence wines. Recommended by Domaine des Launes.
Inexpensive menu weekdays lunch only; otherwise **Moderate**

7   Restaurant de la Maison des Vins des Côtes de Provence
RN7
83460 Les Arcs-sur-Argens
tel: (94) 47 48 47
Closed Sun eve, Mon.
Authentic Provençal cuisine to accompany the 10 wines chosen each fortnight for tasting here and in the *caveau de dégustation* of the *Maison des Vins*. Recommended by Domaines de Rasque de Laval and others.
Moderate

8   Le Logis du Guetteur
place du Château
83460 Les Arcs-sur-Argens
tel: (94) 73 30 82
Closed Fri.
Hotel-restaurant situated in an authentic eleventh-century fort. Recommended by Château de St-Martin.
Moderate

9   Restaurant 'Les Pignatelles'
rte de Bagnols
83920 La Motte
tel: (94) 70 25 70
Closed Wed.
Situated in the Provençal countryside on the route to Bagnols, with a large terrace in front of the restaurant, serving both classic and regional cuisine. Recommended by Domaine du Jas d'Esclans and others.
Moderate

10 Restaurant 'Les Deux Cochers'
7, bd Gabriel Péri
83300 Draguignan
tel: (94) 68 13 97

Open daily (except Mon) at midday and also Fri and Sat eve.
Rustic informal restaurant serving traditional French cuisine and homemade fresh pasta. Recommended by Domaine Castel Roubine.
Inexpensive

11

La Grillade au Feu de Bois
RN7
83340 Le Luc-en-Provence
tel: (94) 69 71 20
Open daily.
Decorated in typical Provençal fashion, this restaurant serves *cèpes, artichaux à la Barigoule, morue aux poireaux*, and *grillades au feu de bois*. Recommended by Commanderie de Peyrassol.
Moderate

12

Hostellerie du Parc
12, rue Jean-Jaurès
83340 Le Luc-en-Provence
tel: (94) 60 70 01
Closed Mon eve, Tue.
This ancient *relais de poste* located in the centre of the *ville* amidst its own shaded park serves fine Provençal cuisine, including *anchoïade, terrine de rascasse, canard aux olives*, together with a good selection of Côtes de Provence wines. Recommended by the Cave 'La Lorguaise' and others.
Moderate to Expensive

13

L'Oustaou du Vin
1, ave Jean-Jaurès
13530 Trets
tel: (42) 61 51 51
Closed Sun eve; Wed eve.
Eighteenth-century *relais de poste* recommended by Mas de Cadenet for its good, simple cooking.
Inexpensive

Coteaux d'Aix-en-Provence (Map p.355)

1

Mas de la Bertrande
Beaurecueil
13100 Aix-en-Provence
tel: (42) 28 90 09
Closed Sun eve, Mon.
This rustic Provençal *mas* located in the heart of Cezanne country just 7 km (4½ miles) south of Aix-en-Provence is a lovely hotel with a fine and highly regarded restaurant. Cuisine is a mixture of local-inspired and lighter imaginative dishes accompanied by wines of the Coteaux d'Aix-en-Provence, Côtes du Rhône, and Bandol.
Expensive

2 Mas d'Entremont
Célony
RN7
13090 Aix-en-Provence
tel: (42) 23 45 32
Restaurant closed Sun eve; Mon midday.
Just outside Aix on the road to Avignon, this grand Provençal *mas* stands
in beautiful gardens with tennis court and swimming pool. Restaurant serves
fine regional-inspired cuisine: *soupe de poissons de roche* and *petite marmite
de rascasses à la Marseillaise.*
Moderate to Expensive

3 Hôtel-Restaurant de l'Esplanade
83560 Rians
tel: (94) 80 31 12
Simple **Inexpensive** *Logis de France* in this typical Provençal village.
Recommended by Château Vignelaure.

'Les Baux' (Map p.354)

1 Le Relais du Coche
place Monnier
13430 Eyguières
tel: (90) 59 86 70
Closed Wed, Sun.
Rustic beamed dining room and pleasant outdoor garden courtyard: specialities
include *pieds et paquets, terrine de lapereau, filet de boeuf aux nouilles.*
Recommended by Domaine de Lauzières.
Moderate

2 Ou Ravi Provençau
34, ave de la Vallée des Baux
13520 Maussane-les-Alpilles
tel: (90) 97 31 11
Closed Mon eve, Tue out of season; open every evening in summer.
Lovely, popular little *bistro* in this small wine town near Les Baux: specialities
include *soupe au pistou, foie gras maison*, and home-smoked salmon.
Moderate

3 Restaurant Berengère
rue du Trencat
13520 Les Baux-de-Provence
tel: (90) 97 35 63
Closed Tue eve, Wed.
This *ancien salon de thé* serves hearty Provençal dishes: *baudroie* (monkfish)
à la tomate et à l'ail doux; noisette d'agneau au romarin, accompanied by

the forthright wines of Les Baux. Recommended by Domaine des Terres Blanches.
Moderate to Expensive

4

Auberge 'La Rigalido'
rue Frédéric Mistral
13990 Fontvieille
tel: (90) 97 60 22
Really pretty *auberge* with rooms and restaurant located in ancient *moulin à huile d'olive*. Recommended by Château d'Estoublon.
Expensive

Cassis (Map p.361)

1

Restaurant La Presqu'île
quartier de Port-Miou
13260 Cassis
tel: (42) 01 03 77
Closed Sun eve, Mon out of high season.
Located on the narrow peninsula separating the *calanque* of Port-Miou from Cassis harbour, this restaurant has an exceptional position with a splendid terrace overlooking the sea. Fish and shellfish are the specialities: *loup farci en feuilletage, salade de homard tiède, poisson cru*. Recommended by La Ferme Blanche and Clos Ste-Magdeleine.
Expensive

2

L'Oustau de la Mer
20, quai des Baux
13260 Cassis
tel: (42) 01 78 22
Closed Thur.
A busy, popular waterfront restaurant with outdoor tables overlooking the port. Specialities include *bourride, bouillabaise*, and an excellent *couscous de poissons*.
Inexpensive

Bandol (Map p.362)

1

Hostellerie Bérard
rue G.-Péri
83740 La Cadière d'Azur
tel: (94) 90 11 43
In the heart of the old village, with a pretty terrace, this restaurant serves good regional cooking: *moules à l'origan, côtes d'agneau, pâtisserie maison*. Recommended by Château Vannières, Moulin des Costes.
Moderate

2

Auberge St Eloi
7, rue de l'Aube
83330 Le Castellet Village
tel: (94) 32 68 98
Closed Wed midday.
Fish restaurant serving *poisson en croûte, bourride, bouillabaisse* on a terrace
with an exceptional view over the vineyards of Bandol to the sea. Recommended
by Mas de la Rouvière.
Moderate

3

Le Poivre d'Ane
83330 Ste-Anne-d'Evenos
tel: (94) 90 37 88
Closed Mon.
Regional foods and wines of Bandol in a typical Provençal atmosphere.
Recommended by Domaine de la Laidière.
Moderate to Expensive

Additional Information

Et pour en savoir plus . . .

Comité Interprofessionnel
  des Vins Côtes de Provence
Maison des Vins
RN7
83460 Les Arcs-sur-Argens
tel: (94) 47 48 47

Syndicat de Defense des
  Coteaux d'Aix-en-Provence
Maison des Agriculteurs
ave Henri Pontier
13626 Aix-en-Provence
tel: (42) 23 57 14

Office Municipal de Tourisme
place du Général de Gaulle
13100 Aix-en-Provence
tel: (42) 26 02 93

Office Municipal du Tourisme
place P. Baragnon
13260 Cassis
tel: (42) 01 71 17

Pavillon du Tourisme
allées Vivien
83150 Bandol
tel: (94) 29 41 35

Office de Tourisme
9, bd Clémenceau
83300 Draguignan
tel: (94) 68 63 30

THE RHÔNE
VALLEY

Introduction

St-Laurent-des-Arbres, a peaceful wine hamlet in the southern Rhône.

*T*he Rhône valley is a great historical corridor, a natural avenue for trade and commerce which has been populated for millennia. The Greeks landed on the Rhône's delta and there founded Massilia (Marseille) in 600 BC; subsequently they sailed further up-river and colonized and established new trading communities. They brought the vine with them and it was soon an established feature of the landscape, for the majestic, scorched environs of the Rhône proved almost perfectly suited to its cultivation.

After the Greeks, the Romans settled the area, leaving behind great monuments of ancient civilization: the magnificent Pont du Gard, the amphitheatre and triumphal arch at Orange, villas at Vaison-la-Romaine, temples at Vienne, and much else. Vienne itself became the capital of the *Provincia Romana* but fine Roman roads led much further north, through the rest of Gaul, and on to the Rhineland Palatinate and to Britain. The Roman legions who were compelled to march up and down this corridor — never ones to suffer thirst for very long — thus did much to encourage viticulture in the region.

Throughout the succeeding Dark Ages, the Church kept alive the cultivation of the vine (presumably the monks needed some solace during what is universally considered a bleak nadir in man's existence). When the papal seat was transferred to Avignon in 1308 the wines of the southern Rhône received an even greater boost; papal patronage, after all, is no mean achievement. Moreover, the Rhône river itself formed the border between the then papal city of Avignon and the frontier of France. Thus, when Philippe-le-Bel founded the opposing city of Villeneuve-lès-Avignon just across across the river, the vineyards on these opposite banks around Roquemaure, Tavel, Lirac, and elsewhere, were soon gracing the tables of kings.

The Rhône today is not by any means the centre of France, let alone Europe as it clearly once was. Yet the region retains its rich historical heritage.

The heritage of the vine is no less proud today than centuries ago, and indeed a full range of prestigious as well as everyday wines are produced all along the length of this mighty river: rare distinguished red and white wines from its northern flanks: Côte-Rôtie, Condrieu, and Château Grillet; powerful old-fashioned reds from Hermitage, Châteauneuf-de-Pape, Gigondas, and elsewhere; probably the finest French rosés from Tavel and Lirac; the magnificent grape-sweet Vin Doux Naturel, Muscat de Beaumes-de-Venise; sparkling wines from St-Péray and Die; and vast rivers of full-flavoured reds, rosés and white bearing the basic *appellation* Côtes du Rhône, or the superior Côtes du Rhône-Villages.

The Rhône valley remains, as in the past, a natural corridor to and from northern France and Europe. On 14 July and throughout the month of August, the so-called *Autoroute du Soleil* is jam-packed with legions of holidaymakers heading to the beaches of the south. Most pass through this historic region as quickly as they can. Let them go. We prefer to stay here, in the thyme-scented and vine-covered *garrigues* where life continues at the civilized and slower pace of a region with a strong sense of its own history.

The Papacy and the Vine

When the Archbishop of Bordeaux was elected to become Pope Clément V he left his own personal vineyard in Graves as a gift to his flock. That vineyard, Château Pape Clément, is still considered among the finest classed Bordeaux properties. God's representative on earth was clearly a lover of wine; when he made the audacious move in 1308 of setting up court at Avignon instead of Rome, he not only altered the entire focal point of medieval Europe, he at the same time gave the vineyards of the southern Rhône a profound boost. It was his successor, Pope John XXII, who restored the nearby 'Châteauneuf', making it a summer residence for the popes. The vineyards around Châteauneuf-du-Pape were soon producing sturdy wines that were to grace the tables of popes and kings for many centuries. Wines from surrounding vineyards flowed into the papal cellars, too, for indeed this was an age not of austerity but of great wealth, when the Church was the equal of even the greatest secular powers.

In 1377 the 'Great Schism' rocked the foundations of Christianity, when 'anti-popes' remained at Avignon while popes were re-established at Rome, each condemning the other to eternal damnation. Certainly Avignon was never to regain the central influence and power that it enjoyed in its brief but glorious heyday. Yet the remains of that splendid age remain for all to see: the Palais des Papes is one of the most remarkable and important Gothic structures in France. Furthermore the papal patronage which the wines of the Rhône received has left them with a status which the finest wines today are still worthy of.

Orientation

The A6 and A7, the main north–south *autoroutes* from Paris to the south of France, pass along the Rhône valley, making access to the region not difficult. The distance from Paris to Lyon is 460 km (290 miles); it is a further 200 km (125 miles) south to Avignon. Reasonable driving time to Lyon is about 4–5 hours. In high season, however, do remember that Lyon is a notorious area for bottlenecks on the *autoroute*. The wine circuit of the northern Rhône begins at Vienne, while the wine roads and vineyards of the southern Rhône are best started from Avignon.

The main Paris–Lyon line has frequent daily trains, the fastest (TGV) covering the distance in less than 3 hours. The Paris–Lyon–Marseille line stops at Valence, Montélimar, Orange, and Avignon. There are motor-rail services from Boulogne to Avignon as well as from Paris to Avignon.

The principal international airports are Lyon Satolas and Marseille Provence.

Michelin Maps 84, 93

The Wines of the Rhône Valley

General *Appellations*

Côtes du Rhône AOC

*T*he basic *appellation* for the Rhône vineyard applies to a vast area extending over 40,000 hectares in six different *départements*: Vaucluse, Gard, Drôme, Ardèche, Rhône, and Loire. The vast majority of wines produced are reds or rosés; white Côtes du Rhône accounts for less than 5 per cent of production. However, this proportion is likely to increase as improved wine-making techniques — slow fermentation at low temperatures in stainless-steel vats — are now resulting in well-made crisp but full-bodied white wines. The characteristic Mediterranean grape varieties as well as some others unique to the region are cultivated: Grenache (the most important and widely planted single variety), Clairette, Syrah, Mourvèdre, Picpoul, Terret Noir, Picardan, Viognier, Cinsault, Roussette, Marsanne, Bourboulenc, and small proportions of a few others. The wines of the Côtes du Rhône must have a minimum alcohol content of 11°: they are, on the whole, strong, robust, and fruity, pleasant quaffing wines to be drunk while relatively young and fresh. A large proportion of wines bearing the basic *appellation* is made in *caves coopératives*.

The southern part of the vineyard, in recent years, has been producing larger amounts of Côtes du Rhône *primeur*: intensely fruity, new wines vinified to be drunk like Beaujolais as early as a few weeks after the vintage. Such wines are traditionally placed on the market on or around 15 November.

Côtes du Rhône-Villages AOC

This superior *appellation* was established in 1967 as a reward for the efforts of wine growers in some 17 villages in the southern half of the Rhône in the *départements* of Drôme, Gard, and Vaucluse. Such red, rosé, and white wines must undergo more rigorous selection and regulations regarding minimum alcohol content, yield per hectare, proportions of grape varieties, and methods of cultivation. On the whole, the wines have more character than basic Côtes du Rhône: deeper colour, more concentration of bouquet and flavour.

The wines may be marketed as Côtes du Rhône-Villages, or they may be labelled under the name of the wine commune alone. Such wines are produced in the following communes: Rochegude, Rousset, Saint-Maurice-sur-Aygues, Saint-Pantaléon-les-Vignes, Vinsobres (Drôme); Cairanne, Rasteau, Roaix, Sablet, Séguret, Vacquéyras, Valréas, Visan, Beaumes-de-Venise (Vaucluse); Chusclan, Laudun, Saint-Gervais (Gard).

Northern Rhône

Château Grillet AOC

Minute and famous estate located within the delimited region of Condrieu but entitled to its own *appellation* for the tiny quantity of fragrant and concentrated dry white wine produced exclusively from the Viognier grape. The vineyard has been owned by the same family for some 300 years and the wine produced is rightly regarded as one of the great white wines of France.

Clairette de Die AOC

The *appellation* applies mainly to sparkling wine produced by traditional methods around this small commune in the Drôme valley (not really in the northern Rhône, though not actually in the southern either). The grapes cultivated are the Clairette and the Muscat, but it is the fragrant latter variety which lends its distinctive, grape-fresh character to the best Clairette de Die *tradition*. Some still white Clairette de Die is also produced entirely from the Clairette grape.

Condrieu AOC

Great but very expensive dry white wine produced entirely from the rare and difficult to cultivate Viognier grapes grown on the granite terraces of the northern Rhône. The Viognier is noted above all for its rather musky, heady aroma of violets which connoisseurs find so seductive; with age its character becomes more compact, more profound.

Cornas AOC

Rich, mighty red wine produced from pure Syrah grown for centuries on vineyards around the village of Cornas: Charlemagne enjoyed Cornas, as did Louis XV. This traditional wine will improve for 20 years and more.

Côte-Rôtie AOC

One of the great wines of the Rhône, produced in northern terraced vineyards below Lyon, and opposite the Roman town of Vienne. The wine must be produced from a minimum of 80 per cent Syrah, with the remaining amount made up from the rare Viognier. Though traditionally Viognier is supposed to add balance and elegance, in truth these days most wine growers eschew this extremely temperamental *cépage* and thus make the wine with pure or almost pure Syrah. Production is small and the wines, favoured in the best local and regional restaurants here and in the Lyonnais, are consequently in great demand and thus very expensive. The vineyard region divides into two stretches: the Côte Brune and the Côte Blonde, said to be named after the two daughters of a medieval Lord of Ampuis.

Crozes-Hermitage AOC

*T*he *appellation* for red and white wines from villages on the right bank of the Rhône opposite Tournon, and around the towns of Crozes-Hermitage, Tain l'Hermitage, Chanos-Curson, Beaumont-Monteux, Pont de l'Isère, and others. Like great Hermitage itself, the red wines are full, powerful, and rather austere, though nowhere near as intense or concentrated as that great heavyweight; white Crozes-Hermitage is a solid, full-bodied wine that can stand up well to full-flavoured foods.

Hermitage AOC

*F*amous red and white wine produced from grapes grown on the superbly exposed granite hill that dominates the town of Tain l'Hermitage in the central Rhône. Red Hermitage is a classic: George Saintsbury and many others have referred to it as 'the manliest of wines': this description may not be in keeping with modern times, and indeed the wine itself is from another age: intensely concentrated, rich in flavours and tannin which necessitate considerable ageing before it is ready to drink. White Hermitage is a rarity, but undoubtedly one of the great white wines of the Rhône.

St-Joseph AOC

A large *appellation* for red and white wines produced from vineyards on the left bank of the Rhône beginning opposite Hermitage around the town of Tournon and extending north nearly to Condrieu. Red St-Joseph, like Hermitage and Cornas, is produced from pure Syrah.

St-Péray AOC

*S*parkling wine produced by the classic *méthode champenoise* from a small vineyard area opposite Valence. Some *nature* (still) wines (praised long ago by Plutarch, Henry IV, and Richard Wagner) continue to be made, though in lesser quantities.

Southern Rhône

Châteauneuf-du-Pape AOC

*O*ne of the great classics of the southern Rhône, the *appellation* applies to both red (mainly) and white wine produced from vineyards around the ruined former summer residence of the popes, and in neighbouring communes such as Courthézon, Bédarrides, Sorgues, and Orange. Châteauneuf-du-Pape is virile, full-bodied, the epitome of a great southern Rhône red wine, balancing its power with a subtle underlying delicacy which is achieved through the

THE RHÔNE VALLEY

skilful *assemblage* of the musts from up to 13 permitted different black and white grape varieties. Traditionally, it is a wine which needs to be laid down for several years — decades even — though many wine producers today are making wines that can be consumed at a much younger age. White Châteauneuf-du-Pape, not widely available outside the region, is a full-bodied traditional Rhône white.

Coteaux du Tricastin AOC

*F*ruity red and rosé wines produced from vineyards of the central Rhône, south of Montélimar. The wines resemble the softer, easy-to-drink Côtes du Rhône when vinified to be drunk young. Very small amounts of white wines are also made.

Côtes du Ventoux AOC

*A*n historic vineyard area on the foothills of the Mt Ventoux range producing red, rosé, and some white wines which are similar in style and quality to the fruity wines of the Côtes du Rhône.

Gigondas AOC

*A*nother classic red from the southern Rhône, produced from grapes grown on the slopes of the Montmirail hills around the picturesque perched village of Gigondas. Like Châteauneuf-du-Pape and the best red wines of the southern Rhône, it is robust, powerful, and concentrated. Some full-bodied rosé Gigondas is also produced.

Lirac AOC

*R*ed, white, and above all rosé wines are produced from grapes grown in vineyards around this typical Gardien village as well as in the neighbouring villages of Saint-Laurent-des-Arbres, Roquemaure, and Saint-Géniés-de-Comolas.

Muscat de Beaumes-de-Venise VDN

*B*eaumes-de-Venise is a Côtes du Rhône-Villages, noted for its powerful red wine, but the commune also produces an unusual Vin Doux Naturel from the Muscat grape. This is a *mistelle*, that is a wine whose natural fermentation has been muted with the addition of alcohol, resulting in a very fragrant, fresh, and powerful dessert wine (though here in the region it is usually drunk as an *apéritif*). At its best, we consider Muscat de Beaumes-de-Venise to be one of the finest of all Vins Doux Naturels.

Rasteau VDN

*A*nother fortified Vin Doux Naturel produced from the Grenache grape. In addition to the limited production of this sweet wine, Rasteau is also entitled to produce Côtes du Rhône-Villages, mainly robust red wines.

Tavel AOC

*Q*uite simply the best rosé wine in France, produced from a variety of different grapes on the stony vineyards around this Gardien town. Its pretty orange-pink colour belies a wine of considerable strength, body, and flavour: it is one of the most refreshing and substantial summer wines to drink, well-chilled with the garlic- and herb-laden foods of Provence.

Côtes du Luberon VDQS	Red, rosé, and white VDQS wines from the Vaucluse *département*.
Côtes du Vivarais VDQS	Red, rosé, and miniscule amounts of white wine produced in the Ardèche and Gard *départements*.
Vin de Pays Coteaux de l'Ardèche	Well-made inexpensive red, white, and rosé Vins de Pays from the Ardèche *département*. The Gamay de l'Ardèche can be particularly good.
Vin de Pays Collines Rhodaniennes	High-quality Vin de Pays red, produced from classic Rhône varieties such as Syrah, can be an interesting alternative to the more concentrated and expensive wines of the northern Rhône. Some rosé and white wines are also made under this classification.

Macération Carbonique

Macération carbonique is an important process of vinification in which, contrary to traditional methods, red grapes are not first crushed before fermentation, but rather are placed in the fermentation vats whole and entirely intact. The vats are then sealed and the grapes consequently ferment from within their skins under the pressure of the natural carbon dioxide gases emitted in the process. In contrast to traditional methods of vinification whereby the crushed grapes and their skins must macerate for long periods to extract not only colour and rich flavouring elements but also harsher tannins (necessary for wines vinified for conservation), by means of the *macération carbonique* the colour is extracted from the skins far more quickly, and, above all, the fresh, fruity aroma of the grape is maintained.

The *macération carbonique* process is essential for the production of the *primeur* and *nouveau* wines from the Rhône, Beaujolais, the Loire, and elsewhere. But 'straight' wines in the Rhône and throughout the Midi often benefit by utilizing this important method of vinification in combination with traditional methods. For by vinifying part of the crop by *macération carbonique* the finished wines gain a fresher character and can be enjoyed far sooner.

The Wine Roads of the Rhône Valley

The *Comité Interprofessionnel des Côtes du Rhône, Côtes du Ventoux, Coteaux du Tricastin* has devised a series of nine '*itinéraires dans le vignoble*', complete with colour-coded *Routes du Vin* signs and rather bizarre modern-art placards announcing all of the wine towns along the route. We have combined the

THE RHÔNE VALLEY

most important vineyard areas into four suggested excursions which broadly follow these sign-posted routes.

The Terraces of the Northern Rhône

In Brief   The vineyards of the northern Rhône begin at Vienne and extend south in a long narrow ribbon all the way to Valence. Either Vienne itself or Condrieu makes an excellent base for exploring the Côte-Rôtie and Condrieu vineyards, but many will follow the *Route du Vin* while travelling south or north. It can easily be covered in a day (or less if pressed for time) and takes in all the great growths of the northern Rhône. This route corresponds with the sign-posted '*Route Rubis*'.

Vienne, by turns a Gaulish town, important Roman metropolis, and flourishing medieval centre, remains today an historic city, located just 24 km (15 miles) south of Lyon. As such, it is just far enough away to be past the main urban sprawl of that great but unmanageable city. Vienne itself rather hugs a bend of the Rhône, sharing it with the A7 '*autoroute du Soleil*'. The city's most important ancient monuments are the Temple of Augustus and Livia, the Temple and Theatre of Cybele, and the tall-pointed Pyramide du Cirque. One other legendary monument should be noted, at once pyramid *and* temple (of gastronomy): La Pyramide, the restaurant of one of France's early culinary 'superstars', the late Fernand Point. Point's disciples learned from the master, and have now spread his gospel of classic, fresh cuisine throughout France; a visit to the source of their inspiration may still be a gastronomic highlight.

To begin the tour of the vineyards of the northern Rhône cross the river and carry on south on the N86 to little Ampuis. This former Greek settlement has been an important wine centre for nearly two and a half millennia, for it was the Phocaeans who probably brought both the Viognier and the Syrah grapes to these steep slopes. Certainly the rare and distinctive Viognier is found nowhere else but here and in the neighbouring wine commune of Condrieu.

The sharp-terraced vineyards which rise above Ampuis and extend through the villages of Tupin and Semons form the Côte Rôtie, the 'roasted slope', a fitting name for this harsh, inhospitable terrain, held together only by a system of ancient retaining walls known as *cheys*. As in many of the greatest vineyards, the vine and *vigneron* both struggle for existence: certainly mechanization here is out of the question as the vineyards can only be tended by hand, a back-breaking labour. Yet presumably the wine produced — and the quite unbelievable prices that it can fetch — make the task worthwhile: Côte-Rôtie AOC is considered the greatest red wine of the Rhône, combining the power and structure of southern wines such as Châteauneuf-du-Pape with a finer elegance, a delicacy even, which is highly appreciated.

Northern Rhône.

Just a few miles further down-river the terraced vineyards continue, around Condrieu, Vérin, and St-Michel. The vineyard of Condrieu is tiny, the entire *appellation* considerably smaller than a single average property in the Médoc. The only grape variety planted is Viognier, a unique rarity which yields fine and unusually fragrant white wine, without doubt the greatest white wine of the Rhône. But scarcity breeds demand: the elegant restaurants of the area (such as the lovely Beau Rivage in Condrieu) as well as throughout the Lyonnais find no problem in selling the meagre output at almost *any* price they care to name. None the less, Condrieu is a classic: wine travellers passing through the town should not miss the chance to stop at Georges Vernay's *caveau* just outside Condrieu, for it provides one of the rare opportunities to taste (at a price) and purchase this marvel.

If Condrieu is rare, consider Château Grillet, a tiny enclave of less than 2 hectares, and the smallest vineyard in the country to be granted its own *appellation d'origine contrôlée*. Curnosky ranked Château Grillet as one of the five greatest white wines in the world: indeed the exposure of this steep natural amphitheatre of Viognier vines is exceptional, and the wine produced is noted above all for its intense concentration of scent (said to be reminiscent of wild violets) and its long, lingering taste. Château Grillet, naturally, is in great demand, but the Neyret-Gachet family, who have owned the vineyard for 300 years, receive visitors by appointment. Understandably, insufficient wine is

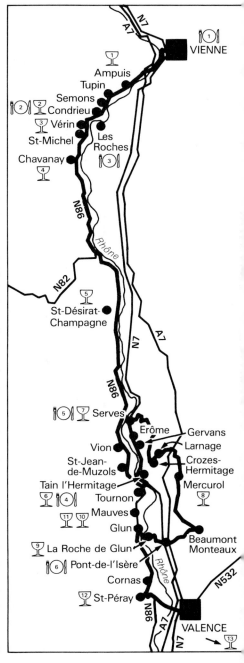

available to hand out tasting samples to all and sundry, but the Neyret-Gachets might be persuaded to part with a few bottles. But beware: even *chez viticulteur* Château Grillet can never be less than very expensive!

Though the wine road continues south for a considerable distance, the areas between Condrieu and Tournon are by no means intensively and solely devoted to viticulture. None the less, along this stretch, quantities of simpler, more accessible wines bearing the basic *appellation* Côtes du Rhône are produced and may be sampled.

By St-Désirat-Champagne, the vine begins to assert itself once more, as we enter the next great *appellation* of the northern Rhône: St-Joseph. The *Cave Coopérative de St-Désirat-Champagne*, located just outside St-Désirat, is noted for its fine example of this big, tannic wine produced entirely from Syrah. The *coopérative* also produces more accessible and ready-for-drinking wines, particularly a fine range of inexpensive Vins du Pays de l'Ardèche from the Gamay and Syrah grapes.

On the way south from St-Désirat-Champagne to Tournon, notice the neglected vineyard terraces at Arras-sur-Rhône: it takes generations and centuries of labour to tame these rugged hills, yet only years or decades of neglect is all that is necessary for nature to reclaim them. Such vineyards are so labour intensive, though, that it is understandable why many farmers have taken to fruit farming on the richer flatter plains instead of viticulture.

The St-Joseph *appellation* is a rather sprawling one, but the concentration of the finest vineyards lies just to the north and south of Tournon, in the wine communes of Vion, St-Jean-de-Muzols, Mauves, and Glun. St-Joseph is generally a somewhat undervalued wine since it is fairly plentiful and not that well known outside the area. White St-Joseph is also produced, though in far smaller quantities.

Tournon itself is a pleasant, somewhat large wine town, nestling on the Rhône opposite Tain l'Hermitage. It is worth stopping here simply to climb up to the fifteenth-century château above the town which gives superb views over the Hermitage vineyards across the Rhône. Emblazoned with large placards bearing the names of some of the most famous producers — Chapoutier, Jaboulet, and others — rearing above the town like a great wave, the hill of Hermitage is indeed one of the great vineyard sights in France.

Hermitage.

Cross the river, then, to explore this prestigious vineyard: Tain itself has its tasting opportunities. Don't miss visiting the fine *cave coopérative* where a full range of northern Rhône wines — Crozes-Hermitage, Cornas, St-Joseph, and Hermitage — can all be tasted and purchased. These wines are heady, immense heavyweights, so do make use of the spittoons which are thoughtfully provided! From Tain,

climb the great granite hill of Hermitage on foot to gain a partial understanding of some of the factors which make this slope so exceptional. The feeling at the top of the steep, craggy hill is strangely reminiscent of the precipitous vineyards of Germany's Mittelmosel.

Red Hermitage is another pure Syrah wine, once as well known as either claret or Burgundy: indeed it remains a classic, old-fashioned wine, immensely deep and rich in colour, full of complex tannins and flavouring elements which need years, decades even, to mellow and knit together. White Hermitage, produced from the Roussanne and Marsanne grapes, shares this essential full-bodied and powerful character: it too is rightly considered one of the great wines of the Rhône.

The vineyards that surround this great hill to the north and south have appended the famous name and thus the wines are marketed under the *appellation* Crozes-Hermitage. Indeed, such wines certainly do bear a family resemblance to Hermitage, though they are necessarily lighter, less concentrated in flavour, generally ready to drink earlier; they are also considerably less expensive. But Crozes-Hermitage is no mere generic wine: it should be appreciated in its own right. Wines such as Paul Jaboulet's Crozes-Hermitage 'Thalabert' and other wines from individual estates can be outstanding heavyweights that take their place alongside the finest of the Rhône.

A circular tour through these less well-known vineyards can thus be a most pleasant introduction to these often undervalued wines: drive north to Gervans, Erôme, and Serves, then back through little Crozes-Hermitage itself and (crossing the *autoroute*) continue on to Mercurol, Beaumont-Monteux, and La Roche de Glun. Recross the river at Tain or La Roche de Glun and continue down to the remaining vineyards of the northern Rhône.

If — like us — you are partial to immense, meaty red wines, then the Rhône in general, and this section of it in particular, will make for most enjoyable wine touring. For in addition to the wines already encountered — Côte-Rôtie, St-Joseph, Crozes-Hermitage, Hermitage — there is yet another classic, but little-known, red wine, produced again from the mighty Syrah grown on vineyards around the little town of Cornas. Cornas is even deeper, tougher, and more rasping than some of those other wines, initially unforthcoming certainly, but splendidly concentrated and powerful after four or five years. The name, apparently, means 'burnt ground' in Celtic; though that may be a perfectly adequate description of this rather austere terrain, it is not clear to me why the Celts should have been the ones to name it.

Finally, the wines of St-Péray, produced from vineyards south of Cornas and opposite Valence, come as a refreshing, mouth-cleansing tonic. For within this sea of predominantly red wines, St-Péray is a clean, delightful sparkling wine produced by the *méthode champenoise*. The white wines of St-Péray have been enjoyed and praised for centuries (Plutarch, Henry IV, and Richard Wagner were all devotees), but in 1929 the wine growers took a collective decision to turn the majority of the crop each year into luminous sparklers. Some smaller amounts of still St-Péray are made, but it is the sparkling St-Péray which is particularly noteworthy.

The wine road ends, finally, at Valence, a large and busy commercial city with a long history dating back to before Roman times. Rabelais studied at Valence University, while the young cadet Napoléon Bonaparte spent a year at the military school of artillery. Valence, though rather sprawling and 'modern' in appearance, has an interesting medieval quarter, and remains an energetic market centre for the luscious fruits and vegetables that are grown in this fertile valley.

To the south-east of Valence, one more important enclave of wine growing should be included on this tour: the vineyards of Die, which extend along the valley of the Drôme. Don't miss the opportunity to sample Clairette de Die *tradition*, a fine fragrant Muscat sparkler, in the local *cave coopérative*, open to all in summer.

Dégustation: Stop to Taste; Stop to Buy

In comparison with the plentiful wines of the southern Rhône, the wines of the northern Rhône — especially Côte-Rôtie AOC, Condrieu AOC, Chateau Grillet AOC, and Hermitage AOC — are rare and correspondingly expensive. None the less, serious wine travellers should take the opportunity at least to try and taste some of these classic wines when in the region. *Cave coopératives* offer good, well-made examples of the more accessible lesser *appellations* as well as Vin de Pays de l'Ardèche and Coteaux de l'Ardèche. St-Joseph AOC and Cornas AOC, though not cheap, are still excellent value.

1

E. Guigal SA
69420 Ampuis
tel: (74) 56 10 22
Hours: Mon–Fri 10–12h; 14–18h. Telephone call preferred.
Closed August.
One of the larger and well-respected producers of Côte-Rôtie AOC, Condrieu AOC, and other northern Rhône wines. Visits to the cellars, and wines available for tasting and purchase.
English spoken.

2

Georges Vernay
1 rte Nationale
69420 Condrieu
tel: (74) 59 52 22
Hours: Mon–Sat 9–12h; 14h30–19h. Appointment preferred.

Georges Vernay is, according to Rhône expert Robin Yapp, '*le gros légume*', the big cheese of Condrieu, a well-known producer of Condrieu AOC as well as Côte-Rôtie AOC, St-Joseph AOC, and Côtes du Rhône AOC wines. The tasting *caveau* is located on the main road before entering the town: visitors should not miss the opportunity of tasting these fine and rare wines when passing by. Charge for *dégustation*.

3

Château Grillet
Vérin
42410 Pelussin
tel: (74) 59 51 56
Hours: Mon–Fri, working hours by appointment.
This tiniest *appellation d'origine contrôlée* in France is entirely exceptional: its position on ancient terraces above the Rhône ensure maximum exposure; the granite soil is perfectly suited to the Viognier; and traditional wine-making methods, including lengthy barrel ageing, ensure that the small quantity of Château Grillet AOC produced is worthy of its reputation.
English spoken.

4

Caveau de Boisseyt
N86
42410 Chavanay
tel: (74) 87 23 45
Hours: Daily except Mon 9–12h; 14–18h. Closed first fortnight in September.
Côte-Rôtie AOC, St-Joseph AOC (red and white), and Côtes du Rhône AOC wines produced by the de Boisseyt family since 1797. In this tasting *caveau* on the main road they offer only wines produced from their own grapes for tasting and sale. The wine-making facilities and vineyards can only be visited by appointment.

5

Cave Coopérative de St-Désirat-Champagne
St-Désirat
07340 Serrières
tel: (75) 34 22 05
Hours: Daily 9–12h; 14–18h.
St-Joseph AOC; Vin de Pays de l'Ardèche *cépages* Syrah and Gamay.

6

Cave Coopérative de Vins Fins
22 rte de Larnage
26600 Tain l'Hermitage
tel: (75) 08 20 87
Hours: Daily 9–11h; 14h30–17h. Appointment not necessary for *dégustation* but preferred for visits to see wine-making facilities.
Hermitage AOC; Crozes-Hermitage AOC; St-Joseph AOC; Cornas AOC; Côtes du Rhône AOC.
One of the best opportunities for tasting the full gamut of Syrah wines from

these prestigious vineyards, as well as for sampling the less well-known white wines of the region.

7
Mme A. Bégot
'Le Village'
Serves-sur-Rhône
26600 Tain l'Hermitage
tel: (75) 03 30 27
Hours: Daily, working hours. Telephone before coming. Open Sat afternoon without appointment.
Crozes-Hermitage AOC.

8
Desmeure Père & Fils
rte de Romans
Mercurol
26600 Tain l'Hermitage
tel: (75) 07 44 28
Hours: Daily by appointment.
Hermitage AOC; Crozes-Hermitage AOC red and white.

9
Paul Jaboulet Aîné
La Roche de Glun
26600 Tain l'Hermitage
tel: (75) 84 68 93
Hours: Mon–Fri 8h30–11h30; 14–17h. Appointment necessary.
Paul Jaboulet is one of the great names of the Rhône, the producer of a full range of wines including the prestigious red Hermitage 'La Chapelle', white Hermitage 'Le Chevalier de Sterimberg', Crozes-Hermitage 'Thalabert', Côte-Rôtie, Châteauneuf-du-Pape and other wines of the Rhône.
English spoken.

10
Pierre Coursodon
place du Marché
Mauves
07300 Tournon
tel: (75) 08 29 27
Hours: Mon–Sat 8–12h; 14–19h. Telephone call in advance preferred.
Though the St-Joseph *appellation* was extended in 1969 to include vineyards all the way north to Chavanay and south to Chateaubourg, the heart of the region remains just to the north as well as south of Tournon, particularly around Mauves. Pierre Coursodon's St-Joseph AOC wines have won many medals. A little English spoken.

11
Bernard Gripa
RN86
Mauves

07300 Tournon
tel: (75) 08 14 96
Hours: Mon–Fri 8–12h; 14–19h. Appointment preferred.
St-Joseph AOC red and white; St-Péray AOC (still).

12

J. F. Chaboud
21, rue Ferdinand Malet
07130 St-Péray
tel: (75) 40 31 63
Hours: Mon–Fri 8–18h. Weekends by appointment.
St-Péray AOC *cépages* Marsanne and Roussanne; St-Péray *méthode champenoise brut* and *demi-sec*.
This *caveau de dégustation* provides a good opportunity to try both the delicious still and the sparkling wines of St-Péray.

13

Cave Coopérative Clairette de Die
ave de la Clairette
BP 79
26150 Die
tel: (75) 22 02 22
Hours: 1 April–30 September daily 8h30–12h30; 13h30–18h30.
Clairette de Die AOC *tradition* (Muscat); Clairette de Die AOC *brut*; and still white wines.
This important *cave coopérative* makes wine from the harvest of 90 per cent of the area's wine growers; it is one of the largest and most important in the Rhône. Die is located south-east of Valence on the banks of the Drôme river. English spoken.

The Wine Roads of the Southern Rhône

In Brief   The Rhône Méridionale, as the southern part of the vineyard is known, is a vast and complex area producing a number of fine wines as well as vast quantities of honest but basic Côtes du Rhône AOC. Avignon, an historic and fascinating city, makes the best base for touring the region, though there are also many fine smaller wine villages to hide out in. The *Comité Interprofessionnel des Côtes du Rhône, Côtes du Ventoux, Coteaux du Tricastin* has devised no fewer than six wine roads through these southern vineyards, all sign-posted and marked with the distinctive abstract placards. We have combined these sign-posted routes into three tours which cover all the principal areas.

The first circuit stays on the east side of the Rhône and takes in the vineyards of Châteauneuf-du-Pape, the historic towns of Orange and Vaison-la-Romaine, and the hill towns which nestle under the Dentelles de Montmirail: Séguret, Gigondas, Vacqueyras, and Beaumes-de-Venise. If sightseeing in Orange or Vaison, as well as stopping at *caveaux de dégustation* then at least two days should be put aside for this tour. It can, however, be completed in a single day. This tour combines the *'Route d'Azur'* and the *'Route Emeraude'*.

The second tour crosses over to the west side of the Rhône and tours the vineyards of Tavel and Lirac, as well as notable Côtes du Rhône-Villages such as Laudun, Chusclan, and St-Gervais. From here, one can continue up to Pont St-Esprit and the beautiful Ardèche gorge, or else make a large circular loop south to Remoulins to visit the Roman aqueduct, Pont du Gard. This tour combines the *'Route d'Azur'* and the *'Route Emeraude'*.

The third tour corresponds roughly with the *'Route Rousse'* and extends from near Bollène (south of Montélimar) across to the olive- and vine-covered *garrigues* of Nyons. It is a fine but brief tour which travellers can incorporate as a break from travels south or north by leaving the A7 *autoroute* at Bollène.

Southern Rhône Tour 1: Châteauneuf-du-Pape and the Dentelles de Montmirail

Avignon is the starting point for the first two tours of the southern Rhône and as such makes a most enjoyable base for it is an important economic and cultural centre for the entire region. Behind its fine and majestic machicolated ramparts that tower over the Rhône lies a busy, prosperous Provençal town of considerable charm and elegance. Of course, it is the monumental fourteenth-century Palais des Papes which continues to dominate Avignon even today; indeed the transference of the papal seat here uplifted a provincial market town into one of the religious and political capitals of Europe. The popes and anti-popes lasted less than 100 years, but the *kudos* which Avignon gained from their presence has proved permanent. Though no longer a strategic centre, Avignon remains one of the most pleasant cities in Provence, with its numerous street cafés dappled with light, its atmospheric medieval craft quarters, its dirt promenades where the men gather for their interminable evening sessions of *pétanque*, and, of course, the Pont St-Bénézet, bridge of nursery fame, half-spanning the mighty Rhône itself (*'sur le pont d'Avignon/On y danse . . .'*).

To begin the first tour of the southern Rhône, leave Avignon on the N7 to Sorgues and there branch left on the D17 to Châteauneuf-du-Pape. As you approach the town, the silhouette of the majestic ruins of the summer residence of the popes will come into view. Though the remains are but a shadow of the château's former grandiose self, the vineyards which were planted around it at that time remain as noble today as in the past. For indeed this is one of the great vineyards of France, and one of the most strictly controlled. Before even the laws of *appellation d'origine contrôlée* came into effect, the wine growers of Châteauneuf-du-Pape laid down strict decrees determining the defined vineyard area (extending over the communes of Châteauneuf-du-Pape, Sorgues, Bédarrides, Courthézon and Orange); the permitted grape varieties (up to 13 different *cépages* are allowed to be cultivated, an unusually high number); the methods of cultivation and pruning; minimum alcohol content

Southern Rhône Tour 1.

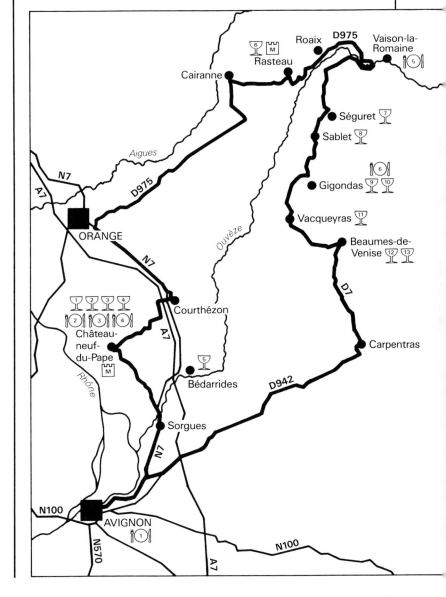

(12.5° by law but often much higher than this); and rules about harvest and vinification (a process known as *triage* must be carried out, for example, whereby less-than-perfect grapes are rejected, ensuring that only untainted bunches are pressed and made into wine). These factors combined with the remarkable *terroir* all determine why Châteauneuf-du-Pape is such a justly famous wine.

'Locals' at Châteauneuf-du-Pape.

Châteauneuf-du-Pape itself is certainly one of the great little wine towns of France, riddled with cellars, oozing with wine-tasting opportunities, full of history and nostalgia, and with a choice of good restaurants to spend the afternoon in. First wander through the old stone streets to the ruined castle: though just a single tower and wall are all that remain, the view from up here over the vineyards of Châteauneuf and the surrounding valley of the Rhône is well worth the effort. Then make your way back and try the wine in any number of tasting *caveaux*: warm, rich, almost peppery, it is the epitome of the southern Rhône, a powerful *vin du soleil*, full of all the energy and the goodness of the sun. Châteauneuf-du-Pape traditionally is a *vin de garde*; in the past, certainly, it needed many years' bottle ageing before it could be approached. Today, though, many examples are drinkable far younger — after, say, only four or five years. Don't miss the opportunity to sample the relatively rare white Châteauneuf-du-Pape on the spot, too.

The stony terrain at Châteauneuf-du-Pape is exceptional.

For those with teetotal drivers, the wine tour presses on, through the vineyards of Châteauneuf-du-Pape via Courthézon, and then on to Orange. These vineyards are indeed some of the most striking in Europe; for although we have seen that the vine can thrive in the most unlikely soils (fine gravel in the Médoc, sand in the Camargue, pure white chalk in Cognac and Champagne, for example), the sight of the stumpy free-standing Grenache, Cinsault, Mourvèdre, and other vines growing amidst fields of enormous smooth stones as large and flat as a size 13 shoe is indeed a shocking one! Needless to say, the task of 'ploughing' such fields is not an easy one (the Père Anselme wine museum has an exhibit of the types of ploughs used). However, the vines clearly benefit from this remarkable environment, for these great stones act as storage heaters, accumulating heat by day, then releasing it at night, thus warming the vines on autumn evenings that can be surprisingly brisk. You can almost taste this warmth, this slow-releasing heat, in a bottle of Châteauneuf-du-Pape.

From Courthézon continue on the N7 to Orange, one of the region's most fascinating towns. The well-preserved triumphal arch commemorates Caesar's victory over Pompey in 49 BC. The Roman amphitheatre is one of the finest and best preserved anywhere in the world. The acoustics of the theatre are still superb: during the summer, numerous dramatic and musical productions take place in this historic open-air setting. In summer, too, there is a small tasting stand in the grotto under the amphitheatre offering refreshment and shade from the unrelenting sun.

From Orange, the vineyard tour continues towards Vaison-la-Romaine, passing through some of the Côtes du Rhône-Villages communes of the Vaucluse. The first such wine town, located just off the D975, is Cairanne, a fine-looking town in the shadow of the imposing range of the Montmirail, and an important wine-growing centre. Then comes little Rasteau, noted not only for its robust red wine, but also for its fragrant Rasteau Vin Doux Naturel, a fortified *apéritif* produced from the Grenache grape. There is a small private wine museum in Rasteau, as well as opportunities to taste both the Côte du Rhône-Villages and the more unusual VDN. Beside Rasteau lies little Roaix, also noted for robust, heavyweight red wines; they can be sampled in the *cave coopérative* for Roaix and Séguret, located along the D977.

Vaison-la-Romaine, though not a wine town as such, should certainly not be overlooked. Set astride the Ouvèze river, this site was inhabited first by the Ligurians in the Bronze Age. Then came the Romans, who turned Vaison into a town of considerable opulence and leisure, as the remains of their villas testify. In the Middle Ages, a castle was built above the town, and the inhabitants huddled below it in the perched village for protection, opposite the flatter town which the Romans had previously inhabited. Indeed, it was during this lawless age that so many of the fortified villages and perched hill towns in Provence developed.

From Vaison, return down the D977 briefly, then branch left on the little D23 which leads to the hill and wine towns under the Dentelles de Montmirail. Séguret, another Côtes du Rhône-Villages of the Vaucluse, is the first reached and also one of the most beautiful. Park below the town and walk up through the stone-paved streets to the *table d'orientation* at the top of the *ville*. It is worth the effort simply for the view alone — on a clear day, you may be able to see the Rhône delta and the Cevennes massif — though you may be further rewarded with a glass of wine, for the *vignerons* of Séguret-Roaix thoughtfully man a tasting *caveau* here in season.

From Séguret, continue on to Sablet (another Côtes du Rhône-Villages) and then on to Gigondas, one of our favourite of all Rhône wine towns. Gigondas, like Séguret, nestles against the steep Montmirail, its ruined ramparts mirroring the jagged teeth of the Dentelles. In truth, there is not that much to do here, once you have climbed up to the steep and dramatic ruined castle. But it is a quiet wine town to linger in; the wines produced here, moreover, are worthy of considerable and extended attention. Gigondas AOC is one of the great wines of the southern Rhône, warm, spicy, rich in flavour and alcohol, and an ample and superb partner to the full-flavoured foods of Provence, such as those served at the Hostellerie Les Florets, located just outside the town.

Vacqueyras, the next wine town encountered, is somewhat larger, located lower down the hills and so more accessible. Vacqueyras, another Côtes du

Rhône-Villages, produces red wines almost exclusively: they can be very good indeed, similar to Gigondas though not as concentrated or as bold.

Finally, the wine tour reaches the hill town of Beaumes-de-Venise, another exceptional wine town in every sense. One of the Côtes du Rhône-Villages noted for its fine red table wines, Beaumes-de-Venise is perhaps more famous for its wonderfully fragrant Muscat Vin Doux Naturel which has no rivals in the Rhône, but rather must be compared with the Muscat wines of the Languedoc and Roussillon, made at Frontignan, Rivesaltes, Lunel, and elsewhere. I wonder, in this vast ocean of red (mainly), rosé, and white table wines, why was the Muscat planted here in the first place? And why was this old-fashioned type of wine — a sweet *mistelle* fortified with grape brandy — made here and in nearby Rasteau but nowhere else in the Rhône? We don't know the answers, but we should gratefully accept Muscat de Beaumes-de-Venise for what it is: a wonderful peachy, honeyed nectar; at its best, drinking Beaumes-de-Venise is as close to drinking sweet fragrant table grapes as you are ever likely to get. Visit the *cave coopérative* along the main road below the town, but also make a point of knocking on the doors of individual *propriétaires-récoltants* in the town itself who make more distinctive estate-bottled examples. Beaumes-de-Venise, itself a lovely hill town, is particularly richly situated, for the olive trees which grow on the scrubby *garrigues* beyond the vines yield a dense, green-gold *huile d'olive* that is considered one of France's finest.

From Beaumes-de-Venise, return to Avignon via Carpentras, a busy little market town, noted not for wine but for its delicious *berlingots* caramels. Purchase a bag in the pretty outdoor market.

Southern Rhône Tour 2: Tavel and Lirac to the Ardèche Gorge; return via the Pont du Gard

This second tour of the southern Rhône concentrates on vineyards on the west bank of the Rhône, mainly in the *département* of the Gard. From Avignon, cross the Rhône to the adjoining town of Villeneuve-lès-Avignon. Though the two towns appear virtually continuous, divided only by the Rhône, they in fact developed historically both in conjunction and in opposition. For when the papal circus, in all its opulence and splendour, came to town, the great entourage of Vatican 'groupies', cardinals and other prelates, built substantial luxurious villas across the river in the then fashionable suburb of Villeneuve. But the Rhône was to prove a boundary as well, for it delineated the frontier between the Holy Roman Empire and the secular realms of the kings and counts of France. Today Villeneuve has much to see in its own right: the St-André fort, the former collegiate church, and the tower of Philippe-le-Bel are all noteworthy. Villeneuve is worth visiting too, simply for the best view (at sunset) of the Palais des Papes across the river.

From Villeneuve, take the river road (D980) north; a lively market often takes place here on the town's outskirts. Continue through the wine town

*Southern Rhône
Tour 2.*

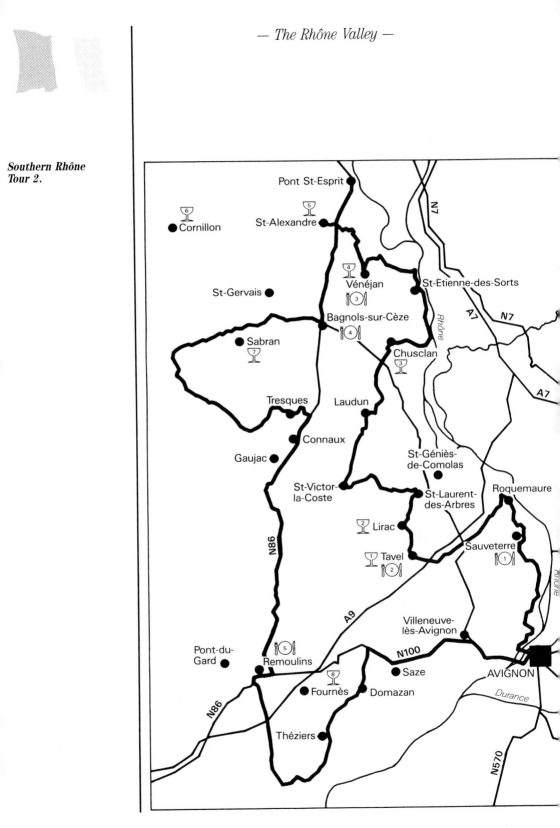

of Sauveterre and then on to Roquemaure, which stands almost opposite Châteauneuf-du-Pape on the opposing flank of the Rhône. Roquemaure was once an important wine-shipping river port in medieval days, though today little evidence of this remains: the main part of this busy town lies to the left of the road, away from the river. However, even long before those days, Hannibal and his elephants came to Roquemaure, set up camp for a brief period, then crossed the Rhône on his long and historic march across the Alps to Rome.

From Roquemaure, find the D976 which leads to Tavel. The vineyard, at first broken up by tall cypresses, then more intensive, with huge heat-retaining stones spread amongst the reddish soil, soon proclaims its pedigree in huge letters: 'TAVEL: *Le Premier Rosé de France*'. Then, as you approach the little wine town itself, the orange-pink terracotta roofs of low-lying Provençal *mas* suggest the delightful beverage that awaits. For the Grenache, Mourvèdre, Cinsault, Syrah, and other grapes, used elsewhere in the Rhône primarily to produce meaty red wines, here combine to create a lovely-to-look-at rosé that has deceptive stamina, body, scent, and alcohol. Stop at the *Cave Coopérative des Vignerons de Tavel* to try the range of wines; the selected '*Cuvée Royale*' is a particular favourite, deep, almost violet-pink, with so much scent and flavour that it is the perfect partner to the pungent, garlic-laden cuisine of the Gard.

In Tavel itself, there are numerous other opportunities for tasting this delectable wine as virtually every house offers *dégustation-vente*. There is also a fine restaurant, the Auberge de Tavel, whose owner is the founder of the *Hostelleries du Vignoble Français*.

From Tavel, find the small road that leads to Lirac, a tiny little wine town which, like so many villages of the Gard, has a quaint covered communal wash house, still in use today. Lirac is also famous for its rosé; though good or even very good, I have not yet drunk examples which can compare with the best Tavel. However, the *vignerons* of Lirac are fortunate in other respects, for the *appellation* also applies to red and white wines, thus making the commune a particularly versatile one. The vineyards of Lirac, which extend to St-Laurent-des-Arbres and St-Géniès-de-Comolas, complete the triangle at Roquemaure.

St-Laurent-des-Arbres is a particularly peaceful hamlet, though its thirteenth-century fortified church is remarkably intimidating and impressive for such a small collection of houses. From St-Laurent follow the wine road signs to St-Victor-la-Coste, then carry on to Laudun. Laudun, nestling under the '*plateau du camp de César*' (Julius Caesar, apparently made this commanding position his base camp), is one of three Côtes du

Rhône-Villages of the Gard. The vineyards of Laudun result in probably one of the best white wines of the southern Rhône, full-bodied but with a certain delicacy and scent often lacking in coarser examples from this hot-house vineyard. Some red and rosé wines are also produced.

The veritable sea of vines continues, bypassing the atomic power station of Marcoule, and then on up to Chusclan, another Côtes de Rhône-Villages of the Gard. Chusclan is noted foremost for its fruity and attractive rosé wines that were said to be favoured by Louis XIV. Much good solid red wine is produced too; one of the best places to sample both is in the town's welcoming *cave coopérative*.

From Chusclan, the wine road continues north to St-Etienne-des-Sorts, Vénéjan, St-Alexandre, and finally Pont St-Esprit. The town of Pont St-Esprit is located just north of where the Ardèche descends to meet the Rhône; it is named after the 'Holy Spirit Bridge' built there in the thirteenth century by the Frères Pontifs (a brotherhood of bridge-builders). Today, the town serves as an important starting point for ascents up the fabulous Ardèche gorge, which, with its vertical cliff walls, rapids, and ravines, remains an area of rare unspoiled and majestic beauty.

The wine tour, however, circles back south to Bagnols-sur-Cèze, a pleasant old town and a good base for excursions into the surrounding grottoes. Take the D980 north-west of town to Aven d'Orgnac. Just a few miles out of Bagnols you will come first to St-Gervais, the third of the Côtes du Rhône-Villages of the Gard. St-Gervais is far less well known than either Laudun or Chusclan but it is the source of some fine red wines. This road then continues through the Gorge de la Cèze before reaching Orgnac, but the wine route returns south of Bagnols through Tresques, Connaux and Gaujac, finally to Remoulins. From Remoulins, an excursion must be made to the Pont du Gard, built nearly 2000 years ago to supply the nearby city of Nîmes with fresh water. The return to Avignon passes through small wine-tasting villages such as Théziers, Domazan, and Saze.

Southern Rhône Tour 3: Bollène to Nyons

This short tour is ideal for travellers heading north or south who may wish to break up their *autoroute* journey with an excursion into the wine country. It is a particularly good route for those who wish to purchase some good, though not particularly expensive or prestigious, wines to take back home. It also provides the opportunity to buy the precious *appellation d'origine contrôlée* Nyons olive oil direct at the source.

Exit the *autoroute* at Bollène, and head east on the D94 to Suze-la-Rousse. Suze-la-Rousse is a most important wine centre. Its *cave coopérative* is the largest in south-east France, an immense wine factory with outdoor storage tanks that look like huge gas or oil containers. Wines from both the Côtes du Rhône and the Coteaux du Tricastin are produced here and can be sampled.

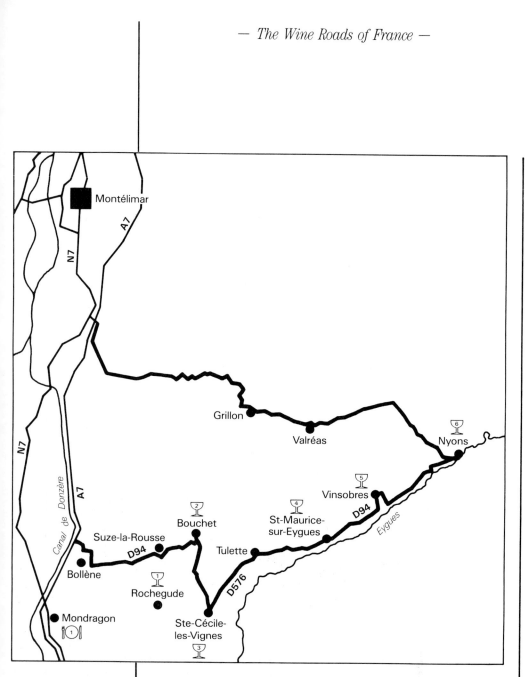

**Southern Rhône
Tour 3.**

The Coteaux du Tricastin is a separate relatively recent *appellation* applying
to wine made from vineyards to the north between Bollène and Montélimar.
Such wines can be very good as well as excellent value.

From Suze-la-Rousse, head out next on the D251 to little Bouchet. Bouchet
is a quiet, unassuming wine town, most remarkable for its twelfth-century
Cistercian abbey, for the local wine growers' union has turned the Abbey into
a great wine store and tasting room, open to the public on weekdays. Another
excellent tasting opportunity is to be had by heading south from Bouchet on
the D141 to Ste-Cécile-les-Vignes where the local *vignerons* have opened up

a fourteenth-century *caveau* which was once used when the village belonged to the papal state. Here in the *Caveau Chantecôtes* an excellent and inexpensive range of wines can be tasted and purchased. This *caveau* is a most convenient source for good but basic wines to purchase to take home on the return journey.

From Ste-Cécile, take the D576 back up to Tulette, then follow the Eygues valley on the D94 to St-Maurice-sur-Eygues. Both these towns are important local wine centres. Tulette has three separate wine *coopérative* organizations, *Costebelle*, *Nouvelle*, and *Le Cellier des Dauphins*, and wines can be tasted and purchased in all of them. The wine growers of St-Maurice claim that they were granted a charter for their wines as long ago as 1333; today the wine commune is one of five Côtes du Rhône-Villages of the Drôme *département*. Its *cave coopérative* is located along the main road.

Beyond St-Maurice-sur-Eygues, the terrain becomes hillier, more complex and rugged. This marks the beginning of the vineyards of Vinsobres, another Côtes du Rhône-Villages, famous for its robust red wines. The town is charming, perched on a steep hill overlooking its vines, while the *cave coopérative* below on the main road is most welcoming; there is a shaded picnic table and swings set up there for passing wine tourists and their children.

Nyons, finally, lies at the end of the Eygues valley, below rugged hills and mountains from which the river descends. Nyons is a fine, unspoiled, little-visited, old town, the surrounding hills covered not just with vines, but also with olive trees. For indeed, Nyons is the most famous olive town in France: the only single one entitled to an *appellation d'origine contrôlée* for its *huile d'olive*. Made from the deep walnut-brown Nyons olive which can be cultivated only in some 41 communes of the Drôme and 19 of the Vaucluse, it is one of the finest of all French olive oils, more yellow than green in colour, with an

Université du Vin

In 1978 a *Université du Vin* was founded with headquarters in the imposing fourteenth-century feudal château of Suze-la-Rousse. This important regional institution offers more than 40 courses and seminars for wine growers in the Rhône as well as from further afield, on subjects such as viticulture, tasting and oenology, technology, marketing, and much else. Extensive sensorial studies on taste have been carried out in the unique tasting facilities comprising 16 individual booths installed in the former chapel of the château. Every year cultural events and exhibitions take place on wine-related themes.

For further information write or telephone:
Université du Vin
Château de Suze
26790 Suze-la-Rousse
tel: (75) 04 86 09

exceptional fruitiness and flavour. Both oils and wines can be tasted and purchased at the *cave coopérative* at the entrance to the town.

From Nyons, travellers heading north can return to the *autoroute* by making a circular tour through Valréas (capital of the Côtes du Rhône wine area known unofficially as the *Enclave des Papes*), and the fortified town of Grillon. Rejoin the *autoroute* south of Montélimar. Travellers heading south may wish to continue on to Vaison-la-Romaine and there join the first southern Rhône wine tour, through the hill towns of the Montmirail to Carpentras and Avignon.

Dégustation: Stop to Taste; Stop to Buy

A full three-quarters of all the wine produced in the southern Côtes du Rhône comes from its *caves coopératives*. Such establishments are thus of vital importance to the local economies: the wines they make, moreover, are, on the whole, of a high standard and should by no means be shunned. However, here as elsewhere, the importance of selection should not be overlooked. Nearly all of the best *caves coopératives* encourage quality by paying the wine growers a higher price per kilo for superior, riper grapes: these are then vinified separately to produce superior *special cuvées* or *cuvées réserves* — wines which may cost a bit more than the 'straight' offerings but which are almost always worth the few extra francs. Don't take our word for it — taste and compare for yourself.

This is a region where direct sales are important to *caves coopératives* and *propriétaires-récoltants* alike, so appointments in advance are rarely necessary. However, if you would like to be shown around the *caves* and wine-making facilities, a telephone call prior to arriving is always appreciated. In addition to the addresses below there will be countless other wine-tasting opportunities.

Southern Rhône Tour 1

Père Anselme
'Le Musée des Outils de Vignerons'
ave Bx-Pierre-de-Luxembourg
84230 Châteauneuf-du-Pape
tel: (90) 83 70 07
Hours: Daily 9–12h; 14–17h30.
The firm of Père Anselme is one of the 'big guns' of the Rhône, a highly respected *négociant-éleveur* producing and marketing the full gamut of wines, including Côte-Rôtie AOC, Châteauneuf-du-Pape AOC, Hermitage AOC, Cornas AOC, St-Joseph AOC, and Côtes du Rhône-Villages AOC.
The 'Père Anselme Musée des Outils de Vignerons' is open every day and it should form an essential part of any visit to Châteauneuf-du-Pape, for it will aid in the understanding of the factors and effort which is necessary to cultivate vines in this unique *terroir* and will also inform about wines and wine making in general. Entrance to the museum is free, and a full range of Père Anselme wines is available for tasting and purchase.

2

Caves Saint Pierre
rte d'Avignon
84230 Châteauneuf-du-Pape
tel: (90) 83 72 14
Hours: Mon–Fri 8–12h; 14–17h. Appointment appreciated but not essential.
Négociant-éleveur producing a full range of respected Rhône wines including Châteauneuf-du-Pape AOC, Gigondas AOC, Tavel AOC, Côtes du Rhône AOC. Visits to the *caves* and free *dégustation*.
English spoken.

3

Paul Coulon & Fils
Domaine de Beaurenard
rte d'Avignon
84230 Châteauneuf-du-Pape
tel: (90) 83 71 79
Hours: Mon–Fri, working hours.
A serious Châteauneuf-du-Pape *propriétaire-récoltant* with premises by the fire station. Also operates the 'Musée du Vigneron' in Rasteau (see below). A little English spoken.

4

Domaine Lucien Barrot & Fils
Chemin du Clos
84230 Châteauneuf-du-Pape
tel: (90) 83 70 90
Hours: Mon–Fri, working hours.
Small *propriétaire-récoltant* producing traditional Châteauneuf-du-Pape AOC from a 15-hectare vineyard. Visits to the *cave* and free *dégustation* for purchasers.

5

Berard Père & Fils
Domaine de Terre Ferme
84370 Bédarrides
tel: (90) 33 02 98
Hours: Mon–Sat, working hours.
Châteauneuf-du-Pape AOC, Gigondas AOC, and other fine wines of the southern Rhône.
English spoken.

6

M

Paul Coulon & Fils
Musée du Vigneron
84110 Rasteau
tel: (90) 46 11 75
Hours: Daily 9–12h30; 13h30–18h30.
This fine private wine museum should not be missed. Good and informative exhibits, as well as tasting of the *vigneron's* own Châteauneuf-du-Pape AOC and Côtes du Rhône AOC. Free entrance to museum and tasting.
A little English spoken.

THE RHÔNE VALLEY

7 Cave Coopérative Les Vignerons de Roaix-Séguret
rte de Vaison
84110 Séguret
tel: (90) 46 91 13
Hours: Mon–Sat, working hours.
Côtes du Rhône-Villages AOC; Côtes du Rhône AOC.

8 Caveau des Vignerons de Sablet
8, rue du Levant
84110 Sablet
tel: (90) 46 95 57
Hours: Open daily including Sun and holidays 9–12h; 14–17h.
Côtes du Rhône-Villages AOC; Côtes du Rhône AOC.

9 Caveau St-Vincent
place de la Mairie
84190 Gigondas
Hours: Mon–Sat, working hours.
Mme Meunier, who runs this village *caveau*, is a great enthusiast and will take you through an interesting comparative tasting of different traditionally made Gigondas AOC wines.

10 Cave des Vignerons
84190 Gigondas
tel: (90) 65 86 27
Hours: Mon–Sat 8–12h; 14–18h; Sun 10–12h; 15–18h.
Two types of red Gigondas AOC are produced: a traditional, which ages 18 months in oak casks and needs a minimum of five years before it is ready to drink, and an example vinified by *macération carbonique* to result in a much lighter, fruitier wine ready to drink as soon as it is sold. Gigondas 'Blanc des Blancs' produced from the Clairette and white Grenache should also be sampled. Telephone in advance only if you would like to see around the installation.

11 Domaine des Lambertins
Cave Lambert
La Grande Fontaine
84190 Vacqueyras
tel: (90) 65 85 54
Hours: Mon–Fri 8–12h; 14–18h. Telephone call appreciated.
Côtes du Rhône-Vacqueyras AOC; Côtes du Rhône AOC red, rosé, and white.
23 hectares of vines around Vacqueyras are worked by the Lambert brothers; their Côtes du Rhône-Vacqueyras AOC and red, rosé, and white Côtes du Rhône AOC wines have been winning medals for many years.

12 Cave des Vignerons de Beaumes-de-Venise
84190 Beaumes-de-Venise

tel: (90) 62 94 45
Hours: Mon–Sat 8h30–12h; 14–18h.
Muscat de Beaumes-de-Venise VDN; Côtes du Rhône-Villages AOC; Côtes du Rhône AOC; Côtes du Ventoux AOC.
A highly respected *cave coopérative* producing a fine range of table wines, as well as the notable Muscat.
English spoken.

13 Domaine des Bernardins
Castaud-Maurin
84190 Beaumes-de-Venise
tel: (90) 62 94 13
Hours: Mon–Sat 9–12h; 14–19h.
Near the centre of town on the road to Malaucène, this family *propriétaire-vigneron* makes an excellent and individual Muscat de Beaumes-de-Venise VDN. Also Côtes du Rhône-Villages AOC and Côtes du Rhône AOC.

Southern Rhône Tour 2

1 Les Vignerons de Tavel
BP 3
30216 Tavel
tel: (66) 50 03 57
Hours: Daily including Sun and holidays 8–12h; 14–18h.
Fine, highly respected *cave coopérative* producing a large proportion of the area's famous Tavel AOC rosé in different quality levels. Consistent winners of many medals.

2 Comte de Régis
Château de Ségriès
30126 Lirac
tel: (66) 21 85 35
Lirac AOC (red, rosé, and white); Tavel AOC; Côtes du Rhône AOC.
Wines from the Château de Ségriès can be tasted and purchased at its '*Caveau de la Fontaine*', situated in the centre of Lirac, and open daily 9–20h.

3 Cave des Vignerons de Chusclan
Chusclan
30200 Bagnols-sur-Cèze
tel: (66) 89 63 03
Hours: Mon–Fri 8h30–12h; 14–18h.
Well-made red and rosé Chusclan AOC in this welcoming *cave*.

4 Cave Coopérative de Vénéjan
Vénéjan
30200 Bagnols-sur-Cèze

tel: (66) 79 25 04
Hours: 8–12h; 14–18h except Wed and Sat afternoons, Sun and holidays.
Red Côtes du Rhône AOC made principally from Syrah and Grenache, and
rosé from Clairette, Cinsault, and Grenache. Vénéjan is an ancient village in
a superb plateau position overlooking the Rhône valley.

5   Alain Robert & Fils
Cave du Frigoulas
30130 St-Alexandre
tel: (66) 39 18 71
Hours: Mon–Sat 9–12h; 14–19h. Sun and holidays by appointment.
Côtes du Rhône-Villages AOC; Côtes du Rhône AOC; Vin de Pays.
Since 1258, some 30 generations of the Robert family have practised viticulture
at the Vieux Manoir du Frigoulas at St-Alexandre. Today the family cultivates
52 hectares by long-standing traditional methods, with no artificial fertilizers,
weedkillers, or other chemicals. The *cave de dégustation* is open at the above
hours, but telephone in advance to visit the wine-making facilities and
vineyards.

6   Mme Castor & Fils
Domaine St-Nabor
30630 Cornillon
tel: (66) 82 20 30
Hours: Daily, working hours. Appointment not essential but appreciated.
Côtes du Rhône AOC red, rosé, and white produced by family *propriétaire-
récoltant* located on the road to the Gorges de la Cèze.
English spoken.

7   de Seresin Père & Fils
Domaine de Bruthel
30200 Sabran
tel: (66) 79 96 24
Hours: Daily except Sun morning, working hours.
Welcoming family *exploitation* producing red, white, and rosé Côtes du Rhône
AOC wines by traditional methods. Ancient *cave* and vineyards surrounding
the domaine.
English spoken.

8   Cave Coopérative 'Les Coteaux de Fournès'
Fournès
30210 Remoulins
tel: (66) 37 02 36
Hours: Mon–Fri 8–12h; 14–18h.
Côtes du Rhône AOC red, rosé, and white wines produced by this large
coopérative near the Pont du Gard.

Southern Rhône Tour 3

1

Cave des Vignerons
26790 Rochegude
tel: (75) 04 81 84
Hours: Daily including Sun and holidays 9–12h; 14–18h.
Rochegude is located not far off the *autoroute* at Bollène; the town's 1000-year-old château is the headquarters for the *Commanderie des Côtes du Rhône*, and wines are aged in its cellars. The local *cave coopérative* produces red, white, and rosé Côtes du Rhône-Villages AOC, sold in bottles and *en vrac*.

2

Abbaye de Bouchet
BP 1
Bouchet
26130 St-Paul-Trois-Châteaux
Hours: Mon–Thur 8–12h; 14–18h. Fri 8–12h.
The former Cistercian Abbaye de Bouchet, founded in 1184, today serves as a wine store for a Rhône wine growers' union. Under its ancient vaulted arches, many hundreds of selected oak barrels of Rhône wines lie ageing: Châteauneuf-du-Pape AOC, Gigondas AOC, Crozes-Hermitage AOC, Côtes du Ventoux AOC, Coteaux de Tricastin AOC and many others, including the Abbaye's own 'Grande Réserve des Côtes du Rhône'. The capitular room is used for professional as well as less formal gatherings.

3

Caveau 'Chantecôtes'
84290 Ste-Cécile-les-Vignes
tel: (90) 30 83 25
Hours: Mon–Sat 8h30–12h15; 14h30–18h30. Sun and holidays 10–12h; 15–18h30.
The vineyards of St-Cécile probably date back to the time of the Templars; today well-made Côtes du Rhône red, rosé, and white wines can be tasted in the vaulted fourteenth-century village tasting room. Wines are sold in bottles and *en vrac*.
Some English spoken.

4

La Cave des Coteaux de St-Maurice
26110 St-Maurice-sur-Eygues
tel: (75) 27 63 44
Hours: Daily including Sun and holidays 8–12h; 14–19h.
The *cave coopérative* produces Côtes du Rhône-Villages red and rosé; the best wines, aged in oak casks, are bottled as 'La Grande Réserve'. Picnic area.

5

Coopérative Vinicole Vinsobraise
26110 Vinsobres
tel: (75) 27 64 22
Hours: Daily 8–12h; 14–18h. Closed Sun in winter.

Located on the main road below the hill town of Vinsobres, this *cave coopérative* produces a particularly full and rich red Côtes du Rhône-Villages. Vinsobres was awarded the village *appellation* in 1957 but its wines have been enjoyed for centuries. Shaded picnic area.

6

Coopérative Agricole du Nyonaise
26110 Nyons
Hours: Mon–Sat 8h30–12h; 14–18h. Sun and holidays 9h30–12h; 14h30–18h.
Come here to purchase not only Côtes du Rhône wines, but also the famous *appellation d'origine contrôlée* olive oil of Nyons, as well as the distinctive, walnut-brown olives themselves.

Wine Festivals

Early May	Fête des Vins	Bagnols-sur-Cèze
Mid July	Fête des Vins des Côtes du Ventoux	Carpentras
End of July	Fête des Vins des Côtes du Rhône Gardoises	Pont St-Esprit
Beginning of September	Le Grand Marché des Côtes du Rhône	St-Péray
End of November	Grande Fête des Côtes du Rhône *Primeurs*	Avignon
End of November	Fête du Vin et de la Musique	Ste-Cécile-les-Vignes

This list is far from complete. From mid-July to mid-August many villages hold small wine festivals. The new wines are usually celebrated in mid-November.

Regional Gastronomy

The Rhône valley, with its head in the Lyonnais, its feet firmly in Provence, has a favourably positioned belly lying somewhere in between.

Certainly the gastronomic traditions of both the Lyonnais and Provence are among the most celebrated in France. The Lyonnais — apart from its handful of super-famous and expensive starred restaurants whose chefs are national and international celebrities — is known foremost as a region for good solid French provincial cooking. This is epitomized by the so-called *bouchons* of Lyon, where copious quantities of honest, well-cooked foods are dished out to workers in blue overalls, truck drivers, and businessmen alike. Such simple meals always begin with platters of Lyonnais *charcuterie*: the famous sausages, *terrines* and *pâtés* of Lyon such as *rosette*, *cervelas*, and much else.

This might then be followed by a simple *galette lyonnaise* (a fried potato and onion pancake), *saucisse en brioche*, poached and boned *pieds de porc* (pig's trotters), *tablier de sapeur* (an 'apron' of tripe, first poached, then breaded and grilled), grilled *andouillette* or boiled chicken and, of course, potatoes (the everyday 'truffle' of Lyon). Afterwards, a groaning cheese-board stocked with a remarkable collection from the surrounding fertile countryside — *bleu de Bresse*, mountain cheeses and *tommes* from the Dauphine, wine-soaked *rigottes* from Condrieu — are accompanied by the ever-present traditional Lyonnais *pot*, a chipped, refillable glass container holding about half a litre of simple *vin du café*. The best such establishments, of course, pride themselves on the quality of this basic draught beverage, simple and inexpensive though it always must be: an anonymous but good Beaujolais, perhaps, or a young gutsy, teeth-staining Côtes du Rhône.

In the northern Rhône, such establishments and indeed such hearty attitudes to eating and drinking may be found in small wine towns and villages. But the great city imparts a more subtle and refined influence, too, for towns such as Vienne and Condrieu are close enough at hand to attract industrialists and their clients, as well as wealthy weekenders, who come to the vineyards to purchase these fabulous wines direct, and to eat in the area's fine restaurants. Here, such delicacies as *quenelle de brochet* (pounded and sieved pike mixed with egg and cream then lightly poached) and *poularde de Bresse truffée*

Le Pique-Nique

Rosette de Lyon Large, attractive, air-dried pork sausage.

Cervelas Smooth, fine sausage, sometimes studded with truffles or pistachios.

Caillette Vauclusienne A type of liver and meat *pâté* highly seasoned, flavoured with *herbes de Provence* and mixed with vegetables such as spinach or lettuce, shaped into a ball and wrapped in a piece of caul. Delicious eaten cold as picnic fare, as well as hot.

Le Tarte des Allymes Pizza-like onion tart.

Jambon au foin Ham cooked in an aromatic mix of herbs and hay.

Rigotte Reddish rind-washed cheese from Condrieu.

Fromage fort du Mont Ventoux Strong cheese from Mont Ventoux, often flavoured with herbs and Marc. Excellent with full-bodied wines.

Picodon Superlative goats' cheese from the Drôme.

Nougat de Montélimar White and/or dark honey and almond nougat confection.

Berlingot Caramel candy from Carpentras.

en vessie (truffled Bresse chicken sewn into a pig's bladder and gently baked or poached) are more fitting accompaniments to the fine selections of Condrieu, Château Grillet, and Côte-Rôtie wines.

As we descend further down the valley, the strength and potency of the wines increases and so does the fuller flavoured, herb- and garlic-laden cuisine until finally, somewhere south of nougat-scented Montélimar, we realize that we are in Provence. Here, in simple Provençal *mas* and in elegant restaurants alike, the *vins du soleil* of the southern Rhône — Châteauneuf-du-Pape, Gigondas, Tavel, and others — are ably matched by one of the most direct and appetizing of all of France's many regional cuisines (see preceding chapter).

Spécialités Régionales:
Stop to Taste; Stop to Buy

Moulin à Huile Autrand
au pied du Pont Roman
26110 Nyons
tel: (75) 26 02 52
Nyons olive oil is undoubtedly one of the top oils of France. Stop to taste and buy at the *coopérative agricole* (address above) or visit this traditional family producer at the foot of the Romanesque bridge.

Montélimar Nougat
It is impossible to drive through this sweet honey-and-almond scented town without stopping to taste and to buy bars of this irresistible candy. Chabert & Guillot and Le Val Roubion both produce good examples.

Restaurants

Northern Rhône (Map p.383)

La Pyramide
14, bd Fernand Point
38200 Vienne
tel: (74) 53 01 96
Not just a restaurant but a mecca, the home of one of France's greatest chefs, the late Fernand Point. The *maître's* specialities are still faithfully prepared: *suprême de turbot au champagne, poularde de Bresse truffée en vessie*, and others, accompanied by the wines of the northern Rhône.
Very Expensive

2 Hôtellerie Beau Rivage
2, rue du Beau Rivage
69420 Condrieu
tel: (74) 59 52 24
This fine hotel-restaurant, situated directly on the Rhône, is famous for its elegant and classic cuisine served in a delightful and warm setting. Recommended by Château Grillet and others.
Expensive

3 Hôtel-Restaurant Bellevue
quai du Rhône
38370 Les Roches-de-Condrieu
tel: (74) 56 41 42
Closed Mon all year; Sun night September–April; Tue lunch April–September.
Located on the opposite bank of the Rhône, looking across the river to the terraces of Condrieu, this comfortable hotel-restaurant serves traditional cooking accompanied by a fine cellar of northern Rhône wines. Recommended by Georges Vernay.
Moderate

4 Restaurant Jean-Marc Reynaud
82, ave Président Roosevelt
26600 Tain l'Hermitage
tel: (75) 07 22 10
Closed Sun eve; Mon.
Fresh produce and regional products from the daily market, served in the dining-room of this grand *maison bourgeoise* with a terrace overlooking the Rhône. Recommended by Paul Jaboulet and others.
Moderate

5 Restaurant-Bar-Hôtel
'La Table du Roy'
Le Village
26600 Serves-sur-Rhône
tel: (75) 03 36 03
Open daily 7–23h.
This simple family restaurant serves a selection of regional menus accompanied by red and white Crozes-Hermitage. Pleasant outdoor eating area in summer. Recommended by Mme Bégot.
Inexpensive

6 Michel Chabran
RN7
26600 Pont de l'Isère
tel: (75) 84 60 09

Elegant *Relais et Châteaux* hotel-restaurant, situated in the main square of the village. Contemporary décor highlights a modern and imaginative cuisine: *le millefeuille de foie gras de canard, le bavarois de saumon mariné aux fines herbes, le pigeonneau des gandels rôti en cocotte.*
Expensive

Southern Rhône Tour 1 (Map p.391)

1

La Fourchette
17, rue Racine
84000 Avignon
tel: (90) 85 20 93
Closed Sat and Sun.
Provençal and personal specialities accompanied by Côtes du Rhône wines in this pleasant **Inexpensive** restaurant.

2

La Mule du Pape
2, rue de la République
84230 Châteauneuf-du-Pape
tel: (90) 83 73 30
Closed Mon eve; Tue.
A well-liked restaurant, owned and run by Père Anselme, situated in the centre of town with a dining-room overlooking the vineyards of Châteauneuf-du-Pape.
Moderate regional and traditional menus.

3

Restaurant Le Pistou
15, rue Joseph Ducos
84230 Châteauneuf-du-Pape
tel: (90) 83 71 75
Closed Tue eve; Wed.
Provençal specialities such as *gibelote de lapin Provençale* and *soupe au pistou* together with local wines served in a comfortable family atmosphere.
Inexpensive

4

Hostellerie Château Fines Roches
84230 Châteauneuf-du-Pape
tel: (90) 83 70 23
Closed Mon; January.
Fine château hotel-restaurant south of the town, in peaceful countryside surrounded by vineyards.
Moderate to Expensive

5

Hostellerie 'Le Beffroi'
rue de l'Evêché BP 85
84110 Vaison-la-Romaine
tel: (90) 36 04 71
Closed Mon; Tue lunch.

Sixteenth-century inn in the centre of the Haute Ville: the 'La Fontaine' restaurant serves **Inexpensive to Moderate** Provençal and classic menus.

6

Hostellerie Les Florets
rte des Dentelles
84190 Gigondas
tel: (90) 65 85 01
Closed Wed.
Quiet and tranquil, under the Dentelles de Montmirail, this favourite serves solid Provençal cuisine — *pieds et paquets maison, aïolade du comtat* — together with own-produced wines. Lovely shaded outdoor terrace. Visits to the family vineyard, Domaine 'La Garrigue' at Vacqueyras can be arranged. Recommended by the Cave des Vignerons.
Inexpensive to Moderate

Southern Rhône Tour 2 (Map p.395)

1

Hostellerie 'La Crémaillère'
BP 14
30150 Sauveterre
tel: (66) 82 55 05
Closed Tue eve; Wed.
Country inn serving seasonal foods and local wines.
Moderate

2

Auberge de Tavel
30125 Tavel
tel: (66) 50 03 41
Closed Mon.
Attractive typical Provençal *mas* on the outskirts of Tavel run by M. Bonnevaux, founder and President of the grouping of *Hostelleries du Vignoble Français*: independent hotel-restaurants in the principal wine-producing regions which specialize in regional foods and local wines. Here the foods of Provence — *morue fraiche en aïoli, caneton rôti au coulis d'orange et miel, blanc de volaille au pistou* — are accompanied by the local wines: a tasting of five different Tavels by the glass is offered to accompany meals. Recommended by Château de Ségriès and others.
Moderate to Expensive

3

Ferme Auberge 'Lou-Caleou'
30200 Vénéjan
tel: (66) 79 25 16
Closed Sun.
Warm *ambiance paysanne* in this comfortable *ferme auberge* serving *grillades au feu de bois* and Côtes du Rhône wines. Recommended by the Cave

Coopérative de Vénéjan.
Inexpensive

4

Château de Coulorgues
rte de Carmignan
30200 Bagnols-sur-Cèze
tel: (66) 89 52 78
Closed Mon out of season; February.
Comfortable hotel-restaurant serves Provençal dishes in a warm dining-room
with open fire in winter. Recommended by Christian de Seresin.
Moderate

5

Auberge des Escaravats
1, rue des Escaravats
30210 Remoulins
tel: (66) 37 10 24
Closed Wed.
Authentic *cuisine Provençale* in an atmospheric vaulted dining-room.
Conveniently located for those visiting the Pont du Gard. Recommended by
the Cave Coopérative 'Les Coteaux de Fournés'.
Inexpensive

Southern Rhône Tour 3 (Map p.398)

1

La Beaugravière
N7
84430 Mondragon
tel: (90) 30 13 40
Another *Hostellerie du Vignoble Français* just south of Bollène: if travelling
north, leave the *autoroute* at Orange to enjoy fresh regional foods together
with one of the best wine lists covering the length of the Rhône.
Inexpensive to Moderate

Additional Information

Comité Interprofessionnel des Côtes du Rhône,
    Côtes du Ventoux, Coteaux du Tricastin
41, cours Jean-Jaurès
84000 Avignon
tel: (90) 86 47 09

Office de Tourisme et Accueil de France
41, cours Jean-Jaurès
84000 Avignon
tel: (90) 82 65 11

SELECT
BIBLIOGRAPHY

Broadbent, Michael, *Wine Tasting* (London: Cassell, 1979).

Delpal, Jacques Louis, *France: A Phaidon Cultural Guide* (Englewood Cliffs: Prentice-Hall, 1985).

Feifer, Maxine, *Everyman's France* (London: J. M. Dent & Sons, 1982).

Johnson, Hugh, *The World Atlas of Wine*, 2nd edition (London: Mitchell Beazley, 1977).

Lichine, Alexis, *Wines and Vineyards of France* (London: Macmillan, 1982).

Michelin Green Tourist Guides: Chateaux of the Loire; Dordogne; French Riviera; Provence (Clermont-Ferrand: Michelin et Cie).

Millau, Christian (ed.), *Guide France 1987* (Paris: Gault-Millau, 1987).

Millon, Marc and Kim, *The Wine and Food of Europe: An Illustrated Guide* (Exeter: Webb & Bower, 1982).

Millon, Marc and Kim, *The Wine Roads of Europe* (London: Robert Nicholson, 1983).

Peppercorn, David, *Pocket Guide to the Wines of Bordeaux* (London: Mitchell Beazley, 1986).

Poupon, Pierre and Pierre Forgeot, *The Wines of Burgundy* (Paris: Presses Universitaires de France, 1979).

Robinson, Jancis, *The Great Wine Book* (London: Sidgwick and Jackson, 1982).

Spurrier, Steven, *French Country Wines* (London: Willow Books, 1984).

Vandyke Price, Pamela, *Guide to the Wines of Bordeaux* (London: Pitman, 1977).

Voss, Roger (ed.), *1987 Which? Wine Guide* (London: Consumers' Association, 1986).

Yapp, Robin and Judith, *Vinegards and Vignerons* (Shaftesbury: Blackmore Press, 1979).

INDEX

Note: Entries in **bold type** refer to maps.